BASIC

GEOMETRY

Second Edition

Deborah A. Hale

Shelby L. Hawthorne

Thomas Nelson Community College
Natural Science and Mathematics Division
P. O. Box 9407
Hampton, Virginia 23670

TABLE OF CONTENTS

Appendices

Preface

Basic Geometry is designed for students enrolled in either a high school or a college class. This textbook is intended for students who have no previous experience with geometry or who need a thorough review. The book is designed for a one semester four credit hour course or a one quarter five credit hour course. The emphasis of the book is on applying geometric concepts as opposed to developing a theoretical axiomatic course. The course builds from beginning to end. Units 11, 12, and 13 can be omitted without disrupting the flow of the material.

It is assumed that the student has a working knowledge of algebra I. Brief reviews of the following topics from algebra and arithmetic are provided for the student's convenience: radicals, Section 7.1, beginning page 201; quadratic equations, Section 7.2, beginning page 210; operations with fractions, Appendix A, beginning page 444; and, solving linear equations, Appendix B, beginning page 450.

There are thirteen units in the text. Each unit begins with learning objectives for the instructor's and student's convenience. Each unit is thoroughly developed using simple, easily understood language. Postulates, theorems, and definitions are clearly identified. Detailed explanations, numerous step-by-step examples, and guiding questions accompany each new topic. Each topic is explained fully. Worked out examples are followed by practice problems for students to work. At the end of major topics, exercises are provided with answers available in Appendix F, beginning on page 462. Arithmetic and algebra are integrated into the presentations of the material to help a student in sharpening these skills. Applications of geometric principles in real life situations are incorporated throughout.

The book is adaptable to a variety of modes of instruction; self paced, lecture-discussion, lab courses, and independent study.

S. Hawthorne wishes to thank the Thomas Nelson Community College Mathematics Department and Essex Community College Mathematics Department for their valuable suggestions for this fourth revision. Special thanks go to my spouse, William, for his many hours of proofreading and to my children for the many hours they watched me in front of the computer.

Unit 1

Angles, Lines and Points

Learning Objectives:

1. The student will list the four elements of a deductive reasoning system.

2. The student will differentiate between deductive and inductive reasoning.

3. The student will differentiate between axioms or postulates, and theorems.

4. The student will demonstrate his mastery of the following definitions and theorems by writing them, or by applying them to solutions of selected problems.

    Definitions: line segment, compass, midpoint, ray, angle, vertex, vertical angles, degrees, perpendicular lines, protractor, right angle, acute angle, obtuse angle, straight angle, complementary angles, supplementary angles, adjacent angles, angle bisector, bisector of a line segment, and perpendicular bisector.

    Theorems: (a) Supplements of the same or equal angles are themselves equal.

    (b) Complements of the same or equal angles are themselves equal.

    (c) Pairs of vertical angles are equal.

The following constructions are required:

(a) Construct the perpendicular bisector of a line segment.

(b) Construct the bisector of a given angle.

(c) Construct a copy of an angle in another position.

ANGLES, LINES AND POINTS

In geometry, the thread that ties one idea with another is called <u>deductive reasoning</u>. Are there other types of reasoning processes? Yes, but these other processes are not used in geometry. One example is called <u>inductive reasoning</u>. For a moment, let us discuss the second type. What exactly is inductive reasoning? How does it differ from deductive reasoning?

1.1 Inductive Reasoning

Example: Study the circles below.

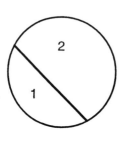 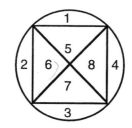

Figure A   Figure B   Figure C

1. In Figure A, two points have been chosen and one straight line drawn between them. The circle has been divided into _____ regions.

1. 2

2. In Figure B, three points determine three straight lines. The circle has been divided into _____ regions.

2. 4

3. In Figure C, four points determine six straight lines. The circle has been divided into _____ regions.

3. 8

Fill in the table below:

Number of points on each circle	2	3	4	
Number or regions resulting	2	4	8	

4. What is the pattern that you see?
    2 points _____2 regions
    3 points _____4 regions
    4 points _____8 regions
    Each time the number of regions seems to _____.

4. double

5. Inductive reasoning involves observing patterns and drawing conclusions based upon this pattern. The patterns in this problem indicate this conclusion. . . "by adding one more point to the circle, the number of regions seems to double."

　　　5 points would indicate _____ regions
　　　6 points would indicate _____ regions

5. 16;32

6. Now demonstrate that your answers are correct. The circle below has five dots. Connect each set of dots with straight lines in every direction. Count the number of resulting regions.

6.

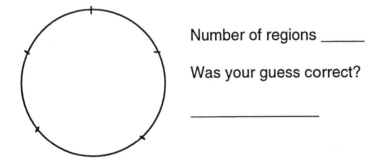

Number of regions _____

Was your guess correct?

_____

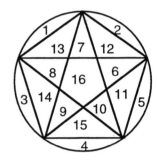

16; yes

7. Draw a large circle having six dots. Connect each pair of dots and count the number of regions resulting.

　　　Number of regions_____

　　　Was your guess correct?

7. 30, if dots are equally spaced 31, if not.

No, your guess in Exercise 5 was 32.

As you demonstrated, using inductive reasoning can lead to <u>false</u> conclusions. Inductive reasoning by itself cannot serve as a mathematical proof for anything.

What are the elements of inductive reasoning? You move from the specific to the general by a three step process.

　　　1) Collect data
　　　2) Observe patterns
　　　3) Draw conclusions based upon these patterns

Here is another example of inductive reasoning. Follow all the instructions listed below.

Choose a number _____
Add four _____
Double the result _____
Subtract six _____
Divide by two _____
Subtract the original number _____

Your result is _____

Try the above process two more times and record your result. Have a friend or relative try a number and record the result.

8. If your addition, subtraction, division, and multiplication have been performed correctly, your result will always be _____.

8. 1 (one)

9. Again you have demonstrated inductive reasoning by (1) starting with specific numbers (collecting data), (2) observing a pattern, and (3) drawing a conclusion based upon this pattern.

What was the conclusion in this problem?

Your answer: _____

9. See exercise 8.

1.2 Deductive Reasoning

The inductive approach does not always give consistent results as answers. Therefore, it cannot be used as a geometric proof for anything.

For a mathematical proof, we need to use the deductive method for reasoning.

Deductive reasoning begins with the general and goes to the specific. Deductive reasoning involves mathematical rules and logic to arrive at its specific conclusions. We will be studying this type of reasoning throughout the course.

One example of deductive reasoning can be demonstrated by using the process above. Remember to start with the general. What is the most general expression for numbers that you have in algebra? _____ Yes, use "x"!

General	Choose a number	___x___	x
	Add four	_____	x + 4
	Double the result	_____	2x + 8
	Subtract six	_____	2x + 2
	Divide by two	_____	x + 1
	Subtract the original number	_____	x + 1 - x
Specific	Your result is	_____	1

You have just used a general expression to prove that your answer will always be one no matter what the original number.

We had to try this process with several specific examples in inductive reasoning before we arrived at this same conclusion.

In order for general statements to have meaning, each individual word or term that it contains must be understood. To get started at some point in our communication, we admit that some terms must be left undefined. However, we will define as many terms as possible.

Definition 1.1 General statements that must be accepted without proof will be called <u>postulates</u>.

Definition 1.2 General statements that have been proven or will be proved will be called <u>theorems</u>.

Note: All theorems are not proved in this text.

Therefore, deductive reasoning involves four elements in moving from the general to the specific.

(1) Undefined terms
(2) Defined terms
(3) Postulates
(4) Theorems

10. What process of reasoning   10.
     (a) Moves from the specific to the general?   (a) Inductive

(b) Moves from the general to the specific?	(b) Deductive
(c) Involves undefined terms, defined terms, postulates, and theorems?	(c) Deductive
(d) Involves collecting data?	(d) Inductive
11. What process of reasoning can be used as mathematical proof?	11. Deductive
12. What process will be used in studying geometry?	12. Deductive
13. Why can't inductive reasoning be used in geometric proof?	13. The conclusion will not always be correct.

We don't always think about the words that we use when we communicate with others in our everyday activities. We <u>assume</u> that the phrases we speak are generally understood and their meanings, we believe, are widely accepted.

Take the word "duck". Just the mere mention of the word "duck" does give rise to a variety of interpretations. Depending upon the perception of the listener, we can expect his (the listener) to interpret the word "duck" to mean one of the following:

1. A bird with webbed feet and a flat bill.

2. A person with an unusual disposition (slang)

3. A sail cloth

4. The act of bending suddenly

Misunderstanding of phrases or terms occurs frequently in the course of a discussion. It is, therefore, very important for the people communicating to <u>agree</u> upon the terms or words involved in their exchange of ideas.

Geometry has its own language and it is important that you know the meanings of the terms involved in order to clearly understand what it is that we may be discussing.

The terms that will be defined in this unit are listed on the next page. As you read through this first unit, jot down definitions beside the respective term. You should refer to this list constantly until you have mastered each and every definition in the unit.

	Term	Definition
1.	postulate	_____
2.	theorem	_____
3.	line segment	_____
4.	midpoint	_____
5.	ray	_____
6.	angle	_____
7.	vertex	_____
8.	right angle	_____
9.	acute angle	_____
10.	obtuse angle	_____
11.	straight angle	_____
12.	adjacent angles	_____
13.	complementary angles	_____
14.	supplementary angles	_____
15.	vertical angles	_____
16.	perpendicular lines	_____
17.	bisector of a line segment	_____
18.	perpendicular bisector	_____
19.	angle bisector	_____

These definitions will be your key to interpreting each new geometric concept. In turn, it will be these concepts that will gracefully unlock the door to your understanding each new unit.

1.3 <u>Point</u>

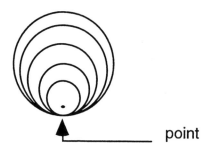

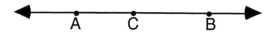
point

The diagram above is a pictorial description of a point. If this figure continues to reduce in size, you will not be able to see it. The dimensions will shrink to no measure at all. It is this small dot that is used to represent a point.

Point is the first term we will not attempt to define because we already have some intuitive knowledge of what it means.

Other undefined terms are listed below:

line, between, closed, figure, intersection, measure, side, interior, exterior, length, height, width, plane, endpoint

1.4 <u>Line Segment</u>

Below is a straight line with points A, B, and C on it. This can be denoted as $\overleftrightarrow{AB}$

A   C   B

Figure 1.1

The <u>line segment</u> where A and B are the <u>endpoints</u> is denoted $\overline{AB}$ or $\overline{BA}$.

Definition 1.3 The <u>line segment</u>, $\overline{AB}$ is the set of all points on the line between A and B including both endpoints.

See Figure 1.1 above.

Point C is a point on $\overline{AB}$ such that it divides $\overline{AB}$ into two smaller sections. These sections, $\overline{AC}$ and $\overline{CB}$ are also line segments.

The sum of these two segments can be expressed as:

$$\overline{AC} + \overline{CB} = \overline{AB}$$

In general, the sum of two (or more) segments of a line equals the measure of the entire segment.

14. Consider the line segment below.

M   X   N

(a) The points M and N are called _____.

(b) The line segment can be denoted as _____ or _____.

(c) Is point X a point on $\overline{MN}$? _____.

(d) Segment $\overline{MN}$ is formed by combining what two smaller segments? _____ and _____.

14.

(a) endpoints

(b) $\overline{MN}$ or $\overline{NM}$

(c) Yes

(d) $\overline{MX}$; $\overline{XN}$

Example:

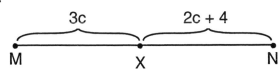

3c   2c + 4

M   X   N

Line segment $\overline{MN}$ = 14 cm. Find the value of c, $\overline{MX}$ and $\overline{XN}$

Solution:
$$3c + (2c + 4) = 14$$
$$5c + 4 = 14 \qquad 2c + 4 = \overline{XN} = 8 \text{ cm.}$$
$$5c = 10 \qquad 3c = \overline{MX} = 6 \text{ cm.}$$
$$c = 2$$

15. (a) In the following two problems, find the value of c, $\overline{MX}$, and $\overline{XN}$ if $\overline{MN}$ equals 25 dm.

(i)

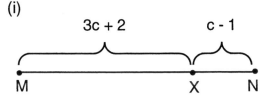

3c + 2   c - 1

M   X   N

15.
(a)

(i)

$$\overline{MX} + \overline{XN} = 25$$
$$(3c + 2) + (c - 1) = 25$$
$$4c + 1 = 25$$
$$4c = 24$$
$$c = 6$$

(ii)

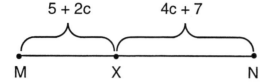

5 + 2c   4c + 7

M   X   N

(b) If $\overline{XN}$ = 30 ft., find the value of c, $\overline{XY}$, $\overline{YZ}$, and $\overline{ZN}$.

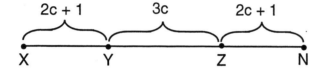

2c + 1   3c   2c + 1

X   Y   Z   N

(c) If $\overline{AC}$ = 10 inches, find the value of x, $\overline{AB}$, and $\overline{BC}$.

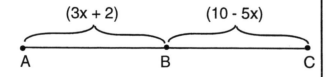

(3x + 2)   (10 - 5x)

A   B   C

$\overline{MX} = 20$ dm.

$\overline{XN} = 5$ dm.

(ii)
$(5 + 2c) + (4c + 7) = 25$

$6c + 12 = 25$

$6c = 13$

$c = 2\dfrac{1}{6}$

$c = 2.1\overline{6}$

$\overline{MX} = 9\dfrac{1}{3} = 9.\overline{3}$ dm.

$\overline{XN} = 15\dfrac{2}{3} = 15.\overline{6}$ dm.

(b)

$2(2c + 1) + 3c = 30$

$7c + 2 = 30$

$7c = 28$

$c = 4$

$\overline{XY} = 9$ ft.

$\overline{YZ} = 12$ ft.

$\overline{ZN} = 9$ ft.

(c)

$\overline{AB} + \overline{BC} = 10$

$(3x + 2) + (10 - 5x) = 10$

$12 - 2x = 10$

$-2x = -2$

$x = 1$

$\overline{AB} = 5$ in.

$\overline{BC} = 5$ in.

The sum of these two segments can be expressed as:

$$\overline{AC} + \overline{CB} = \overline{AB}$$

In general, the sum of two (or more) segments of a line equals the measure of the entire segment.

14. Consider the line segment below.

M   X   N

    (a) The points M and N are called _____.

    (b) The line segment can be denoted as _____ or _____.

    (c) Is point X a point on $\overline{MN}$? _____.

    (d) Segment $\overline{MN}$ is formed by combining what two smaller segments? _____ and _____.

14.

    (a) endpoints

    (b) $\overline{MN}$ or $\overline{NM}$

    (c) Yes

    (d) $\overline{MX}$; $\overline{XN}$

Example:

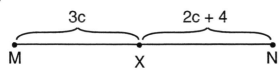

Line segment $\overline{MN}$ = 14 cm. Find the value of c, $\overline{MX}$ and $\overline{XN}$

Solution:

$$3c + (2c + 4) = 14$$
$$5c + 4 = 14 \qquad 2c + 4 = \overline{XN} = 8 \text{ cm.}$$
$$5c = 10 \qquad 3c = \overline{MX} = 6 \text{ cm.}$$
$$c = 2$$

15. (a) In the following two problems, find the value of c, $\overline{MX}$, and $\overline{XN}$ if $\overline{MN}$ equals 25 dm.

    (i)

3c + 2   c - 1

M   X   N

15.

(a)

(i)

$$\overline{MX} + \overline{XN} = 25$$
$$(3c + 2) + (c - 1) = 25$$
$$4c + 1 = 25$$
$$4c = 24$$
$$c = 6$$

$\overline{MX} = 20$ dm.

$\overline{XN} = 5$ dm.

(ii)

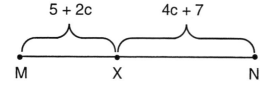

M   X   N

(ii)
$(5+2c)+(4c+7)=25$

$6c+12=25$

$6c=13$

$c=2\dfrac{1}{6}$

$c=2.1\overline{6}$

$\overline{MX}=9\dfrac{1}{3}=9.\overline{3}$ dm.

$\overline{XN}=15\dfrac{2}{3}=15.\overline{6}$ dm.

(b) If $\overline{XN}$ = 30 ft., find the value of c, $\overline{XY}$, $\overline{YZ}$, and $\overline{ZN}$.

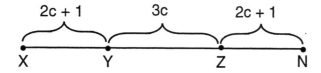

X   Y   Z   N

(b)

$2(2c+1)+3c=30$

$7c+2=30$

$7c=28$

$c=4$

$\overline{XY}=9$ ft.

$\overline{YZ}=12$ ft.

$\overline{ZN}=9$ ft.

(c) If $\overline{AC}$ = 10 inches, find the value of x, $\overline{AB}$, and $\overline{BC}$.

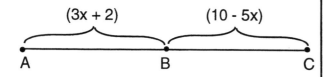

A   B   C

(c)

$\overline{AB}+\overline{BC}=10$

$(3x+2)+(10-5x)=10$

$12-2x=10$

$-2x=-2$

$x=1$

$\overline{AB}=5$ in.

$\overline{BC}=5$ in.

Two line segments are <u>equal</u> if they have the same measure. In the figure below $\overline{AT}$ has the same measure as $\overline{TB}$ Therefore, $\overline{AT} = \overline{TB}$.

16.

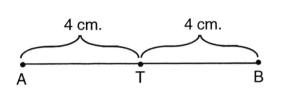

(a)   What point falls halfway between A and B? _____ .

(b)   What is the length of $\overline{AB}$?_____ .

16.

(a)   T

(b)   8 cm.

Point T is called the midpoint of $\overline{AB}$. The midpoint lies exactly in the middle of the segment. It is the point that divides a line segment into two equal parts.

> Definition 1.4 A <u>midpoint</u> is a point that divides a line segment into two equal parts.

Exercise 1.1

1. Given line segment $\overline{AB}$.

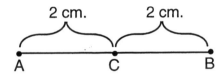

a. What are the endpoints of $\overline{AB}$?

b. Is $\overline{AB} = \overline{BA}$?

c. Find the measure of $\overline{AB}$. Is C the midpoint?

2. In the figure below, if $\overline{XW}$ = 12 cm., find the length of $\overline{XY}$, $\overline{YZ}$, and $\overline{ZW}$ using algebra. (Hint: First find the value of c.)

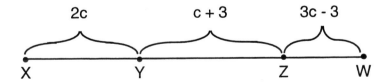

1.5 <u>Rays</u>

The figure T •————————S •—————————▶ is denoted as $\overrightarrow{TS}$ and is called a <u>ray</u>.

Ray $\overrightarrow{TS}$ is the set of all points beginning at T on the same side as S and continuing indefinitely through S. (Notation $\overrightarrow{TS}$ or $\overleftarrow{ST}$.) Point T is called the endpoint of $\overrightarrow{TS}$.

> Definition 1.5 A <u>ray</u> is the set of all points beginning with an endpoint and continuing infinitely far in one direction.

17. The symbol $\overrightarrow{AB}$ indicates a _____.

A •————————B •—————————▶

The endpoint of the ray is _____.

17. ray

    Point A

18. The symbol $\overleftarrow{QR}$ indicated that the endpoint of

$\overleftarrow{QR}$ is_____ and the ray extends _____.

18.

    Point R;
    indefinitely
    beyond Q.

19. In the figure

M •——N •——O •—————▶

(a) Is $\overrightarrow{MN}$ the same ray as $\overrightarrow{MO}$?

(b) Is $\overrightarrow{MN}$ the same ray as $\overrightarrow{NO}$?

(c) Is $\overrightarrow{MO}$ the same ray as $\overleftarrow{MO}$?

19.

(a) Yes, same
    endpoint
    and same
    direction

(b) No, not the
    same end-
    points

(c) No, not the
    same end-
    points

20. Distinguish between a ray and a line segment in regards to endpoints.

20. A ray has only
    one endpoint

and a line segment has two endpoints.

21. Answer yes or no to the following statements.

C   D   E

(a) $\overrightarrow{CD}$ = $\overrightarrow{DE}$

(b) $\overrightarrow{CD}$ = $\overline{CD}$

(c) $\overrightarrow{DE}$ = $\overrightarrow{ED}$

(d) $\overrightarrow{DE}$ = $\overrightarrow{EC}$

(e) $\overrightarrow{CD}$ = $\overrightarrow{CE}$

21.

(a) no

(b) no

(c) no

(d) no

(e) yes

1.6 Angles

Two rays may have a common endpoint as illustrated here.

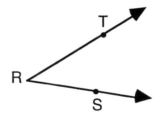

Rays $\overrightarrow{RT}$ and $\overrightarrow{RS}$ share a common endpoint R, The rays form a figure called an angle. The common endpoint R is called the vertex of the angle. The symbol for an angle is $\angle$. The above figure can be denoted as $\angle$TRS and read as "angle TRS".

Definition 1.6 An <u>angle</u> is the union of two rays with a common endpoint.
The common endpoint is called the <u>vertex</u>.

22.

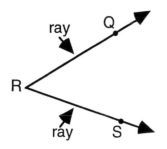

$\overrightarrow{RS}$ and $\overrightarrow{RQ}$ are the rays forming the angle QRS. Point R is called the _____ or the common endpoint of the two rays.

22.

Vertex

23. Point M is the vertex to what two rays?

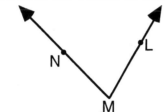

23. $\overrightarrow{ML}$ and $\overrightarrow{MN}$

24. If $\overrightarrow{TS}$ and $\overrightarrow{TU}$ form a straight line, is the figure an angle?

24. Yes, it fits the definition of an angle.

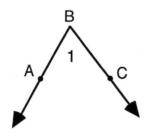

Figure 1.2

The middle letter of the notation ∠ABC is the vertex. The angle may be written as either ∠ABC, ∠CBA, or ∠B.

Numbers may also be used to name an angle. Therefore, Figure 1.2 may be named in four different ways: ∠1, ∠ABC, ∠CBA, or ∠B.

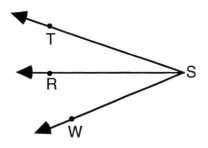

Figure 1.3

If the vertices of more than one angle meet at a point, then three letters or a number must be used to name the angle. In Figure 1.3, ∠S refers to which angle? To avoid confusion, be very specific in problems where more than one vertex is involved. Instead of using only one letter, ∠S, be specific. Name ∠TSW, ∠TSR, or ∠RSW if those are the angles you want to indicate.

25.

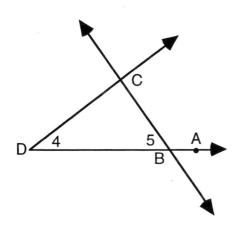

(a) Name ∠D in five other ways. ____, ____, ____, ____, or ____

(b) Show how many other ways you can, name ∠5. _____, _____

25.

(a) ∠4, ∠CDB, ∠BDC, ∠CDA, ∠ADC

(b) ∠DBC, ∠CBD

1.7 Angular Measure

Definition 1.7	A protractor is an instrument used to measure angles.

Definition 1.8	The unit of measure used in measuring angles is called degree.

Angles are measured with an instrument called a protractor. The number of degrees in an angle is called its measure. Your instructor will demonstrate the method used in measuring angles with a protractor. In Appendix E, a detailed explanation of this procedure can be found.

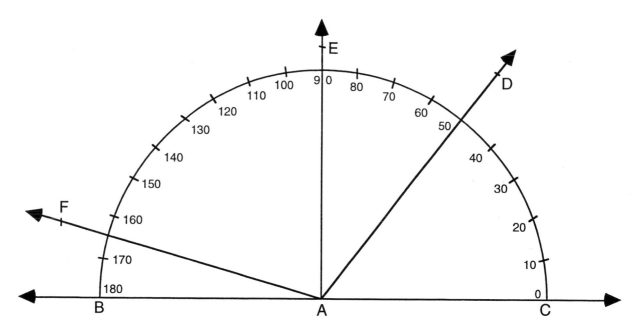

The measure of ∠CAD is equal to 50° (degrees).

∠CAE = 90°   ∠CAF = 165°   ∠CAB = 180°

26. Using a protractor, measure the given angles. (You may extend the sides of the angle if necessary.)

i.

ii.

26.

i. 80°

ii. 30°

iii.

The measure of an angle in this text may vary anywhere from any degree greater than 0° through 180°. Angles are placed in categories depending upon their degree measure.

1.8 Basic Definitions

Definition 1.9   A right angle is an angle that measures exactly 90°.

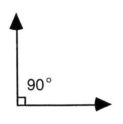

You may compare this measure of 90 degrees to the 3 o'clock position on your watch. Note the box symbol at the vertex used to denote a right angle.

Definition 1.10   An acute angle is an angle which measures more than 0° but less than 90°.

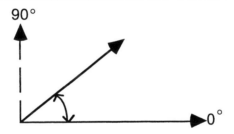

Definition 1.11   An obtuse angle is an angle which measures greater than 90° but less than 180°.

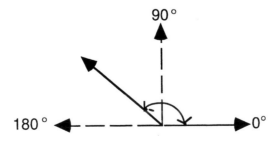

Definition 1.12   A <u>straight angle</u> is an angle which measures exactly 180°

180° ◄————————————•————————————► 0°

27. Using the preceding definitions, classify each of
    the following angles by the measures given:

    (a) 160°   (e) 110°
    (b) 180°   (f) 89°
    (c) 3°   (g) 91°
    (d) 90°

27.
    (a) obtuse
    (b) straight
    (c) acute
    (d) right
    (e) obtuse
    (f) acute
    (h) obtuse

28. Use a protractor to measure the angles
    given below:

28. (a) 120°
     (b) 90°

    (a)

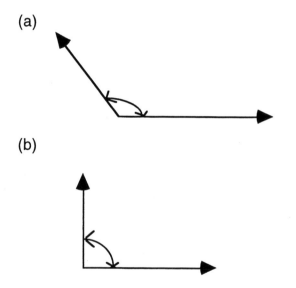

    (b)

Definition 1.13   <u>Adjacent angles</u> are two angles that share a common vertex and a common side between them.

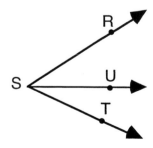

∠RSU and ∠UST are adjacent angles. Common vertex is S. Common side between ∠RSU and ∠UST is $\overrightarrow{SU}$.

29.

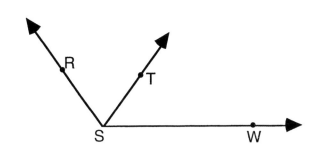

(a)   ∠RST and ∠TSW share what common vertex?

(b)   ∠RST and ∠TSW share what common side?

(c)   ∠RST and ∠TSW are called adjacent angles because _____.

(d)   Are ∠RSW and ∠TSW called adjacent angles?

29.

(a)   Point S

(b) $\overrightarrow{ST}$

(c)   Common side between them and a common vertex.

(d)   No, they share a common vertex but their common side, $\overrightarrow{SW}$, doesn't lie between the two angles.

Example:

∠XYZ is a straight angle. Find the measures of each angle.

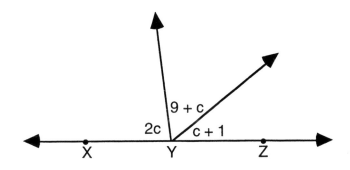

Solution:

$$(2c)+(9+c)+(c+1)=180°$$
$$4c+10=180$$
$$4c=170$$
$$c=42\frac{1}{2}°=42.5°$$

$$2c=85°$$
$$9+c=51\frac{1}{2}°=51.5°$$
$$c+1=43\frac{1}{2}°=43.5°$$

30. Find the measure of each angle if $\overleftrightarrow{OP}$ is a straight line. $\angle 1$, $\angle 2$, and $\angle 3$ are given the respective values in each part.

30.

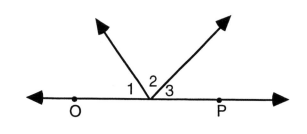

(a) c; 4c; 7c

(a)
$$c+4c+7c=180°$$
$$12c=180$$
$$c=15$$
$$4c=60°$$
$$7c=105°$$

(b) 8c + 3; 3c + 12; c − 3

(b)
$$(8c+3)+(3c+12)+(c-3)=180°$$
$$12c+12=180$$
$$12c=168$$
$$c=14$$
$$8c+3=115°$$
$$3c+12=54°$$
$$c-3=11°$$

1.9 Supplementary and Complementary Angles

The measure of two angles may be added together to illustrate two relationships between angles. These angles may be adjacent or they may be on different planes but the relationship will continue.

The first relationship is as follows:

Definition 1.14	Two angles are said to be <u>complementary</u> if their sum is 90°. That is, if ∠A + ∠B = 90°, ∠A and ∠B are complementary.

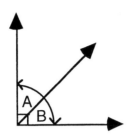

In the figure to the left angle A and angle B are complementary.

31. Two angles are said to be _____ if the sum of their measures equals 90°.

31. complementary

32. Angles A and B are called complements of one another. If ∠A = 50°, then the complement, ∠B, must equal _____.

32. ∠B = 40°, since 50° + 40° = 90°

33. If ∠A = 70° and ∠B = 70° are they complementary?

33. No, 70°+70° ≠ 90°

34. If ∠B = 35°, how do you find its complement?

The complement, ∠A, must equal what measure?

34. Subtract 35° from 90° 55°

Example:

∠ABC and ∠CBD are complementary angles. Find the measure of each.

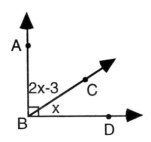

Solution:

$$(x)+(2x-3)=90°$$
$$3x-3=90$$
$$3x=93$$
$$x=31° \text{ equals the measure of } \angle CBD$$
$$2x-3=59° \text{ equals the measure of } \angle ABC$$

35. Find the measure of each angle if these rays, $\overleftarrow{MN}$ and $\overrightarrow{NO}$, form a right angle at their intersection. $\angle 1$ and $\angle 2$ are the respective values in each part.

35.

(a)   3x and 4x

(a)
$$3x+4x=90°$$
$$7x=90°$$
$$x=12\frac{6°}{7}$$
$$3x=38\frac{4°}{7} \text{ or } 38.\overline{571428}°$$
$$4x=51\frac{3°}{7} \text{ or } 51.\overline{428571}°$$

(b)   (3x + 2) and (3+2x)

(b)
$$(3x+2)+(3+2x)=90°$$
$$5x+5=90°$$
$$x=17°$$
$$3x+2=53°$$
$$3+2x=37°$$

The second relationship is as follows:

Definition 1.15   Two angles are <u>supplementary</u> if their sum is 180°. That is, if $\angle A + \angle B = 180°$, then $\angle A$ and $\angle B$ are supplementary.

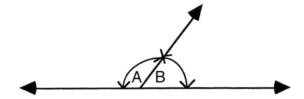

In the figure to the left, angle A and angle B are supplementary.

36. Two angles are supplementary if the sum of their measures is _____ .

36. 180°

37. Angles A and B are called supplements of each other. If ∠B = 50°, then the supplement, ∠A, must equal _____ .

37. 130°

38. If ∠B = 100° and ∠A = 80° are they complementary angles?

38. No, they are supplementary.

39. (a) If ∠A = 110° , how do you find its supplement?

     ∠B = _____ .

    (b) How do you find the complement of ∠A?

39. (a) Subtract 110° from 180°
             70°

    (b) 110° has no comple- ment since 90° - 110° cannot be the measure- ment of an angle.

Supplementary and complementary angles can be expressed in verbal problems. Study the following example.

Example: Two angles are complementary and one is 60° smaller than the other. Find the measure of the two angles.

Solution: x = first angle (unknown value)
           x – 60 = second angle

$(x) + (x - 60) = 90$ since they are complementary angles

$2x - 60 = 90$ simplifying algebraic expressions

$2x = 150$ adding 60 to both members and simplifying

$x = 75$ solving for "x", the first angle's measure

$(x - 60) = 15$ evaluating x - 60 to find the second angle's measure

40. Two angles are complementary. One angle is forty more than four times another. Find the measures of the two angles.

    Solution:

    x = one angle

    _____ = second angle   (a) _____   40.

    The equation   x + (4x+40) = _____   (b) _____   (a) 4x+40
    Simplifying   _____ = 90°   (c) _____   (b) 90°
                                5x = _____   (d) _____   (c) 5x+40
                                 x = _____   (e) _____   (d) 50°
    The first angle is _____.   (f) _____   (e) 10°
    The second angle is   (f) 10°
        4(10) + 40 = _____   (g) _____   (g) 80°

41. One angle is thirty-nine more than twice its supplement. Find the measure of both angles.

    _____ = the supplement   (a) _____   41.
    _____ = first angle   (b) _____   (a) x
    x + (2x + 39) = 180°   (b) 2x+39
        _____ = 180°   (c) _____   (c) 3x+39=180
           3x = _____   (d) _____   (d) 141
            x = _____   (e) _____   (e) 47
    The supplement equals _____.   (f) _____   (f) 47°
    The first angle equals _____.   (g) _____   (g) 133°

Exercise 1.2

1.

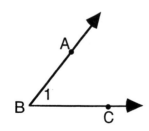

Indicate three possible labels for this angle.

_____

_____

_____

2.

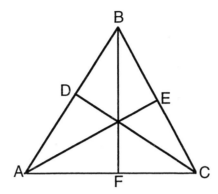

The angles listed below are numbered 1 through 8. Using the figure above, locate each angle and write its number on the figure in the order given.

1) ∠BAE   5) ∠BEA
2) ∠ADC   6) ∠EAC
3) ∠BDC   7) ∠BFC
4) ∠ABF   8) ∠DCF

3. Using a protractor, measure the given angles. Label each angle as straight, right, acute, or obtuse. Use a straightedge to extend the sides of the angles if necessary.

a.   b.   c.

d.

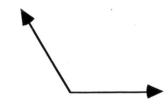

4. Find the supplement and complement of the given angle.

	Supplement	Complement
a. 30°	_____	_____
b. 120°	_____	_____

c.   x°   _____   _____

d.   45°   _____   _____

5. ∠XYZ is a straight angle. Find the measures of each angle and classify
    each as straight, acute, obtuse, or right angle.

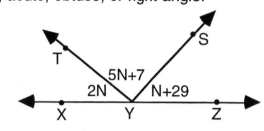

           N = _____

     ∠XYT = _____   _____

     ∠TYS = _____   _____

     ∠SYZ = _____   _____

6. Two angles are complementary and one is 30° less than the other. How
    many degrees are there in each angle?

7. Two angles are complementary. One angle is twelve more than five times
    the other. Find the measures of the two angles.

8. Two supplementary angles are equal in measure. Find their measure.

9. Two angles are supplementary. One angle is ten more than two-thirds the
    other. Find the measures of both angles.

10. Find the measure of each angle.

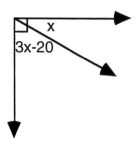

1.10 **Related Theorems**

> Theorem 1.1   Supplements of the <u>same</u> (or <u>equal</u>) angles are themselves
> equal.

Each condition below is illustrated with an example.

> Condition 1   Supplements of the <u>same</u> angle are equal.

Condition 1 compares the measures of different supplements to the same
angle. Let $\angle A$ and $\angle C$ be supplements of $\angle B$. Let $\angle B = 150°$. If
$\angle B = 150°$, then $\angle A = 30°$.

$\angle B + \angle A = 180°$ by the definition of supplementary angles.

$$\angle B + \angle A = 180°$$
$$150° + 30° = 180°$$

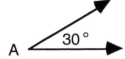 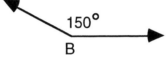

$\angle A$ is supplementary to $\angle B$.

Likewise, $\angle C = 30°$.

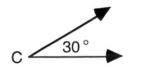 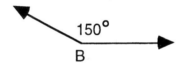

$\angle C$ is supplementary to $\angle B$.

$\angle A$ and $\angle C$ have the same measure, $30°$; therefore, they are equal.

> Condition 2 Supplements of <u>equal</u> angles are themselves equal.

In this condition we discuss angles that are equal and compare the
measures of the supplements to these angles.

$\angle S = \angle U$, $\angle S = 25°$, and $\angle U = 25°$. If $\angle S$ is supplementary to an
angle, say $\angle T$, then $\angle S + \angle T = 180°$ by the definition of supplementary
angles.

$$25 + \angle T = 180°$$
$$\angle T = 155°$$

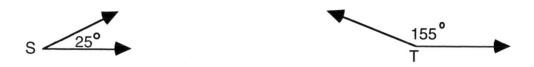

∠S is supplementary to ∠T.

If ∠U is supplementary to ∠W, then ∠U + ∠W = 180° by the definition of supplementary.

$$\angle U + \angle W = 180°$$
$$25° + \angle W = 180°$$
$$\angle W = 155°$$

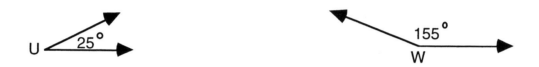

∠U is supplementary to ∠W.

∠T = 155° , ∠W = 155° , so ∠T = ∠W. This demonstrates that supplements of equal angles are equal.

Theorem 1.2 Complements of the <u>same</u> (or <u>equal</u>) angles are themselves equal.

Each condition below will be illustrated with an example.

Condition 1 Complements of the <u>same</u> angles are equal.

Condition 1 compares the measures of different complements of a single angle. Let ∠W and ∠Y be complements of ∠X. Let ∠X = 70°. If ∠X = 70°, then ∠W = 20°. ∠X + ∠W = 90° by the definition of complementary angles.

$$\angle X + \angle W = 90°$$
$$70° + \angle W = 90°$$
$$\angle W = 20°$$

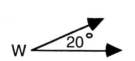

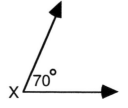

∠W is complementary to ∠X.

Likewise, ∠Y = 20°.

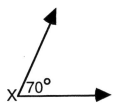

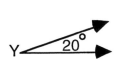

∠Y is complementary to ∠X.

∠W and ∠Y have the same measure, 20°; therefore, they are equal.

| Condition 2 Complements of <u>equal</u> angles are themselves equal. |

In this condition we discuss angles that are equal and compare the measures of the complements to these angles. Let ∠R = ∠Q, ∠R = 40° and ∠Q = 40°. If ∠R is complementary to ∠P, then ∠R + ∠P = 90° by the definition of complementary angles.

$$∠R + ∠P = 90°$$
$$40° + ∠P = 90°$$
$$∠P = 50°$$

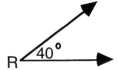

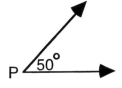

∠R is complementary to ∠P.

If ∠Q is complementary to ∠T, then ∠Q + ∠T = 90° by the definition of complementary angles.

$$∠Q + ∠T = 90°$$
$$40° + ∠T = 90°$$
$$∠T = 50°$$

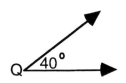

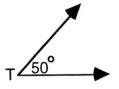

∠Q is complementary to ∠T.

∠P = 50° and ∠T = 50°. Therefore, ∠P = ∠T. This demonstrates that complements of equal angles are equal.

Example: ∠ABC and ∠EBD are right angles. If ∠2 = 25°, show that ∠1 equals ∠3.

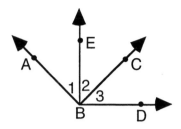

Solution:

1. ∠1 and ∠2 are complementary angles; ∠1 = 65°.

2. ∠3 and ∠2 are complementary angles; ∠3 = 65°.

3. ∠1 = ∠3 because complements of the same angle are themselves equal.

42. In the figure below, ∠XYN and ∠NYZ are right angles. Also, ∠2 = 44° and ∠3 = 44°. Show that ∠1 = ∠4. For statements 2-4, give the reason why each statement is true.

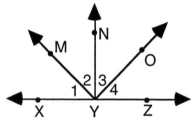

1. ∠2 = ∠3 Why?

2. ∠1 and ∠2 are _____.

3. ∠3 and ∠4 are _____.

4. ∠1 = ∠4 because _____.

42.

1. Given

2. complementary angles; ∠1=46°

3. complementary angles; ∠4=46°

4. complements of equal angles are themselves equal.

Example:

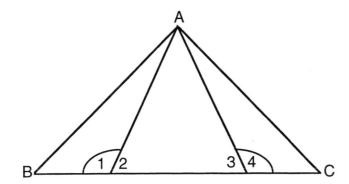

In the figure, $\overline{BC}$ is a straight line segment, $\angle 1 = 110°$, and $\angle 4 = 110°$.
Show that $\angle 2$ equals $\angle 3$.

Solution:

1. $\angle 1 = \angle 4$ because the information was given.

2. $\angle 1$ and $\angle 2$ are supplementary angles; $\angle 2 = 70°$.

3. $\angle 3$ and $\angle 4$ are supplementary angles; $\angle 3 = 70°$.

4. $\angle 2 = \angle 3$ because supplements of equal angles are themselves equal.

43.

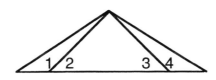

In the figure $\angle 2 = \angle 3$. If $\angle 2 = 40°$, show
that $\angle 1$ and $\angle 4$ are equal and find the value
of $\angle 1$ and $\angle 4$.

Fill in the correct response below.

1. $\angle 2 = \angle 3$ Why?
2. $\angle 1$ and $\angle 2$ are _____.
3. $\angle 4$ and $\angle 3$ are _____.
4. $\angle 1 = \angle 4$ because _____.

5. $\angle 1 = $ _____
    $\angle 4 = $ _____

43.

1. given
2. supplementary
3. supplementary
4. supplements of
   equal angles
   are themselves
   equal.
5. $\angle 1 = 140°$
    $\angle 4 = 140°$

44.

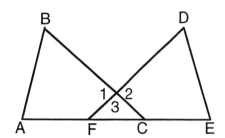

44.

In the figure, if ∠3 = 100°, show that ∠1 equals ∠2 and find the value of ∠1 and ∠2.

Fill in the correct response below.

1. ∠1 and ∠3 are _____.
2. ∠2 and ∠3 are _____.
3. ∠1 = ∠2 because _____.

4. ∠1 = _____.
    ∠2 = _____.

1. supplementary
2. supplementary
3. supplements of the same angle are themselves equal.
4. ∠1 = 80°
    ∠2 = 80°

Problems similar to #43-44 can be applied to <u>complementary</u> angles.

Definition 1.16	A pair of non adjacent angles formed by two intersecting lines is called a pair of <u>vertical angles</u>.

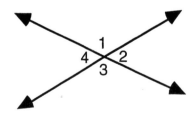

Figure 1.4

∠1 and ∠3 are vertical angles.
∠2 and ∠4 are vertical angles.

Theorem 1.3   Pairs of vertical angles are equal.

Proof: (Note: The statements refer to Figure 1.4.)

Statements	Reasons
1. ∠1 and ∠3 are vertical angles.	1. Definition of vertical angles.
2. ∠1 and ∠2 are supplementary angles. ∠2 and ∠3 are supplementary angles.	2. Definition of supplementary angles.
3. ∠1 = ∠3	3. Supplements of the same angle are equal.

Definition 1.17   Two lines are <u>perpendicular</u> if they form right angles at their intersection.

The symbol for perpendicular is ⊥. Each angle formed at the intersection of perpendicular lines is 90°.

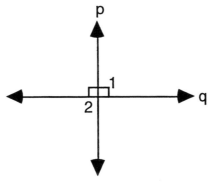

p ⊥ q

45. In the figure above, show that ∠1 and ∠2 are right angles.

45.

1. Lines p ⊥ q. Why?	1. Given
2. ∠1 is a right angle. Why?	2. Perpendicular lines form right angles.
3. ∠1 and ∠2 are what kind of angles?	3. Vertical angles by definition.
4. ∠1 = ∠2. Why?	4. Pairs of vertical angles are equal.

46. If $\overleftrightarrow{EF}$ and $\overleftrightarrow{XY}$ are perpendicular and $\angle 3 = \angle 5$, find the measure of $\angle 1$, $\angle 2$, $\angle 3$, $\angle 4$, $\angle 5$, and $\angle 6$.

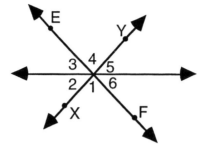

46.

1. $\overleftrightarrow{EF} \perp \overleftrightarrow{XY}$ Why?
2. $\angle 4 = 90°$ Why?

1. Given
2. Perpendicular lines form right angles.

3. $\angle 1$ and $\angle 4$ are what kind of angles?

3. Vertical angles by definition.

4. $\angle 1 = 90°$ Why?

4. Pairs of vertical angles are equal.

5. $\angle 3 = \angle 5$ Why?
6.

5. Given
6.

    $\angle 3 + \angle 4 + \angle 5 = 180°$ and

      $x + 90° + x = 180°$ by substitution

        $2x + 90 = 180$

          $2x = 90$

The angles all together form a straight line.

            $x = \underline{}$

7. $\angle 3$ and $\angle 6$ are what kind of angles?

$45°$

7. Vertical angles by definition.

8. $\angle 6 = \underline{}$ because pairs of vertical angles are equal.

8. $45°$

9. $\angle 5$ and $\angle 2$ are what kind of angles?

9. Vertical angles by definition.

10. $\angle 2 = \underline{}$ because $\underline{}$.

10. $45°$
Pairs of vertical angles are equal.

Definition 1.18   A line that divides a line segment into two equal parts is called the <u>bisector</u> of a line segment.

Segment $\overline{EF}$ is bisected by line p in the following figure. Hence, $\overline{EM} = \overline{MF}$. M is the midpoint of $\overline{EF}$. A bisector of a line segment and a midpoint both divide a line segment into two equal parts. However, a <u>bisector</u> of a line segment is a <u>line</u>; a <u>midpoint</u> is a <u>point</u>.

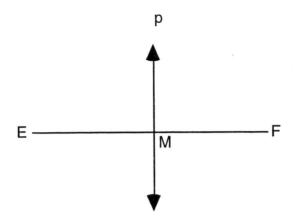

1.11 **Constructions**

With every geometric concept, there is a physical application of this concept. Constructions are only one method of demonstrating such applications. Since we are to make no measurements in a construction, we are limited to the use of two instruments...an unmarked ruler (straight edge) and compass. The straight edge will be used for drawing a line through two points and the compass will be used to draw circles to make arcs.

Definition 1.19   The perpendicular bisector of a line segment is a line which is perpendicular to that segment and divides that segment into two equal parts.

Construction 1.1   To Find the Perpendicular Bisector of a Line Segment

Procedure:

Step 1:   Draw a line segment $\overline{MN}$.
Estimate the radius of your compass to be more than 1/2 the length of $\overline{MN}$.

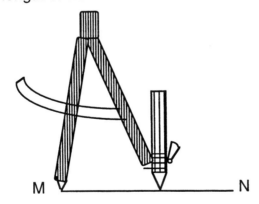

Step 2:   With M as the center on your compass, draw a partial circle (arc) on the right side of the letter M.

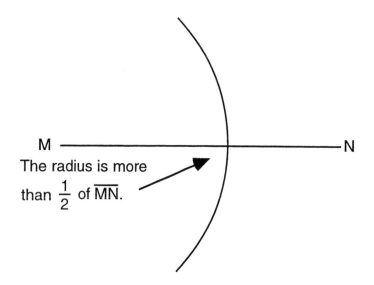

M ────────────────────────────────N

The radius is more

than $\frac{1}{2}$ of $\overline{MN}$.

Step 3:   With N as the center and using the same radius, draw a partial circle on the left side of letter N. (Note: If the arcs do not intersect the radius selected is less than half of $\overline{MN}$ and needs to be increased.)

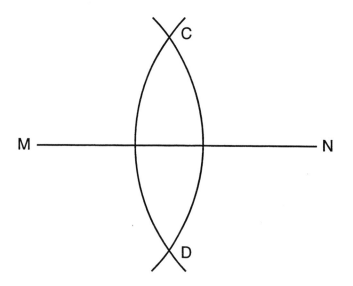

Step 4:   With your straight edge, draw a line from point C to point D.

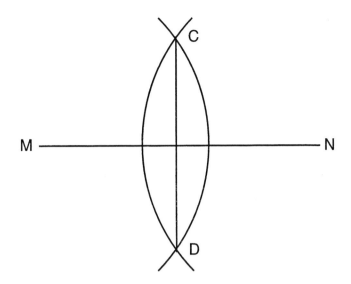

Step 5: $\overleftrightarrow{CD}$ intersects $\overline{MN}$ at a point we will call E. Point E is the midpoint of $\overline{MN}$ and line $\overleftrightarrow{CD}$ is the bisector of $\overline{MN}$.

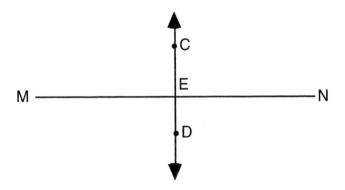

$\overleftrightarrow{CD}$ bisects $\overline{MN}$ and is perpendicular to $\overline{MN}$. $\overleftrightarrow{CD}$ is called the perpendicular bisector of the line segment.

47. Follow Steps 1-5 of Construction 1.1. Find the midpoint and the perpendicular bisector of the segment $\overline{XY}$.

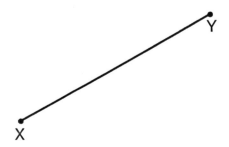

Definition 1.20	The <u>angle bisector</u> is a ray that divides an angle into two smaller angles having equal measure.

Construction 1.2	To Find the Angle Bisector

Procedure:

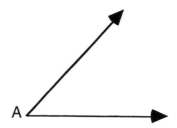

Step 1   With A as the center, draw a partial circle (arc) that crosses both rays of the angle and plot points B and C at the intersection.

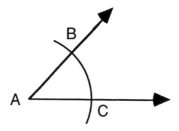

Step 2   With B and C as centers, using a radius greater than half the distance between B and C draw two arcs in the interior of the angle. Plot point D at the intersection.

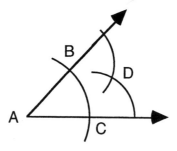

Step 3   Draw ray $\overrightarrow{AD}$. This ray divides ∠A into two equal parts.

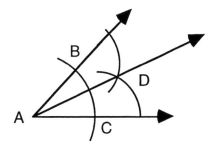

48. Using the procedure in Construction 1.2, find the angle bisector of ∠X below.

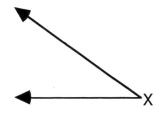

Construction 1.3   To Copy an Angle

Step 1

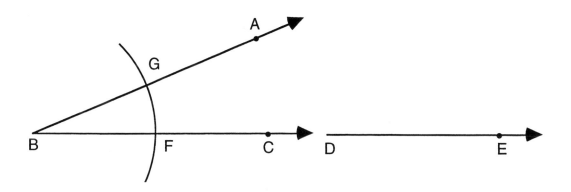

Figure 1.5

With B as center, draw an arc which intersects $\overrightarrow{BA}$ and $\overrightarrow{BC}$ at points G and F, respectively.

Step 2   With the same radius and with D as center, draw an arc which intersects $\overrightarrow{DE}$ (at point H) and extends above $\overrightarrow{DE}$ as shown.

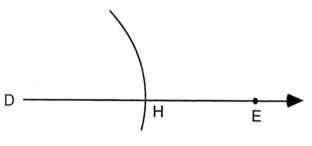

Figure 1.6

Step 3   In Figure 1.5, place one point of the compass at F and adjust the radius of the compass so the other point is at G. With this radius and using H as center in Figure 1.6, draw a second arc to intersect the previous arc to form point I as shown below.

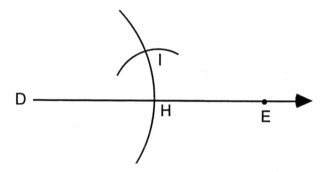

Step 4   Draw a ray from D through I.

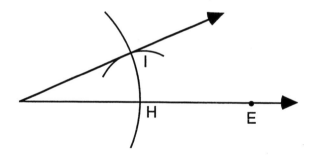

49. Follow Steps 1-4 and copy ∠XYZ onto the ray $\overrightarrow{NO}$ by construction.

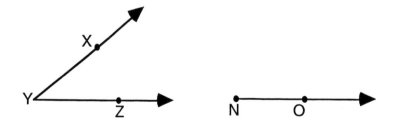

Exercise 1.3

1. Draw an acute angle and copy it onto segment $\overline{TR}$.

T ———————————————————— R

2. Find the perpendicular bisector of segments $\overline{MN}$ and $\overline{NO}$ by using only a straight edge and a compass.

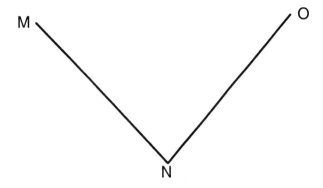

3. Using only a straight edge and compass, bisect $\angle ABC$.

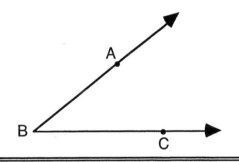

Unit 1 Review

1. a. <u>Define</u> the following:

postulate	deductive reasoning	straight angle
theorem	adjacent angles	midpoint
degrees	complementary angles	line segment
right angle	vertical angles	angle bisector
acute angle	perpendicular bisector	vertex
angle	bisector of a line segment	inductive reasoning
ray	supplementary angles	perpendicular lines
obtuse angle		

  b. <u>Describe</u> the use of the following:

  compass   straight edge   protractor

2. Fill in the blanks with the appropriate word or phrase to complete the definition.

  a. An _____ is formed by a pair of rays with a common endpoint called a _____. The symbol for this figure is _____.

  b. If $\angle A + \angle B = 90°$, the angles are said to be _____.

  c. If $\angle A + \angle B = 180°$, the angles are said to be _____.

3. The four elements of the deductive reasoning system are: _____, _____, _____, and _____.

4. a. What is the degree of an angle whose measure is $\dfrac{2}{3}$ of its complement?

  b. Two angles are supplementary. One angle is five times the measure of the other angle. Find the two angles.

  c. Two angles are complementary. One angle is 20 more than four times as much as the other. Find the two angles.

  d. Two angles are supplementary. One angle is twice the other. Find the angles.

5. Use only a straightedge and compass in the following constructions.

  a. Find the midpoint of $\overline{AB}$ by construction.

A   B

  b. Construct the bisector of the given angle.

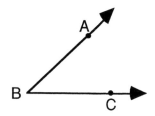

c. Copy the given angle.

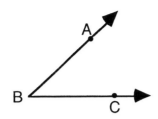

6. Using a protractor, find the measures of the given angles. Label each has straight, acute, obtuse, or right and write each of their degrees.

(i)

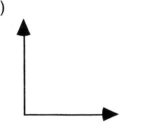

(ii)

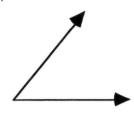

(iii)

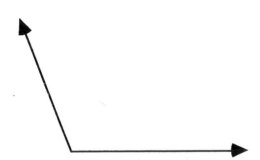

(iv)

7. Given the line segment $\overline{DX}$.

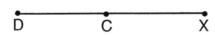

D   C   X

(i)   What are the endpoints of $\overline{DX}$?

(ii)   Is $\overline{DX} = \overline{XD}$?

(iii)   If $\overline{DC} = \overline{CX}$ then point C is called the _____.

8.

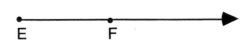

E   F

(i) In $\overrightarrow{EF}$, E is called the _____.

(ii) Is $\overrightarrow{EF}$ the same as $\overrightarrow{FE}$? Why or why not?

9. Find the indicated values.

a. Given that $\overleftrightarrow{AD}$ is a straight line, find $\angle ABC$, $\angle CBE$, and $\angle DBE$.

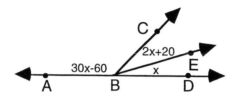

b. Given $\overleftrightarrow{AB} \perp \overrightarrow{BC}$, find $\angle ABD$, $\angle DBC$, $\angle ABC$.

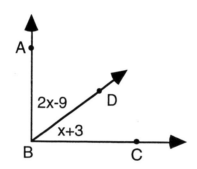

10. a. In the figure $\angle 1 = \angle 4$ and $\angle 4 = 110°$. Show that $\angle 2 = \angle 3$ and find the measure of $\angle 1$, $\angle 2$, and $\angle 3$. $\overline{AD}$ is a straight line segment.

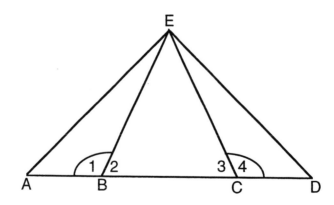

b. Given two straight lines, p and q, if $\angle 5 = 85°$, then find the measures of the other angles. Give reasons for your answers.

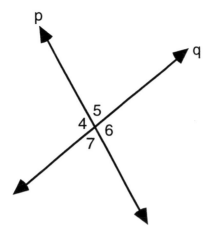

Unit 2

Triangles and Congruence

Learning Objectives:

1. The student will demonstrate his mastery of the following definitions and postulates by writing them and by applying them to solutions of selected problems:

    <u>Definitions</u>: triangle, vertices, perimeter, isosceles triangle, equilateral triangle, scalene triangle, right triangle, obtuse triangle, acute triangle, equiangular triangle, hypotenuse, legs, altitude, median, overlapping triangles, congruent triangles, and " $\cong$ ".

    <u>Postulates</u>: (a) If three sides of one triangle are equal to three corresponding sides of a second triangle, then the triangles are said to be congruent. (SSS = SSS)

    (b) If two sides and an included angle of one triangle are equal to two sides and an included angle of a second triangle, then the triangles are congruent. (SAS = SAS)

    (c) If two angles and an included side of one triangle are equal to two angles and an included side of a second triangle, then the triangles are congruent. (ASA = ASA)

2. The following constructions are required:

    (a) Construct the three medians of any triangle.

    (b) Construct the three altitudes of any triangle.

TRIANGLES AND CONGRUENCE

2.1 Basic Definitions

> Definition 2.1   A <u>triangle</u> is the union of three line segments determined by three points that are all not on the same line (noncollinear points). The three noncollinear points are called the <u>vertices</u> of the triangle. The symbol for a triangle is $\triangle$.

A triangle is a figure that is shaped like one of the following. It is a closed three-sided figure.

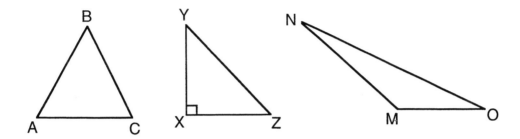

We name the first triangle by writing, $\triangle ABC$. It may also be denoted an $\triangle BCA$ or $\triangle CAB$. The order of the vertices does not matter. The three sides of $\triangle ABC$ are $\overline{AB}$, $\overline{BC}$, and $\overline{AC}$. A triangle also has three angles, $\angle A$, $\angle B$, and $\angle C$. In $\triangle ABC$ the points A, B, and C are the vertices. A is called a vertex of $\triangle ABC$.

1. What are the three sides of the second triangle, $\triangle XYZ$?

1. $\overline{XY}$, $\overline{YX}$, $\overline{XZ}$

2. What are the angles in $\triangle XYZ$?

2. $\angle X$, $\angle Y$, $\angle Z$

3.

F
7 cm.   4 cm.
D _____ E
      8 cm.

3.

a. Name the vertices of $\triangle DEF$.

a. points D, E, F

b. Name the sides of $\triangle FED$ (same as $\triangle DEF$).

b. $\overline{DE}$, $\overline{EF}$, $\overline{DF}$

c. Name the angles of $\triangle EFD$ (same as $\triangle DEF$).

c. $\angle D$, $\angle E$, $\angle F$

4.

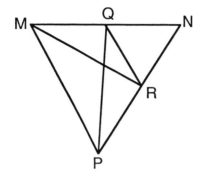

a. With your pencil, shade in △NQR.

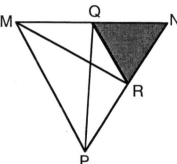

b. Find ∠NQR and number it with a 1.

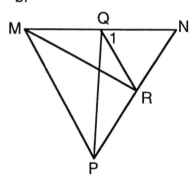

c. With your pencil, shade in △MPQ.

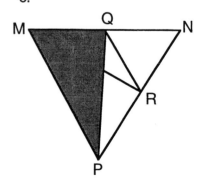

4.

a.

b.

c.

d. Find ∠MPQ and number it with a 2.

d.

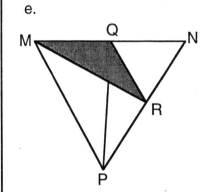

e. With your pencil, shade in △MRQ.

e.

Definition 2.2 The <u>perimeter</u> of a triangle is the sum of the measures of the sides of the triangle.

5. a. What is the perimeter of △DEF in #3?

5. a. 19 cm.

b. Find the perimeter of a triangle with sides

$7\frac{1}{2}$ in., 3 in., and $5\frac{2}{3}$ in.

b. $16\frac{1}{6} = 16.1\overline{6}$ in.

c. Find the perimeter of a triangular garden with

sides $4\frac{1}{2}$ ft., $5\frac{1}{4}$ ft. and $8\frac{1}{5}$ ft. If a homeowner has 6 yds. of fence, could he enclose the garden with fencing?

c. $17\frac{19}{20} = 17.95$ ft.

Yes

Exercise 2.1

1.

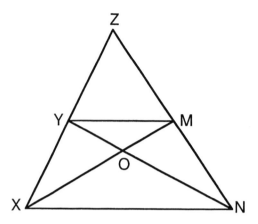

 a. Name the vertices of △XZN.

 b. Name twelve triangles that are in △XZN. (Triangles can overlap one
   another.)

2. Find the perimeter of △ABC.

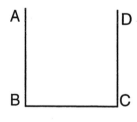

3. Is Figure 2.1 a triangle?
  Why or why not?

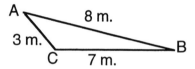

Figure 2.1

2.2 Classification of Triangles

Triangles may be classified by two methods: length of sides or measure of
angles.

The following definitions (2.3, 2.4, and 2.5) give the classification of triangles by
lengths of the sides.

> Definition 2.3 An <u>isosceles triangle</u> is a triangle that has at least two sides equal.

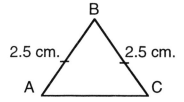

△ABC is isosceles with sides $\overline{AB} = \overline{BC}$. Note how △ABC is marked to note that two sides are equal.

> Definition 2.4 An <u>equilateral triangle</u> is a triangle that has all the sides equal.

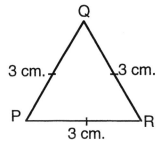

△PQR is an equilateral triangle with sides $\overline{PQ} = \overline{QR} = \overline{PR}$. Note how △PQR is marked to note that three sides are equal.

Can an equilateral triangle also be isosceles? Yes. An equilateral triangle has at least two sides equal.

Can an isosceles triangle also be equilateral? Yes. However, not all isosceles triangles have all the sides of equal measure.

> Definition 2.5 A <u>scalene triangle</u> is a triangle that has no two sides of equal measure.

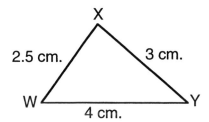

△WXY is scalene. No two sides are of equal measure.

Using the previous definitions, consider the following three triangles and classify each by its sides.

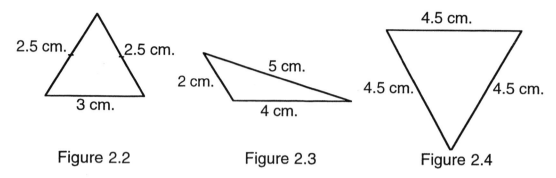

Figure 2.2   Figure 2.3   Figure 2.4

Figure 2.2 has exactly two sides the same length. This triangle is called isosceles. The equal sides are often called the legs of the triangle and the third side is called the base.

Figure 2.3 has no two sides equal. When all three sides of the triangle have different lengths, the triangle is called scalene.

Figure 2.4 has each side of 4.5 cm. An equilateral triangle fits this description with all three sides the same measure.

6. Classify the triangles below according to the lengths of their sides.
   a.

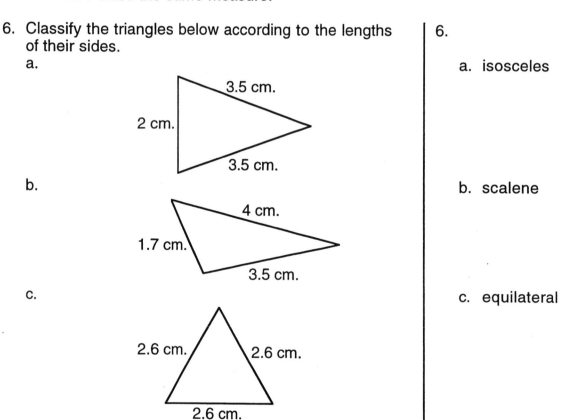

6.

a. isosceles

b. scalene

c. equilateral

7. Classify each triangle by the length of its sides.

7.

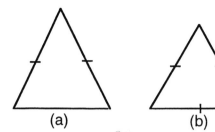

(a)   (b)   (c)

(a) isosceles
(b) equilateral
(c) scalene

8. Can an equilateral triangle also be an isosceles triangle?
   Why?

8. Yes, because an isosceles triangle has at least two equal sides.

9. Can a scalene triangle also be isosceles?

9. No, because an isosceles triangle has at least two sides equal.

Classifying triangles by the measure of their angles is the second method of identifying types of triangle. The following definitions (2.6, 2.7, 2.8, and 2.9) give the classification of triangles by the measure of the angles.

Definition 2.6 A right triangle is a triangle that has one right angle. The side opposite the right angle is called the hypotenuse. The other two sides are called legs.

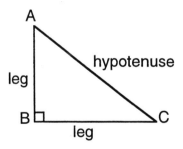

In right triangle ABC, sides $\overline{AB}$ and $\overline{BC}$ are the legs. The hypotenuse is $\overline{AC}$. The longest side of a right triangle is the hypotenuse.

Definition 2.7   An <u>obtuse triangle</u> is a triangle with one obtuse angle.

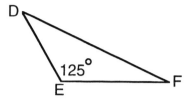

△DEF is an obtuse triangle with obtuse angle, ∠E.

Definition 2.8   An <u>acute triangle</u> is a triangle with all acute angles.

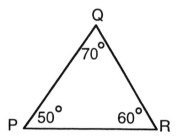

△PQR is an acute triangle.   ∠P, ∠Q, and ∠R are acute angles.

Definition 2.9   If an acute triangle has all the angles of equal measure,
the triangle is called an <u>equiangular triangle</u>.

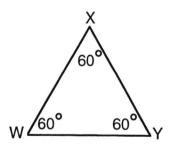

△WXY is an equiangular triangle.   ∠W, ∠X, and ∠Y are all three acute angles
and equal to 60°.

10.   Classify the triangles below according to their angles
or their sides.

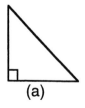   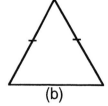   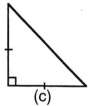

10.

(a) right
triangle
(b) isosceles
triangle
(c) isosceles
right
triangle

11. Classify the triangles below according to their angles or their sides.

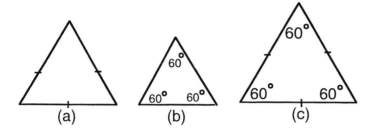

(a)   (b)   (c)

11.

    (a) equilateral
        triangle
    (b) equiangular
        triangle
    (c) equilateral
        and equi-
        angular
        triangle

12. Classify the triangle below according to their angles or their sides.

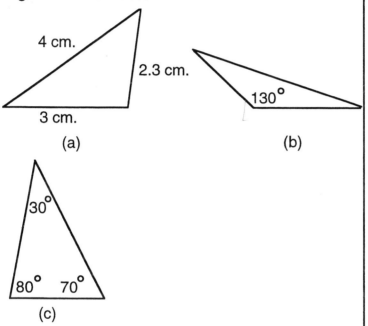

(a)   (b)

(c)

12.

    (a) scalene
        triangle
    (b) obtuse
        triangle
    (c) acute
        triangle

13. Find the hypotenuse in each of the following right triangles.

(a)

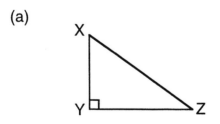

13.

    (a) $\overline{XZ}$ is
        opposite
        the right
        angle so
        $\overline{XZ}$ is the
        hypotenuse.

(b)

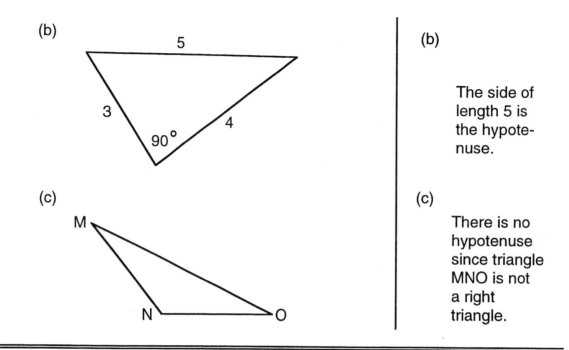

(b)

The side of length 5 is the hypotenuse.

(c)

There is no hypotenuse since triangle MNO is not a right triangle.

Exercise 2.2

1. Give two classifications for each of the following triangles, one based on length of sides and one based on measure of angles.

a.

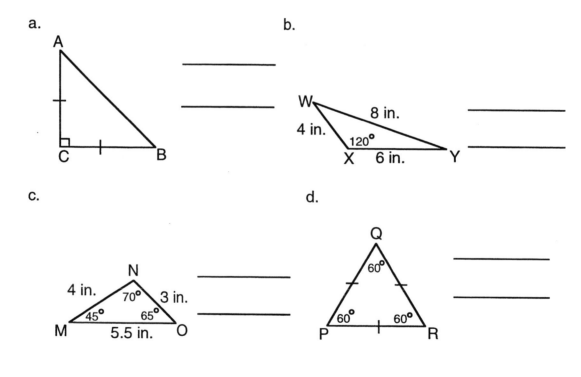

b.

c.

d.

2.3 <u>Altitude of a Triangle</u>

> Definition 2.10   An <u>altitude</u> of a triangle is a line segment that is drawn from the vertex perpendicular to the opposite side (or extension of that side).

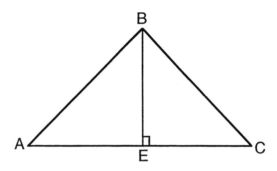

Figure 2.5

In Figure 2.5, $\overline{BE}$ is one altitude of $\triangle ABC$. It originates at vertex B and is perpendicular to side $\overline{AC}$. Please note that $\triangle ABC$ has three vertices. It also has three altitudes, one from each vertex.

14.   In Figure 2.5

    (a)   If you were to draw an altitude from vertex C, this altitude would be perpendicular to what side?

    (b)   The altitude drawn from point A would be perpendicular to what side of the triangle?

15.

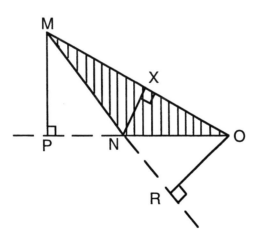

Figure 2.6

In Figure 2.6 the altitude, $\overline{MP}$, from vertex M is perpendicular to the extension of side $\overline{NO}$.

14.

    (a) $\overline{AB}$

    (b) $\overline{BC}$

15.

What are the other altitudes found in △MNO?

$\overline{NX}$ from
vertex N
$\overline{OR}$ from
vertex O

Construction   2.1 Construct an altitude of a triangle.

To construct an altitude of a triangle follow the steps illustrated below:

Step 1: To construct an altitude from point M, extend side $\overline{NO}$.

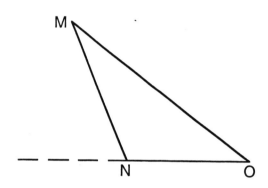

Step 2: Using point M as the center select a radius wide enough to intersect $\overline{NO}$ at two points, A and B.

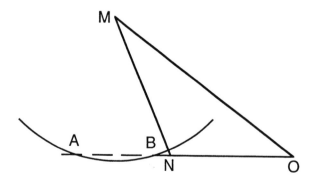

Step 3: Using points A and B as centers, construct point C below $\overline{NO}$ and draw a line from point M to P. $\overline{MP}$ is called the altitude.

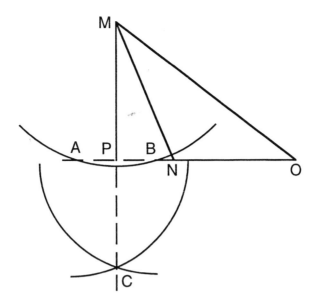

16. Now turn triangle MNO so that $\overline{MO}$ is horizontal. Using steps 1, 2, and 3, construct the altitude from point N to $\overline{MO}$. (You will not have to extend the base line for this vertex.) $\overline{NQ}$ is the altitude.

16.

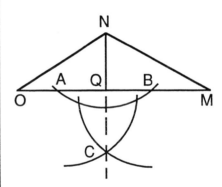

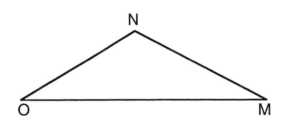

17. Finally turn triangle MNO again with side $\overline{MN}$ horizontal. (Note that the triangle does not have to be rotated. It is being rotated here for convenience in construction.) Using steps 1, 2, and 3, construct the altitude from point O to $\overline{MN}$. $\overline{OR}$ is the altitude.

17.

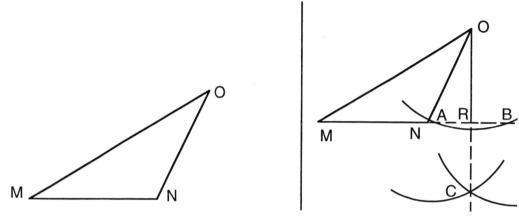

2.4 Median of a Triangle

Definition 2.11   A median of a triangle is a line segment that is drawn from the vertex to the midpoint of the opposite side.

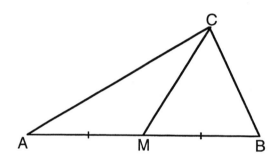

M is the midpoint of $\overline{AB}$ and $\overline{CM}$ is called the median of $\triangle ABC$.

A triangle has three altitudes and it has three medians.

18. (a)   An altitude drawn from point C in $\triangle ABC$ is _____ to side $\overline{AB}$.

18. (a)   perpendicular

    (b)   A median drawn from point C in $\triangle ABC$ is drawn to the _____ of side $\overline{AB}$.

    (b)   midpoint

Construction 2.2   Construct a median of a triangle

To construct a median from point A to segment $\overline{BC}$ follow steps 1 and 2 as illustrated.

Step 1: Construct the perpendicular bisector of $\overline{BC}$ to find the midpoint of $\overline{BC}$. (For the perpendicular construction, see Unit 1, Construction 1.1).

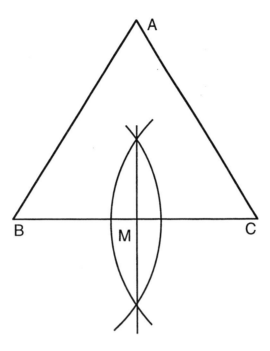

Step 2: Draw the line segment from the midpoint M to point A. $\overline{AM}$ is the median of △ABC.

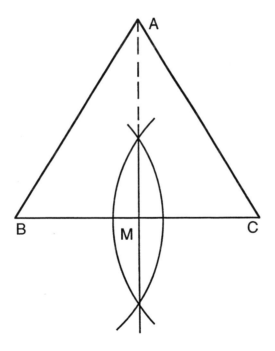

19. Using the same triangle as in Figure 2.6, construct the three medians of that triangle. Copies of triangle MNO are provided for your convenience.

19.

(a) Construct the median from
     vertex M.

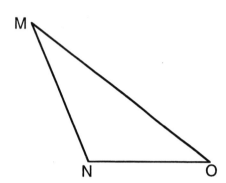

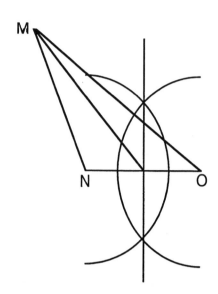

(b) Construct the median from
     vertex O.

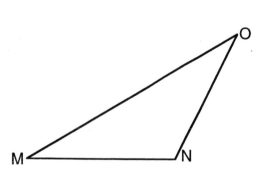

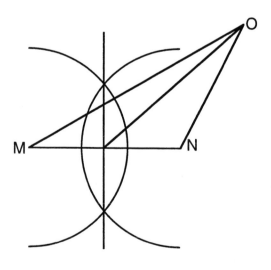

(c) Construct the median from vertex N.

(a)

(b)

(c)

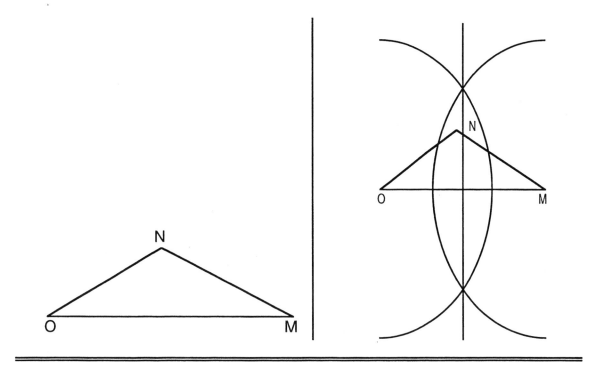

Exercise 2.3

1. Draw a triangle and construct the medians from each of its vertices.

2. Draw an obtuse triangle and construct the altitudes from each of its vertices.

3. Find the perimeter of an equilateral triangle with a side of 15 inches.

4. The perimeter of an isosceles triangle is 32 inches and its base is 8 inches. Find the length of one of its equal sides.

5. The base of an isosceles triangle is half the length of one of the equal sides. The perimeter is $41\frac{1}{2}$ inches. Find the length of the base.

6. If the perimeter of an equilateral triangle is 69 inches, find the length of one of its sides.

7. a. Can a triangle have more than one right angle?

   b. More than one obtuse angle?

   c. More than one acute angle?

2.5 <u>Overlapping Triangles</u>

Geometric figures may overlap. It is important that you are able to see more than one figure in a drawing that overlaps such as the picture below. There are two ladies in this picture. Which do you see, the old lady or the young woman? Concentrate on trying to see each (one at a time). In order to recognize both, you must perceive a portion of the drawing in different relationships. Each figure is illustrated separately as well.

The young lady turned looking back over her right shoulder.

The old lady

The ability to see these relationships is important to geometry. Without this ability you will be unable to see the relationship of figures or the relationship of how parts in deductive reasoning fit together in a geometric proof.

Definition 2.12 Two triangles are called <u>overlapping triangles</u> if they share some of the same space.

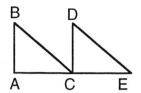

$\triangle ABC$ and $\triangle CDE$ are not overlapping.

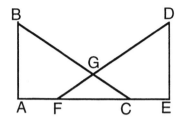

$\triangle ABC$ and $\triangle EDF$ are overlapping. They share the space in $\triangle FGC$.

Study each of the following figures and indicate which two triangles are overlapping.

20.

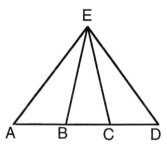

$\triangle ACE$ and _____

20. $\triangle DBE$ or $\triangle BCE$

21.

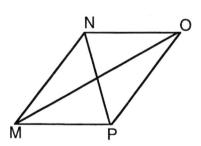

$\triangle MNO$ and _____

21. $\triangle PON$ or $\triangle MNP$

22.   △XZW and _____ | 22. △VYZ

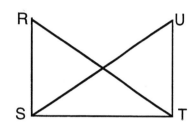

23.   △RST and _____ | 23. △UTS

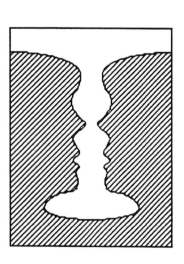

24. What do you see in this drawing? | 24. Two things can
                                             be seen: two
                                             heads facing
                                             each other or a
                                             vase.

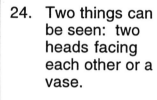

2.6 Definition of Congruence

Is △DEF the same size and shape as △ABC?

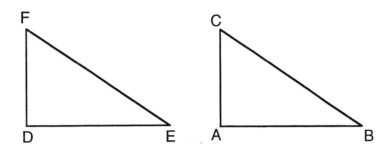

How would one be able to tell? One way, of course, would be to cut the first triangle out and position it directly on top of the second triangle, matching it exactly. This method, however, is not always feasible. In this unit we will discuss other ways to compare the measures of two triangles.

> Definition 2.13   Two figures which have the same size and shape are said to be <u>congruent</u> figures. The symbol used for this property is ≅.

The question arises, why is the concept of congruence studied? In the physical world, there are many examples of congruent figures. A machine that seals cans in a mass production line must use circular tops that are all congruent. A paper press that cuts and prints notebook paper will make each sheet exactly the same. All 9 x 10 glass window panes are produced in the same shape in order that each may fit a standard window.

In considering industry and its output of appliances, furnishings, paper and machine supplies, food production, transport vehicles and all other processes, it is no wonder why "congruence" is considered the single most outstanding geometric principle permeating every facet of each of our daily lives.

This unit will limit its discussions of congruence to comparing two triangles. Below are illustrated △RST and △ABC.

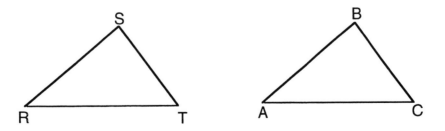

∠R and ∠A are said to be corresponding parts of these triangles. Why?

Answer:

They are in the same relative positions with regard to the sides of the compared triangles. Likewise ∠S corresponds to ∠B and ∠T corresponds to ∠C. The same relationship exists between the sides. $\overline{RS}$ corresponds to $\overline{AB}$, $\overline{ST}$ corresponds to $\overline{BC}$ and $\overline{RT}$ to $\overline{AC}$.

25. In △PQR and △XYZ, give the corresponding parts.

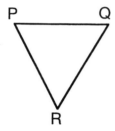 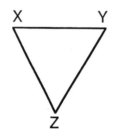

25. ∠P corr. ∠X
     ∠Q corr. ∠Y
     ∠R corr. ∠Z

     $\overline{PR}$ corr. $\overline{XZ}$
     $\overline{PQ}$ corr. $\overline{XY}$
     $\overline{RQ}$ corr. $\overline{ZY}$

Definition 2.14 Two triangles are <u>congruent</u> if and only if all corresponding parts are of equal measure.

If △LMN ≅ △PAC,

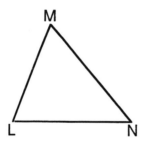 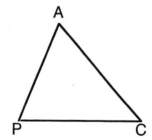

then the corresponding angles are equal (∠L = ∠P, ∠M = ∠A, ∠N = ∠C) and the corresponding sides are equal. ($\overline{LM} = \overline{PA}, \overline{LN} = \overline{PC}, \overline{MN} = \overline{AC}$) Note the position of the letters as listed in △LMN ≅ △PAC. The triangles are named in the order of their corresponding vertices. For example, ∠L corresponds to ∠P so if letter L is first in the listing of one triangle's name then P must be first in the listing of the second triangle's name. Next, if M is listed then A would correspond and so on. The congruence can be indicated as △MNL ≅ △ACP or △NLM ≅ △CPA as well as △LMN ≅ △PAC.

26. In each of the following, record the congruence symbolically for the given triangle.

26.

a.

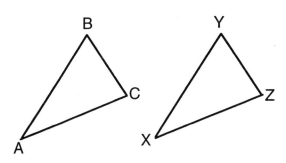

b.

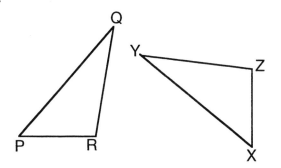

a.

$\triangle ABC \cong \triangle XYZ$
or $\triangle BCA \cong \triangle YZX$
or $\triangle CAB \cong \triangle ZXY$

b.

$\triangle PQR \cong \triangle XYZ$
or $\triangle QRP \cong \triangle YZX$
or $\triangle RPQ \cong \triangle ZXY$

Exercise 2.4

1.   If $\triangle MNO \cong \triangle PNO$, complete the following statements.

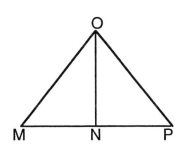

$\angle M = \text{\_\_\_\_\_}$
$\angle MNO = \text{\_\_\_\_\_}$
$\angle PON = \text{\_\_\_\_\_}$
$\overline{OP} = \text{\_\_\_\_\_}$
$\overline{MN} = \text{\_\_\_\_\_}$
$\overline{ON} = \text{\_\_\_\_\_}$

2.   List the six pairs of corresponding congruent parts for the following congruences. Use a sketch if necessary.

   a. $\triangle PRQ \cong \triangle ABC$

   b. $\triangle LMN \cong \triangle CUT$

3.   Write the congruence from studying each of the six pairs of corresponding congruent parts.

$$\overline{DC} = \overline{AB}$$

$$\overline{AE} = \overline{DF}$$

$$\angle D = \angle A$$

$$\angle C = \angle B$$

$$\angle E = \angle F$$

$$\overline{CF} = \overline{BE}$$

Therefore, Δ _____ ≅ Δ _____.

2.7   Markings in Triangles

Markings can be used to indicate corresponding parts of congruent triangles. For example, it △ABC ≅ △ WHN,

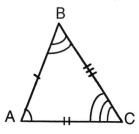

then ∠A = ∠W. To indicate this a single mark could be used; ∠B = ∠H, a double mark; and, ∠C = ∠N, a triple mark. This same process applies to the corresponding sides.

27.   If △DEF ≅ △GHI, mark the triangles to indicate the equal parts.

27.   One possible marking may be as below:

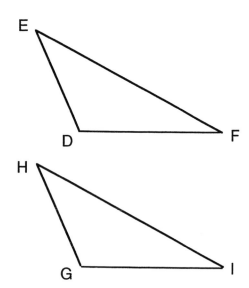

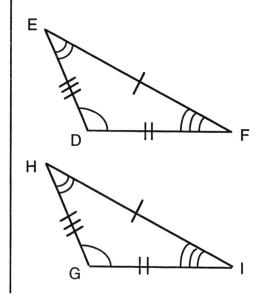

Markings can also be helpful in writing the congruence relationship. For example, study the diagram below with the indicated markings. ∠J = ∠M, ∠K = ∠N, ∠L = ∠O, $\overline{JK} = \overline{MN}$, $\overline{KL} = \overline{NO}$, and $\overline{JL} = \overline{MO}$.

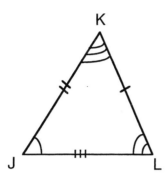
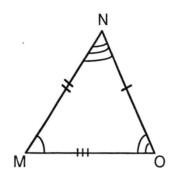

Since all the corresponding sides and angles of both figures are equal then △JKL ≅ △ MNO

28.   From the given diagram, write the congruence relationship.

28.

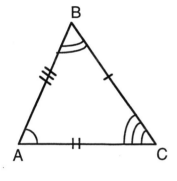
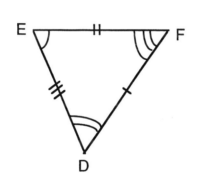

△ABC ≅ △EDF

This is the same as

△BCA ≅ △DFE

△CAB ≅ △FED

Study this figure!

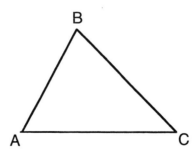

∠A is referred to as the included angle between sides $\overline{AB}$ and $\overline{AC}$ because sides $\overline{AB}$ and $\overline{AC}$ intersect to form ∠A. ∠B is the included angle between sides $\overline{AB}$ and $\overline{BC}$.

29.   ∠C is the included angle between which   29. $\overline{BC}$ and $\overline{AC}$
       two sides?

Below is a marked diagram to indicate an included angle between two sides.

The marked diagram below indicates an angle which is <u>not</u> an included angle.

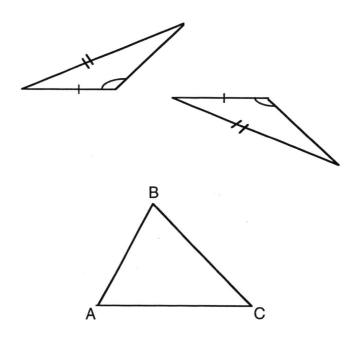

Referring to △ABC above, similarly, $\overline{AB}$ is the included side between ∠A and ∠B and $\overline{BC}$ is the included side between ∠B and ∠C.

30. $\overline{AC}$ is the included side between which   30. ∠A and ∠C
       two angles?

The diagram which follows is a marked diagram to indicate an included side between two angles.

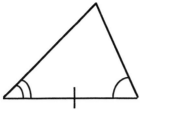
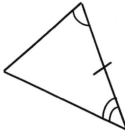

The marked diagram below indicates a side which is <u>not</u> an included side.

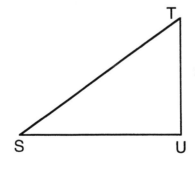
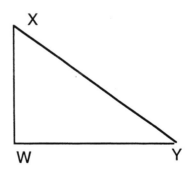

Exercise 2.5

1. ΔSTU ≅ ΔYXW Show all the equal parts by marking the triangles
    accordingly.

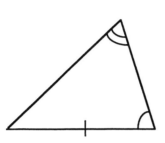
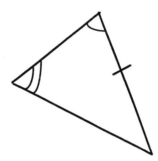

2. Write the congruence that is indicated by the markings on the two triangles.

Δ_____ ≅ Δ _____

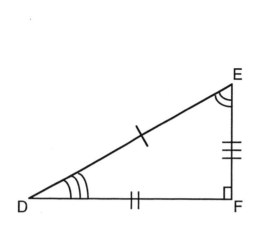

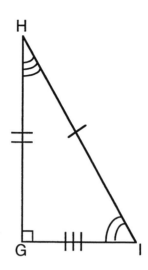

3. Which of the following markings indicate included angle? Write "yes" or "no" for each illustration.

   a. _____

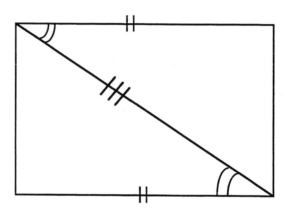

   b. _____

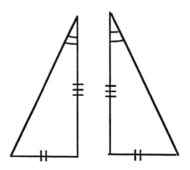

c. _____

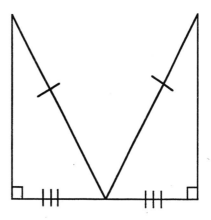

d. _____

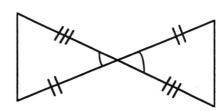

4. Which of the following markings indicate <u>included side</u>? Write "yes" or "no" for each illustration.

a. _____

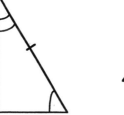 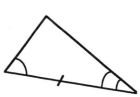

b. _____

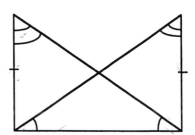

c. _____

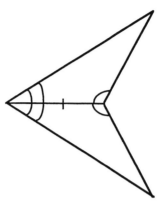

d. _____

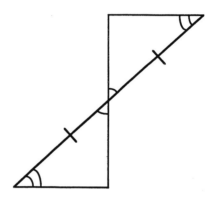

5. Draw a △RUT and answer the following questions.

    a. Which angles include $\overline{RU}$?

    b. Which sides include ∠R?

    c. Which side is included by ∠R and ∠T?

    d. Which angle is included by $\overline{RT}$ and $\overline{UT}$?

2.8   Congruence Postulates

In order for triangles to be congruent, must all corresponding parts be known to be equal? No. There are certain conditions that can be shown without all parts of one triangle equal to all parts of another triangle. These conditions will be stated in the form of postulates. As you recall, a postulate is a statement whose truth is accepted without proof.

Postulate 2.1   If three sides of one triangle are equal to three corresponding sides of a second triangle, then the triangles are said to be congruent. (Abbreviated SSS = SSS)

Examples:

a.

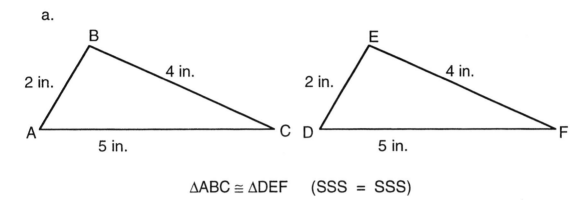

$\triangle ABC \cong \triangle DEF$ (SSS = SSS)

b.

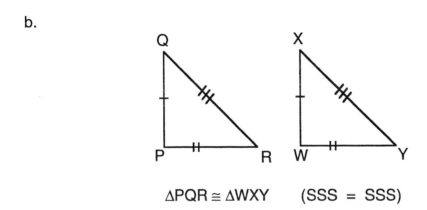

$\triangle PQR \cong \triangle WXY$ (SSS = SSS)

31.

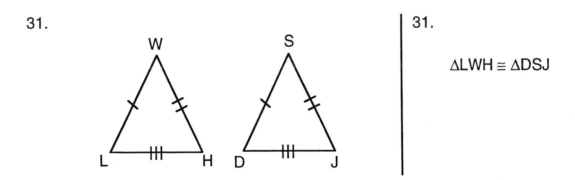

31.

$\triangle LWH \cong \triangle DSJ$

Postulate 2.2:   If two sides and an included angle of one triangle are equal to two sides and an included angle of a second triangle, then the triangles are congruent. (SAS = SAS)

Examples:

a.

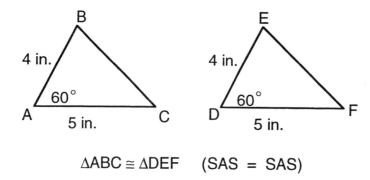

$$\triangle ABC \cong \triangle DEF \quad (SAS = SAS)$$

b.

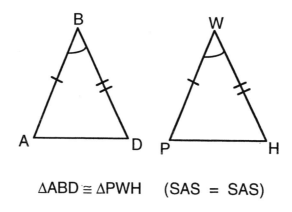

$$\triangle ABD \cong \triangle PWH \quad (SAS = SAS)$$

32.

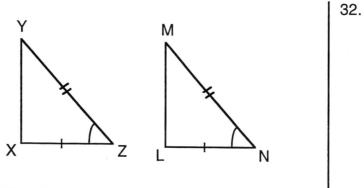

Give the congruence relationship.

32.

$$\triangle YZX \cong \triangle MNL$$

Postulate 2.3:   If two angles and an included side of one triangle are equal to two angles and an included side of a second triangle, then the triangles are congruent. (ASA = ASA)

Examples:

a.

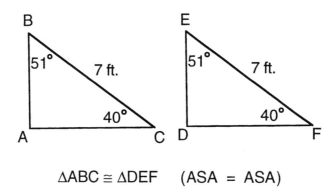

$$\triangle ABC \cong \triangle DEF \quad (ASA = ASA)$$

b.

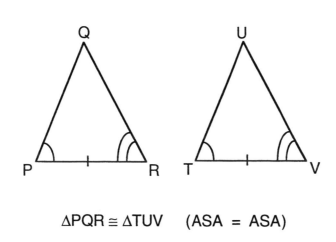

$$\triangle PQR \cong \triangle TUV \quad (ASA = ASA)$$

33. | 33.

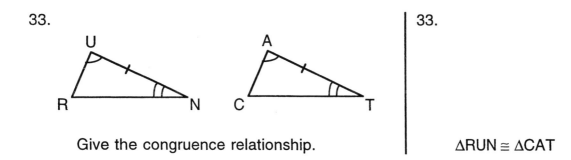

Give the congruence relationship. | $\triangle RUN \cong \triangle CAT$

The three postulates were illustrated separately and with examples that gave the appropriate data. Study the following examples.

Examples:

a.

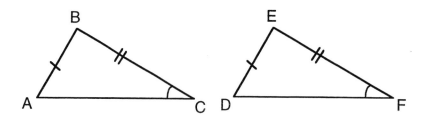

Can we conclude these triangles are congruent? No. Why not? The two triangles are not congruent because two sides and an angle of one triangle are equal to two sides and an angle of the second but the known angle is <u>not the included angle</u>. Actually, when this set of conditions is known, the triangle may not even appear the same as illustrated below.

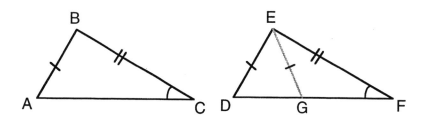

∠C = ∠F, $\overline{BC} = \overline{EF}$, and $\overline{AB} = \overline{DE}$. △ABC and △DEF look alike and may be congruent. However, observe that the two sides and given angle may also occur as follows: ∠C = ∠F, $\overline{BC} = \overline{EF}$, and $\overline{AB} = \overline{EG}$. Obviously, △ABC and △GEF are not congruent. Consequently, the conditions, SSA = SSA, do not give congruence in all cases and cannot be used as a reason for showing congruence.

b.

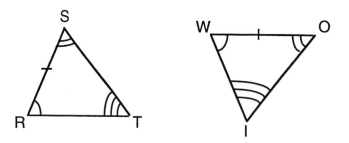

Can we conclude these triangles are congruent? Yes. ∠R = ∠W, ∠S = ∠O, and $\overline{RS} = \overline{WO}$ so △RST ≅ △WOI by ASA = ASA. The information that ∠T = ∠I was not needed.

c.

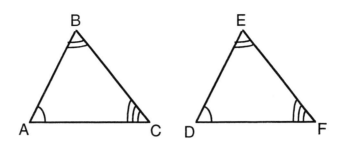

In this example the triangles are not congruent. Three angles of one triangle equal the corresponding three angles of a second triangle but nothing is known about any of its sides. We do <u>not</u> have an AAA = AAA postulate.

34.

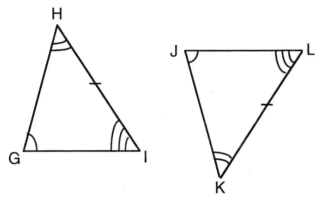

Can we conclude these triangles are congruent?

34. Yes, ASA = ASA

Exercise 2.6

State whether or not you have sufficient information to determine if the triangles are congruent by Postulate 1, 2, or 3. If the triangles are congruent, state which postulate.

1.

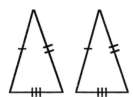

2.

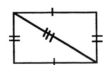

3.

4.

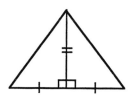

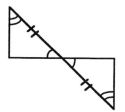

5.

6.

Unit 2 Review

1. Define the following:

triangle
obtuse triangle
perimeter
isosceles triangle
equilateral triangle
scalene triangle
right triangle
overlapping triangles

acute triangle
equiangular triangle
hypotenuse
legs
altitude
median
congruent
"≅"

2. Which of the following pairs of triangles are congruent by the SAS, ASA, or SSS postulate? Indicate whether or not the triangles are congruent and why.

a.

b.

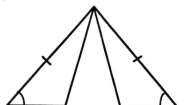

c.

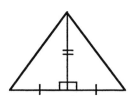

d.

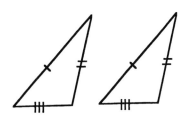

e.

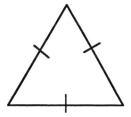

f.

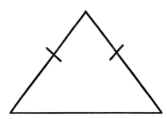

3. Classify each of the following triangles by the lengths of their sides or the measure of their angles as indicated in the figures.

a.

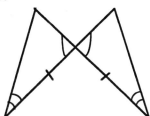

b.

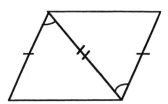

c.

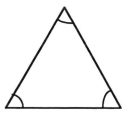

d.

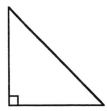

e.

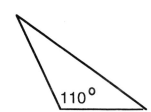

110°

f.

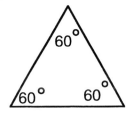

60°

60°   60°

4. Identify the corresponding parts that are equal in the following pairs of congruent triangles.

a.   △ACD ≅ △BDC

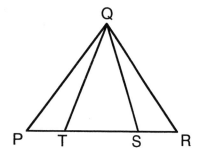

equal sides   equal angles

_____   _____

_____   _____

_____   _____

b.   △PQT ≅ △RQS

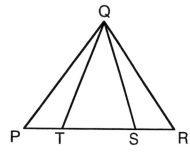

equal sides   equal angles

_____   _____

_____   _____

_____   _____

c.   △PQS ≅ △RQT

equal sides   equal angles

_____   _____

_____   _____

_____   _____

5. Indicate what two triangles are congruent using the proper correspondence.

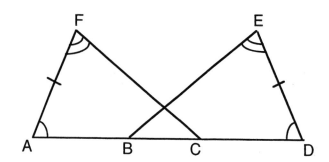

6. The base of an isosceles triangle measures 5 inches. Find the length of one of the equal sides of the triangle if the perimeter equals 23 inches.

7. This triangular garden spot has 59 feet of fencing surrounding it. What are the lengths of each side of the plot?

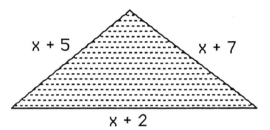

x + 5   x + 7

x + 2

8. Construct the altitude and median from ∠C to base $\overline{AB}$ in the triangle ABC.

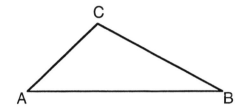

C

A   B

9. Study each of the following figures and indicate two triangles that are overlapping.

a.   b.

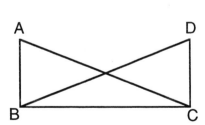

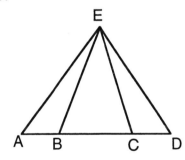

Unit 3

Simple Proofs

Learning objectives:

1. The student will differentiate between the hypothesis and conclusion of a conditional statement.

2. The student will demonstrate his mastery of the converse, inverse, and contrapositive by writing these statements given a conditional statement.

3. The student will review and use in simple proofs statements of equality about angles and line segments.

4. The student will demonstrate his mastery of three congruence postulates by applying them to simple proofs.

5. The student will demonstrate his mastery of the following theorems by writing them, by applying them to selected problems and by using them in simple proofs:

    a. If two sides of a triangle are equal, then the angles opposite these sides are equal.

    b. If two angles of a triangle are equal, then the sides opposite these angles are equal.

6. The student will demonstrate the concept of corresponding parts of congruent triangles are equal (abbreviated CPCTE) by applying it to selected problems and by using it in simple proofs.

SIMPLE PROOFS

3.1 Introduction

There are two major reasons for understanding and writing simple proofs. One reason is to strengthen your understanding of the concepts involved in the previous units. The second reason, even more important is to demonstrate that common sense is fallible and that there is a real need to use proofs in mathematics.

1. Study the pictures below and answer the following questions:

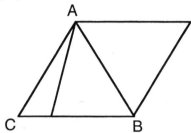

    a. Which is longer, $\overline{AC}$ or $\overline{AB}$?

    b.

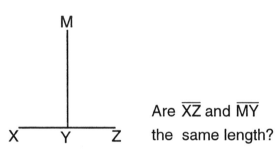

Are $\overline{XZ}$ and $\overline{MY}$ the same length?

1.

    a. Neither, they are the same length.

    b.

Yes

No two people will always arrive at exactly the same conclusions when they are depending solely upon their senses. As illustrated in example 1 above, some senses can be fooled simply by the use of optical illusions.

Even basic common sense can be fallible and can also lead you to incorrect conclusions. Study the following examples.

2. Use only your common sense to identify which of the following algebraic expressions are prime?

    a. 13

    b. $x^2 + 9$

2.

    a. prime

    b. prime

c. $5x^2 - 3x - 14$ | c. not prime

$(5x + 7)(x - 2)$

3. a. The sum of two numbers is 10. The product | 3. a. 4,6
        of these two numbers is 24. What are the
        numbers?

    b. The distance between two hospitals is 20 | b. $20\frac{2}{3}$ or $20.\overline{6}$

        miles more than one-fourth of the distance
        between them. What is the distance between
        them?

You were asked to only use common sense to arrive at your answers.
Examples 2 and 3 involved a few examples that could be worked out quite
easily. However, the more difficult examples required algebraic manipulations
and could not be solved by simple opinion or emotion. In geometry we must
eliminate personal emotions and depend upon proofs as a basis for drawing
conclusions. These proofs are derived from a logical sequence of steps. This
sequence of steps is not innate and most students will have to <u>learn</u> to think
logically.

From Unit 1, we discussed that the system of logic that we employ in geometry
is called deductive reasoning. The four elements of the deductive reasoning
system are postulates, theorems, defined terms, and undefined terms. Recall
that in deductive reasoning you are given very general statements with which to
begin. You then draw upon the four elements in developing a very specific
conclusion. Deductive reasoning involves a logical connection between "what
is given" and "what is to be proven".

Logical Connection

| What is given | ──────────────▶ | What is to be proven |

To start you must be <u>given</u> some information. This given information is the "if"
part of the conditional statement and is called the <u>hypothesis</u>. From this given
hypothesis as well as by using previously proven theorems, postulates, defined
terms, and undefined terms, we develop a valid chain of reasoning to reach a
logical conclusion. The conclusion is the "then" part of the statement. If we
succeed at constructing a logical connection between the hypothesis and the
conclusion, then the IF-THEN statement has been proven. This type of "if-then"
statement is a <u>conditional statement</u>.

The following is an example of an if-then statement.

If today is December first, then first semester will end soon.

If _____ , then _____ .

     p   q

4. p represents what part of the statement?

4. "if" or hypothesis

5. q represents what part of the statement?

5. "then" or conclusion

6. In the following statement identify the hypothesis and conclusion.

If I study hard, then I will pass geometry.

6. Hypothesis
   If I study hard
Conclusion
   then I will pass geometry

Other relationships can be formed between the hypothesis and conclusion by introducing the converse, inverse, and contrapositive of statements. Study the relationships below.

Statement: If p, then q.

Converse: If q, then p.

Inverse: If not p, then not q.

Contrapositive: If not q, then not p.

Use the statement below in filling in the blanks for 7-9 that follow.

If Sam is a man, then Sam is a human being.
      p   q

7. The <u>converse</u> is started below. Please complete the statement using -- If q, then p.

If Sam is a human being, then _____.
      q   p

7.

Sam is a man.

8. The <u>inverse</u> is started below. Please complete the statement using -- If not p, then not q.

If Sam is not a man, then _____.
   not p   not q

8.

Sam is not a human being.

9. Complete the <u>contrapositive</u> statement using -- If not q, then not p.

If Sam is not a human being, then _____.
    not q   not p

9.

Sam is not a man.

Exercise 3.1

Find the converse, inverse, and contrapositive for each of the following statements. (The statements may or may not be true statements.)

1. If you live in Virginia, then you live in the United States.

2. If you can operate a car, then you can fly an airplane.

3. If a triangle is not scalene, then it is equilateral.

4. If a triangle is an acute triangle, then it is not a right triangle.

5. If it is raining, then it is cloudy.

3.2   Relationships Between Conditional Statements

You have undoubtedly discovered that some statements may or may not be valid. For example, let's discuss the statement given below:

If Sam is a man, then Sam is a human being.

The statement is truthful. It is valid in its logic because you can not possibly be a man and not be human at the same time.

The contrapositive is also valid. If Sam is not at all human then he could not possibly be a man.

Statements and their contrapositives are, indeed, logical equivalents of one another. If the statement is true, so follows the contrapositive. If the statement is false, the contrapositive will also be false. Therefore, it follows that once you've proven a theorem to be true, you need not do a second proof for the contrapositive. A theorem and its contrapositive are logical equivalents.

However, the same does not apply to the converse. A converse of a statement is not always true even though the original statement may be valid. For example, in the statement above, the converse indicates that if Sam is a human being then Sam is a man. I'm sure that the female portion of the human race will have something to say about the gross oversight implied in the statement.

If a theorem is proven to be true, its converse is not necessarily true and must be proven with a second proof.

3.3   Review of Basic Concepts

The previous units have provided a sturdy foundation upon which you will build your understanding of simple proofs.

Let's review some concepts about equality that you will be using in writing simple proofs.

A. You can prove that two angles are equal if:

1. They are equal to the same or equal angles.

2. They are supplements of the same or equal angles.

3. They are complements of the same or equal angles.

4. They are right angles. All right angles are equal.

5. They are vertical angles. Pairs of vertical angles are equal.

6. They are the same angle. Any angle is equal to itself. (Reflexive)

7. They are parts of a bisected angle.

B. You can prove that two line segments are equal if:

1. They are equal to the same or equal line segments.

2. They are parts of a bisected line segment.

3. They are the equal sides of an isosceles triangle. (Definition of isosceles triangle.)

4. They are the same line segment. Any line segment is equal to itself. (Reflexive)

5. They are the results of adding or subtracting equal line segments.

6. They are multiples or halves of equal line segments.

Given the following information, show why the angles or line segments in problems 10-17 are equal. State why they are equal using any of the previous statements that would logically apply.

10.

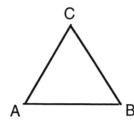

Given: △ABC is isosceles

$\overline{AC}$ is the base

Why does $\overline{AB} = \overline{BC}$?

10.

Part B-#3

$\overline{AB}$ and $\overline{BC}$ are the equal sides of an isosceles triangle.

11.

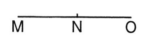

Given: N is the midpoint of $\overline{MO}$.

Why does $\overline{MN} = \overline{NO}$?

11.

Part B-#2

$\overline{MN}$ and $\overline{NO}$ are parts of a bisected line segment since the midpoint divides a line segment into two equal parts.

12.

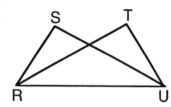

Given: △RSU and △UTR

Why does $\overline{RU} = \overline{RU}$?

12.

Part B-#4
Reflexive Law- any quantity is equal to itself.

13.

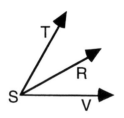

Given: $\overrightarrow{SR}$ bisects ∠TSV

Why does ∠TSR = ∠RSV?

13.

Part A-#7
∠TSR and ∠RSV are parts of a bisected angle.

14.

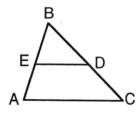

Given: △ABC and △EBD

Why does ∠B = ∠B?

14.

Part A-#6
Reflexive law- any quantity is equal to itself.

15.

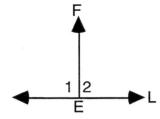

Given: $\overrightarrow{EF} \perp$ line L
Why does $\angle 1 = \angle 2$?

15.

Part A-#4
$\angle 1$ and $\angle 2$ are
right angles and
all right angles are
equal.

16.

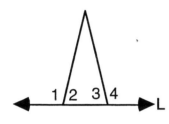

Given: Line L and
$\angle 2 = \angle 3$
Why does $\angle 1 = \angle 4$?

16.

Part A-#2
$\angle 1$ and $\angle 2$ are
supplementary
angles. $\angle 3$ and
$\angle 4$ are supple-
mentary angles.
$\angle 1 = \angle 4$ since
supplements of
equal angles
are themselves
equal.

17.

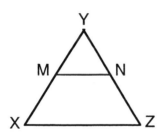

Given: $\triangle XYZ$ is isosceles
with base $\overline{XZ}$ and
$\overline{MX} = \overline{NZ}$.
Why does $\overline{MY} = \overline{NY}$?

17.

Part B-#5
$\overline{XY}$ and $\overline{YZ}$ are
equal since $\triangle XYZ$
is isosceles. If
$\overline{MX} = \overline{NZ}$ are
subtracted from
$\overline{XY}$ and $\overline{YZ}$, then
the result of sub-
tracting equal
quantities from
equal quantities
are equal. There-
fore, $\overline{MY} = \overline{NY}$.

Exercise 3.2

1.

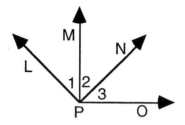

Given: ray L ⊥ ray N
              ray M ⊥ ray O
Why does ∠1 = ∠3?

2.

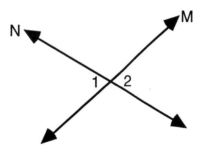

Given: △RSU and △TSU
Why does $\overline{SU} = \overline{SU}$?

3.

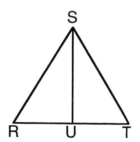

Given: line M intersects line N
Why does ∠1 = ∠2?

4.

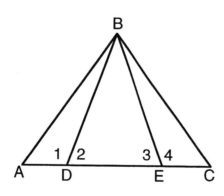

Given: △ABC and △DBE
              ∠2 = ∠3
Why does ∠1 = ∠4?

5.

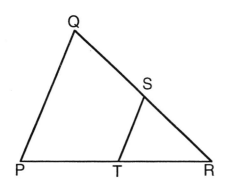

Given: ΔPQR is isosceles with base $\overline{PQ}$

ΔPQR and ΔSTR

S is the midpoint of $\overline{QR}$

T is the midpoint of $\overline{PR}$

a. Why does $\overline{QR} = \overline{PR}$?

b. Why does $\overline{QS} = \overline{PT}$?

3.4   Anatomy of a Proof

In most cases the problems that you have just completed could be answered simply. Those problems were merely an introduction to the next set of proofs that involve more than one or two steps to arrive at the conclusion. So, what does a complete proof look like?

For this section you will need to review the unit on congruence. Three ways to prove triangles congruent are SSS = SSS, SAS = SAS, and ASA = ASA.

(In the proof of statements, the use of approved symbols and abbreviations is acceptable.)

Procedure:	Example of a proof:
I. Divide the problem up into what is given and what is to be proven.	I. Given: Δ ABC with $\overline{AB} = \overline{BC}$, $\overline{BD}$ bisects ∠B, ∠A = ∠C Prove: ΔABD ≅ ΔCBD
II. Use the given to mark your diagram.	II. 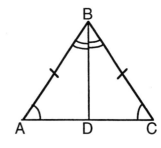

III. Present a plan to prove your hypothesis.	III. Plan: Since two triangles can be proven congruent only by SSS = SSS, SAS = SAS, and ASA = ASA, you must select the one that best fits the information that you were given. You were given two angles and an included side. Therefore, the ASA postulate would be the one that you would select.
IV. Set up your t-table. Provide logical statements on the left. Provide valid reasons for each statement to the right of the statement.	IV. <table><tr><td>Statements</td><td>Reasons</td></tr><tr><td>1. $\overline{AB} = \overline{BC}$ (side)</td><td>1. Given</td></tr><tr><td>2. $\overline{BD}$ bisects $\angle B$</td><td>2. Given</td></tr><tr><td>3. $\angle ABD = \angle CBD$ (angle)</td><td>3. Def. of bisector</td></tr><tr><td>4. $\angle A = \angle C$ (angle)</td><td>4. Given</td></tr><tr><td>5. $\triangle ABD \cong \triangle CBD$</td><td>5. ASA = ASA</td></tr></table>

Using postulates, definitions, and theorems, examine the following proofs. In some you will be asked to supply the reasons.

18.

Given: $\triangle ABC$ with $\overline{AB} = \overline{BC}$

$\overline{AD} = \overline{DC}$

Prove: $\triangle ABD \cong \triangle CBD$

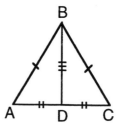

Statements	Reasons
1. $\overline{AB} = \overline{BC}$ $\overline{AD} = \overline{DC}$	1. Given
2. $\overline{BD} = \overline{BD}$	2. Reflexive Law
3. $\triangle ABD \cong \triangle CBD$	3. SSS = SSS

Note: Markings generally help in demonstrating the given and pointing out what is still needed. Examine the markings on the figure above. In statement 1, $\overline{AB} = \overline{BC}$. On the diagram notice each of these has a single dash. In statement 1, $\overline{AD} = \overline{DC}$. On the diagram notice each of these has a double dash. Then in examining the two triangles, congruence can be obtained by SSS = SSS. This is only one of many methods of marking. Colored pencils may also be beneficial.

19.

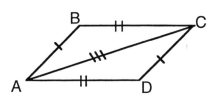

Given: Figure ABCD with $\overline{AB} = \overline{DC}$ and $\overline{BC} = \overline{AD}$

Prove: △ABC ≅ △CDA

Statements	Reasons
1. $\overline{AB} = \overline{DC}$ $\overline{BC} = \overline{AD}$	1. Given
2. $\overline{AC} = \overline{AC}$	2. Why?
3. △ABC ≅ △CDA	3. SSS = SSS

19.

2. Reflexive Law

20.

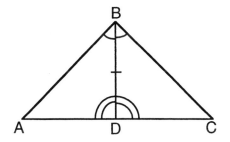

Given: △ABC with ∠ABD = ∠CBD and
              ∠ADB = ∠CDB

Prove: △ABD ≅ △CBD

Statements	Reasons
1. ∠ABD = ∠CBD ∠ADB = ∠CDB	1. Given
2. $\overline{BD} = \overline{BD}$	2. Why?
3. △ABD ≅ △CBD	3. Why?

20.

2. Reflexive Law
3. ASA = ASA

21.

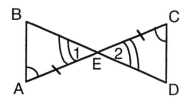

Given: $\overline{BD}$ bisects $\overline{AC}$ at E, $\angle A = \angle C$
Prove: $\triangle ABE \cong \triangle CDE$

Statements	Reasons
1. $\overline{BD}$ bisects $\overline{AC}$ at E $\angle A = \angle C$	1. Given
2. $\overline{AE} = \overline{EC}$	2. Why?
3. $\angle 1$ and $\angle 2$ are vertical angles.	3. Def. of vertical angles
4. $\angle 1 = \angle 2$	4. Pairs of vertical angles are equal.
5. $\triangle ABE \cong \triangle CDE$	5. Why?

21.

2. Def. of bisector

5. ASA = ASA

22.

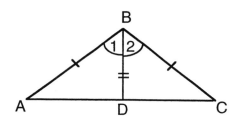

Given: $\triangle ABC$ is isosceles with base $\overline{AC}$
              $\overline{BD}$ bisects $\angle B$
Prove: $\triangle ABD \cong \triangle CBD$

Statements	Reasons
1. $\triangle ABC$ is isosceles with base $\overline{AC}$ $\overline{BD}$ bisects $\angle B$	1. Given
2. $\overline{AB} = \overline{BC}$	2. Why?
3. $\angle 1 = \angle 2$	3. Why?
4. $\overline{BD} = \overline{BD}$	4. Reflexive Law
5. $\triangle ABD \cong \triangle CBD$	5. Why?

22.

2. Def. of isosceles
3. Def. of angle bisector

5. SAS = SAS

23.

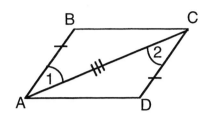

Given: $\overline{AB} = \overline{DC}$, $\angle 1 = \angle 2$
Prove: $\triangle ABC \cong \triangle CDA$

Statements	Reasons
1. $\overline{AB} = \overline{DC}$, $\angle 1 = \angle 2$	1. Given
2. $\overline{AC} = \overline{AC}$	2. Why?
3. $\triangle ABC \cong \triangle CDA$	3. Why?

23.

2. Reflexive Law
3. SAS = SAS

Exercise 3.3

Set up a t-table and prove the following exercises.

1.

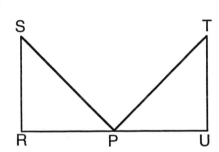

Given: $\angle S = \angle T$, $\overline{SR} = \overline{TU}$
$\overline{SR} \perp \overline{RU}$ and $\overline{TU} \perp \overline{RU}$

Prove: $\triangle SRP \cong \triangle TUP$

2.

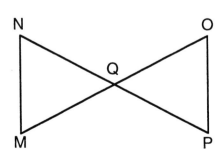

Given: $\overline{MO}$ and $\overline{NP}$ bisect
one another at their
point of intersection.

Prove: $\triangle NMQ \cong \triangle POQ$

3.

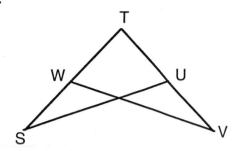

Given: $\overline{WT} = \overline{UT}$, $\overline{ST} = \overline{TV}$

Prove: $\triangle STU \cong \triangle VTW$

4.

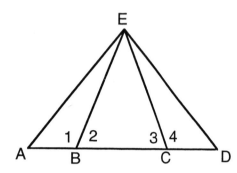

Given: $\angle 2 = \angle 3$, $\overline{AB} = \overline{CD}$,
$\qquad \angle A = \angle D$

Prove: $\triangle ABE \cong \triangle DCE$

5.

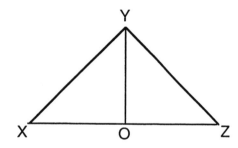

Given: $\triangle XYZ$ is isosceles with
$\qquad$ base $\overline{XZ}$ and $\overline{XO} = \overline{OZ}$

Prove: $\triangle XYO \cong \triangle ZYO$

3.5 <u>Corresponding Parts of Congruent Triangles</u>

In proving two triangles congruent, you have proven that these two figures have the same size and shape. Therefore, each pair of corresponding sides and each pair of corresponding angles are also equal. <u>Corresponding parts of congruent triangles are equal.</u> This complete statement may be abbreviated as CPCTE. Remember that you must <u>first</u> prove the triangles congruent before you can use CPCTE. Study the following examples.

Example:

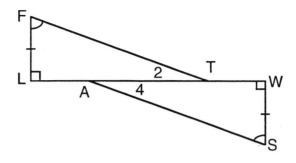

Given: $\overline{FL} \perp \overline{LT}$, $\overline{WS} \perp \overline{WA}$, $\angle F = \angle S$ and $\overline{FL} = \overline{WS}$

Prove: $\angle 2 = \angle 4$

Statements	Reasons
1. $\overline{FL} \perp \overline{LT}$, $\overline{WS} \perp \overline{WA}$, $\overline{WS} = \overline{FL}$ $\angle F = \angle S$	1. Given
2. $\angle L$ and $\angle W$ are right angles.	2. Definition of perpendicular lines.
3. $\angle L = \angle W$	3. All right angles are equal.
4. $\triangle FLT \cong \triangle SWA$	4. ASA = ASA
5. $\angle 2 = \angle 4$	5. CPCTE

Example:

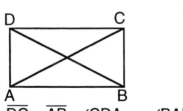

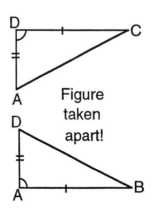

Figure taken apart!

Given: $\overline{DC} = \overline{AB}$, $\angle CDA = \angle BAD$

Prove: $\overline{AC} = \overline{BD}$

Statements	Reasons
1. $\overline{DC} = \overline{AB}$, $\angle CDA = \angle BAD$	1. Given
2. $\overline{AD} = \overline{AD}$	2. Reflexive law
3. $\triangle ADC \cong \triangle DAB$	3. SAS = SAS
4. $\overline{AC} = \overline{BD}$	4. CPCTE

3.6 Proof of a Theorem

| Theorem 3.1   If two sides of a triangle are equal, then the angles opposite these sides are equal. |

Remember the _____ is the given, | "if" part
and the _____ is the part to prove. | "then" part

So, if we use a triangle ABC with $\overline{AB} = \overline{BC}$ as the two equal sides, then we would need to prove which two angles are equal? The "given" is $\overline{AB} = \overline{BC}$ and the "to prove" is $\angle A = \angle C$.

This proof will be slightly different from the others. Before beginning, construct the bisector of $\angle B$. This can be done without altering the given or doing anything to what is to be proven. Constructing the bisector of an angle is one of our basic constructions. It is very important to remember that this can be done only if the "given" and the "to prove" are not altered.

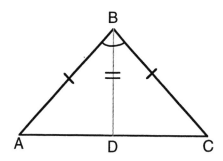

Statements	Reasons
1. $\overline{AB} = \overline{BC}$	1. Given
2. $\overline{BD}$ bisects $\angle B$.	2. By construction
3. $\angle ABD = \angle CBD$	3. Definition of angle bisector
4. $\overline{BD} = \overline{BD}$	4. Reflexive Law
5. $\triangle ABD \cong \triangle CBD$	5. SAS = SAS
6. $\angle A = \angle C$	6. CPCTE

Looking at the converse of this theorem, we have:

| Theorem 3.2   If two angles of a triangle are equal, then the sides opposite these angles are equal. |

Note: The converse of a theorem should also be proven. The proof of this theorem is not included since it is more difficult and would require more background to develop the logical steps. We will, however, use this theorem in proofs further along in this unit. These two theorems are very useful in proving relationships between other triangles.

24. Given: $\triangle ABC$ with $\angle 1 = \angle 2$ and $\overline{AE} = \overline{DC}$ 24.

     Prove: $\overline{AB} = \overline{CB}$

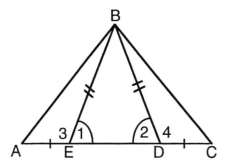

Statements	Reasons	
1. $\angle 1 = \angle 2$, $\overline{AE} = \overline{DC}$	1. Given	
2. $\overline{BE} = \overline{BD}$	2. Why?	2. If two angles of a triangle are equal, then the sides opposite these angles are equal.
3. $\angle 1$ and $\angle 3$ are supplementary angles. $\angle 2$ and $\angle 4$ are supplementary angles.	3. $\angle 1$ and $\angle 3$ and $\angle 2$ and $\angle 4$ form a straight angle. (Definition of of supplementary angles.)	
4. $\angle 3 = \angle 4$	4. Supplements of equal angles are themselves equal.	
5. $\triangle AEB \cong \triangle CDB$	5. Why?	5. SAS = SAS
6. $\overline{AB} = \overline{CB}$	6. Why?	6. CPCTE

===

Exercise 3.4

1. Given: $\angle B = \angle E$, $\overline{BC} = \overline{EC}$
    Prove: $\angle A = \angle D$

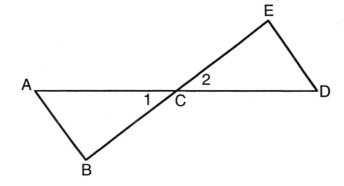

Statements	Reasons
1. ∠B = ∠E, $\overline{BC}$ = $\overline{EC}$	1. _____.
2. ∠1 and ∠2 are vertical angles.	2. _____.
3. ∠1 = ∠2	3. _____.
4. △ABC ≅ △DEC	4. _____.
5. ∠A = ∠D	5. _____.

2. Given: ∠A = ∠D, ∠AEB = ∠DEC
    Prove: ∠ABE = ∠DCE

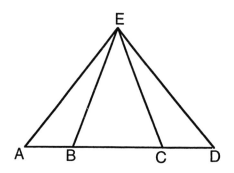

Statements	Reasons
1. ∠A = ∠D, ∠AEB = ∠DEC	1. _____.
2. $\overline{AE}$ = $\overline{DE}$	2. _____.
3. △AEB ≅ △DEC	3. _____.
4. ∠ABE = ∠DCE	4. _____.

3. Given: $\overline{AB}$ = $\overline{CD}$, $\overline{BC}$ = $\overline{AD}$
    Prove: ∠B = ∠D

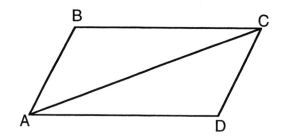

Statements	Reasons
1. $\overline{AB}$ = $\overline{CD}$, $\overline{BC}$ = $\overline{AD}$	1. _____.
2. $\overline{AC}$ = $\overline{AC}$	2. _____.
3. △ABC ≅ △CDA	3. _____.
4. ∠B = ∠D	4. _____.

4. Given: $\overline{AE} = \overline{DC}$, $\angle 1 = \angle 2$
    Prove: $\angle A = \angle C$

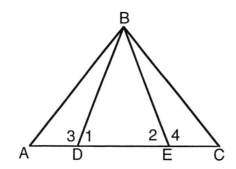

Statements	Reasons
1. $\overline{AE} = \overline{DC}$, $\angle 1 = \angle 2$	1. _____.
2. $\overline{BD} = \overline{BE}$	2. _____.
3. $\overline{DE} = \overline{DE}$	3. _____.
4. $\overline{AD} = \overline{EC}$	4. _____.
5. $\angle 1$ and $\angle 3$ are supplementary. $\angle 2$ and $\angle 4$ are supplementary.	5. _____.
6. $\angle 3 = \angle 4$	6. _____.
7. $\triangle ABD \cong \triangle CBE$	7. _____.
8. $\angle A = \angle C$	8. _____.

5. Given: C is the midpoint of both $\overline{BE}$ and $\overline{AD}$.
    Prove: $\angle B = \angle E$

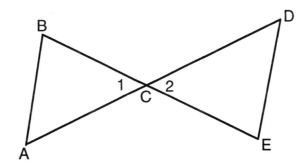

Statements	Reasons
1. C is the midpoint of both $\overline{BE}$ and $\overline{AD}$.	1. _____.
2. $\overline{BC} = \overline{CE}$	2. _____.
3. $\overline{AC} = \overline{CD}$	3. _____.
4. $\angle 1$ and $\angle 2$ are vertical angles.	4. _____.
5. $\angle 1 = \angle 2$	5. _____.

6. △ABC ≅ △DEC   6. _____.
7. ∠B = ∠E   7. _____.

6. Given: ∠1 = ∠2, $\overline{WY}$ bisects ∠XYZ
   Prove: ∠X = ∠Z

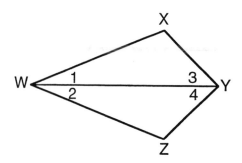

Statements	Reasons
1. ∠1 = ∠2, $\overline{WY}$ bisects ∠XYZ	1. _____.
2. ∠3 = ∠4	2. _____.
3. $\overline{WY} = \overline{WY}$	3. _____.
4. △WXY ≅ △WZY	4. _____.
5. ∠X = ∠Z	5. _____.

7. Given: $\overline{BD}$ is the perpendicular bisector of $\overline{AC}$
   Prove: ∠ABD = ∠CBD

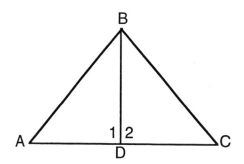

Statements	Reasons
1. $\overline{BD}$ is the perpendicular bisector of $\overline{AC}$	1. _____.
2. ∠1 and ∠2 are right angles.	2. _____.
3. ∠1 = ∠2	3. _____.
4. $\overline{AD} = \overline{DC}$	4. _____.
5. $\overline{BD} = \overline{BD}$	5. _____.

6. $\triangle ABD \cong \triangle CBD$ 6. _____.
7. $\angle ABD = \angle CBD$ 7. _____.

Unit 3 Review

1. The "if" part of a conditional statement is called the _____ and the "then" part is called the _____.

2. Write the converse, inverse, and contrapositive of the following conditional statement.

    "If I study hard, then I will pass geometry."

3. Does the converse of a theorem need to be proven if the theorem has already been proven? Why or why not?

4. Three ways to prove two triangles are congruent are _____, _____, and _____.

5. Given: $\overline{AG} = \overline{FE}$, $\overline{BF} = \overline{DG}$, $\angle DGE = \angle BFA$
    Prove: $\triangle ABF \cong \triangle EDG$

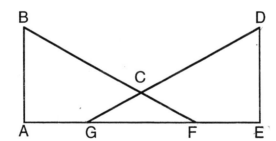

Statements	Reasons
1. $\overline{AG} = \overline{FE}$, $\overline{BF} = \overline{DG}$, $\angle DGE = \angle BFA$	1. _____.
2. $\overline{GF} = \overline{GF}$	2. _____.
3. $\overline{AF} = \overline{GE}$	3. _____.
4. $\triangle ABF \cong \triangle EDG$	4. _____.

6. Given: $\angle 1 = \angle 4$, $\angle 2 = \angle 3$
    Prove: $\triangle ABD \cong \triangle CDB$

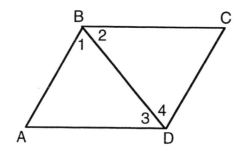

Statements	Reasons
1. ∠1 = ∠4, ∠2 = ∠3	1. _____.
2. $\overline{BD} = \overline{BD}$	2. _____.
3. △ABD ≅ △CDB	3. _____.

7. Given: Figure ABCD, with E as midpoint of $\overline{AB}$. $\overline{AD} = \overline{BC}$, ∠A = ∠B

Prove: ∠1 = ∠2

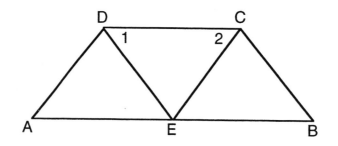

Statements	Reasons
1. E is the midpoint of $\overline{AB}$, $\overline{AD} = \overline{BC}$, ∠A = ∠B	1. _____.
2. $\overline{AE} = \overline{BE}$	2. _____.
3. △ADE ≅ △BCE	3. _____.
4. $\overline{DE} = \overline{CE}$	4. _____.
5. ∠1 = ∠2	5. _____.

8. Given: $\overline{CD}$ bisects $\overline{AB}$, $\overline{CD} \perp \overline{AB}$

Prove: △ABC is isosceles.

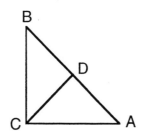

Statements	Reasons
1. $\overline{CD} = \overline{CD}$	1. _____.
2. $\overline{CD}$ bisects $\overline{AB}$	2. _____.
3. $\overline{BD} = \overline{DA}$	3. _____.
4. $\overline{CD} \perp \overline{AB}$	4. _____.
5. $\angle CDB$ and $\angle CDA$ are right angles.	5. _____.
6. $\angle CDB = \angle CDA$	6. _____.
7. $\triangle CDB \cong \triangle CDA$	7. _____.
8. $\overline{BC} = \overline{CA}$	8. _____.
9. $\triangle ABC$ is isosceles.	9. _____.

9. Given: $\overrightarrow{AC}$ bisects $\angle DAB$ and $\angle DCB$
    Prove: $\angle D = \angle B$

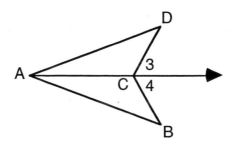

Statements	Reasons
1. $\overrightarrow{AC}$ bisects $\angle DAB$ and $\angle DCB$	1. _____.
2. $\angle DAC = \angle BAC$ and $\angle 3 = \angle 4$	2. _____.
3. $\angle DCA$ and $\angle 3$ are supplementary angles. $\angle BCA$ and $\angle 4$ are supplementary angles.	3. _____.
4. $\angle DCA = \angle BCA$	4. _____.
5. $\overline{AC} = \overline{AC}$	5. _____.
6. $\triangle ACD \cong \triangle ACB$	6. _____.
7. $\angle D = \angle B$	7. _____.

Unit 4

Parallel Lines

Learning objectives:

The student will demonstrate his mastery of the following definitions, postulates, and theorems by writing them, by applying them to solutions of selected problems, or using them as reasons in a proof.

Definitions: parallel lines, skew lines, transversal, alternate interior angles, alternate exterior angles, corresponding angles, corollary, and exterior angle

Postulates:

1. Parallel Postulate. Through any point, P, not on line L there can be constructed one and only one line, M, that is parallel to L.

2. Two lines are parallel if they are both perpendicular to a third line.

Theorems and their converses:

If two parallel lines are cut by a transversal, then

1. Nonadjacent angles on the opposite sides of the transversal but interior to the two lines (alternate interior angles) are equal.

2. Nonadjacent angles on the opposite sides of the transversal but exterior to the two lines (alternate exterior angles) are equal.

3. Angles on the same side of the transversal but interior to the two lines are supplementary.

4. Angles on the same side of the transversal and in the same position relative to the two lines (corresponding angles) are equal.

Theorems:

5. The sum of the interior angles of a triangle is 180°.

6. If a line segment joins the midpoints of two sides of a triangle, that line segment is parallel to and equal to one-half the measure of the third side.

Corollaries:

1. In a right triangle, the two acute angles are complementary.

2. Each exterior angle of a triangle equals the sum of its non-adjacent interior angles.

Constructions:

1. Construct parallel lines using equal alternate interior angles.

2. Construct parallel lines by constructing two lines perpendicular to a third line.

PARALLEL LINES

4.1 Basic Definitions

Have you ever noticed that the horizontal lines on a piece of notebook paper never intersect or that teeth on a comb never cross one another? The environment is abundant with examples of parallel lines. The rows of mortar between bricks, railroad tracks, the horizontal bars in a five-barred gate, and the center and outer edge markings on an interstate highway provide a few illustrations of parallel lines.

Definition 4.1   Lines that are (1) in the same plane and (2) do not intersect are called <u>parallel lines</u>.

A plane can be described as a flat surface that extends indefinitely in every direction.

The first relationship of parallel lines refers to the fact that these lines must lie totally within the same plane.

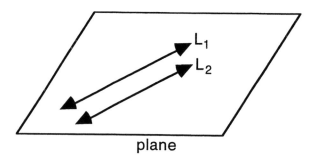

plane

Figure 4.1

Line L_1 is parallel to L_2. The symbol for parallel is ‖. Therefore, $L_1 \parallel L_2$.

That is, we should be able to lay a piece of paper flat against both lines. If one line passes through the paper and the other lies on the paper, these lines are not contained in the same plane and, therefore, are not parallel.

Definition 4.2   Lines that are (1) not in the same plane and (2) do not intersect are called <u>skew</u>.

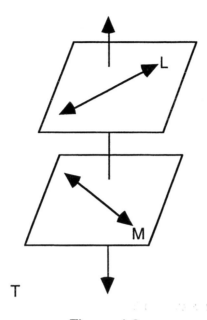

Figure 4.2

Lines L and M are not in the same plane and do not intersect. Lines L and M are skew lines.

Lines that are not parallel but are in the same plane must intersect at some point within that plane. See L and M in Figure 4.3.

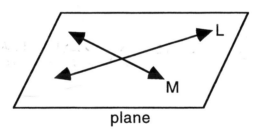

plane

Figure 4.3

1. Which of the following lines appear to be intersecting lines and which ones are parallel?

    a.   b.

1. a. parallel

    b. intersecting

c.

d.

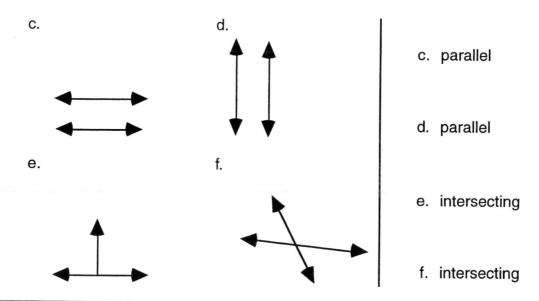

c. parallel

d. parallel

e.

f.

e. intersecting

f. intersecting

Definition 4.3   A <u>transversal</u> is a line that intersects two other lines in two
distinct places.

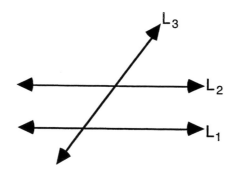

$L_1 \parallel L_2$ and L_3 is the transversal.

Figure 4.4

Is line L_3 in Figure 4.5 a transversal?

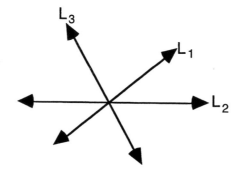

Figure 4.5

No, L_3 is not a transversal. It is a line but it does not intersect two other lines in <u>two</u> distinct places. It intersects L_1 and L_3 in only one point.

4.2 <u>Angles Related To Two Lines Intersected By a Transversal</u>

> Definition 4.4   <u>Alternate interior angles</u> are nonadjacent angles on opposite sides of the transversal but "interior" to the two lines.

Given: L_1 and L_2 with transversal L_3

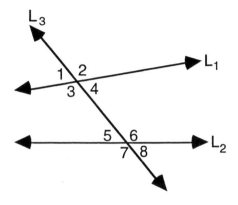

Figure 4.6

The pairs of angles $\angle 3$ and $\angle 6$; $\angle 4$ and $\angle 5$ are called alternate interior angles.

> Definition 4.5   <u>Alternate exterior angles</u> are nonadjacent angles on opposite sides of the transversal but "exterior" to the two lines.

In Figure 4.6, the pairs of angles that fit this description are $\angle 1$ and $\angle 8$; $\angle 2$ and $\angle 7$.

> Definition 4.6   <u>Corresponding angles</u> are angles on the same side of the transversal and in the same relative position to the given lines.

In Figure 4.6, $\angle 1$ and $\angle 5$; $\angle 2$ and $\angle 6$; $\angle 3$ and $\angle 7$; $\angle 4$ and $\angle 8$ are all pairs of corresponding angles.

Example:

   Given: L II M and $\angle 1 = 48°$
   With the use of your protractor, find the other numbered angles.

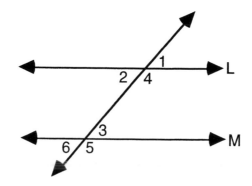

$\angle 1 = 48°$ $\angle 2 = 48°$ $\angle 3 = 48°$

$\angle 4 = 132°$ $\angle 5 = 132°$ $\angle 6 = 48°$

Note that from your data, $\angle 2 = \angle 3$ (pair of alternate interior angles); $\angle 1 = \angle 6$ (pair of alternate exterior angles); and, $\angle 1 = \angle 3$, $\angle 4 = \angle 5$, and $\angle 2 = \angle 6$ (pairs of corresponding angles). If two lines are parallel, you have discovered that the pairs of alternate interior angles, the pairs of alternate exterior angles, and the pairs of corresponding angles are <u>equal</u>. Observe also, $\angle 3 = 48°$, $\angle 4 = 132°$ and $48°+132°=180°$. This equation indicated that $\angle 3$ and $\angle 4$ are <u>supplementary</u>.

2.

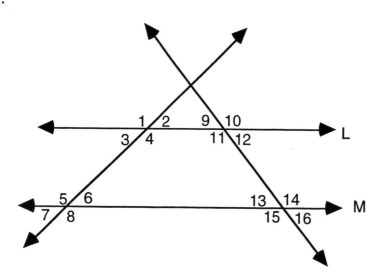

L ‖ M and $\angle 2 = 44°$ and $\angle 13 = 53°$. By using your protractor, find the following measures:

$\angle 1 =$ _____ $\angle 9\ \ =$ _____
$\angle 3 =$ _____ $\angle 10 =$ _____
$\angle 4 =$ _____ $\angle 11 =$ _____
$\angle 5 =$ _____ $\angle 12 =$ _____

2.

$\angle 1 = 136°$

$\angle 3 = 44°$

$\angle 4 = 136°$

$\angle 5 = 136°$

$\angle 6 = 44°$

$\angle 7 = 44$

$\angle 8 = 136°$

$\angle 9 = 53°$

$\angle 10 = 127°$

$\angle 11 = 127°$

$\angle 12 = 53°$

$\angle 14 = 127°$

$\angle 15 = 127°$

$\angle 16 = 53°$

∠6 = _____   ∠14 = _____
∠7 = _____   ∠15 =_____
∠8 = _____   ∠16 = _____

By using your protractor in answering the steps in problem 2, you should have discovered the following four theorems:

If two parallel lines are cut by a transversal, then ...

Theorem 4.1   Nonadjacent angles on the opposite sides of the transversal but interior to the two lines (alternate interior angles) are equal.

Theorem 4.2   Nonadjacent angles on the opposite sides of the transversal but exterior to the two lines (alternate exterior angles) are equal.

Theorem 4.3   Angles on the same side of the transversal but interior to the two lines are supplementary.

Theorem 4.4   Angles on the same side of the transversal and in the same position relative to the two lines (corresponding angles) are equal.

Now, re-work problem 2. This time do not use your protractor. Use the four theorems for parallel lines and other definitions and theorems about angles to find the measure of each angle. One possible set of reasons for the angle measures follows:

∠1 = 136°	Supplementary to ∠2
∠3 = 44°	Vertical to ∠2
∠4 = 136°	Vertical to ∠1
∠5 = 136°	Alternate interior to ∠4
∠6 = 44°	Alternate interior to ∠3
∠7 = 44°	Corresponding to ∠3
∠8 = 136°	Corresponding to ∠4
∠9 = 53°	Corresponding to ∠13
∠10 = 127°	Supplementary to ∠9
∠11 = 127°	Vertical to ∠10
∠12 = 53°	Vertical to ∠9
∠14 = 127°	Corresponding to ∠10
∠15 = 127°	Corresponding to ∠11
∠16 = 53°	Corresponding to ∠12

Algebraic expressions may be used in the evaluation of angles and parallel lines.

Example:

Given: P ‖ Q

Find the value of x and the measures of each angle as shown in the figure.

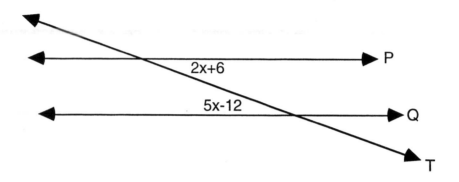

Solution:

Since alternate interior angles are equal,

then $2x + 6 = 5x - 12$

Now, solve

$$2x + 6 = 5x - 12$$
$$-3x + 6 = -12$$
$$-3x = -18$$
$$x = 6$$

By substituting 6 into each expression, we find:

2x + 6	(or)	5x - 12
2(6) + 6		5(6) - 12
12 + 6		30 - 12
18°		18°

The value of x is 6 and the angles both measure 18°.

3. Given: L ‖ M   3.

   Find x and the measure of the angles.

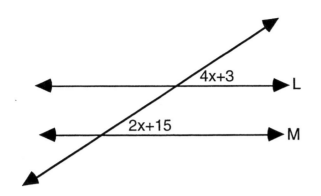

a. The two angles are called _____
    and are equal.
b. 4x + 3 = _____.

Simplify to

c. x = _____
d. One angle is 4x + 3 which equals _____.

a. corresponding
    angles
b. 2x + 15

c. 6
d. 4(6) + 3
    24 + 3
    27°

4. Given: L ‖ M

    Find x and the measure of the angles

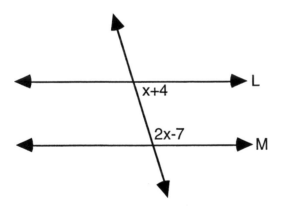

a. The two angles are called _____.
b. (x + 4) + (2x - 7) = _____

Simplify to

c. x = _____
d. One angle is x + 4 which equals _____.
e. The other angle equals _____.

4.

a. supplementary
b. 180°

    3x - 3 = 180
        3x = 183
c.   x = 61
d. (61) + 4 = 65°
e. 2(61) - 7 = 115°

Parallel lines give us four new theorems that can be applied to simple proofs such as the ones that follow.

Example:

Given: $\overline{AD} \parallel \overline{BC}$, $\overline{DC} \parallel \overline{AB}$

Prove: $\triangle ADB \cong \triangle CBD$

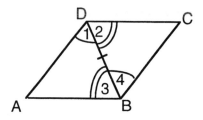

Statements	Reasons
1. $\overline{AD} \parallel \overline{BC}$, $\overline{DC} \parallel \overline{AB}$	1. Given
2. $\angle 1$ and $\angle 4$, $\angle 2$ and $\angle 3$ are alternate interior angles.	2. Definition of alternate interior angles.
3. $\angle 1 = \angle 4$	3. If lines are parallel, then pairs of alternate interior angles are equal. ($\overline{AD} \parallel \overline{BC}$, $\overline{BD}$ is the transversal.) 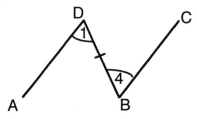
4. $\angle 2 = \angle 3$	4. If lines are parallel, then pairs of alternate interior angles are equal. ($\overline{DC} \parallel \overline{AB}$, $\overline{BD}$ is the transversal.) 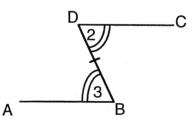
5. $\overline{BD} = \overline{BD}$	5. Reflexive Law
6. $\triangle ADB \cong \triangle CBD$	6. ASA = ASA

5. Given: $\overline{AB} \parallel \overline{DC}$, E is the midpoint of $\overline{BD}$.   5.

Prove: $\triangle ABE \cong \triangle CDE$

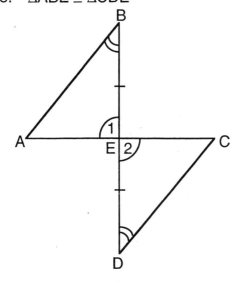

Statements	Reasons	
1. $\overline{AB} \parallel \overline{DC}$ E is the midpoint of $\overline{BD}$.	1. Given	
2. $\angle 1$ and $\angle 2$ are vertical angles.	2. Why?	2. Definition of vertical angles.
3. $\angle 1 = \angle 2$	3. Why?	3. Pairs of vertical angles are equal.
4. $\overline{BE} = \overline{ED}$	4. Why?	4. Definition of midpoint
5. $\angle B$ and $\angle D$ are alternate interior angles.	5. Why?	5. Definition of alternate interior angles
6. $\angle B = \angle D$	6. Why?	6. If lines are parallel, then pairs of alternate interior angles are equal.
7. $\triangle ABE \cong \triangle CDE$	7. Why?	7. ASA = ASA

Converses of conditional statements have been mentioned earlier. Recall that the converse interchanges the hypothesis and conclusion of a conditional statement. The four theorems studied thus far in this unit have true converses. The theorems are as follows:

Theorem 4.1   If two parallel lines are cut by a transversal, then pairs of alternate interior angles are equal.

Theorem 4.2   If two parallel lines are cut by a transversal, then pairs of alternate exterior angles are equal.

Theorem 4.3   If two parallel lines are cut by a transversal, then angles on the same side of the transversal but interior to the two lines are supplementary.

Theorem 4.4   If two parallel lines are cut by a transversal, then pairs of corresponding angles are equal.

6. The converse of the first theorem reads as follows:

Theorem 4.5   If two lines cut by a transversal form equal alternate interior angles, then the lines are parallel.

Write the converses of the other three theorems below:

Theorem 4.6   _____,
              _____.

Theorem 4.7   _____,
              _____.

Theorem 4.8   _____,
              _____.

7.

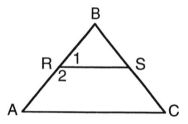

Let's consider the following conditions:

a. If ∠1 = ∠A, is $\overline{RS}$ ∥ $\overline{AC}$? Why?

b. If ∠1 = ∠C and $\overline{AB}$ = $\overline{BC}$, is $\overline{RS}$ ∥ $\overline{AC}$? Why?

7.

a. Yes. If corresponding angles are equal, then the lines are parallel.

b. Yes, if $\overline{AB}$ = $\overline{BC}$, then ∠A = ∠C. (Angles opposite equal sides of a triangle are equal.) By substitution, ∠1 = ∠A plus ∠1 and ∠A are corre-

c. If ∠RSC = 103° and ∠C = 77°, is $\overline{RS}$ ‖ $\overline{AC}$?
    Why?

sponding angles;
hence, the lines are
parallel.

c. Yes, ∠RSC and
    ∠C are supple-
    mentary; therefore,
    $\overline{RS}$ ‖ $\overline{AC}$.

Exercise 4.1

1. Lines P ‖ Q. ∠2 = 57° Find the measure of each angle and give a reason
    for each answer.

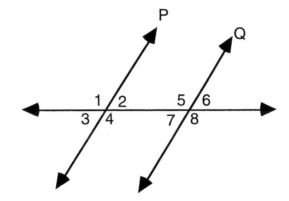

2. In problem 1, find x and the measure of each angle if ∠4 = 2x and
    ∠7 = x + 4.

3. In problem 1, find x and the measure of each angle if ∠2 = 3x - 2 and
    ∠7 = x + 4.

4. In problem 1, find x and the measure of each angle if ∠3 = 2x - 10 and
    ∠7 = x + 4.

5. Lines L and M are not in the same plane. (See illustration.) They are called
    what type of lines?

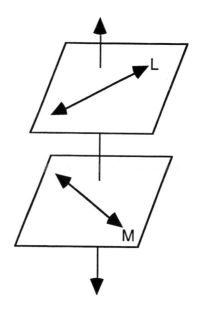

6. If two lines are parallel and are cut by a transversal, what pairs of equal angles are formed? (Name three types.)

7. If two lines are parallel and are cut by a transversal, what pairs of angles are supplementary only because the lines are parallel? Demonstrate your answer with examples.

8.

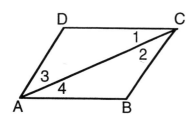

Given: $\overline{AD} \parallel \overline{CB}$ and $\overline{AD} = \overline{CB}$

Prove: $\triangle ADC \cong \triangle CBA$

Statements	Reasons
1. $\overline{AD} \parallel \overline{CB}$ and $\overline{AD} = \overline{CB}$	1. _____.
2. $\angle 2$ and $\angle 3$ are alternate interior angles.	2. _____.
3. $\angle 2 = \angle 3$	3. _____.
4. $\overline{AC} = \overline{AC}$	4. _____.
5. $\triangle ADC \cong \triangle CBA$	5. _____.

9. Given: $\overline{AC}$ and $\overline{DE}$ intersect at B, $\overline{AB} = \overline{BC}$, $\overline{AD} \parallel \overline{CE}$
    Prove: $\overline{AD} = \overline{CE}$

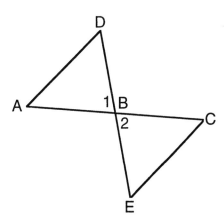

Statements	Reasons
1. $\overline{AC}$ and $\overline{DE}$ intersect at B $\overline{AB} = \overline{BC}$, $\overline{AD} \parallel \overline{CE}$	1. _____.
2. $\angle A$ and $\angle C$ are alternate interior angles.	2. _____.
3. $\angle A = \angle C$	3. _____.
4. $\angle 1$ and $\angle 2$ are vertical angles.	4. _____.
5. $\angle 1 = \angle 2$	5. _____.
6. $\triangle ADB \cong \triangle CEB$	6. _____.
7. $\overline{AD} = \overline{CE}$	7. _____.

4.3 Euclid's Parallel Postulate

Euclid, a famous ancient mathematician, put fourth a theoretical principle presently called the Parallel Postulate. This postulate has become well known in math circles and much discussion has centered around its attempted proof.

However, it remains a postulate and we will demonstrate the parallel postulate by construction.

Postulate 4.1   Parallel Postulate
Through any point, P, not on line L, there can be constructed one and only one line, M, that is parallel to L.

Construction 4.1   To Construct Parallel Lines Using the Parallel Postulate And Equal Alternate Interior Angles

Given: Line L and point, P, not on L.

·P

Step 1:   Through P draw a line, T, that also intersects line L. Notice that the intersection of Lines T and L form ∠1.

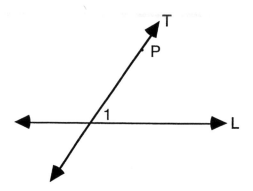

Step 2:   Copy ∠1 on the opposite side of the transversal using P as the vertex and T as one side of the new angle. Draw line M through P and the arc intersection as shown.

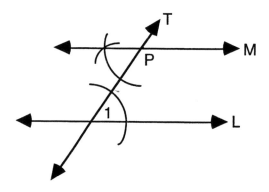

Since the new angle and ∠1 are constructed as equal alternate interior angles, then line L is indeed parallel to line M by Theorem 4.5.

4.4 <u>Triangles and Parallel Lines</u>

Theorem 4.9   The sum of the interior angles of a triangle is 180°.

The proof of this theorem requires the use of the Parallel Postulate as well as theorems related to parallel lines.

Given: △ABC
Prove: ∠A + ∠2 + ∠C = 180°

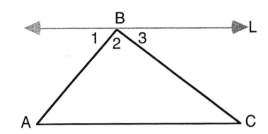

Statements	Reasons
1. △ABC	1. Given
2. L ‖ $\overline{AC}$	2. Parallel Postulate By construction
3. ∠1 and ∠A are alternate interior angles. ∠3 and ∠C are alternate interior angles.	3. Definition of alternate interior angles
4. ∠1 = ∠A, ∠3 = ∠C	4. If two lines are parallel, then pairs of alternate interior angles are equal.
5. ∠1 + ∠2 + ∠3 = 180°	5. Definition of straight angle
6. ∠A + ∠2 + ∠C = 180°	6. Substitution

8. In △XYZ, ∠X = 45°, ∠Z = 62°, find ∠Y.

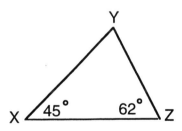

8.

$$45° + 62° + ∠Y = 180°$$
$$107° + ∠Y = 180°$$
$$∠Y = 73°$$

9. If ∠Q = x° and ∠R = (91 − x)°, find ∠P.

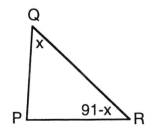

9.

$$x° + (91 − x)° + ∠P = 180°$$
$$∠P + 91° = 180°$$
$$∠P = 89°$$

10. In the given triangle solve for the three angles.

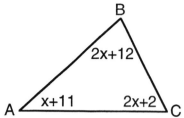

10.

Solution:

$(x+11)+(2x+12)+(2x+2) = 180°$
Why?
Solving:

$$5x + 25 = 180$$
$$5x = 155$$
$$x = 31$$

The sum of the interior angles of a triangle is $180°$.

X has been found to be 31. We still have to find the angles. Substituting, the solutions are as follows:

$\angle A = x+11 = 31+11 = 42°$

$\angle B = 2x+12 = 2(31)+12 = 62+12 = 74°$

$\angle C = 2x+2 = 2(31)+2 = 64+2 = 64°$

11. Given triangle ABC, find x and the value of each angle.

11.

$(2x-6)+(x-3)+(2x+4) = 180°$
$$5x - 5 = 180$$
$$x = 37$$
$\angle A = x-3 = 37-3 = 34°$
$\angle B = 2x-6 = 2(37)-6$
$\angle B = 74-6 = 68°$
$\angle C = 2x+4 = 2(37)+4$

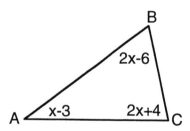

Example:

One angle of a triangle is five more than twice a second. A third is ten less than twice the second angle. Find the value of the angles of the triangle.

Solution:

x = second angle

<u>five</u> <u>more than</u> <u>twice a second</u> is the first angle
  5   +   2 .   x   = first angle

<u>ten less than</u> <u>twice a second</u> is the third angle
                2 .   x   - 10   = third angle

Since the sum of the angles of a triangle is 180°, we obtain our equation:

$$(x) + (5 + 2x) + (2x - 10) = 180$$
$$5x - 5 = 180$$
$$5x = 185$$
$$x = 37$$

Now the first angle $= 5 + 2x$
$= 5 + 2(37)$
$= 5 + 74$
$= 79°$
and the third angle $= 2x - 10$
$= 2(37) - 10$
$= 74 - 10$
$= 64°$

12. Given the following problem, find the solution.

In a triangle one angle is three times a second. The third angle is six less than twice the second. Find the angles.

Let x = second angle
_____ = first angle
_____ = third angle

The equation is _____ .

The angles are _____, _____, and _____.

12.

$3x$ = first angle
$2x-6$ = third angle
$x + (3x) + (2x - 6) = 180°$
$$6x = 186$$
$$x = 31$$
31°, 93°, 56°

13. Given: $\overline{MN} \parallel \overline{OP}$, $\overline{NO} \parallel \overline{MP}$, $\angle ONP = 30°$,
        $\angle OPN = 70°$
   Find: $\angle PNM$, $\angle NPM$, and $\angle M$.

13.

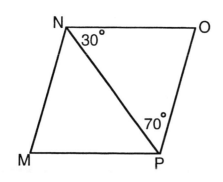

a. ∠OPN = ∠PNM because _____ and
    ∠PNM = _____.

b. ∠ONP = ∠NPM because _____ and
    ∠NPM = _____.

c. ∠PNM + ∠NPM + ∠M = 180°
        70° + 30° + ∠M = 180°
             ∠M = _____.

a. If two lines are
    parallel, then the
    alternate interior
    angles are equal.
    70°

b. If two lines are
    parallel, then the
    alternate interior
    angles are equal.
    30°

c. The sum of the
    interior angles of
    a triangle equals
    180°.
    ∠M = 80°

Theorem 4.9 has several interesting conclusions which can be drawn with minimal effort.

Definition 4.7   Statements which are theorems but are easily obtained as an extension of another theorem are called <u>corollaries</u>.

Corollary 4.1   In a right triangle, the two acute angles are complementary.

Given: Triangle ABC is a right triangle with ∠C as right angle.

Prove: ∠A and ∠B are complementary.

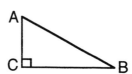

Statements	Reasons
1. △ABC is a right triangle with	1. Given

∠C a right angle.

2. $\angle A + \angle B + \angle C = 180°$	2. The sum of the interior angles of a triangle is 180°.
3. $\angle C = 90°$	3. Definition of a right angle
4. $\angle A + \angle B + 90° = 180°$	4. Substitution
5. $\angle A + \angle B = 90°$	5. Equals subtracted from equals give equals.
6. ∠A and ∠B are complementary.	6. Definition of complementary

14. Solve for the other two angles in the following triangle.

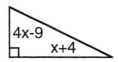

$$(x+4)+(4x-9) = 90° \text{Why?}$$
$$5x - 5 = 90$$
$$5x = 95$$
$$x = 19$$
$$x + 4 = 19 + 4 = 23°$$
$$4x - 9 = 4(19) - 9 = 76 - 9 = 67°$$

14.

The acute angle of a right triangle are complementary.

15. Using Corollary 4.1, solve for x in △ABC.

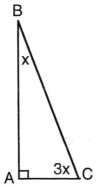

$$x + 3x = 90$$
$$4x = \underline{}$$
$$x = \underline{}$$

15.

$$4x = 90$$
$$x = \frac{90}{4} = 22\frac{1}{2}°$$

16. Solve for ∠D in △CDE.

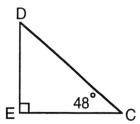

16.

$$48° + ∠D = 90°$$
$$∠D = 42°$$

17. In a right triangle, the two complementary angles are 2x + 5 and 50 - x. Find the value of x and the measures of each complementary angle.

17.

$$(2x+5)+(50-x) = 90°$$
$$x+55 = 90$$
$$x = 35$$
$$angle\ 1 = 2(35)+5 = 75°$$
$$angle\ 2 = 50 - 35 = 15°$$

Another extension of the theorem on "the sum of the interior angles of a triangle" pertains to the definition of exterior angles.

Definition 4.8 An exterior angle of a triangle is formed whenever one of the sides of a triangle is extended through its vertex. An exterior angle is adjacent to an interior angle of a triangle.

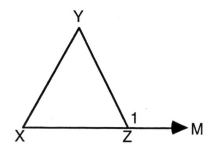

∠1 is formed by extending side $\overline{XZ}$ of the triangle.

∠1 is also supplementary to ∠XZY.

Example:

Given: △ABC with ∠A = 25° and ∠B = 60°

Find the measures of ∠ACB and the exterior angle, ∠BCD.

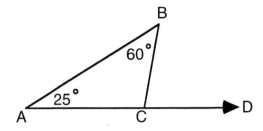

Solution:

$\angle A = 25°$ and $\angle B = 60°$ Information given

$\angle A + \angle B + \angle ACB = 180°$ The sum of the interior angles of a triangle is 180°.

$25° + 60° + \angle ACB = 180°$ Substitution

$85° + \angle ACB = 180°$ By addition

$\angle ACB = 95°$ By subtraction

We have already obtained the measure of $\angle ACB = 95°$. In finding the second angle's measure, recall the definition of supplementary angles.

$\angle BCD$ is supplementary to $\angle ACB$.

$\angle BCD + \angle ACB = 180°$

$\angle BCD + 95° = 180°$

$\angle BCD = 85°$

$\angle BCD$ is called an exterior angle to $\triangle ABC$ which is also supplementary to $\angle ACB$.

18. Given: $\triangle MNO$, $\angle 2 = 40°$

Find the measure of $\angle 1$.

18. $\angle 1$ is an exterior angle and is supplementary to $\angle 2$.

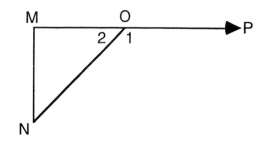

$$\angle 1 + \angle 2 = 180°$$
$$\angle 1 + 40° = 180°$$
$$\angle 1 = 140°$$

19. Given: $\angle HMT = 15°$ and $\angle U = 64°$

    Find $\angle R$ and $\angle RMU$.

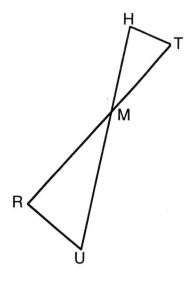

    a. $\angle HMT = \angle RMU$

        $\angle RMU = $ _____

    b. $\angle RMU + \angle U + \angle R = 180°$
        $\angle R = $ _____

20. Given: $\triangle XYZ$ is isosceles and $\overline{YT}$ is an
             altitude of $\triangle$.

    Find: $\angle X$, $\angle XYT$, and $\angle YTX$

19.

    a. Pairs of vertical
        angles are
        equal.
        $15°$

    b. $15 + 64 + \angle R = 180°$
        $\angle R = 101°$

20.

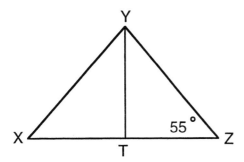

a. ∠X = ∠Z
    ∠X = _____

b. ∠YTX = 90° because _____.

c. ∠X + ∠YTX + ∠XYT = 180°
              ∠XYT = _____

21. Given: $\overline{CD}$ ‖ $\overline{AB}$, ∠2 = 70°, ∠3 = 81°
    Find the measures of the other angles.

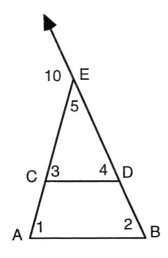

a. Angles opposite
    equal sides in a
    triangle are equal.
    55°

b. $\overline{YT}$ ⊥ $\overline{XZ}$ by the
    definition of
    altitude and
    perpendicular
    lines form right
    angles.

c. 35°

21. ∠1 = ∠3 = 81°
     ∠2 = ∠4 = 70°

If two lines are
parallel, then the
corresponding angles
are equal.
The sum of the interior
angles of a triangle
equals 180°.
81° + 70° + ∠5 = 180°
    151° + ∠5 = 180°
          ∠5 = 29°
∠10 is an exterior
angle to △ABE.
          ∠10 = 151°

In problem 21, note that the measure of ∠10 equals the sum of the measures
of ∠3 and ∠4.

$$\angle 10 = \angle 3 + \angle 4$$
$$\angle 10 = 81° + 70°$$
$$\angle 10 = 151°$$

Corollary 4.2 Each exterior angle of a triangle equals the sum of its two nonadjacent interior angles.

Given: $\triangle ABC$ with exterior angle, $\angle 1$
Prove: $\angle 1 = \angle A + \angle B$

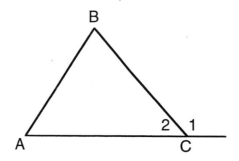

Statements	Reasons
1. $\triangle ABC$ with exterior angle, $\angle 1$	1. Given
2. $\angle A + \angle B + \angle 2 = 180°$	2. The sum of the interior angles of a triangle equals $180°$.
3. $\angle 1$ and $\angle 2$ are supplementary.	3. Definition of supplementary
4. $\angle 1 + \angle 2 = 180°$	4. Definition of supplementary
5. $\angle A + \angle B + \angle 2 = \angle 1 + \angle 2$	5. Substitution
6. $\angle A + \angle B = \angle 1$	6. Equals subtracted from equals give equals.

22. Using the measures given, find $\angle 1$, $\angle 2$, and $\angle 3$.

22. $\angle 1 + \angle ONM = 180°$
$\angle 1 + 20° = 180°$
$\angle 1 = 160°$

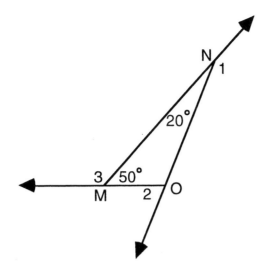

$\angle 3 + \angle NMO = 180°$

$\angle 3 + 50° = 180°$

$\angle 3 = 130°$

$\angle 2 = \angle NMO + \angle MNO$

$\angle 2 = 50° + 20°$

$\angle 2 = 70°$

The exterior angle, $\angle 2$, equals the sum of the nonadjacent interior angles.

23. Given: $\triangle$ RST
    Is $\angle 5$ an exterior angle to $\triangle$ RST? Why?

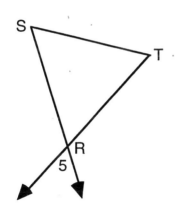

23.

No, by definition an exterior angle is formed by the extension of only one side of a triangle. $\angle 5$ is not an exterior angle but it is a vertical angle to $\angle SRT$.

Exercise 4.2

1. If $\angle A = 70°$ and $\angle B = 60°$, find $\angle BCA$ and $\angle BCD$.

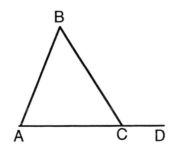

2. In the given triangle find the three angles.

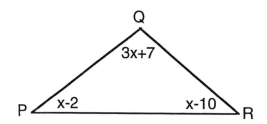

3. One angle is twice a second in a triangle. A third is ten less than six times the second. Find the angles of this triangle.

4. Solve for x and find the measures of ∠A and ∠B.

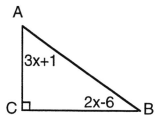

5.

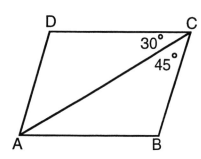

Given: $\overline{AD}$ II $\overline{BC}$, $\overline{AB}$ II $\overline{DC}$

∠DCA = 30°, ∠ACB = 45°

Find: ∠DAC, ∠CAB, ∠D and ∠B

Justify your answer.

6. Given: ∠A = 43°, $\overline{AB}$ = 6 in., $\overline{BC}$ = 6 in
   Find: ∠C and ∠B
   What kind of triangle is △ABC?

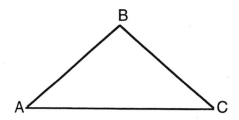

7. Find the measures of all the numbered angles. Name all the angles exterior to △CGE.

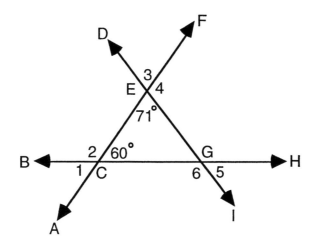

8. Construct a line that passes through H and is parallel to line N by using the steps outlined in Construction 4.1.

·H

N

9. Given: ∠A = ∠D, ∠C = ∠F, $\overline{AB} = \overline{DE}$
    Prove: △ABC ≅ △DEF

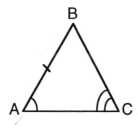 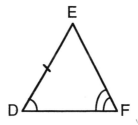

Fill in the appropriate reasons for each statement listed below:

Statements	Reasons
1. ∠A = ∠D, ∠C = ∠F, $\overline{AB} = \overline{DE}$	1.
2. ∠A + ∠B + ∠C = 180° ∠D + ∠E + ∠F = 180°	2.
3. ∠A + ∠B + ∠C = ∠D + ∠E + ∠F	3.
4. ∠B = ∠E	4.
5. △ABC ≅ △DEF	5. *

* Note: Recall the three methods discussed to prove triangles congruent
were ASA = ASA, SAS = SAS, and SSS = SSS. This exercise is
actually another method to prove congruence. This is AAS = AAS.
If two angles of a triangle are given, the third angle can always be
found. When any side is given, enough data is known to obtain
congruence by ASA = ASA.

This exercise is actually a theorem.

Theorem 4.10	If two angles and a side of one triangle are equal to two angles and a side of another triangle, then the triangles are congruent. (AAS = AAS)

4.5 Additional Theorem Concerning Triangles

Theorem 4.11	If a line segment joins the midpoints of two sides of a triangle, then that line segment is parallel to and equal to one-half the measure of the third side.

Example: In $\triangle ABC$, D is the midpoint of $\overline{AB}$ and E is the midpoint of $\overline{AC}$. If
$\overline{DE} = 10\frac{1}{4}$ in., find $\overline{BC}$.

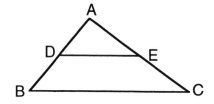

Solution:

$\overline{BC} = 2\overline{DE}$ from the theorem

$\overline{BC} = 2\left(10\frac{1}{4}\right)$

$\overline{BC} = 2\left(\frac{41}{4}\right)$

$\overline{BC} = \frac{82}{4} = 20\frac{1}{2} = 20.5$ in.

24. In $\triangle XYZ$, A is the midpoint of $\overline{XY}$ and B is
the midpoint of $\overline{YZ}$. If $\overline{AB} = 5$ in., find
$\overline{XZ}$.

24.

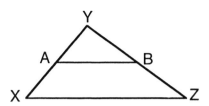

Solution:

$$\overline{XZ} = 2\overline{AB}$$
$$\overline{XZ} = 2(5)$$
$$\overline{XZ} = \underline{\hspace{1cm}}$$

10 in.

25. In UVW, P is the midpoint of $\overline{UV}$ and Q is the midpoint of $\overline{VW}$. If $\overline{UW} = 7\frac{1}{3}$ cm., find $\overline{PQ}$.

25.

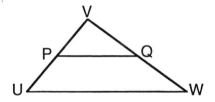

Solution:

$$2\overline{PQ} = \overline{UW}$$
$$2\overline{PQ} = 7\frac{1}{3} \text{ cm.}$$
$$\left(\frac{1}{2}\right)\left(2\overline{PQ}\right) = \left(\frac{1}{2}\right)\left(\frac{22}{3}\right)$$
$$\overline{PQ} = \underline{\hspace{1cm}}$$

$\frac{11}{3} = 3\frac{2}{3} = 3.\overline{6}$ cm.

26. In $\triangle$MNO, C and D are midpoints of $\overline{MN}$ and $\overline{NO}$, respectively. If $\overline{MO} = 5.7$ dm., find $\overline{CD}$.

26.

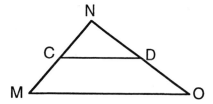

Solution:

$$2\overline{CD} = \overline{MO}$$
$$2\overline{CD} = 5.7$$
$$\overline{CD} = \underline{\qquad}$$

$$\frac{1}{2}\left(2\overline{CD}\right) = \frac{1}{2}(5.7)$$
$$\overline{CD} = 2.85 \text{ dm.}$$

27. D is the midpoint of $\overline{AB}$. E is the midpoint of $\overline{BC}$.

27.

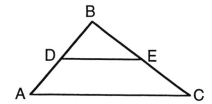

a. If $\overline{AD} = 6$ in., find $\overline{BD}$.

Solution: Since D is the midpoint of $\overline{AB}$, $\overline{BD} = \overline{AD} = 6$ in.

b. If $\angle BDE = 60°$ and $\angle C = 35°$, find $\angle A$ and $\angle B$.

Solution: Theorem 4.11 tells us that $\overline{DE} \parallel \overline{AC}$. Therefore, $\angle BDE = \angle A$. (Corresponding angles) Hence, $\angle A = 60°$.

$\angle A + \angle B + \angle C = 180°$
(The sum of the interior angles of a triangle equals 180°.)
If $\angle A = 60°$ and $\angle C = 35°$,
$60° + \angle B + 35° = 180°$

$$\angle B + 95° = 180°$$
$$\angle B = 85°$$

c. If $\overline{DE}$ = 8 in., find $\overline{AC}$.
    Solution: By Theorem 4.11
$$\overline{AC} = 2\overline{DE}$$
$$\overline{AC} = 2(8)$$
$$\overline{AC} = \underline{\quad}$$

c.

    16 in.

28. S and T are midpoints of $\overline{PQ}$ and $\overline{QR}$, respectively.

28.

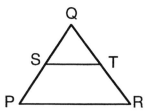

a. If $\overline{QT}$ = 9 cm., find $\overline{QR}$.
    $\overline{QR}$ = _____

a.
    18 cm.

b. If $\angle QTS$ = 50° and $\angle P$ = 65°, find $\angle R$ and $\angle Q$.

    i. $\angle R$ =

b.

    i. $\angle R$ = 50°
       $\overline{ST}$ ‖ $\overline{PR}$ and
       $\angle R$ and $\angle QTS$
       are correspond-
       ing angles. If
       lines are
       parallel, then
       pairs of corre-
       sponding
       angles are
       equal.

    ii. $\angle P + \angle Q + \angle R = 180°$
       $65 + \angle Q + 50 = 180$
       $\angle Q + 115 = 180$
       $\angle Q = \underline{\quad}$

    ii.

    65°
    The sum of
    the interior
    angles of
    a triangle is
    180°.

c. If $\overline{ST} = 4\dfrac{3}{5}$ ft., find $\overline{PR}$.

c.

$$\overline{PR} = 2\overline{ST}$$

$$\overline{PR} = 2\left(4\frac{3}{5}\right)$$

$$\overline{PR} = 2\left(-\right)$$

$$\overline{PR} = \underline{\quad\quad}$$

$$\overline{PR} = 2\left(\frac{23}{5}\right) = \frac{45}{5}$$

$$\overline{PR} = 9\frac{1}{5} = 9.2 \text{ ft.}$$

Exercise 4.3

1.

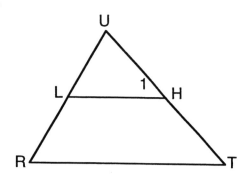

N, M, and O are midpoints of $\overline{AC}$, $\overline{AB}$, and $\overline{BC}$, respectively.
$\overline{MO} = 2.7$ cm. and $\overline{NM} = 3$ cm.
Find the lengths of $\overline{AC}$ and $\overline{BC}$.

2.

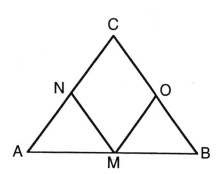

E, F, and G are midpoints of their respective sides. Find the perimeter of $\triangle EFG$ if $\overline{XZ} = 22$ cm., $\overline{XY} = 31$ cm., and $\overline{ZY} = 27$ cm.

3.

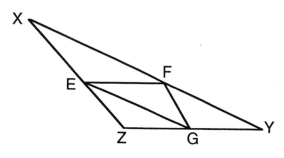

H is the midpoint of $\overline{UT}$ and L is the midpoint of $\overline{RU}$. $\overline{RT} = 13$ ft.
$\angle R = 58°$, $\angle 1 = 47°$
Find $\angle U$, $\angle ULH$, $\angle T$, and $\overline{LH}$.

4.6 <u>Constructing Parallel Lines Using Another Postulate</u>

In Construction 4.1, the alternate interior angles were drawn as acute angles. If the alternate interior angles were both 90°, they would be equal; and, therefore, would form two parallel lines.

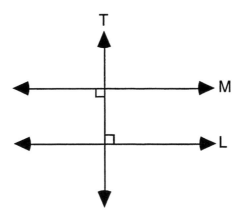

Postulate 4.2   Two lines are parallel if they are both perpendicular to a third line.

Since T ⊥ M and T ⊥ L, then M ‖ L.

We will use Postulate 4.2 to construct two lines that are parallel to one another and perpendicular to the same line.

Construction 4.2   Constructing two parallel lines by constructing two lines perpendicular to the same line.

Step 1:   Draw line L and select two distinct points, P and Q, on L.

Step 2:   Select a radius on your compass. Using Q, then P, as centers, make arcs on each side of each point.

Step 3:   With Q as the midpoint of the segment, $\overline{XY}$, formed at Q, construct a perpendicular bisector of $\overline{XY}$. Do the same construction for the segment, $\overline{RS}$, formed at P.

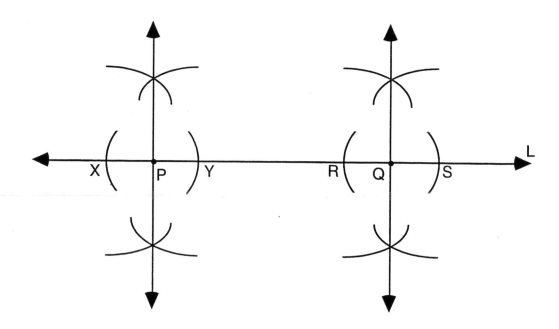

The two lines formed are perpendicular to the same line; and, therefore, are themselves parallel.

Exercise 4.4

1. How do you know that lines M and N are parallel?

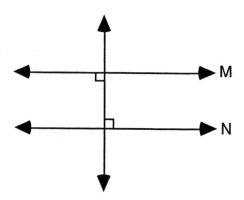

2. Given line L and points A and B on L. Construct lines that are parallel, one through A and one through B.

Unit 4 Review

1. If two lines are cut by a transversal, then name four ways you can prove that the two lines are parallel.

2. Given: $\overline{AB} \parallel \overline{DC}, \overline{AD} \parallel \overline{BC}$
   Find the measures of all the angles if $\angle 1 = 30°$ and $\angle 3 = 60°$.

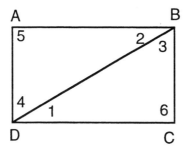

3. If $\overrightarrow{PD} \parallel \overleftrightarrow{EF}$, $\overleftrightarrow{CF} \perp \overleftrightarrow{AE}$, $\overrightarrow{PD} \perp \overrightarrow{PB}$ and $\angle 5 = 30°$, find the other numbered angles.

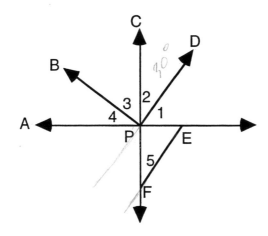

4. Define the following terms: parallel lines, skew lines, alternate interior angles, alternate exterior angles, corresponding angles, transversal and exterior angle.

5. Draw a line and select two distinct points on the line. Construct a line through each of these two points to obtain parallel lines using Postulate 4.2.

6. Given: Lines O ∥ P
   If $\angle 14 = 25°$ and $\angle 6 = 44°$, find the measure of each of the numbered angles. Justify each answer. There is more than one correct reason for each answer.

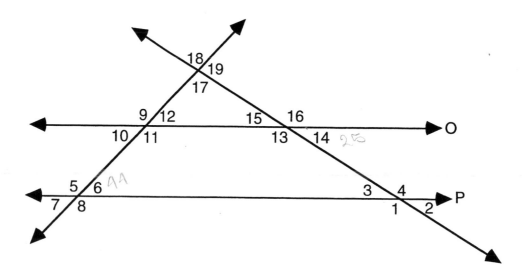

7. Given: $\overline{AB} \perp \overline{AD}$, $\overline{DE} \perp \overline{AD}$, $\overline{AB} = \overline{DE}$
   Prove: $\triangle ABC \cong \triangle EDC$

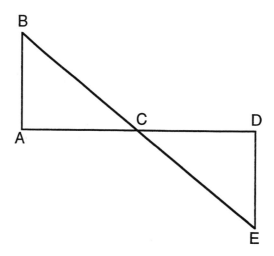

Statements	Reasons
1. $\overline{AB} \perp \overline{AD}$, $\overline{DE} \perp \overline{AD}$, $\overline{AB} = \overline{DE}$	1. Given
2. $\angle A$ and $\angle D$ are right angles.	2. _____.
3. $\angle A = \angle D$	3. _____.
4. $\overline{AB} \parallel \overline{DE}$	4. _____.
5. $\overline{BE}$ is a transversal.	5. _____.
6. $\angle B$ and $\angle E$ are alternate interior angles.	6. _____.
7. $\angle B = \angle E$	7. _____.
8. $\triangle ABC \cong \triangle EDC$	8. _____.

8. Given: L ‖ M
    Find the value of "x" and the measure of the angles.

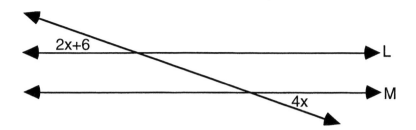

9. S, T, and U are midpoints of $\overline{PQ}$, $\overline{QR}$, and $\overline{PR}$, respectively. If $\overline{PQ}$ = 10 in.,
    $\overline{QR}$ = 12 in., and $\overline{PR}$ = 8 in., find the perimeter of △STU.

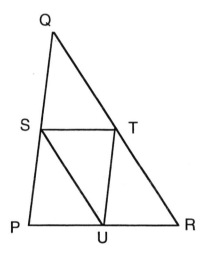

10. Using Postulate 4.1, construct a line through point M that is parallel to the
    given line.

 M

11. In a triangle, the first angle is eleven more than three times the second.
    The third is one less than twice the second. Find the angles.

12. In △ABC, ∠A is a right angle. Find ∠B and ∠C.

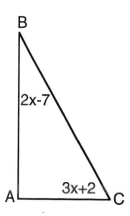

13. In the figure, line O⊥L, O⊥M, L ‖ M ‖ N, and ∠9 = 130°. Find the measure of each of the other angles and state the reason for each answer.

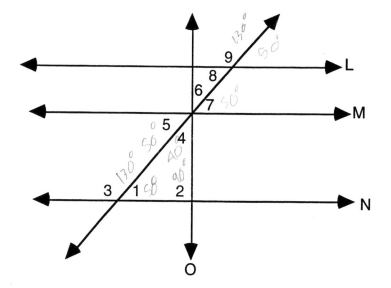

Unit 5

Quadrilaterals

Learning Objectives:

The student will demonstrate his mastery of the following definitions and theorems by writing them and by applying them to the solution of selected problems:

Definitions: quadrilateral, convex, vertices, sides, consecutive angles, consecutive sides, opposite angles, opposite sides, diagonal, parallelogram, rectangle, square, rhombus, trapezoid, base, median of a trapezoid, and isosceles trapezoid

Theorems:

1. If a quadrilateral is a parallelogram, then the diagonal divides the parallelogram into two congruent triangles.

2. If a quadrilateral is a parallelogram, then both pairs of opposite sides are equal.

3. If the quadrilateral is a parallelogram, then both pairs of opposite angles are equal.

4. Consecutive angles of a parallelogram are supplementary.

5. The diagonals of a rectangle are equal.

6. The diagonals of a parallelogram bisect each other.

7. The diagonals of a rhombus are perpendicular.

8. The diagonals of a rhombus bisect the angles of a rhombus.

9. The median of a trapezoid is parallel to the bases and is equal to one-half of the sum of the two bases.

Converses:

1. If both pairs of opposite sides of a quadrilateral are equal, then the quadrilateral is a parallelogram.

2. If both pairs of opposite angles of a quadrilateral are equal, then the quadrilateral is a parallelogram.

3. If consecutive angles of a quadrilateral are supplementary, then the quadrilateral is a parallelogram.

QUADRILATERALS

5.1 <u>Definitions</u>

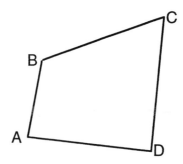

| Definition 5.1 | If A, B, C, and D are points, no three of which are collinear and if sides $\overline{AB}$, $\overline{BC}$, $\overline{CD}$, and $\overline{AD}$ intersect only at these points, then the figure so formed is called a <u>quadrilateral</u> . |

The illustrations below are two examples of a four sided closed figures (quadrilaterals).

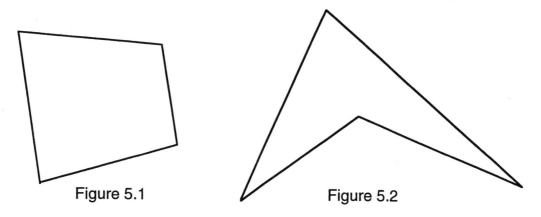

Figure 5.1   Figure 5.2

Figure 5.1 represents a convex quadrilateral. Figure 5.2 is not a convex figure but is a quadrilateral.

| Definition 5.2 | A quadrilateral is <u>convex</u> if one may connect any two points belonging to the figure without any portion of the line segment lying in the exterior of the figure. |

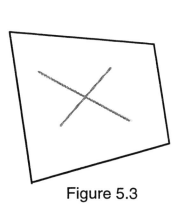

Figure 5.3

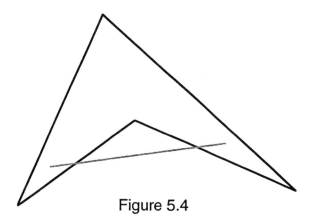

Figure 5.4

Figure 5.3 is convex. The dotted lines connecting any two points in this figure are also contained within the figure. Figure 5.4 is not convex. The dotted lines connecting the two points in this figure are not contained within the figure.

1. Which of the following are convex quadrilaterals? Tell why or why not.

a.

b.

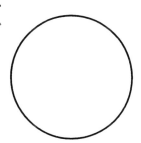

c.

1.

a. not convex

b.

It is convex but is not a quadrilateral.

c. convex

d.

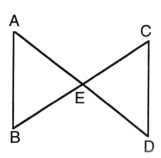

d. not convex, not a
    quadrilateral

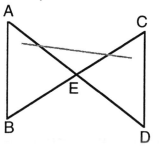

e.

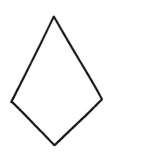

e. convex

f.

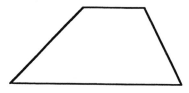

f. convex

g.

g. not convex, not a
    quadrilateral

The quadrilaterals that we will be discussing are all closed, four-sided convex figures.

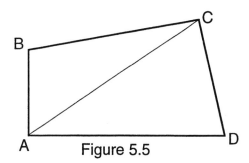

Figure 5.5

Figure 5.5 is one example of this type of quadrilateral. Points A, B, C, and D are called the <u>vertices</u> of the quadrilateral and the line segments, $\overline{AB}$, $\overline{BC}$, $\overline{CD}$, and $\overline{AD}$ are called the <u>sides</u>. The sides that intersect one another are called <u>consecutive</u>. $\overline{CD}$ and $\overline{AD}$ are examples of <u>consecutive sides</u>. The angles are consecutive if they have a side in common. ∠A and ∠B are examples of consecutive angles. Angles A and C are called <u>opposite angles</u> because they do not share a common side. $\overline{BC}$ and $\overline{AD}$ are <u>opposite sides</u> because they do not intersect. The <u>diagonal</u> of a quadrilateral is a line segment that connects pairs of opposite vertices. $\overline{AC}$ is the diagonal in Figure 5.5.

2.

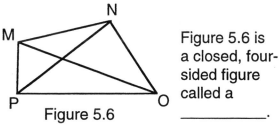

Figure 5.6

Figure 5.6 is a closed, four-sided figure called a _____.

2. quadrilateral

3. Name the consecutive angles and and consecutive sides of the quadrilateral in Figure 5.6.

3. Consecutive angles: ∠M and ∠N, ∠N and ∠O, ∠O and ∠P, and ∠P and ∠M
Consecutive sides: $\overline{MN}$ and $\overline{NO}$, $\overline{NO}$ and $\overline{PO}$, $\overline{PO}$ and $\overline{MP}$, $\overline{MP}$ and $\overline{MN}$

4. Name the opposite angles and opposite sides of the quadrilateral in Figure 5.6.

4. Opposite angles: ∠M and ∠O, ∠P and ∠N
Opposite sides: $\overline{MN}$ and $\overline{PO}$, $\overline{MP}$ and $\overline{NO}$

5. Name the two diagonals of the quadrilateral | 5. $\overline{MO}$ and $\overline{PN}$

The most common types of quadrilaterals are defined as follows:

Definition 5.3	A <u>parallelogram</u> is a quadrilateral in which each pair of opposite sides are parallel to one another.

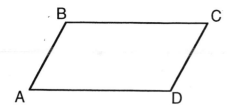

ABCD is a parallelogram. From the definition side $\overline{AB}$ is parallel to $\overline{CD}$ and side $\overline{BC}$ is parallel to $\overline{AD}$.

Definition 5.4	A <u>rectangle</u> is a parallelogram having one right angle.

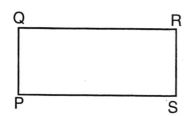

PQRS is a rectangle with right angle P. Using Theorem 4.3 it can be shown that all the angles of a rectangle are right angles. Because a rectangle is a parallelogram, the opposite sides are parallel.

Definition 5.5	A <u>square</u> is a rectangle all of whose sides are equal.

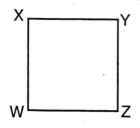

WXYZ is a square. By definition all of its sides are equal. Since it is a rectangle, all of its angles are right angles. Since a rectangle is a parallelogram, then WXYZ has opposite sides parallel. --

Definition 5.6	A <u>rhombus</u> is a parallelogram all of whose sides are equal.

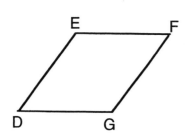

DEFG is a rhombus. By definition all sides are equal. Since it is also a parallelogram, the opposite sides are parallel. Note: The angles are not necessarily right angles.

Definition 5.7	A <u>trapezoid</u> is a quadrilateral having a single pair of opposite sides that are parallel. The sides that are parallel are called <u>bases</u>.

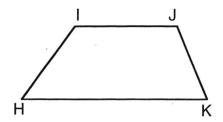

HIJK is a trapezoid. $\overline{IJ}$ ‖ $\overline{HK}$.

$\overline{IJ}$ and $\overline{HK}$ are called bases.

$\overline{HI}$ and $\overline{JK}$ are not parallel.

They are legs of the trapezoid.

The schematic diagram below illustrates the relationships of these common types of quadrilaterals.

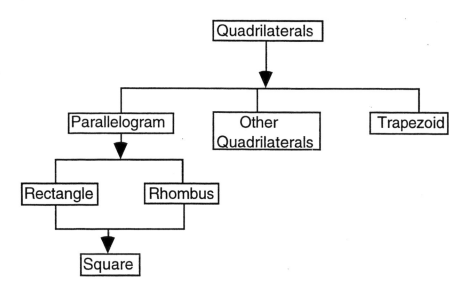

6. Using the diagram, answer the following statements about quadrilaterals. (Use yes or no.)

  a. A rectangle is trapezoid.

  b. A square is a parallelogram.

  c. A rhombus is a square.

  d. A square is a rectangle.

  e. A rectangle is a square.

  f.   A square is a rhombus.

  g. A trapezoid is a quadrilateral.

  h. A rhombus is a parallelogram.

6.

  a. no

  b. yes

  c. no

  d. yes

  e. no

  f.   yes

  g. yes

  h. yes

7. Using the definitions, which quadrilaterals fit these given conditions?

    a. Has one right angle and is a parallelogram.

    b. Has all the sides equal and is a parallelogram.

    c. Has a right angle, all sides equal, and is a parallelogram.

    d. Has both pairs of opposite sides parallel.

    e. Has only one pair of parallel sides.

7.

    a. rectangle

    b. rhombus

    c. square

    d. parallelogram

    e. trapezoid

5.2 Parallelograms

There are many theorems concerning parallelograms. We will examine a few of them in this section.

Theorem 5.1	If a quadrilateral is a parallelogram, then the diagonal divides the parallelogram into two congruent triangles.

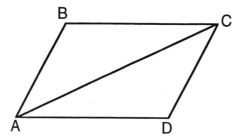

Given: ABCD is a parallelogram

Prove: △ABC ≅ △CDA

Statements	Reasons
1. ABCD is a parallelogram.	1. Given
2. $\overline{AB} \parallel \overline{CD}$, $\overline{BC} \parallel \overline{AD}$	2. Definition of parallelogram
3. $\overline{AC}$ is a diagonal.	3. Definition of diagonal.
4. ∠BAC and ∠DCA are alternate interior angles. ∠BCA and ∠DAC are alternate interior angles.	4. Definition of alternate interior angles.

5. ∠BAC = ∠DCA, ∠BCA = ∠DAC	5. If two parallel lines are cut by a transversal, then pairs of alternate interior angles are equal.
6. $\overline{AC} = \overline{AC}$	6. Reflexive
7. ΔABC ≅ ΔCDA	7. ASA = ASA

Theorem 5.2	If a quadrilateral is a parallelogram, then both pairs of opposite sides are equal.

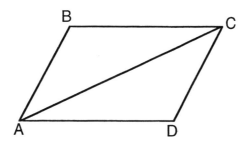

Given: ABCD is a parallelogram.

Prove: $\overline{AB} = \overline{CD}$ and $\overline{BC} = \overline{AD}$

Statements	Reasons
1. ABCD is a parallelogram	1. Given
2. $\overline{AC}$ is a diagonal.	2. Definition of diagonal.
3. ΔABC ≅ ΔCDA	3. If a quadrilateral is a parallelogram, then the diagonal divides the parallelogram into two congruent triangles.
4. $\overline{AB} = \overline{CD}$, $\overline{BC} = \overline{AD}$	4. CPCTE

The converse of Theorem 5.2 is also a theorem.

8. Write the converse in the space provided:

Converse of Theorem 5.2:
_____
_____
_____

8.

If both pairs of opposite sides of a quadrilateral are equal, then the quadrilateral is a parallelogram.

Theorem 5.3   If a quadrilateral is a parallelogram, then both pairs of opposite angles are equal.

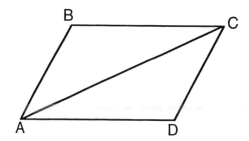

Given: ABCD is a parallelogram with diagonal $\overline{AC}$.

Prove: ∠BAD = ∠BCD and ∠B = ∠D

Statements	Reasons
1. ABCD is a parallelogram.	1. Given
2. $\overline{AC}$ is a diagonal.	2. Given
3. ΔABC ≅ ΔCDA	3. If a quadrilateral is a parallelogram, then the diagonal divides the parallelogram into two congruent triangles.
4. ∠B = ∠D, ∠BAC = ∠DCA ∠BCA = ∠DAC	4. CPCTE
5. ∠BAD = ∠BCD	5. Equals added to equals give equals.

9. Write the converse in the space provided: 9.

Converse of Theorem 5.3:

_____

_____

_____

If both pairs of opposite angles of a quadrilateral are equal, then the quadrilateral is a parallelogram.

Theorem 5.4   Consecutive angles of a parallelogram are supplementary.

10. Use the following steps to prove Theorem 5.4. | 10.

Given: MNOP is a parallelogram.

Prove: ∠M and ∠P are supplementary angles.

Statements	Reasons
a. MNOP is a parallelogram.	a. Given
b. $\overline{MN} \parallel \overline{PO}$	b. _____
c. $\overline{MP}$ is a transversal.	c. _____
d. ∠M and ∠P are supplementary	d. _____

b. Definition of parallelogram

c. Definition of transversal

d. If two parallel lines are cut by a transversal, two angles on the same side of the the transversal interior to the two lines are supplementary.

Likewise, it can be shown that ∠M and ∠N are supplementary, ∠N and ∠O are supplementary, and ∠O and ∠P are supplementary.

11. Write the converse in the space provided: | 11.

Converse of Theorem 5.4:

_____

_____

_____

If consecutive angles of a quadrilateral are supplementary, then the quadrilateral is a parallelogram.

Theorem 5.5   The diagonals of a rectangle are equal.

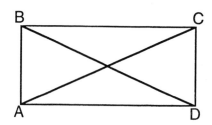

Given: Rectangle ABCD with diagonals $\overline{AC}$ and $\overline{BD}$

Prove: $\overline{AC} = \overline{BD}$

Statements	Reasons
1. Rectangle ABCD with diagonals $\overline{AC}$ and $\overline{BD}$	1. Given
2. ∠BAD and ∠CDA are right angles.	2. Definition of rectangle
3. ∠BAD = ∠CDA	3. All right angles are equal.
4. $\overline{AB} = \overline{CD}$	4. If a quadrilateral is a parallelogram, then both pairs of opposite sides are equal.
5. $\overline{AD} = \overline{AD}$	5. Reflexive
6. ΔBAD ≅ ΔCDA	6. SAS = SAS
7. $\overline{AC} = \overline{BD}$	7. CPCTE

Theorem 5.6   The diagonals of a parallelogram bisect each other.

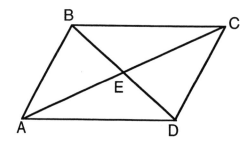

Given: ABCD is a parallelogram with diagonals $\overline{AC}$ and $\overline{BD}$.

Prove: $\overline{AC}$ and $\overline{BD}$ bisect each other.

Statements	Reasons
1. ABCD is a parallelogram with diagonals $\overline{AC}$ and $\overline{BD}$.	1. Given
2. $\overline{BC} \parallel \overline{AD}$	2. Definition of parallelogram.
3. ∠CBD and ∠ADB are alternate interior angles. ∠BCA and ∠DAC are alternate interior angles.	3. Definition of alternate interior angles.
4. ∠CBD = ∠ADB ∠BCA = ∠DAC	4. If two parallel lines are cut by a transversal, then pairs of alternate interior angles are equal.
5. ∠CBD = ∠CBE, ∠ADB = ∠ADE, ∠BCE=∠BCA, ∠DAC = ∠DAE	5. Substitution
6. $\overline{BC} = \overline{AD}$	6. Opposite sides of a parallelogram are equal.
7. △BEC ≅ △DEA	7. ASA = ASA
8. $\overline{BE} = \overline{ED}$, $\overline{AE} = \overline{EC}$	8. CPCTE
9. $\overline{AC}$ and $\overline{BD}$ bisect each other.	9. Definition of bisector.

Theorem 5.7   The diagonals of a rhombus are perpendicular.

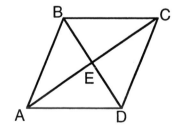

Given: ABCD is a rhombus with diagonals $\overline{AC}$ and $\overline{BD}$

Prove: $\overline{BD} \perp \overline{AC}$

Statements	Reasons
1. ABCD is a rhombus with diagonals $\overline{AC}$ and $\overline{BD}$.	1. Given
2. $\overline{AB} = \overline{BC} = \overline{CD} = \overline{AD}$	2. Definition of rhombus
3. $\angle CBD = \angle CDB$	3. If two sides of a triangle are equal ($\triangle BCD$), then the angles opposite those sides are equal.
4. $\overline{BE} = \overline{DE}$	4. The diagonals of a parallelogram bisect each other.
5. $\triangle BCE \cong \triangle DCE$	5. SAS = SAS
6. $\angle BEC = \angle DEC$	6. CPCTE
7. $\angle BED = 180°$	7. Definition of a straight angle
8. $\angle BEC = \angle DEC = 90°$	8. $\frac{1}{2}(180°) = 90°$
9. $\overline{BD} \perp \overline{AC}$	9. Definition of perpendicular

Theorem 5.8   The diagonals of a rhombus bisect the angles of the rhombus.

12. Use the following steps to prove Theorem 5.8. | 12.

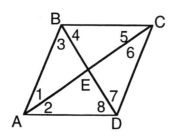

Given: Rhombus ABCD with diagonals $\overline{AC}$ and $\overline{BD}$

Prove: $\overline{AC}$ bisects $\angle BAD$ and $\angle BCD$
$\overline{BD}$ bisects $\angle ABC$ and $\angle ADC$

Statements	Reasons	
a. Rhombus ABCD with diagonals $\overline{AC}$ and $\overline{BD}$	a. _____	a. Given
b. $\overline{BE} = \overline{DE}$ $\overline{AE} = \overline{CE}$	b. _____ _____	b. The diagonals of a parallelogram bisect each other.
c. $\overline{AB} = \overline{BC} = \overline{CD} = \overline{AD}$		c. Definition of rhombus.
d. $\triangle AEB \cong \triangle AED$ $\triangle AEB \cong \triangle CEB$ $\triangle CEB \cong \triangle CED$ $\triangle CED \cong \triangle AED$	c. _____	d. SSS = SSS
e. $\angle 1 = \angle 2$ $\angle 3 = \angle 4$ $\angle 5 = \angle 6$ $\angle 7 = \angle 8$	d. _____	e. CPCTE
f. $\overline{AC}$ bisects $\angle BAD$ and $\angle BCD$, $\overline{BD}$ bisects $\angle ABC$ and $\angle ADC$	e. _____	f. Definition of angle bisector.

Now, let's look at some problems.

13. If the measure of one angle of a rhombus is 40°, find the measures of the other angles.

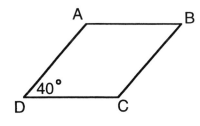

ABCD is a rhombus.

	13.
a. $\angle B = \angle D$	a. If a quadrilateral is a parallelo-gram, then both pairs of opposite angles are equal.
b. $\angle B = $ _____	b. 40°
c. $\angle A$ and $\angle B$ are supplementary.	c. Consecutive

d. ∠A = _____
e. ∠A = ∠C

f. ∠C = _____

angles of a
parallelogram
are supple-
mentary.
d. 140°
e. If a quadrilateral
is a parallelo-
gram, then both
pairs of opposite
angles are equal.
f. 140°

14. Find the length of each side of a parallelogram
if one of its sides has length 5 in., and its
perimeter is 38 in.

14.

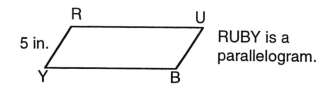

RUBY is a
parallelogram.

a. $\overline{RY} = \overline{UB}$
    $\overline{RU} = \overline{YB}$

a. If a quadrilateral
is a parallelo-
gram, then both
pairs of opposite
sides are equal.

b. $\overline{UB}$ = _____
    $\overline{RU}$ = _____
c. 38 = 2x + 2(5)

d. Solve for x.

b. 5 in.
    x
c. Definition of
perimeter
d.   38 = 2x + 10
        28 = 2x
      14 in. = x

15. Find the value of x and the measure of the
two angles shown in the parallelogram.

15.

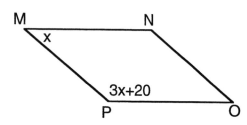

∠M and ∠P are supplementary because they
are consecutive angles of a parallelogram.

Therefore:

$$\angle M + \angle P = 180°$$
$$x + (3x + 20) = 180$$
$$4x + 20 = 180$$
$$4x = 160$$
$$x = 40°$$

3x + 20 = _____   140°

16. The statements in the proof of the converse of   16.
     Theorem 5.2 are given below. Fill in the
     reasons in the blanks provided.

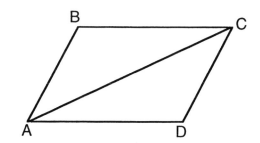

     Given: $\overline{AB} = \overline{CD}$, $\overline{BC} = \overline{AD}$

     Prove: ABCD is a parallelogram.

	Statements		Reasons		Reasons
a.	$\overline{AB} = \overline{CD}$, $\overline{BC} = \overline{AD}$	a. _____	a.	Given	
b.	$\overline{AC}$ is a diagonal.	b. _____	b.	Definition of diagonal.	
c.	$\overline{AC} = \overline{AC}$	c. _____	c.	Reflexive	
d.	$\triangle ABC \cong \triangle CDA$	d. _____	d.	SSS = SSS	
e	$\angle BCA = \angle CAD$ $\angle BAC = \angle DCA$	e. _____	e.	CPCTE	
f.	$\angle BCA$ and $\angle CAD$ are alternate interior angles. $\angle BAC$ and $\angle DCA$ are alternate interior angles.	f. _____	f.	Definition of alternate interior angles.	
g.	$\overline{AB} \parallel \overline{CD}$ $\overline{BC} \parallel \overline{AD}$	g. _____	g.	If two lines cut by a transversal form	

equal alternate interior angles, then the lines are parallel.

h. ABCD is a parallelogram.

h. _____

h. Definition of parallelogram.

17. RSTU is a rectangle. Solve for x.

17.

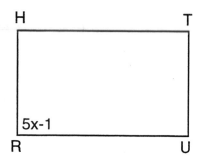

∠R is a right angle since RSTU is a rectangle. Therefore,

$$5x - 1 = 90°$$

$$5x = 91$$

$$x = ?$$

$$18\frac{1°}{5} = 18.2°$$

18. Find the value of x for the angles shown in parallelogram ABCD.

18.

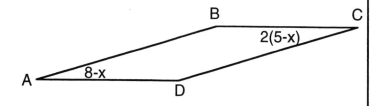

a. ∠A = ∠C, why?

a. If a quadrilateral is a parallelogram, then both pairs of opposite angles are equal.

b. Therefore,

$$(8 - x) = 2(5 - x)$$

$$x = ?$$

b. $x = 2°$

Exercise 5.1

1. If the measure of one angle of a rhombus is 86°, find the measure of the other angles.

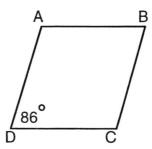

2. Find the length of each side of a parallelogram if one of its sides has length 8 in. and its perimeter is 46 in.

3. Given ABCD is a parallelogram, find x.

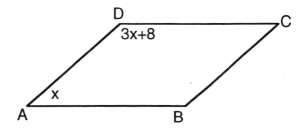

4. Given ABCD is a square with perimeter 75 m., find the length of a side and also the value of x.

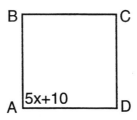

5. Given ABCD is a parallelogram, find the value of each angle.

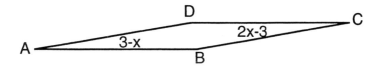

6. Supply the reasons for the following proof of the converse of Theorem 5.4.

   If consecutive angles of a quadrilateral are supplementary, then the quadrilateral is a parallelogram.

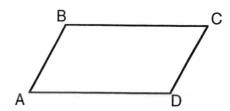

   Given: ∠A and ∠B are supplementary. ∠B and ∠C are supplementary.

   Prove: ABCD is a parallelogram.

Statements	Reasons
1. ∠A and ∠B are supplementary. ∠B and ∠C are supplementary.	1. _____
2. $\overline{AB}$ is a transversal. $\overline{BC}$ is a transversal.	2. _____
3. $\overline{AB} \parallel \overline{CD}$, $\overline{BC} \parallel \overline{AD}$	3. _____
4. ABCD is a parallelogram.	4. _____

7. In parallelogram ABCD, $\overline{AB}$ = x - 1, $\overline{BC}$ = 3x - 17, and $\overline{CD}$ = 2x - 9. Show that ABCD is a rhombus.

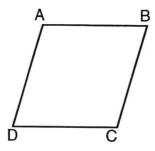

8. Given: PQRS is a rectangle with diagonals $\overline{PR}$ and $\overline{QS}$.
   If $\overline{PR}$ = 6 in., what is the length of $\overline{QS}$? Why? What is the length of $\overline{QT}$?
   Why? What is the length of $\overline{PT}$? Why?

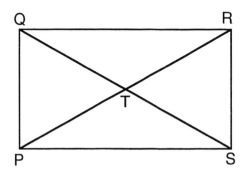

9. Given: ABCD is a rhombus.
   If ∠C = 60°, find the measure of ∠1, ∠2, ∠3, ∠4, ∠5, ∠6, ∠A, and ∠D.

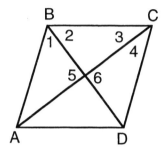

5.3 Trapezoids

The trapezoid is a quadrilateral that does not come under the heading of parallelogram. (See diagram on page 159.)

Recall from the definition that a trapezoid is a quadrilateral that has only one pair of opposite sides that are parallel. These parallel sides are called bases. The non-parallel sides of a trapezoid are called legs.

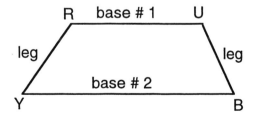

$\overline{RY}$ and $\overline{UB}$ are legs of the figure. $\overline{RU}$ and $\overline{YB}$ are bases.

Definition 5.8   An isosceles trapezoid is a trapezoid whose legs are equal.

Definition 5.9	The line that joins the midpoints of the legs of any trapezoid is called the <u>median of a trapezoid</u>.

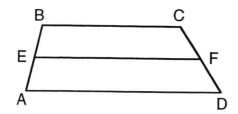

E is the midpoint of leg $\overline{AB}$. F is the midpoint of $\overline{CD}$. $\overline{EF}$ is the median of trapezoid ABCD.

Theorem 5.9	The median of a trapezoid is parallel to the bases and is equal to one-half of the sum of the two bases.

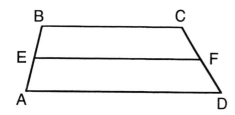

Given: $\overline{EF}$ is the median of trapezoid ABCD.

Prove: $\overline{EF} \parallel \overline{BC} \parallel \overline{AD}$

$$\overline{EF} = \frac{1}{2}(\overline{BC} + \overline{AD})$$

19. Given trapezoid ABCD with median $\overline{MN}$.
     If $\overline{AB}$ = 10 ft. and $\overline{CD}$ = 40 ft, find the measure of $\overline{MN}$.

19.

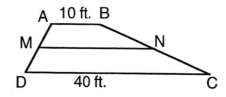

$\overline{MN} = \frac{1}{2}(\overline{AB} + \overline{DC})$ or, by eliminating fractions

$2\overline{MN} = \overline{AB} + \overline{CD}$

$2\overline{MN} = 10 + 40$

$2\overline{MN} = 50$

$\overline{MN} =$ _____

25 ft.

20. $\overline{SP}$ is the median for trapezoid RUTH. If | 20.
$\overline{SP}$ = 11 in. and $\overline{RU}$ = 15 in., find $\overline{HT}$. |

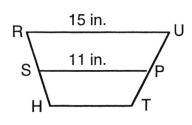

$2\,\overline{SP} = \overline{RU} + \overline{HT}$ $2(11) = 15 + \overline{HT}$

___ = $\overline{HT}$ $22 = 15 + \overline{HT}$

7 in. = $\overline{HT}$

Exercise 5.2

1. Find the length of the unknown median or base in the following trapezoids.

    a.

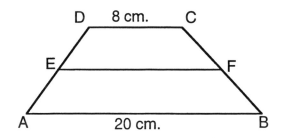

    b.

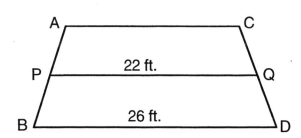

c.

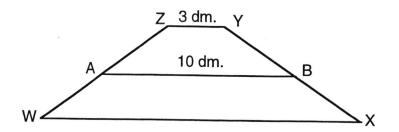

2. Given trapezoid ABCD with median $\overline{EF}$, find x in each of the following.

a.

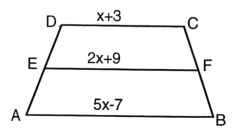

b.

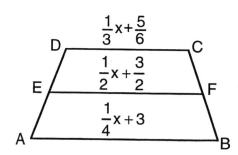

c.

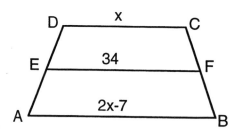

3. $\overline{EF}$ is the median of isosceles trapezoid ABCD. $\overline{BC}$ = 10 in., $\overline{AD}$ = 40 in.,
    and the perimeter is 100 in. Find the length of the legs. If ∠A = 35°, find
    ∠1 and ∠B. Find $\overline{EF}$.

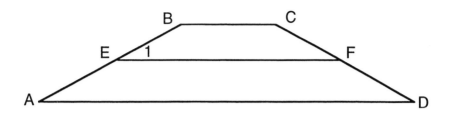

Unit 5 Review

I. Fill in the blanks with the appropriate word or phrase as studied in this unit.

1. A _____ is a closed, four-sided convex figure.

2. In quadrilateral ABCD the vertices are _____, _____,
    _____, and _____. The sides are _____,
    _____, _____, and _____. ∠A and ∠C are
    called _____ angles. ∠A and ∠D are called _____
    angles.

3. A _____ is a quadrilateral in which each pair of opposite
    sides is parallel.

4. A _____ is a parallelogram having at least one right angle.

5. A _____ is a rectangle all of whose sides are equal.

6. A _____ is a parallelogram all of whose sides are equal.

7. A _____ is a quadrilateral having only one pair of parallel
    sides which are called _____.

8. An _____ _____ is a trapezoid whose legs are equal.

9. The line that joins the midpoints of the legs of a trapezoid is called the _____ of a trapezoid.

II. Solve the following.

1. In parallelogram ABCD, $\overline{AB}$ = 3x - 7 and $\overline{DC}$ = 2x + 30. Find x.

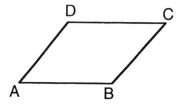

2. In parallelogram ABCD, ∠CAB = 2x - 3 and ∠DCA = 3x - 7. Find x. If ∠D = 105°, find ∠B and ∠DAB.

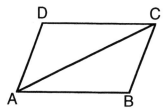

3. Find the length of each side of the parallelogram below if one of its sides has length 8 dm. and its perimeter is 60 dm.

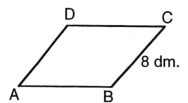

4. Find the value of x and the measure of the angles shown in the parallelogram.

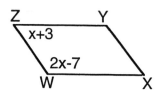

5. RSTU is a rectangle. Solve for x

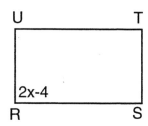

6. PQRS is a rectangle. If $\overline{PR}$ = 8 in., find $\overline{QS}$.

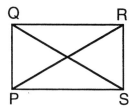

7. ABCD is a parallelogram. $\overline{BD}$ = 10 in. and $\overline{AC}$ = 16 in. Find the measure of $\overline{BE}$ and $\overline{CE}$. Justify your answer.

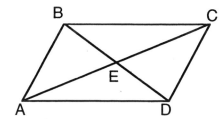

8. ABCD is a rhombus with diagonal $\overline{AC}$ = 16 in. and $\overline{BD}$ = 12 in. Find $\overline{BE}$ and $\overline{CE}$. If ∠BAD= 60°, find ∠ABC, ∠1, ∠2, ∠3, ∠4, and ∠5.

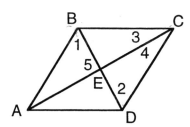

9. $\overline{AB}$ is a median of trapezoid PQRS. $\overline{SR}$ = 6 cm. and $\overline{PQ}$ = 20 cm. Find $\overline{AB}$. If $\angle 1$ = 60°, $\angle 2$ = _____? Why?

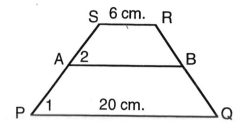

10. $\overline{FC}$ is the median of isosceles trapezoid ABDE. Find $\overline{AB}$, $\overline{BD}$, and $\overline{AE}$ if the perimeter is 100 ft.

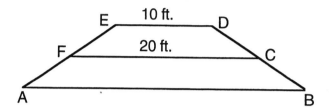

11. Given trapezoid WRYZ. Find x, $\overline{WR}$, and $\overline{YZ}$ if $\overline{AB}$ is the median.

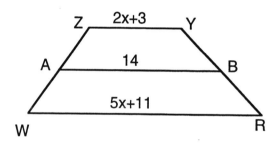

Unit 6

Inequalities

Learning Objectives:

1. The student will write the meanings for ">" and "<".

2. The student will write an algebraic open sentence for an English sentence involving inequalities.

3. The student will use the following properties to solve linear, certain quadratic, some cubic inequalities, and other selected problems.

    a. Order Property I: The Possibilities Postulate (Trichotomy Law) In comparing any two numbers only one of the following can exist at any one time. Either $a = b$, $a > b$, or $a < b$.

    b. Order Property II: Transitive Law. In comparing two real numbers, with a third real number c, the following order will exist: If a is greater than b and b is greater than c, then a is greater than c.

    c. Order Property III: The Addition Property. If equals are added to unequals, then the sums are unequal in the same order.

    d. Order Property IV: The Subtraction Property. If equals are subtracted from unequals, then the differences are unequal in the same order.

    e. Order Property V: The Multiplication Property.
        Part 1: If unequals are multiplied by the same positive number, then the products are unequal in the same order.
        Part 2: If unequals are multiplied by the same negative number, then the products are unequal in the opposite order.

4. Using definitions, postulates, and previously proven theorems, the student will apply the following theorems to the solution of related problems:

    a. The whole is greater than any of its parts.

    b. If two sides of a triangle are unequal, then the angles opposite them are unequal and the larger angle is opposite the longer side.

    c. If two angles of a triangle are unequal, then the sides opposite them are unequal and longer side is opposite the larger angle.

INEQUALITIES

6.1 Introduction

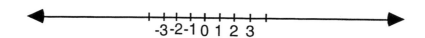

In comparing numbers on the number line, the furthest number to the right has the greatest value. For example, -2 and 0. The number that has the greater value is zero since it is further to the right on the number line than -2.

Similarly, a number furthest to the left on the number line has the lesser value. For example, 1 and 4. The number that has the lesser value is one since it is further to the left on the number line than 4.

The symbols used for inequality are > for "is greater than" and < for "is less than". These symbols compare any two numbers whose values are not equal.

Example 1: 0 is greater than -2 may be written as 0 > -2.

Example 2: 1 is less than 4 may be written as 1 < 4.

You complete the following using the correct symbol.

1. -5 _____ -3	1. -5 < -3
2. -3 _____ 0	2. -3 < 0
3. 1 _____ 0	3. 1 > 0
4. -2 _____ 6	4. -2 < 6
5. -10 _____ -19	5. -10 > -19
6. 3 _____ -3	6. 3 > -3
7. 0 _____ 9	7. 0 < 9

Any number greater than zero is <u>positive</u> and may be written as x > 0 (x representing any number greater than zero).

If x were a negative number, then it would be expressed as x < 0 (x representing any number less than zero).

8. A negative number, x, may be expressed as _____.	8. x < 0
9. 4 is less than 6 may be expressed as _____.	9. 4 < 6

10. Is 6 > 4 a correct response to problem 9? _____ Why or why not? _____

10. Yes, 6 is greater than 4 has the same meaning as 4 is less than 6.

11. 23 is greater than 22. _____

11. 23 > 22 or 22 < 23

12. 0 is less than 15. _____

12. 0 < 15 or 15 > 0

13. Y is a positive number. _____

13. Y > 0

14. Twice a number is greater than 3. _____

14. 2x > 3

15. The sum of a number and -5 is greater than 2. _____

15. [x + (-5)] > 2

16. 8z is a negative number. _____

16. 8z < 0

The inequality symbol, in combination with the equal sign, will result in two possible conditions to be considered in studying the example.

Example:

$$x \leq 0 \text{ means } \begin{cases} 1. & x \text{ may be negative} \\ & \text{or} \\ 2. & x \text{ may be equal to zero.} \end{cases}$$

$$x \geq 0 \text{ means } \begin{cases} 1. & x \text{ may be positive} \\ & \text{or} \\ 2. & x \text{ may be equal to zero.} \end{cases}$$

Complete these problems:

17. x is negative.

17. x < 0

18. x is zero.

18. x = 0

19. x may be negative or zero.

19. x ≤ 0

20. x may be positive or zero.

20. x ≥ 0

21. x may be greater than or equal to 10.

21. x ≥ 10

22. x may be less than or equal to 10.

22. x ≤ 10

If one numbers falls between two other numbers, the expression is written as follows:

Example: 7 falls between 6 and 9 and may be expressed as "7 is greater than 6 and also less than 9".

$$6 < 7 < 9$$

23. Write a number that is between -1 and 15 using the inequality symbol and x.

23. $-1 < x < 15$

24. A number is less than 1 and greater than 0.

24. $0 < x < 1$

25. x is greater than 8 and less than or equal to 200.

25. $8 < x \leq 200$

26. x is less than -5 and greater than or equal to -9.

26. $-9 \leq x < -5$

27. x is a positive number and has a value less than or equal to 2.

27. $0 < x \leq 2$

6.2 Order Properties of Inequality

Order Property I: The Three Possibilities Postulate (Trichotomy Law)

In comparing any two numbers only one of the following can exist at any one time. Compare two numbers, a and b, real numbers, either
1. a is greater than b _____ $a > b$
2. a is less than b _____ $a < b$
3. a is equal to b _____ $a = b$

28. Compare 10 and $\dfrac{20}{2}$. Can 10 equal $\dfrac{20}{2}$ $\left(10 = \dfrac{20}{2}\right)$ and can 10 be less than $\dfrac{20}{2}$ $\left(10 < \dfrac{20}{2}\right)$ at the same time?

28. no

29. Compare x and 0. What are the three possible values of x in relation to zero? Either _____ or _____ or _____.

29. Either $x < 0$, or $x > 0$, or $x = 0$.

30. If x is not negative (non-negative) then what are the other two possible values of x? (See # 29 above.)

30. x can be positive or x can be zero.

31. If x is not positive (non-positive) then what are the other two possible values of x?

31. x can be negative or x can be zero.

32. x ≥ 0 means that x is non-negative. If x is non-positive, then how would you write that in symbols?

32. x ≤ 0

33. If x is not zero, then x must be _____ or _____.

33. x > 0 or x < 0

34. Write m is non-negative in symbols.

34. m ≥ 0

35. Write three times z increased by 4 is non-positive.

35. 3z + 4 ≤ 0

36. y is non-positive and greater than -11.

36. -11 < y ≤ 0

Order Property II: Transitive Law
In comparing two real numbers, a and b, with a third real number c, the following order will exist:

If a is greater than b and b is greater than c, then a is greater than c. In symbols, if a > b and b > c, then a > c.

Consider the order as it applies to the number line.

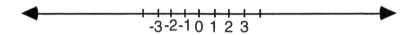

-3 -2 -1 0 1 2 3

If 2 is greater than -1 and -1 is greater than -4, then 2 must be greater than -4 also. In symbols, if 2 > -1 and -1 > -4, then 2 > -4.

37. If 12 > 7 and 7 > -14, what is the relationship of 12 and -14?

37. 12 > -14

38. If 0 > -4 and -4 > -11, then _____.

38. 0 > -11

39. If -3 < 6 and 6 < 39, then _____.

39. -3 < 39

40. If x > y and y > 0, then is x also positive?

40. Yes, because x > 0.

41. If x < y and y < 0, then _____.

41. x < 0

42. If x < m and m = 7, then _____.
(by substitution)

42. x < 7

Order Property III: The Addition Property
If equals are added to unequals, then the sums are unequal in the same order.

In symbols, if a > b and c = d, then a + c > b + d.

For example: If 5 > 3 and 2 = 2, then (5 + 2) > (3 + 2).

Order Property IV: The Subtraction Property
If equals are subtracted from unequals, then the
differences are unequal in the same order.

In symbols, if a > b and c = d, then a - c > b - d.

For example: If 5 > 3 and 2 = 2, then 5 - 2 > 3 - 2.

43. If 16 > 5 and 3 = 3, then is 16 - 3 > 5 - 3?
Show why or why not.

43. Yes
     16 - 3 > 5 - 3
         13 > 5 - 3
         13 > 2

44. If 16 > 5 and 3 = 3, then is 16 + 3 > 5 + 3?
Show why or why not

44. Yes
     16 + 3 > 5 + 3
         19 > 5 + 3
         19 > 8

45. If equal quantities are subtracted from unequal
quantities, will the difference be unequal in
in the same order?

45. Yes
     Order Property IV

Order Property V: The Multiplication Property

Part 1:   If unequals are multiplied by the same positive
number, then the products are unequal in the
same order.

In symbols, if a > b and c > 0, then ac > bc.

Part 2:   If unequals are multiplied by the same negative
number, the products are unequal in the
OPPOSITE order.

In symbols, if a > b and c < 0, then ac < bc.

Example of part 1:   If 5 > 3 and 2 is positive, then (5)(2) > (3)(2), since
10 > 6.

Example of part 2:   If 5 > 3 and -1 is negative, then (5)(-1) < (3)(-1)
since -5 < -3.

46. If c is -2 and 11 < 41, then how do the products
11c and 41c compare?

46. The products are
     unequal in the
     opposite order.
     (11)(-2) > (41)(-2)
         -22 > -82

47. If c is positive 2 and 11 < 41, then how do the products 11c and 41c compare?

47. $(11)(2) < (41)(2)$
$22 < 82$
Order Property V, Part 1

Order Property V, Part 2

48. If $\frac{1}{4}x > 5$ and 4 is positive, then is x > 20?

48. Yes

$$(4)\left(\frac{1}{4}x\right) > (5)(4)$$

$$x > 20$$

49. If -2x > 16 and $\frac{-1}{2}$ is negative, then is x > -8?

49. No

$$\left(\frac{-1}{2}\right)(-2x) < \left(\frac{-1}{2}\right)(16)$$

$$\frac{+2}{2}x < \frac{-16}{2}$$

$$x < -8$$

Order Property V, Part 2

Exercise 6.1

1. Identify the order property illustrated in each of the following:

   a. If 6 > 4 and 4 > 2, then 6 > 2.

   b. If 8 > 2 and .5 = .5, the 8 + .5 > 2 + .5.

   c. If 9 > 6 and 2 = 2, then 9 - 2 > 6 - 2.

   d. If 10 > 2 and 3 is positive, then 30 > 6.

   e. If 4 < 6 and -1 is negative, then -4 > -6.

   f. If 2x > 3 and y is negative, then 2xy < 3y.

   g. If B < 10, then B can not equal 10.

   h. If Y > 3 and 5 = 5, then y + 5 > 3 + 5.

   i. If x > y and y > z, the x > z.

j. If m < n and c < 0, them mc > nc.

k. If c ≠ d, then c > d or c < d.

l. If y < 8 and 1 = 1, then y - 1 < 8 - 1.

m. If 7 < m and m < n, then 7 < n.

n. If p > 11 and 5 is positive, then (p)(5) > (11)(5).

2. Fill in with the appropriate word, phrase, or algebraic expression.

   a. If -6 < 0 and 0 < 5, then _____. (Transitive Law)

   b. If x and y are real numbers, then _____, _____, or _____. (Trichotomy Law)

   c. If 6 < 8 and -2 is negative, then -12 _____ -16. (Order Property V, Part 2)

   d. If 3x + 1 > 0 and 1 = 1, then _____. (Subtraction Property)

3. Write an open sentence with the same meaning as the following statements.

   a. Twice x increased by two is positive.

   b. Y is non-negative.

   c. W is non-positive.

   d. Z is positive and less than or equal to 78.

   e. X is between 2 and 10.

   f. The square of x is greater than 4.

   g. X is between -3 and 7 and may equal to 7.

6.3 Solving Inequalities

Using the properties on the preceding pages, solve the following inequalities.

Example 1:

$$2x + 5 < 4x - 3$$

a. $\underline{-2x} + 2x + 5 < \underline{-2x} + 4x - 3$ Order Property IV

b. $5 < 2x - 3$ Simplify

c. $5 \underline{+3} < 2x - 3 \underline{+3}$ Order Property III

d. $8 < 2x$ Simplify

e. $\frac{1}{2}(8) < \frac{1}{2}(2x)$ Order Property V, Part 1

f. $4 < x$ Simplify

Therefore, $2x + 5 < 4x - 3$ simplifies to $4 < x$. Any value of x greater than 4 will be a solution to the inequality in Example 1.

Example 2:

$x(x^2 + 5) < 8x - 12 + x^3$

a. $x^3 + 5x < 8x - 12 + x^3$ Distributive Law

b. $x^3 - x^3 + 5x < 8x - 12 + x^3 - x^3$ Order Property IV

c. $5x < 8x - 12$ Simplify

d. $5x - 8x < 8x - 8x - 12$ Order Property IV

e. $5x - 8x < -12$ Simplify

f. $-3x < -12$ Simplify

g. * $\frac{-1}{3}(-3x) > \frac{-1}{3}(-12)$ Order Property V, Part 2

h. * $x > 4$ Simplify

* Note the change in order! See Order Property V, Part 2.

50. Solve by filling in the blank spaces.   50.

$2(x - 5) > 7x - 2$

a.   _____ $> 7x - 2$ Distributive   a. $2x - 10$
                                    Law
b. $2x - 7x - 10 > 7x - 7x - 2$ Why?   b. Order Property IV

c. $-5x - 10 > -2$ Why?   c. Simplify

d.   _____ > _____   Order Pro-   d. -5x-10+10 > -2+10
                              perty III

e.   -5x > _____   Simplify   e. 8

f. $\frac{-1}{5}(-5x) < \frac{-1}{5}(8)$ Why?   f. Order Property V,
                                                        Part 2

g.   x < _____   Simplify   g. $x < \frac{-8}{5}$ or $x < -1\frac{3}{5}$ or
                                                    x < -1.6

51. Solve: $\frac{5x}{3} < 7 + x$ 51.

$$\frac{5x}{3} < 7 + x$$

$$3\left(\frac{5x}{3}\right) < 3(7) + 3(x)$$

$$5x < 21 + 3x$$

$$2x < 21$$

$$x < \frac{21}{2}$$

$$x < 10\frac{1}{2}$$

or x < 10.5

52. Solve: $8x - 4 > \frac{3}{5}x + 2$ 52.

$$8x - 4 > \frac{3}{5}x + 2$$

$$5(8x) - 5(4) > 5\left(\frac{3}{5}x\right) + 5(2)$$

$$40x - 20 > 3x + 10$$

$$37x - 20 > 10$$

$$37x > 30$$

$$x > \frac{30}{37}$$

or $x > 0.\overline{810}$

Exercise 6.2

1. Solve the following inequalities.

   a. $11x > -22$

   b. $-3x < 18$

   c. $10x + 3 \geq 9 + 13x$

   d. $2 + 4(x + 3) \geq 2(x + 3)$

   e. $3x + 7(x + 1) \geq -2(x - 7)$

   f. $\dfrac{3x}{4} - \dfrac{x}{2} > \dfrac{3}{8} + \dfrac{5x}{4}$

   g. $\dfrac{1}{2}x + \dfrac{1}{3}x \leq -7$

   h. $4(5 - 2y) - 7 \geq 6(y + 3) - 3(y + 4) + y$

   i. $3x - \dfrac{x - 2}{2} \geq 5(2 - x)$

   j. $3(x - 2) > -6$

   k. $\dfrac{-13}{15} + \dfrac{x + 2}{3} - \dfrac{4x - 1}{5} < 0$

   l. $\dfrac{1}{2}x - \dfrac{x - 2}{3} \leq \dfrac{1}{12}$

6.4 Theorems of Inequality

Theorem 6.1   The whole is greater than any of its parts. In symbols, if $a = b + c$ and $a > 0$, $b > 0$, and $c > 0$, then $a > b$ and $a > c$.

Example: For Theorem 6.1 use these line segments to illustrate the theorem by construction. Add line segment b to c by using only a straightedge and compass.

Given: The measures for segments a, b, and c

_____
a

_____
b

_____
c

Copy the above segments to construct the sum of (b + c) equal to a. What are your results?

_____
a

_____)_____
b   c

b + c = a

Now compare <u>a</u> to each of the original segments.

_____
a

_____
b

a > b

_____
a

_____
c

a > c

53. Using Theorem 6.1, compare the line segments below:

A   B   C

$\overline{AC}$ equals $\overline{AB}$ added to $\overline{BC}$

a. Is $\overline{AC}$ greater than $\overline{AB}$?

b. Is $\overline{BC}$ greater than $\overline{AC}$?

53.

a. yes

b. no, $\overline{AC} > \overline{BC}$

54. Given: △ABC with exterior angle, ∠1.

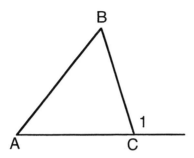

a. Is ∠1 greater than ∠B?

b. Is ∠1 greater than ∠A?

c. How does ∠1 relate to ∠BCA?

54.

a. Yes, the whole is greater than any of its parts.

b. Yes

c. ∠BCA is supplementary to ∠1.

Theorem 6.2	If two sides of a triangle are unequal, the angles opposite them are unequal and the larger angle is opposite the longer side.

Example: Given: In △MNO, $\overline{NM} < \overline{NO}$.

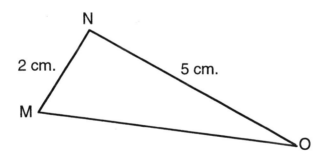

How do ∠O and ∠M compare?

The measure of ∠O is less than the measure of ∠M since it is opposite the shorter side.

Theorem 6.3	If two angles of a triangle are unequal, then the sides opposite them are unequal and the longer side is opposite the larger angle.

Example: Given: △XYZ with ∠Y having measure less than ∠X

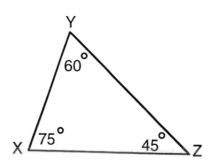

How does side $\overline{XZ}$ compare to side $\overline{YZ}$?

Side $\overline{XZ}$ is shorter than $\overline{YZ}$ since it is opposite the smaller angle.

55.

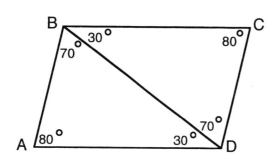

On the basis of the drawing, answer the questions below:

a. In △ABD which is the longest side?

b. In △BCD which is the shortest side?

56.

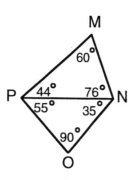

In the figure, the angle measures are given. Show that $\overline{PM}$ is the longest side.

55.

a. $\overline{BD}$

b. $\overline{DC}$

56.

In △PON, side $\overline{PN}$ is is the longest but in △PMN $\overline{PN}$ is

opposite the 60°
angle. Therefore, $\overline{PN}$
is not the longest
side in △PMN. The
longest side in
△PMN is opposite
the 76° angle, side
$\overline{PM}$.

57. Given: △ABC with exterior angle, ∠1

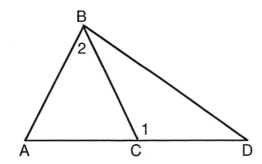

If ∠1 = 125° and ∠2 = 60°, what side is the
longest in △ABC?

57.

$$\angle BCA + \angle 1 = 180°$$
$$\angle BCA + 125° = 180°$$
$$\angle BCA = 55°$$
$$\angle A + \angle 2 = \angle 1$$
$$\angle A + 60° = 125°$$
$$\angle A = 65°$$

∠A is the largest
angle in △ABC. By
Theorem 6.3, $\overline{BC}$ is
the longest side.

58.

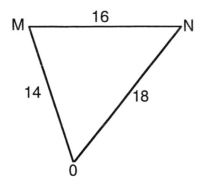

Tell why ∠N is the smallest angle.

58.

By Theorem 6.2, ∠N
is opposite the
smallest side.

59. Tell why ∠WXY is not the smallest or the
largest of △WXY.

59.

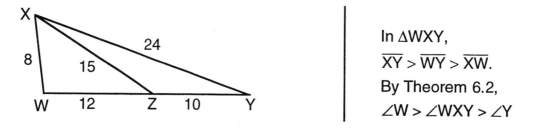

In △WXY,

$\overline{XY} > \overline{WY} > \overline{XW}$.

By Theorem 6.2,

$\angle W > \angle WXY > \angle Y$

Exercise 6.3

1. ABCD is a parallelogram. In △DCB which side is the longest? Which side is the shortest? Justify your answer.

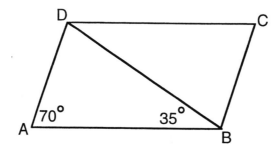

2. In △ABC which is the longest side? Which is the shortest side?

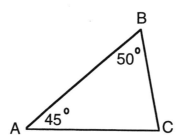

3. In △PQR, find the longest SIDE.

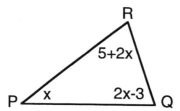

4. $\overline{XY} = 14$. In △ZNY, which angle is the largest angle? Which is the smallest? Justify your answer.

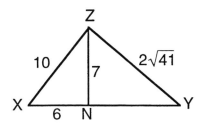

5. Is ∠CBD larger than ∠A? Why or why not?

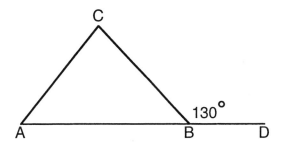

Unit 6 Review

1. Identify the order property illustrated in each of the following:

    a. If 10 > 2 and 2 > -5, then 10 > -5.

    b. If 2 > -3 and $\frac{1}{4}$ = .25, then 2 + $\frac{1}{4}$ > -3 + .25.

    c. If 10 > 3 and 8 = $\frac{16}{2}$, then 10 - 8 > 3 - $\frac{16}{2}$.

    d. If 3 > 2 and 5 is positive, then 15 > 10.

    e. If 4 < 10 and -2 is negative, then -8 > -20.

2. Fill in with the appropriate word, phrase, or algebraic expression.

    a. If -4 < 0 and 0 < 8, then _____. (Transitive Law)

    b. If c and d are real numbers, then _____, _____, or _____.
        (Law of Trichotomy)

    c. If 3 < 8 and 4 is positive, then 12 _____ 32. (Multiplication Property,
        Part 1)

3. Write an open sentence with the same meaning as the following statements.

    a. Three times x decreased by five is positive.

    b. Y is non-positive.

    c. Z is negative and greater than or equal to -21.

    d. Y is between 3 and 11.

4. Solve the following inequalities.

    a. $3(x + 4) - 2(7 - x) > 0$

    b. $6 - \dfrac{3y - 4}{7} \geq 0$

    c. $2(x + 2) > x - 3$

    d. $1 - \dfrac{y}{2} \geq 4$

    e. $1 - (x - 1) < 2 + (x + 1)$

    f. $2x - \dfrac{1}{2} > x + \dfrac{1}{2}$

    g. $\dfrac{1}{2}x + \dfrac{3}{8} \leq \dfrac{1}{4}(x + 5)$

    h. $3 - (1 - 2c) \leq 4(c - 1)$

    i. $\dfrac{3x}{4} - \dfrac{2}{3} > x + 1$

5. a. ABCD is a parallelogram. In $\triangle ACD$ which is the longest side and why? Which is the shortest?

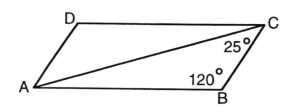

b. In △ABC, which side is the longest?

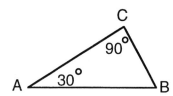

c. Which angle is the largest? Which is the smallest angle? Justify your answer.

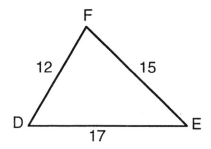

d. ∠9 = 108° and ∠5 = 54°. ∠9 is an exterior angle to △XYZ. Explain why $\overline{YZ}$ is longer than $\overline{XZ}$ and $\overline{XY}$

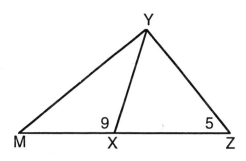

Unit 7

Area

Learning Objectives:

1. Given real number values the student will compute the area of each of the following: rectangle, square, parallelogram, triangle, trapezoid, and circle.

2. Given real values for all but one of the variables in the formula for a given area, the student will find the remaining variable.

3. Using combinations of the area formulae, the student will find the area of various geometric figures.

4. Using the area formulae, the student will use them to solve real world application problems.

5. The student will demonstrate his mastery of the definitions of circumference, circle, radius, and diameter by writing them and applying them to selected problems.

6. The student will demonstrate his mastery of the following theorem by writing it and applying it to selected problems.

    Theorem: The ratio of the circumference to the diameter is the same for all circles.

AREA

7.1 Radicals Review

Before discussing the concept of area, some rules concerning radicals need to be refreshed.

Rule # 1: $\sqrt{ab} = \sqrt{a} \cdot \sqrt{b}$

Two major applications for this rule are as follows:

    I. Simplifying radicals

        Example: $\sqrt{98}$

                First, split the radical into two radicals. In the first radical place all the perfect squares and, in the second, place all other factors. In $\sqrt{98}$, 49 is a perfect square.

$$\sqrt{98} = \sqrt{49}\sqrt{2}$$
$$= \sqrt{7 \cdot 7}\sqrt{2}$$
$$= 7\sqrt{2}$$

        Example: $\sqrt{75}$

$$\sqrt{75} = \sqrt{25}\sqrt{3}$$
$$= \sqrt{5 \cdot 5}\sqrt{3}$$
$$= 5\sqrt{3}$$

      1. $\sqrt{27}$

        1.

$$\sqrt{27} = \sqrt{9}\sqrt{3}$$
$$= \sqrt{3 \cdot 3}\sqrt{3}$$
$$= 3\sqrt{3}$$

        Example: $\sqrt{81}$

$$\sqrt{81} = \sqrt{9 \cdot 9}$$
$$= 9$$

2. $\sqrt{64}$

2.

$$\sqrt{64} = \sqrt{8 \cdot 8}$$
$$= 8$$

Example: $\sqrt{252}$

The factors of 252 are not readily apparent. Prime factorization is useful here.

```
2 | 252
2 | 126
3 | 63
3 | 21
    7
```

$$\sqrt{252} = \sqrt{2 \cdot 2 \cdot 3 \cdot 3 \cdot 7}$$

Note 252 has a pair of two's and a pair of three's. The product of these pairs is 36 which is a perfect square. Then,

$$\sqrt{252} = \sqrt{36}\sqrt{7} = \sqrt{6 \cdot 6}\sqrt{7} = 6\sqrt{7}$$

Example: $\sqrt{192}$

Prime factoring:

```
2 | 192
2 | 96
2 | 48
2 | 24
2 | 12
2 | 6
    3
```

$$\sqrt{192} = \sqrt{2 \cdot 2 \cdot 2 \cdot 2 \cdot 2 \cdot 2 \cdot 3}$$

Note there are three pairs of two's. Multiplying these three pairs of factors, you can obtain the perfect square factor of 192.

$$\sqrt{192} = \sqrt{64}\sqrt{3} = \sqrt{8 \cdot 8}\sqrt{3} = 8\sqrt{3}$$

3. $\sqrt{250}$

3.

   a. Prime factor first.

   a.

$$5 \underline{|250}$$
$$5 \underline{|50}$$
$$5 \underline{|10}$$
$$2$$

b. $\sqrt{250}$

b. $\sqrt{5 \cdot 5} \sqrt{5 \cdot 2}$
$= \sqrt{25} \sqrt{10}$
$= 5\sqrt{10}$

4. $\sqrt{147}$

4. $\sqrt{7 \cdot 7 \cdot 3}$
$= \sqrt{49} \sqrt{3}$
$= 7\sqrt{3}$

II.   Multiplying Radicals

Example: $\sqrt{2} \cdot \sqrt{8} = \sqrt{16} = 4$

Example: $\sqrt{3} \cdot \sqrt{12} = \sqrt{36} = 6$

5. $\sqrt{5} \cdot \sqrt{20}$

5. $\sqrt{100} = \sqrt{10 \cdot 10} = 10$

6. $\sqrt{2} \cdot \sqrt{18}$

6. $\sqrt{36} = \sqrt{6 \cdot 6} = 6$

Example: $\sqrt{6} \cdot \sqrt{3} = \sqrt{18}$
$= \sqrt{9} \sqrt{2}$
$= \sqrt{3 \cdot 3} \sqrt{2}$
$= 3\sqrt{2}$

7. $\sqrt{8} \cdot \sqrt{3}$

7. $\sqrt{24} = \sqrt{2 \cdot 2} \sqrt{2 \cdot 3}$
$= 2\sqrt{6}$

Rule #2: $\sqrt{\dfrac{a}{b}} = \dfrac{\sqrt{a}}{\sqrt{b}}$

Use Rule # 2 for simplifying quotients of radicals and for simplifying the square roots of fractions under the radical sign.

Example: $\sqrt{\dfrac{1}{9}} = \dfrac{\sqrt{1}}{\sqrt{9}} = \dfrac{1}{3}$

Example: $\sqrt{\dfrac{4}{25}} = \dfrac{\sqrt{4}}{\sqrt{25}} = \dfrac{2}{5}$

8. $\sqrt{\dfrac{81}{121}}$

8. $\sqrt{\dfrac{81}{121}} = \dfrac{\sqrt{81}}{\sqrt{121}} = \dfrac{9}{11}$

9. $\sqrt{\dfrac{9}{16}}$

9. $\sqrt{\dfrac{9}{16}} = \dfrac{\sqrt{9}}{\sqrt{16}} = \dfrac{3}{4}$

Example: $\sqrt{\dfrac{1}{3}} = \dfrac{\sqrt{1}}{\sqrt{3}} = \dfrac{1}{\sqrt{3}}$

The answer $\dfrac{1}{\sqrt{3}}$ is not considered in its simplest form since there is a square root in the denominator. Since any number can be multiplied by 1 without changing the value of the number, in a problem like this, we multiply by $\dfrac{\sqrt{3}}{\sqrt{3}} = 1$.

$\dfrac{1}{\sqrt{3}} \cdot \dfrac{\sqrt{3}}{\sqrt{3}} = \dfrac{\sqrt{3}}{\sqrt{9}}$

$\dfrac{\sqrt{3}}{\sqrt{3}}$ was chosen so the denominator will become the square root of a perfect square.

$\dfrac{\sqrt{3}}{\sqrt{9}} = \dfrac{\sqrt{3}}{\sqrt{3 \cdot 3}} = \dfrac{\sqrt{3}}{3}$

With the square root eliminated from the denominator, the answer is now in its simplest form.

Example: $\sqrt{\dfrac{2}{5}} = \dfrac{\sqrt{2}}{\sqrt{5}} \cdot \dfrac{\sqrt{5}}{\sqrt{5}} = \dfrac{\sqrt{10}}{\sqrt{25}} = \dfrac{\sqrt{10}}{\sqrt{5 \cdot 5}} = \dfrac{\sqrt{10}}{5}$

10. $\sqrt{\dfrac{5}{6}}$

10. $\sqrt{\dfrac{5}{6}} = \dfrac{\sqrt{5}}{\sqrt{6}} \cdot \dfrac{\sqrt{6}}{\sqrt{6}}$

$= \dfrac{\sqrt{5 \cdot 6}}{\sqrt{6 \cdot 6}} = \dfrac{\sqrt{30}}{\sqrt{36}}$

$= \dfrac{\sqrt{30}}{6}$

Note: This answer does not reduce because 30 is under the radical and 6 is not.

Example: $\sqrt{\dfrac{4}{5}} = \dfrac{\sqrt{4}}{\sqrt{5}} = \dfrac{2}{\sqrt{5}} = \dfrac{2}{\sqrt{5}} \cdot \dfrac{\sqrt{5}}{\sqrt{5}} = \dfrac{2\sqrt{5}}{\sqrt{25}} = \dfrac{2\sqrt{5}}{\sqrt{5 \cdot 5}} = \dfrac{2\sqrt{5}}{5}$

Note: The 2 remains outside the radical sign. It is a whole number and not a square root.

11. $\sqrt{\dfrac{64}{7}} = \dfrac{\sqrt{}}{\sqrt{}}$

$= \left(\dfrac{8}{}\right)\cdot\left(\dfrac{}{}\right)$

$= \underline{\hspace{2cm}}$

$= \underline{\hspace{2cm}}$

11. $\dfrac{\sqrt{64}}{\sqrt{7}}$

$= \left(\dfrac{8}{\sqrt{7}}\right)\cdot\left(\dfrac{\sqrt{7}}{\sqrt{7}}\right)$

$= \dfrac{8\sqrt{7}}{\sqrt{7\cdot 7}}$

$= \dfrac{8\sqrt{7}}{7}$

Some problems take a slightly different twist. The denominator can be partially simplified before completely removing the radical.

Example: $\dfrac{\sqrt{7}}{\sqrt{8}}$

First $\sqrt{8} = \sqrt{4}\cdot\sqrt{2} = 2\sqrt{2}$. Thus, $\dfrac{\sqrt{7}}{\sqrt{8}} = \dfrac{\sqrt{7}}{2\sqrt{2}}$.

Now multiplying by $\dfrac{\sqrt{2}}{\sqrt{2}}$ will rationalize the denominator as

follows: $\dfrac{\sqrt{7}}{2\sqrt{2}}\cdot\dfrac{\sqrt{2}}{\sqrt{2}} = \dfrac{\sqrt{7\cdot 2}}{2\cdot\sqrt{2\cdot 2}} = \dfrac{\sqrt{14}}{2\cdot 2} = \dfrac{\sqrt{14}}{4}$.

Observe the final answer cannot be further simplified. True 2 divides 4 and also 14. However, observe that 14 is under the radical sign and 4 is not.

12. $\dfrac{\sqrt{5}}{\sqrt{27}} = \dfrac{\sqrt{5}}{\sqrt{9}\sqrt{3}} = \underline{\hspace{3cm}}$

$= \underline{\hspace{3cm}}$

$= \underline{\hspace{3cm}}$

$= \underline{\hspace{3cm}}$

$= \underline{\hspace{3cm}}$

12. $\dfrac{\sqrt{5}}{\sqrt{9}\sqrt{3}} = \dfrac{\sqrt{5}}{3\sqrt{3}}$

$\dfrac{\sqrt{5}}{3\sqrt{3}}\cdot\dfrac{\sqrt{3}}{\sqrt{3}}$

$\dfrac{\sqrt{5\cdot 3}}{3\sqrt{3\cdot 3}}$

$\dfrac{\sqrt{15}}{3\cdot 3}$

$\dfrac{\sqrt{15}}{9}$

Example: $\sqrt{\dfrac{4}{6}} = \dfrac{\sqrt{4}}{\sqrt{6}} = \dfrac{2}{\sqrt{6}}\cdot\dfrac{\sqrt{6}}{\sqrt{6}} = \dfrac{2\sqrt{6}}{\sqrt{6\cdot 6}} = \dfrac{2\sqrt{6}}{6} = \dfrac{\sqrt{6}}{3}$

In this example, the 2 in the numerator and the 6 in the denominator have a common factor of 2. Both 2 and 6 are not under a radical sign. Consequently, $\dfrac{2\sqrt{6}}{6}$ can be reduced to $\dfrac{\sqrt{6}}{3}$.

13. $\sqrt{\dfrac{25}{10}} = \dfrac{\sqrt{25}}{\sqrt{10}} = \dfrac{5}{\sqrt{10}} = \left(-\right)\cdot\left(-\right)$

$= \underline{\hphantom{xxxx}}$

$= \underline{\hphantom{xxxx}}$

$= \underline{\hphantom{xxxx}}$

13. $\dfrac{5}{\sqrt{10}}\cdot\dfrac{\sqrt{10}}{\sqrt{10}}$

$\dfrac{5\sqrt{10}}{\sqrt{100}}$

$\dfrac{5\sqrt{10}}{10}$

$\dfrac{\sqrt{10}}{2}$

Rule # 3: $x\sqrt{a} + y\sqrt{a} = (x+y)\sqrt{a}$

Example: $4\sqrt{2} + 6\sqrt{2} = (4+6)\sqrt{2} = 10\sqrt{2}$

Notice these radical expressions are added as "like terms". The radicands must be the <u>same</u> in order to add the coefficients to obtain the answer.

Example: $3\sqrt{3} + 2\sqrt{5}$ cannot be simplified since $\sqrt{3}$ and $\sqrt{5}$ do not have the same radicand.

Example: $7\sqrt{5} + 3\sqrt{5} = (7+3)\sqrt{5} = 10\sqrt{5}$

14. $8\sqrt{3} + 7\sqrt{3}$

14. $(8+7)\sqrt{3} = 15\sqrt{3}$

15. $20\sqrt{6} - 8\sqrt{6}$

15. $(20-8)\sqrt{6} = 12\sqrt{6}$

Example: $\sqrt{45} + \sqrt{80}$

At first glance these radicals appear as though they cannot be added together. Simplify each radical, then combine.

$\sqrt{45} = \sqrt{9}\sqrt{5} = 3\sqrt{5}$
$\sqrt{80} = \sqrt{16}\sqrt{5} = 4\sqrt{5}$

$$\sqrt{45} + \sqrt{80} = 3\sqrt{5} + 4\sqrt{5}$$

So,
$$= (3+4)\sqrt{5}$$
$$= 7\sqrt{5}$$

16. $5\sqrt{7} + \sqrt{28}$ = _____

= _____

= _____

= _____

16. $5\sqrt{7} + \sqrt{4}\sqrt{7}$

$5\sqrt{7} + 2\sqrt{7}$

$(5+2)\sqrt{7}$

$7\sqrt{7}$

Example: $3\sqrt{20} + 4\sqrt{5} = 3\sqrt{4}\sqrt{5} + 4\sqrt{5}$
$$= 3 \cdot 2\sqrt{5} + 4\sqrt{5}$$
$$= 6\sqrt{5} + 4\sqrt{5}$$
$$= (6+4)\sqrt{5}$$
$$= 10\sqrt{5}$$

17.

$\sqrt{12} + \sqrt{27} + \sqrt{75}$ = _____

= _____

= _____

= _____

17.

$\sqrt{4}\sqrt{3} + \sqrt{9}\sqrt{3} + \sqrt{25}\sqrt{3}$

$2\sqrt{3} + 3\sqrt{3} + 5\sqrt{3}$

$(2+3+5)\sqrt{3}$

$10\sqrt{3}$

Rule # 4: $\left(x\sqrt{a}\right)\left(y\sqrt{b}\right) = xy\sqrt{ab}$

Example: $5\sqrt{2} \cdot 3\sqrt{6}$
Multiplying coefficients gives $5 \cdot 3 = 15$.
Multiplying radicals gives $\sqrt{2} \cdot \sqrt{6} = \sqrt{12}$.
Hence,
$5\sqrt{2} \cdot 3\sqrt{6} = 15\sqrt{12}$

$$= 15\left(2\sqrt{3}\right) \text{ Rule \# 1 }\left(\sqrt{12} \text{ simplifies to } 2\sqrt{3}\right)$$

$$= 30\sqrt{3}$$

Example: $4\sqrt{8} \cdot 5\sqrt{6}$
$4\sqrt{8} \cdot 5\sqrt{6} = 4 \cdot 5\sqrt{8}\sqrt{6}$ using commutative and associative laws to group coefficients and radicals

$= 20\sqrt{48}$ multiplying coefficients and radicals

$= 20\sqrt{16}\sqrt{3}$ simplifying the radical

$= 20 \cdot 4\sqrt{3}$ taking the square root

$= 80\sqrt{3}$ multiplying coefficients

Example: $\left(3\sqrt{3}\right)\left(\dfrac{-1}{2}\sqrt{12}\right)$

Multiplying coefficients: $3\cdot\dfrac{-1}{2}=\dfrac{-3}{2}$

Multiplying radicands: $\sqrt{3}\cdot\sqrt{12}=\sqrt{36}=6$

Hence, $\left(3\sqrt{3}\right)\left(\dfrac{-1}{2}\sqrt{12}\right)=\dfrac{-3}{2}\cdot 6=-9$

18. $3\sqrt{7}\cdot 5\sqrt{14}=$ _____

= _____

= _____

= _____

= _____

18. $3\cdot 5\sqrt{7}\sqrt{14}$

$15\sqrt{98}$

$15\sqrt{49}\sqrt{2}$

$15\cdot 7\sqrt{2}$

$105\sqrt{2}$

19. $\left(25\sqrt{3}\right)\left(\dfrac{-1}{5}\sqrt{6}\right)=$ _____

= _____

= _____

= _____

= _____

19. $25\cdot\dfrac{-1}{5}\sqrt{3}\sqrt{6}$

$-5\sqrt{18}$

$-5\sqrt{9}\sqrt{2}$

$-5\cdot 3\sqrt{2}$

$-15\sqrt{2}$

Example: $\left(4\sqrt{2}\right)^{3}$

$=\left(4\sqrt{2}\right)\left(4\sqrt{2}\right)\left(4\sqrt{2}\right)$ using the definition of exponent

$=64\sqrt{8}$ using Rule # 4

$=64\sqrt{4}\sqrt{2}$ using Rule # 1

$=64\cdot 2\sqrt{2}$ simplifying

$=128\sqrt{2}$ multiplying coefficients

20. $\left(2\sqrt{3}\right)^{3}=$ _____

= _____

= _____

= _____

= _____

20. $\left(2\sqrt{3}\right)\left(2\sqrt{3}\right)\left(2\sqrt{3}\right)$

$8\sqrt{27}$

$8\sqrt{9}\sqrt{3}$

$8\cdot 3\sqrt{3}$

$24\sqrt{3}$

Rule # 5:   Distributive Law $a\sqrt{b}\left(c\sqrt{d}+e\sqrt{f}\right)=ac\sqrt{bd}+ae\sqrt{bf}$

Example: $5\sqrt{6}\left(4\sqrt{3}+2\sqrt{10}\right)$

$= 5\cdot4\sqrt{6}\sqrt{3}+5\cdot2\sqrt{6}\sqrt{10}$ using Rule #5
$= 20\sqrt{18}+10\sqrt{60}$ using Rule #4 and Rule #5
$= 20\sqrt{9}\sqrt{2}+10\sqrt{4}\sqrt{15}$ using Rule #1
$= 20\cdot3\sqrt{2}+10\cdot2\sqrt{15}$ taking the square root
$= 60\sqrt{2}+20\sqrt{15}$ multiplying coefficients

(Note: These radicals cannot be added since the radicands are different.)

21. $3\sqrt{2}\left(4\sqrt{2}+5\sqrt{6}\right)$ = _____

= _____

= _____

= _____

21.	$12\sqrt{4}+15\sqrt{12}$
	$12\cdot2+15\sqrt{4}\sqrt{3}$
	$24+15\cdot2\sqrt{3}$
	$24+30\sqrt{3}$

Exercise 7.1

I.   Simplify each of the following. Leave the final answer in simple radical form.

1. $\sqrt{32}$

2. $3\sqrt{8}$

3. $\sqrt{\dfrac{3}{16}}$

4. $\sqrt{128}$

5. $\dfrac{1}{\sqrt{3}}$

6. $\dfrac{7}{\sqrt{7}}$

7. $\left(5\sqrt{3}\right)\left(4\sqrt{2}\right)$

8. $\left(2\sqrt{3}\right)\left(3\sqrt{3}\right)$

9. $\sqrt{125}-\sqrt{20}$

10. $\dfrac{\sqrt{15}}{\sqrt{5}}$

11. $3\sqrt{5}\cdot\sqrt{15}$

12. $5\sqrt{3}\cdot8\sqrt{2}$

13. $\sqrt{20}+\sqrt{45}-4\sqrt{5}$

14. $\sqrt{12}+\sqrt{27}+\sqrt{48}$

15. $\left(8\sqrt{3}\right)\left(5\sqrt{27}\right)$

16. $6\sqrt{2}\left(5\sqrt{3}+4\sqrt{2}\right)$

17. $\dfrac{1}{2}\sqrt{3}\left(5\dfrac{1}{2}+2\sqrt{3}\right)$

18. $\dfrac{7}{3}\left(6\sqrt{2}\right)\left(5\sqrt{6}\right)$

19. $\dfrac{4}{3}\left(4\sqrt{3}\right)^{3}$

20. $\sqrt{448}$

7.2 Quadratic Equations Review

The general form of a quadratic equation is $Ax^2 + Bx + C = 0$. Three methods for solving will be reviewed: using the square root method, factoring, and using the formula.

I.   Only quadratic equations of the type $Ax^2 + C = 0$ will be considered for the first method. To solve a quadratic equation by the square root method, follow the procedure below.

Example: $16x^2 - 3 = 0$

a. Isolate the squared term in one member.

a. $16x^2 = 3$

b. Divide both members of the equation by the coefficient of the of the squared term.

b. $\dfrac{16x^2}{16} = \dfrac{3}{16}$

$x^2 = \dfrac{3}{16}$

c. Take the square root of both members of the equation.

c. $x = \pm\sqrt{\dfrac{3}{16}}$

d. Simplify your answer. Leave the answer in simple radical form. The answer approximated to the nearest hundredth would be _____.

d. $x = \pm\dfrac{\sqrt{3}}{4}$

$x = \pm 0.43$

22.   Solve $24x^2 - 25 = 0$.

$24x^2 =$

$x^2 =$

$x =$

22.

$24x^2 = 25$

$x^2 = \dfrac{25}{24}$

$x = \pm\dfrac{\sqrt{25}}{\sqrt{24}}$

$$x = \pm \frac{5}{\sqrt{4}\sqrt{6}}$$

$$x = \pm \frac{5}{2\sqrt{6}}$$

$$x = \pm \frac{5}{2\sqrt{6}} \cdot \frac{\sqrt{6}}{\sqrt{6}}$$

$$x = \pm \frac{5\sqrt{6}}{2\sqrt{36}}$$

$$x = \pm \frac{5\sqrt{6}}{2 \cdot 6}$$

$$x = \pm \frac{5\sqrt{6}}{12}$$

To the nearest hundredth the answer would be _____.

$$x = \pm 1.02$$

II. To solve a quadratic equation by factoring, follow the procedure below.

Example: $4x^2 = 13x - 3$

a. Set the equation equal to zero.

a. $4x^2 - 13x + 3 = 0$

b. Factor the left member of the equation.

b. $(x - 3)(4x - 1) = 0$

c. Set each factor equal to zero and solve for x.

c. $x - 3 = 0$
$x = 3$
$4x - 1 = 0$
$4x = 1$
$x = \frac{1}{4}$

The solution set is $\left\{ \frac{1}{4}, 3 \right\}$.

You can check your answer by substitution.

If x = 3, then $\qquad$ $4x^2 = 13x - 3$ becomes

$$4(3)^2 = 13(3) - 3$$

$$4(9) = 39 - 3$$

$$36 = 36$$

If $x = \dfrac{1}{4}$, then $\qquad$ $4x^2 = 13x - 3$ becomes

$$4\left(\dfrac{1}{4}\right)^2 = 13\left(\dfrac{1}{4}\right) - 3$$

$$4\left(\dfrac{1}{16}\right) = \dfrac{13}{4} - \dfrac{3}{1}$$

$$\dfrac{4}{16} = \dfrac{13}{4} - \dfrac{12}{4}$$

$$\dfrac{1}{4} = \dfrac{1}{4}$$

23. Solve $x^2 - 2x - 15 = 0$ by factoring.

(   )(   ) = 0

(   ) = 0 and (   ) = 0

x = _____ and x = _____

The solution set is _____.

Now, check your solution.

23.

$(x + 3)(x - 5) = 0$

$(x + 3) = 0$ and
$(x - 5) = 0$

x = -3 and x = 5

{-3,5}

Checking x = -3:
$$(-3)^2 - 2(-3) - 15 = 0$$
$$9 + 6 - 15 = 0$$
$$0 = 0$$
Checking x = 5:
$$(5)^2 - 2(5) - 15 = 0$$
$$25 - 10 - 15 = 0$$
$$0 = 0$$

III. You will discover very quickly in step (b) of the factoring method above whether or not a quadratic equation is factorable. If the equation is not factorable, then use the quadratic formula to obtain the solutions. If the equation is in general form, $Ax^2 + Bx + C = 0$, the formula is given by

$$x = \frac{-B \pm \sqrt{B^2 - 4AC}}{2A}$$

where A is the coefficient of x^2; B is the coefficient of x; and, C is the constant term.

Example: $3x^2 - 11x = -6$

a. Set the equation equal to zero.

$3x^2 - 11x + 6 = 0$

b. Select A = 3, B = -11, and C = 6. Substitute these values directly into the formula.

$$x = \frac{-(-11) \pm \sqrt{(-11)^2 - 4(3)(6)}}{2(3)}$$

c. Solve for x.

$$x = \frac{11 \pm \sqrt{121 - 72}}{6}$$

$$x = \frac{11 \pm \sqrt{49}}{6}$$

$$x = \frac{11 \pm 7}{6}$$

Splitting the two solutions apart to simplify gives the following:

$$x = \frac{11 + 7}{6}$$

$$x = \frac{18}{6}$$ and

$$x = 3$$

$$x = \frac{11 - 7}{6}$$

$$x = \frac{4}{6}$$

$$x = \frac{2}{3}$$

d. Write the solution set in set notation: $\left\{ \frac{2}{3}, 3 \right\}$

24. Solve $2x^2 - 5x - 6 = 0$ by using the quadratic formula.
A = _____; B = _____;
C = _____

24.

A = 2; B = -5; C = -6

$2x^2 - 5x - 6 = 0$

$$X = \frac{-(-5) \pm \sqrt{(-5)^2 - 4 \cdot 2 \cdot (-6)}}{2 \cdot 2}$$

X = _____

$$X = \frac{5 \pm \sqrt{25 + 48}}{4}$$

$$X = \frac{5 \pm \sqrt{73}}{4}$$

The solution set is _____.

$$\left\{ \frac{5 - \sqrt{73}}{4}, \frac{5 + \sqrt{73}}{4} \right\}$$

The solution set approximated to the nearest hundredth is ____.

{-0.89, 3.39}

Exercise 7.2

In I, II, and III, leave answers in exact form and also round off non integer answers to the nearest hundredth.

I. Solve the following quadratic equations by using the square root method.

1. $x^2 - 4 = 0$ 5. $3x^2 - 4 = 0$

2. $4x^2 - 9 = 0$ 6. $16x^2 - 27 = 0$

3. $25x^2 = 1$ 7. $12x^2 = 5$

4. $36x^2 - 5 = 0$ 8. $32x^2 - 45 = 0$

II. Solve each of the following equations by factoring.

1. $x^2 - 8x + 15 = 0$ 5. $4x^2 - 9 = 0$

2. $12x^2 - 19x + 5 = 0$ 6. $2x^2 = x + 6$

3. $5x^2 = -2x$ 7. $4x^2 + 9 = 12x$

4. $6x^2 + 11x - 30 = 0$ 8. $10x^2 + 21x - 10 = 0$

III. Solve each of the following equations using the quadratic formula.

1. $x^2 + 6x + 5 = 0$ 4. $x^2 + 2x - 11 = 0$

2. $2x^2 - 7 = 0$ 5. $3x^2 = 7$

3. $2x^2 - 5x + 3 = 0$ 6. $3x^2 - 2x = 6$

7. $x(x-8)+2(2x-5)=3(x^2-3)$ 8. $8x^2-8x+2=0$

7.3   Introduction to Area

Area deals with the number of square units in a figure. For example, in a rectangle 3 feet by 4 feet, there will be 12 square feet (abbreviated sq. ft. or ft.^{2}) or 12 blocks 1 ft. by 1 ft. This number can be obtained by counting in the figure below.

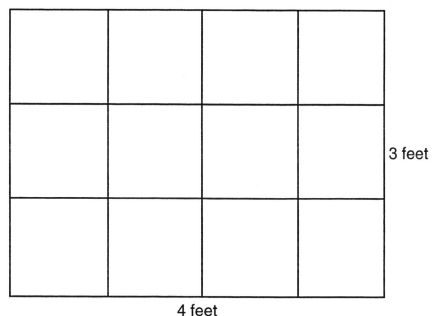

3 feet

4 feet

The procedure of dividing a figure into square blocks and counting these units is tedious, not to mention time consuming as well. A procedure needs to be developed to do this for all figures whose area will be of concern. As you progress through these sections you will need to make a list of the formulas for the area of certain figures.

AREA	FORMULA
Rectangle	_____
Square	_____
Parallelogram	_____
Triangle	_____
Trapezoid	_____
Circle	_____

7.4   Area of a Rectangle

Postulate 7.1   The area of a rectangle is the product of the length and the width. If L = length, W = width, and A = area, then A = LW.

Note: Unless otherwise specified in this unit non integer answers will be expressed to the nearest hundredth.

Example:

If the length of a rectangle is 5 in. and the width is 6 in. Find the area.

$$A = LW$$
$$A = (5 \text{ in.})(6 \text{ in.})$$
$$A = 30 \text{ sq.in. or } 30 \text{ in.}^2$$

Example:

If the length of a rectangle is $4\frac{3}{4}$ ft. and the width is $5\frac{1}{8}$ ft., find the area.

$$A = LW$$
$$A = \left(4\frac{3}{4}\right)\left(5\frac{1}{8}\right)$$
$$A = \left(\frac{19}{4}\right)\left(\frac{41}{8}\right)$$
$$A = \frac{779}{32}$$
$$A = 24\frac{11}{32} \text{ sq. ft. or approximately } 24.34 \text{ sq.ft}$$

25.   If the length of a rectangle is 12 ft. and the width is 8.7 ft., find the area.

$$A = LW$$
$$A = \underline{\quad}$$
$$A = \underline{\quad}\text{sq.ft.}$$

25.
$$A = (12)(8.7)$$
$$A = 104.4 \text{ sq.ft.}$$

Example:

Find the cost of covering a rectangular floor 5 yd. by 4 yd. if the carpeting cost $9 per sq. yd.

Solution:

First, determine the area of the rectangle.

$A = (5 \text{ yd.})(4 \text{ yd.}) = 20 \text{ sq. yd.}$

Second, find the cost to carpet the room.

Each square yard cost $9 and we have 20 sq. yd. Therefore, $(20)(9) = \$180 =$ cost of carpeting the room.

26.   A hallway 20 ft. by $4\frac{1}{2}$ ft. is to be covered with carpeting that costs $4 a square foot Determine the cost of carpeting the hallway.

a. Area of the hall = _____	26.
	a. $A = (20)\left(4\frac{1}{2}\right)$
	$\quad\; A = (20)\left(\frac{9}{2}\right)$
	$\quad\quad = 90 \text{ sq. ft.}$
b. Cost of carpeting = $\quad$ (Area) $\cdot$ (Cost per square foot)	b. $\quad (4)\cdot(90) = \$360$

Example:

Mr. Brown owns a farm that is 16 miles longer than it is wide. If the area of the farm is 80 square miles, find the dimensions of his rectangular farm.

$$x = \text{width}$$
$$x + 16 = \text{length}$$
$$\text{Area} = \text{length} \cdot \text{width}$$
$$80 = (x + 16)x$$
$$80 = x^2 + 16x$$
$$0 = x^2 + 16x - 80$$
$$0 = (x + 20)(x - 4)$$
$$x + 20 = 0 \text{ and } x - 4 = 0$$
$$x = \text{-}20 \qquad x = 4$$

$x = $ -20 is not a suitable choice for width since we measure figures with positives numbers only.

x = 4 is the width.

x + 16 = 4 + 16 = 20 is the length.

27.   Mr. Smith owns a farm whose length if five | 27.
      times its width and whose area is 320 square |
      miles. Find the dimensions of his rectangular |
      garden. |
                                                         |
      _____ = width | x
                                                         |
      _____ = length | 5x
                                                         |
      _____ is the equation. |
                                                         | $5x^2 = 320$
                                                         | $x^2 = 64$
                                                         | $x = \pm\sqrt{64}$
                                                         | $x = \pm 8$
      The solution is _____ . | 8

      Note: The negative root is discarded
      since dimensions are expressed in
      positive numbers only.

      width = _____ | 8 miles

      length = _____ | 40 miles

Example:

The Wildlife Service has a rectangular park they wish to fence. The
rangers know the park is three times longer than it is wide and the area is
75 sq. mi. How much fence will they need to purchase?

Solution:

This problem deals with both area and perimeter. The fencing is placed
on the perimeter of the park. Before determining the perimeter, the
length and width need to be obtained.

From the problem:

    x = width

    3x = length

$$(\text{width})(\text{length}) = \text{area}$$
$$(x)(3x) = 75$$
$$3x^2 = 75$$
$$x^2 = 25$$
$$x = \pm 5$$
$$x = 5 \quad \text{width}$$
$$3x = 15 \quad \text{length}$$

The perimeter of a rectangle is the distance around the rectangle. It takes two lengths and two widths to equal the perimeter.

$$2 \text{ widths} + 2 \text{ lengths} = \text{perimeter}$$
$$2(5) + 2(15) = 10 + 30$$
$$= 40 \text{ mi. of fence needed for the park.}$$

28. Tom and Betty wish to fence in their yard so they can get a puppy. Their lot is twice as long as it is wide and is 20,000 sq. ft. in area. How much fence will they need for their rectangular yard?

28.

_____ = width

x

_____ = length

$2x$

Equation: _____

$(x)(2x) = 20{,}000$

$$2x^2 = 20{,}000$$
$$x^2 = 10{,}000$$
$$x = \pm 100$$

Solution: _____

Width = _____

100

Length = _____

200

Perimeter = 2 lengths + 2 widths

$$2(200) + 2(100)$$
$$400 + 200$$
$$600 \text{ ft.}$$

= _____

Amount of fencing needed: _____

600 ft.

Example:

Find the area of the given region.

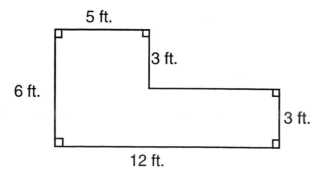

Method I:

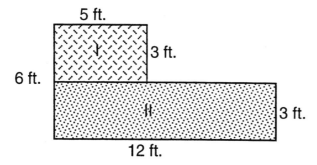

The region can be divided into two rectangles. (See the illustration above.) The top region (I) is 5 ft. by 3 ft. The lower region (II) is 12 ft. by 3 ft.

Area I =   5 ft. X 3 ft. = 15 sq. ft.

Area II = 12 ft. X 3 ft. = 36 sq. ft.

Total area of entire figure = 15 + 36 = 51 sq. ft.

Method II:

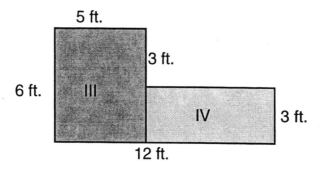

A second way to divide into regions is illustrated above. The left region (III) is 6 ft. by 5 ft. The right region (IV) is 3 ft. by 7 ft. (12 - 5).

Area III = 6 ft. X 5 ft. = 30 sq. ft.

Area IV = 3 ft. X 7 ft. = 21 sq. ft.

Total area of entire region = 51 sq. ft.

Which method is best? Either method is acceptable.

29. Determine the area of the region below.

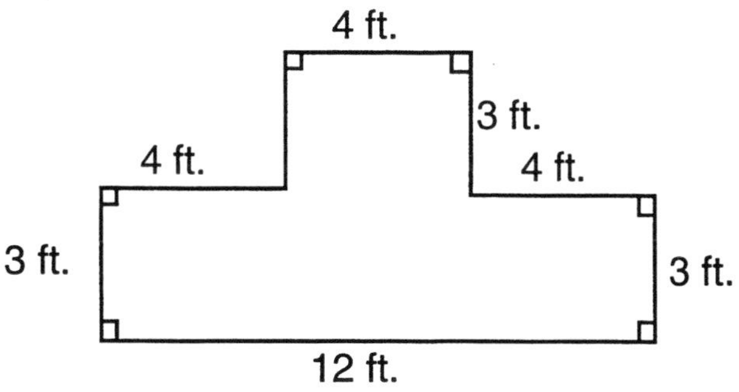

29. One possible method is:

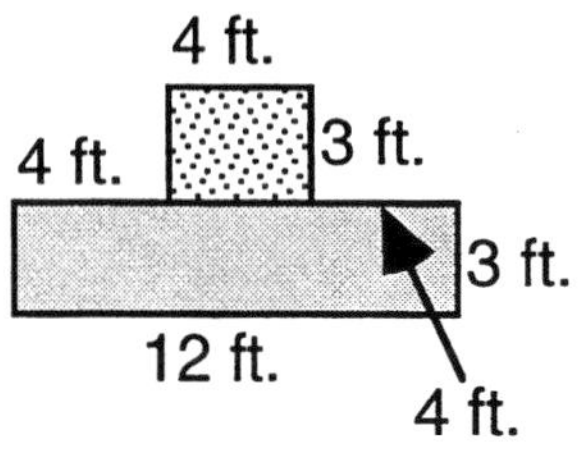

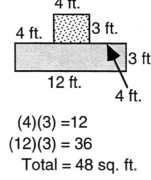

(4)(3) =12
(12)(3) = 36
Total = 48 sq. ft.

Theorem 7.1	The area of a square with side, s, is given by the formula $A = s^2$.

A square is a special type of rectangle. It is a rectangle with two adjacent sides equal. The area of a rectangle is length times the width. In a square the length equals the width; therefore, we can readily see why the area of a square is side times side or side squared.

Example:

If the side of a square is 7 ft., find its area.

$$A = (7 \text{ ft.})^2 = (7 \text{ ft.})(7 \text{ ft.}) = 49 \text{ sq. ft.}$$

Example:

If the side of a square is $4\sqrt{2}$ in., find the area.

$$A = \left(4\sqrt{2}\right)^2 = \left(4\sqrt{2}\right)\left(4\sqrt{2}\right) = 16\sqrt{4} = 32 \text{ sq. in.}$$

30.   If the side of a square is $4\frac{1}{2}$ ft., find its area.

30.

$$A = \left(4\frac{1}{2}\right)^2$$

$$= \left(\frac{9}{2}\right)^2$$

$$= \frac{81}{4}$$

$$= 20\frac{1}{4} = 20.25 \text{ ft.}^2$$

Example:

The perimeter of a square is 48 in. Find its area.

Since the distance all the way around a figure is the perimeter and all four sides of the square are equal, then

$$P = 2x + 2x$$
$$P = 4x$$

where x is the length of the side of the square.

$$P = 4x$$
$$48 = 4x$$
$$12 = x$$

If x = 12, then

$$A = x^2$$
$$A = 12^2$$
$$\text{Area} = 144 \text{ sq. in.}$$

31.   If the perimeter of a square is 40 ft., find its area.

Let x be the length of a side.

Equation: _____

The length of a side is _____ ft.

31.

$$P = 4x$$
$$40 = 4x$$
$$10 = x$$

10

The area of the square is _____ . | (10)(10)=100 sq. ft.

Exercise 7.3

In this exercise, round each final answer to the nearest hundredth.

1.   Find the area of the following rectangles.

   a. L = 12 in., W = 10 in.

   b. L = 20 ft., W = 6 ft.

   c. L = √7 yd., W = √7 yd.

   d. L = $3\frac{1}{2}$ m., W = $\frac{77}{5}$ m.

2.   In a rectangle, if:

   a. A = 12 sq. in., L = 6 in., find W.

   b. A = √14 sq. cm., L = 5 cm., find W.

   c. A = $3\frac{1}{3}$ sq. mm., W = $2\frac{1}{2}$ mm., find L.

3.   Find the area of each geometric figure depicted below:

   a.

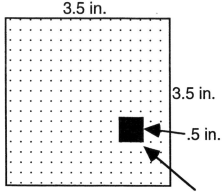

3.5 in.

3.5 in.

.5 in.

hole (The hole is a square.)

The larger figure is a square.

b.

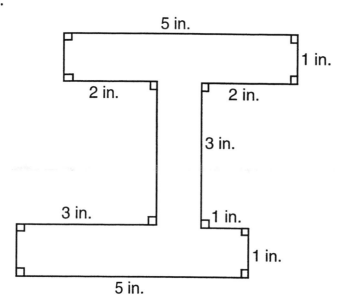

c.

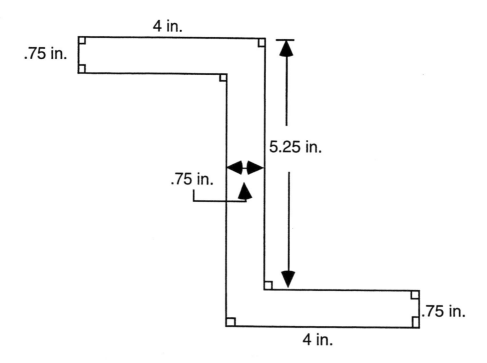

4. Find the measures of the sides of a rectangular room if the length is three feet longer than the width and the area equals 180 sq. ft.

5. To completely border a rectangular lot that measures 54 ft by 90 ft., the owner must purchase at least how many feet of fencing?

6.   Tonya wishes to carpet a room that is 20 ft. by 15 ft. in carpeting that costs $3 a square foot. How much will it cost to carpet this room?

7.   If the side of a square is 5 ft., find its area.

8.   If the perimeter of a square is 6 in., find its area.

7.5 Area of a Parallelogram

> Theorem 7.2   The area of a parallelogram is the product of the base and height. In symbols A = bh, where b is the base; h is the height; and, A is the area.

The height of a parallelogram is the length of the line drawn from a vertex perpendicular to the other side (base).

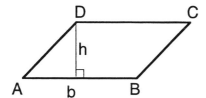

In parallelogram ABCD, h is the height and b is the base.

Let's examine the formula closer.

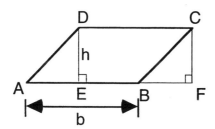

In parallelogram ABCD a perpendicular line ($\overline{CF}$) is dropped to the extended base. By doing this, a rectangle, DCFE, is formed having the same base (b) and altitude (h) as the parallelogram. Since $\triangle ADE \cong \triangle BCF$ and $\triangle BCF$ is added on one side of the parallelogram and $\triangle ADE$ is removed from the other, the area is unchanged. Consequently, the formula for the area of a parallelogram is concluded:

$$A = bh$$

Example:

In parallelogram ABCD, the height is 6 ft. and the base is $10\frac{1}{2}$ ft. Find the area.

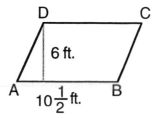

$$A = (6 \text{ ft.})\left(10\frac{1}{2} \text{ ft.}\right)$$

$$A = 6 \cdot \frac{21}{2} \text{ sq. ft.}$$

$$A = 63 \text{ sq. ft.}$$

32. In a parallelogram, h = 5 ft. and b = 20 ft. Find the area.

$$A = bh$$
$$A = \underline{\hspace{2cm}} \text{ sq. ft.}$$

32.

$$A = (5)(20)$$
$$A = 100 \text{ sq. ft.}$$

Example:

In a parallelogram, find the height if the area is 48 sq. in. and the base is 6 in.

$$A = bh$$
$$48 = 6h$$
$$\frac{1}{6} \cdot 48 = \frac{1}{6} \cdot 6h$$
$$8 \text{ in.} = h$$

33. In a parallelogram, find the height, if the area is $10\frac{1}{2}$ sq. mi. and the base is $4\frac{1}{2}$ mi.

$$A = bh$$
$$10\frac{1}{2} = 4\frac{1}{2}h$$
$$\underline{\hspace{1.5cm}} = h$$

33.

$$\frac{21}{2} = \frac{9}{2}h$$
$$21 = 9h$$
$$\frac{1}{9} \cdot 21 = \frac{1}{9} \cdot 9h$$
$$\frac{21}{9} = h$$
$$2\frac{1}{3} \text{ mi.} = h$$
$$2.33 \text{ mi.} = h$$

Example:

In a parallelogram find the base if the area is 81 sq. m. and the height is three times the base.

$$x = \text{base}$$
$$3x = \text{height}$$
$$A = bh$$
$$81 = x \cdot 3x$$
$$81 = 3x^2$$
$$27 = x^2$$
$$3\sqrt{3} \text{ mi.} = x \text{ or}$$
$$5.20 \text{ mi.} = x$$

34. In a parallelogram find the base if the area is 100 sq. cm. and the height is five times the base.

$$x = \text{base}$$
$$\underline{\quad\quad} = \text{height}$$

34.

$$5x$$
$$100 = x \cdot 5x$$
$$100 = 5x^2$$
$$20 = x^2$$
$$2\sqrt{5} = x \text{ or}$$
$$4.47 \text{ cm.} = x$$

Exercise 7.4

In this exercise, round each final answer to the nearest hundredth.

1.   Find the area of the following parallelogram.

  a. b = 6 in., h = 4 in.

  b. b = $13\frac{1}{3}$ ft., h = 1.7 ft.

  c. b = $3\sqrt{5}$ yd., h = $7\sqrt{72}$ yd.

  d. b = 7 cm., h = $3\frac{2}{3}$ cm.

e. $b = 8\frac{1}{5}$ dm., h = 25 dm.

2. Find the missing dimension in the following.

a. A = 40 sq. m., h = 5 m., find b.

b. A=$17\sqrt{3}$ sq. cm., b = $\sqrt{3}$ cm., find h.

c. A = $16\frac{2}{3}$ sq. mi., b = 5 mi., find h.

d. A = 17.1 sq. m., h = .03 m, find b.

3. In a parallelogram the base is three more than the height. If the area is 108 sq. ft., find the height and the base.

4. In a parallelogram the height is 2 less than three times the base. If the area is 21 sq. yd., find the height and the base.

7.6   Area of a Triangle

From the parallelogram, the formula for the area of a triangle can be obtained.

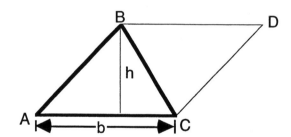

In parallelogram ABCD with base, b, and height, h, the diagonal $\overline{BC}$ divides the parallelogram into two congruent triangles. Congruent triangles have the same shape and same size. Consequently, they will have the same area. The area of the parallelogram ABDC is A = bh. The area of $\triangle$ABC is

$$A = \frac{1}{2}bh.$$

Note that parallelogram ABCD and $\triangle$ABC have the same base and the same height.

Theorem 7.3   The area, A, of a triangle is given by $A = \frac{1}{2}bh$, where h is the height and b is the base.

Example:

In triangle ABC if h = 6 ft. and b = $7\frac{1}{2}$ ft. find the area.

$$A = \frac{1}{2}bh$$

$$A = \frac{1}{2} \cdot 6 \cdot 7\frac{1}{2}$$

$$A = \frac{1}{2} \cdot 6 \cdot \frac{15}{2}$$

$$A = \frac{45}{2}$$

$$A = 22\frac{1}{2} \text{ or } 22.5 \text{ sq. ft.}$$

35.   In a triangle if h = 12 ft. and b = $7\frac{1}{5}$ ft., find the area.

$$A = \frac{1}{2}bh$$

35.

$$A = \frac{1}{2} \cdot 12 \cdot 7\frac{1}{5}$$

$$A = 6 \cdot \frac{36}{5}$$

$$= \frac{216}{5}$$

$$= 43\frac{1}{5}$$

or 43.2 sq. ft.

Example:

If the area of a triangle is 40 sq. in. and the base is 8 in., find the height.

$$A = \frac{1}{2}bh$$

$$40 = \frac{1}{2} \cdot 8 \cdot h$$

$$40 = 4h$$

$$10 \text{ in. } = h$$

36.   If the area of a triangle is 75 sq. m. and the base is 5 m., find the height.

$$A = \frac{1}{2}bh$$

36.

$$75 = \frac{1}{2} \cdot 5 \cdot h$$

$$75 = \frac{5}{2} \cdot h$$

$$30 \text{ m.} = h$$

Example:

The height of a triangle is five more than twice the base. If the area is 12 sq.m., find the base.

$$x = \text{base}$$
$$2x + 5 = \text{height}$$

$$12 = \frac{1}{2}(x)(2x + 5)$$

$$0 = 2x^2 + 5x - 24$$

$$x = \frac{-5 \pm \sqrt{25 - 4 \cdot 2 \cdot -24}}{4}$$

$$x = \frac{-5 \pm \sqrt{25 + 192}}{4}$$

$$x = \frac{-5 \pm \sqrt{217}}{4}$$

$$x = \frac{-5 \pm 14.73}{4}$$

The solution for the base is $x = \dfrac{-5 + 14.73}{4}$ or $x = 2.43$ m. since dimensions are measured in positive numbers.

37.   The height of a triangle is five more than four times the base. Find the height and base if the area is $25\frac{1}{2}$.

37.

$$x = \text{base}$$
$$4x + 5 = \text{height}$$

$$\frac{1}{2}x(4x+5)=25\frac{1}{2}$$

$$4x^2+5x-51=0$$

$$(4x+17)(x-3)=0$$

$$4x+17=0$$

$$4x=-17$$

or $\begin{array}{c}x-3=0\\ x=3\end{array}$

$$x=\frac{-17}{4}$$

$$x=-4.25$$

base $= 3$ m.

height $= 4(3)+5$

or

height $= 17$ m.

Exercise 7.5

In this exercise round the final answer to each problem to hundredths.

1. Find the area of the following triangles:

    a. $b = 6$ in., $h = 10$ in.

    b. $b = 5$ ft., $h = 3$ ft.

    c. $b = \sqrt{7}$ cm., $h = \sqrt{5}$ cm.

    d. $b = \sqrt{2}$ m., $h = 2\sqrt{2}$ m.

    e. $b = \frac{2}{3}$ mi., $h = \frac{1}{2}$ mi.

2. In a triangle, if:

    a. $A = 16$ sq. ft., $b = 4$ ft., find h.

    b. $A = 14$ sq. in., $b = \sqrt{3}$ in., find h.

    c. $A = 2\frac{1}{4}$ sq. yd., $b = \frac{1}{2}$ yd., find h.

3. The base of a triangle is 8.6 m. and the height is 4.4 m., find the area.

4. If the base is 3 more inches than the height of the triangle and the area equals 90 sq. in., find the measure of the base.

5. The area of a triangle is 40 sq. cm. If the base is 5 cm. then find the measure of the height.

6. The floor of a triangular bathroom is illustrated below:

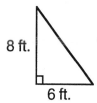

8 ft.

6 ft.

How many tiles are needed to cover the floor if each tile is 1 sq. ft.?

7.7   Area of a Trapezoid

Recall that a trapezoid is a quadrilateral with only one pair of sides parallel. Examining a trapezoid, let us determine a way to find the area. Begin with trapezoid ABCD.

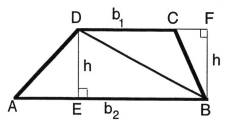

Divide trapezoid ABCD into triangles by drawing in diagonal $\overline{BD}$. For $\triangle ABD$ draw altitude $\overline{DE}$ and call its length h. The area of $\triangle ABD$ is $\frac{1}{2}hb_2$. Likewise, for $\triangle BCD$ draw altitude $\overline{BF}$. Note $\overline{BF}$ is exterior to the triangle and is perpendicular to the extension of $\overline{DC}$. The length of $\overline{BF}$ is equal to h since $\overline{AB} \| \overline{DF}$ and the perpendicular segments between parallel lines are everywhere the same length. The area of $\triangle DBC$ is $\frac{1}{2}hb_1$. The area of trapezoid ABCD = the area of $\triangle ABD$ plus the area of $\triangle DBC$.

Therefore,

$$A = \frac{1}{2}hb_2 + \frac{1}{2}hb_1$$

$$= \frac{1}{2}h(b_2 + b_1) \qquad \text{(factoring)}$$

Theorem 7.4 The area, A, of a trapezoid is given by the formula

$$A = \frac{1}{2}h(b_1 + b_2)$$

where h is the altitude and b_1 and b_2 are the bases.

Example:

Find the area of a trapezoid with b_1 = 10 in. and b_2 = 18 in, and h = 9 in.

$$A = \frac{1}{2}h(b_1 + b_2)$$

$$A = \frac{1}{2} \cdot 9(10 + 18)$$

$$A = \frac{9}{2} \cdot 28$$

$$A = 126 \text{ sq. in. or } 126 \text{ in.}^2$$

38. Find the area of a trapezoid with b_1 = 15 in., b_2 = 20 in., and h = 10 in.

38.

$$A = \frac{1}{2}h(b_1 + b_2)$$

$$A = \frac{1}{2} \cdot 10(15 + 20)$$

$$= \frac{1}{2} \cdot 10(35)$$

$$= 5(35)$$

$$= 175 \text{ sq.in.}$$

Example:

Find the height of a trapezoid if the bases are 12 inches and 14 inches and the area is 60 square inches.

$$A = \frac{1}{2}h(b_1 + b_2)$$

$$60 = \frac{1}{2} \cdot h(12 + 14)$$

$$60 = \frac{1}{2} \cdot h(26)$$

$$60 = 13h$$

$$4\frac{8}{13} \text{ in. or } 4.62 \text{ in.} = h$$

39.   Find the height of a trapezoid, if the bases are
      8 meters and 10 meters and the area is 72
      square meters.

39.

$$A = \frac{1}{2}h(b_1 + b_2)$$

$$72 = \frac{1}{2} \cdot h(8 + 10)$$

$$72 = \frac{1}{2} \cdot h(18)$$

$$72 = 9h$$

$$8 \text{ m.} = h$$

Example:

Find each base of a trapezoid in which the larger base is four more than
the smaller, the height is 6 inches, and the area is 20 sq. in.

$$x = \text{smaller base (base 1)}$$

$$x + 4 = \text{larger base (base 2)}$$

$$A = \frac{1}{2}h(b_1 + b_2)$$

$$20 = \frac{1}{2} \cdot 6[x + (x + 4)]$$

$$20 = 3(2x + 4)$$

$$20 = 6x + 12$$

$$8 = 6x$$

$$1\frac{1}{3} \text{ in. } = x$$

$$\begin{cases} \text{base}_1 = 1\frac{1}{3} \text{ in. or 1.33 in.} \\ \text{base}_2 = 5\frac{1}{3} \text{ in. or 5.33 in.} \end{cases}$$

40.   Find each base of a trapezoid in which the
      smaller base is three less than the larger
      base, the height is 4 ft., and the area is 42
      sq. ft.

      smaller base = _____

      larger base = _____

40.

$$x - 3$$

$$x$$

$$42 = \frac{1}{2} \cdot 4[x + (x - 3)]$$
$$42 = 2(2x - 3)$$
$$42 = 4x - 6$$
$$48 = 4x$$
$$12 = x$$

9 ft. = smaller base

12 ft. = larger base

Exercise 7.6

In this exercise round the final answer to each problem to hundredths.

1. Find the area of the following trapezoids:

    a. $b_1 = 12$ m., $b_2 = 14$ m., $h = 7$ m.

    b. $b_1 = 30$ cm., $b_2 = 40$ cm., $h = 10$ cm.

    c. $b_1 = 3\sqrt{5}$ mm., $b_2 = 5\sqrt{5}$ mm., $h = 6\sqrt{5}$ mm.

    d. $b_1 = 7\frac{1}{2}$ in., $b_2 = 3\frac{1}{3}$ in., $h = \frac{1}{2}$ in.

2. In a trapezoid, if:

    a. $b_1 = 12$ mi., $b_2 = 10$ mi., find h if A = 55 sq. mi.

    b. h = 12 m., $b_1 = 14$ m., find b_2 if A = 180 sq. m.

3. Find the bases of a trapezoid if the upper base is 2 less than the lower base; the altitude is 7 ft. and the area is 35 sq. ft.

4. Find the sum of the bases of a trapezoid if the area is 63 sq. ft. and the altitude is 3 ft.

5. A base is one less than twice the second base and the area is 40 sq. cm. Find the altitude of the trapezoid if the altitude is the length of the second base.

6. In a trapezoid the second base is three times the first. The height is 10 cm. If the area is 100 sq. cm., find the length of the two bases.

7.   Cindy wants to cover a trapezoidal table with 1 in. square tiles. If the top of the table has one side of 48 in., a second side of 72 in., and height of the trapezoidal top (width of the table) of 24 in., how many tiles will be needed?

7.8   Introduction to Circles

The topic of area is not complete without including the area of a circle. A brief discussion of the definition and circumference of a circle will precede the topic of area of a circle.

The top of a can, the end of a pipe, the end of pistons in automobile engines, the tires on cars, and the burner on the gas range are a few examples of circles we all encounter.

One could simply say that a circle is a flat round object. But that description is certainly not the definition for a circle. For our discussion, let's draw a picture of this object.

Take your ruler and pencil and do the following:

From point P below, make dots all a distance of 2 cm. from P.

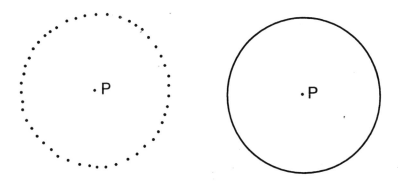

Notice these dots, when connected, form a 'round' figure. Note two things about this figure: (1) we started with a fixed point (P) and (2) we used a fixed distance (2 cm.) each time. This exercise leads us to the following definition.

Definition 7.1   A circle is the set of all possible points in a plane a fixed distance from a given point. The fixed distance is called the radius of the circle and the given point is the center.

41. a. In the diagram below what is the radius?   41. a. $\overline{OW}$

     b. What is the center?   b. O

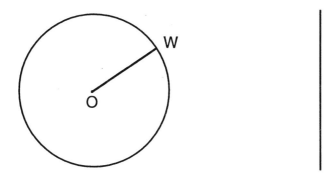

Definition 7.2   The <u>diameter</u> of a circle is a line segment that divides a circle into two equal parts. It is equal in measure to two radii of a circle.

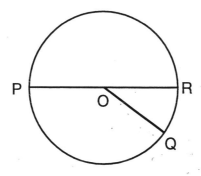

Radii $\overline{OP}$ and $\overline{OR}$ form diameter $\overline{PR}$. $\overline{OR}$ and $\overline{OQ}$ do not form a diameter. A diameter divides a complete circle into two equal parts. Each part is called a <u>semicircle</u>.

42. Does a diameter always pass through the center of a circle?

42. yes

43. Is a diameter equal to the length of two radii?

43. yes

7.9 <u>Circumference of a Circle</u>

The circumference is to a circle as perimeter is to a rectangle. However, circumference can not be defined in the same way as perimeter. Perimeter is defined in terms of adding the lengths of line segments that make up the sides of a figure. Since a circle is not composed of line segments, the definition of perimeter is not quite satisfactory.

Definition 7.3   The <u>circumference</u> of a circle is the distance around the rim of the circle.

Theorem 7.5   The ratio of the circumference to the diameter is the same for all circles.

The theorem tells us that for a circle of radius r, circumference C, and diameter d, the ratio of circumference to diameter, $\frac{C}{d}$, equals a constant number. This constant number has been traditionally symbolized by the Greek letter π, pronounced as "pi". Therefore $\frac{C}{d} = \pi$ or $C = \pi d$. This formula may sometimes be stated in terms of radius r.

$$\frac{C}{d} = d \text{ or } C = \pi d$$

replacing d with 2r the formula becomes

$$\frac{C}{2r} = \pi \text{ or } C = 2\pi r$$

The number, π, which relates the circumference to the diameter of a circle, is an irrational number. π is a constant number that in its decimal form it never ends nor repeats. Values such as $3\frac{1}{7}$, 3.14, and $\frac{22}{7}$ are most commonly used for π but π is not exactly equal to any of these numbers. The value of pi has been calculated on modern computers to 500,000 decimal places. Rounded to only the first nine decimal places, π equals approximately 3.141592654. However, in this unit we will express all answers in terms of π and approximate the final answer to hundredths using $\pi = 3.14$.

Example:

In a circle if the diameter is 6 cm., find the circumference.

The formula is $C = \pi d$. Substituting $d = 6$ into the formula given:

$$C = \pi d$$
$$C = 6\pi \text{ ft.}$$

or approximating to hundredth

$$C = 18.84 \text{ ft.}$$

44.   Find the circumference of a circle if d = 8 ft.

44.
$$C = \pi d$$
$$C = 8\pi \text{ ft.}$$
or
$$C = 25.12 \text{ ft.}$$

Example:

In a circle with $r = 2\frac{1}{5}$ m., find the circumference

$C = 2\pi r$	formula
$C = 2\pi\left(2\frac{1}{5}\right)$	substitution
$C = 2\pi\left(\frac{11}{5}\right)$	simplify
$C = \left(\frac{22}{5}\right)\pi$ m.	simplify
$C = 4.4\pi$ m.	decimal form
$C = 13.82$ m	substituting and rounding

45. If the radius of a circle is $6\sqrt{3}$ in., find the circumference.

45.

$$C = 2\pi r$$
$$C = 2 \cdot \pi \cdot 6\sqrt{3}$$
$$C = 12\pi\sqrt{3}$$
$$C = 65.26 \text{ in.}$$

46. If the radius of a circle is $9\frac{1}{4}$ in., find the circumference.

46.

$$C = 2\pi r$$
$$C = 2 \cdot 9\frac{1}{4}\pi$$
$$C = 2 \cdot \left(\frac{37}{4}\right)\pi$$
$$C = \frac{37}{2}\pi = 18.5\pi \text{ in.}$$
$$C = 58.09 \text{ in.}$$

Example:

If the circumference is 28π cm., find the radius.

$$C = 2\pi r$$
$$28\pi = 2\pi r$$
$$\frac{28\pi}{2\pi} = \frac{2\pi r}{2\pi}$$
$$14 \text{ cm.} = r$$

47.   If the circumference is 48π cm., find the
       radius.

47.

$$C = 2\pi r$$
$$48\pi = 2\pi r$$
$$24 \text{ cm. } = r$$

48.   If the circumference is 10π ft., find the
       diameter.

48.

$$10\pi = \pi d$$
$$10 \text{ ft. } = d$$

7.10 Area of a Circle

The area of a circle is represented by the shaded area in the figure below.

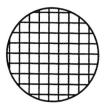

Theorem 7.6	The area of a circle is given by the formula $A = \pi r^2$, where A is the area, π is an irrational constant, and r is the radius of the circle.

Example:

Find the area of a circle with radius 5 ft.

$$A = \pi r^2$$
$$A = \pi \cdot 5^2$$
$$A = 25\pi \text{ sq. ft.}$$
$$A = 78.5 \text{ sq. ft.}$$

Example:

Find the area of a circle with diameter 21 cm.

Recall that a diameter equal two radii, so

$$21 = 2r$$
$$\frac{21}{2} = r$$
$$10.5 = r$$

Now, substitute r into the formula,

$$A = \pi r^2$$

$$A = \pi \left(\frac{21}{2}\right)^2$$

$$A = \frac{441}{4} \pi \text{ sq. cm.}$$

or

$$A = 110.25\pi \text{ cm.}^2$$

or

$$A = 346.19 \text{ cm.}^2$$

49. Find the area of a circle with radius 4 m.

49.
$$A = \pi 4^2$$
$$A = 16\pi \text{ sq. m.}$$
or
$$A = 50.24 \text{ m.}^2$$

50. Find the area of a circle with diameter $4\sqrt{2}$ cm.

50.
$$A = \pi r^2$$
$$4\sqrt{2} = 2r$$
$$2\sqrt{2} = r$$
$$A = \pi \left(2\sqrt{2}\right)^2$$
$$A = 8\pi \text{ sq. cm.}$$
$$A = 25.12 \text{ sq. cm.}$$

Example:

If the area of a circle is 25π sq. in., find the radius.

$$A = \pi r^2$$
$$25\pi = \pi r^2$$
$$\frac{1}{\pi} \cdot 25\pi = \frac{1}{\pi} \cdot \pi r^2$$
$$25 = r^2$$
$$5 \text{ in.} = r$$

51.   If the area of a circle is 64π sq. m., find the radius.

51.

$$A = \pi r^2$$

$$64\pi = \pi r^2$$

$$\frac{1}{\pi} \cdot 64\pi = \frac{1}{\pi} \cdot \pi r^2$$

$$64 = r^2$$

$$8 \text{ m.} = r$$

Exercise 7.7

1.   Find the area and circumference of the following circles. Use $\pi = 3.14$ and round off the final answer to hundredths.

a. $d = 30$ m.

b. $r = 2\sqrt{3}$ cm.

c. $r = \dfrac{3}{2}$ ft.

2.   Find r in each of the following. Round off the final answer to hundredths.

a. $C = 24\pi$ m.

b. $C = 45\pi$ cm.

c. $A = 25\pi$ sq. m.

d. $A = 48\pi$ sq. in.

3.   A country club built a jogging track by putting a semicircle on each end of a rectangle. Find the area of the jogging track. Use $\pi = 3.14$ and round off the final answer to hundredths.

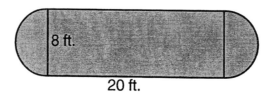

8 ft.

20 ft.

7.11 **Formulae Summary**

In summary, the formulae you have studied in this unit are as follows:

<u>Figure</u>	<u>Area Formula</u>
Rectangle	$A = LW$
Square	$A = s^2$
Parallelogram	$A = bh$
Triangle	$A = \dfrac{1}{2}bh$
Trapezoid	$A = \dfrac{1}{2}h(b_1 + b_2)$
Circle	$A = \pi r^2$
Perimeter of a rectangle	$P = 2L + 2W$
Circumference of a circle	$C = 2\pi r$ or $C = \pi d$

Unit 7 Review

1.   Find the areas of the figures depicted below:

a.

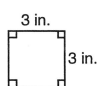

3 in.

3 in.

b.

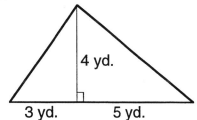

4 yd.

3 yd.   5 yd.

c.

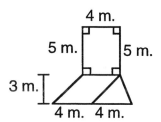

4 m.

5 m.   5 m.

3 m.

4 m. 4 m.

d.

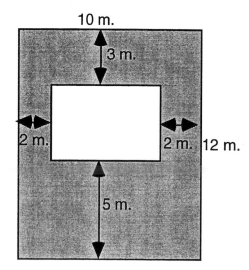

e.

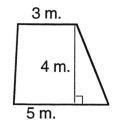

2.   If the area of a square is 12 sq. in, find the length of the sides. Find the perimeter of the square. Round the final answer to hundredths.

3.   Find the length of a rectangle if its width is 5 m. and its area is 105 m.^{2}.

4.   Find the base of a triangle with area 30 sq. cm. and altitude 10 cm.

5.   Find the base of a triangle with area 45 sq. ft. and altitude that is eight more than twice the base.

6.   Find the area of a triangle with base and altitude both equal to 9 in.

7.   In a parallelogram, find the altitude if the base is seven less than one-half the measure of the altitude and the area is 10 sq. cm. Round the final answer to hundredths.

8.   Find the area of a rhombus whose perimeter is 56 ft. and whose altitude is 3 ft.

9.   In a parallelogram, find the base and altitude if the base is $(4x + 1)$, the altitude is $(3x + 2)$, and the area is represented as $(12x^2 + 35)$.

10. In a trapezoid find the area if $b_1 = 25$ inches, $b_2 = 15$ inches and $h = 7$ inches.

11. In a trapezoid find the bases if the lower base is twice the upper base, the altitude is 9 inches and the area is 27 sq. in.

12. In a trapezoid find the altitude if the bases are 5 ft. and 13 ft. and the area is 11 sq.ft. Round the final answer to hundredths.

13. Jose' plans to paint a room that is 14 ft. by 12 ft. The walls are 7 ft. tall. He plans to paint the walls and not the ceiling. He plans to apply two coats of paint to each wall. Each gallon covers 200 sq. ft. and costs $15. Assuming the paint only comes in gallons, how many gallons will he need to do the job and how much will it cost?

14. Tonya has a garden which is a rectangle with a triangle on one end and a semicircle on the other. See diagram below.

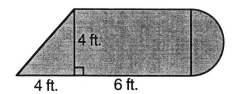

She plans to fertilize her garden. If 1 lb. of fertilizer will cover 20 sq. ft., how many 1 lb. bags does she need? (Use $\pi = 3.14$.)

15. Find the circumference and area of the following circles. Use $\pi = 3.14$ and round off the final answer to hundredths.

   a. $r = 2\frac{1}{3}$ cm.

   b. $r = 5\sqrt{2}$ ft.

   c. $d = 1.6$ dm.

   d. $d = 12$ in.

16. Find the radius in each of the following circles.

   a. $C = 6\pi$ m.

   b. $A = 25\pi$ sq. ft.

   c. $d = 9.4$ cm.

   d. $A = 128\pi$ sq. in. (Round off the final answer to hundredths.)

17.   A high school built a track field by putting a semicircle on one end of a rectangle. Find the area of the field to the nearest hundredth. (Use π = 3.14.)

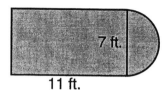

7 ft.

11 ft.

18.   Fill in the blanks with an appropriate word or phrase as discussed in this unit.

a. A _____ is the set of points a given distance from a fixed point. The given distance is a _____ of the circle and the fixed point is the _____.

b. If two radii are put together to form a straight line segment, this line segment is called a _____.

c. The _____ of a circle is the distance around the outer rim.

Unit 8

Planes in Space, Volume, and Surface Area

Learning Objectives:

1. The student will list the three methods to determine a plane.

   a. Three non-collinear points determine a plane.

   b. A line and a point not on that line determine a plane.

   c. Two intersecting lines determine a plane.

2. The student will demonstrate his mastery of the following definitions and concepts by writing them and by applying them to the solutions of selected problems.

   Definitions: coplanar, parallel planes, solid, prism, rectangular solid, cube, right pyramid, right circular cylinder, right circular cone, sphere, volume, and surface area.

   Concepts: 1. The intersection of two planes will form a straight line.

   2. Two lines perpendicular to the same plane are parallel.

   3. The intersection of a plane and a line not in that plane is a point.

3. Given real number values the student will compute the volume of each of the following: rectangular solid, right pyramid, right circular cylinder, right circular cone, and sphere.

4. Given real number values for all but one of the variables in the formula for a given volume the student will find the remaining variable.

5. Given real number values the student will compute the surface area of the following: rectangular solid, right pyramid, right circular cylinder, right circular cone, and sphere.

6. Given real number values for all but one of the variables in the formula for a given surface area, the student will find the remaining variable.

Planes in Space, Volume, and Surface Area

8.1   Planes in Space

A plane is a flat surface that extends indefinitely in every direction. A very crude representation of a plane is illustrated in Figure 8.1.

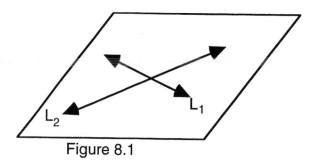

Figure 8.1

A plane is determined by the following methods:

a. Three non-collinear points will determine a plane.

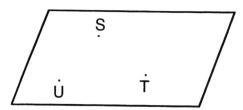

b. A line and a point not on that line will determine a plane.

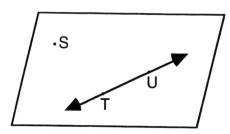

c. Two intersecting lines will determine a plane.

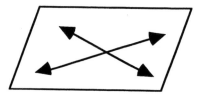

Definition 8.1	A set of points is <u>coplanar</u> if and only if all the points in the set lie in the same plane.

For example, the set of points of line L are coplanar to the plane P in Figure 8.2.

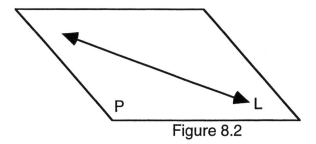

Figure 8.2

1. Points G and H lie in plane P. Is line L_1 in plane P? Tell why or why not.

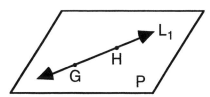

1. Yes, points G and H determine line L_1. Since G and H lie in plane P, then L_1 lies in plane P.

2. From the illustration, which line is not in plane Q? Tell why.

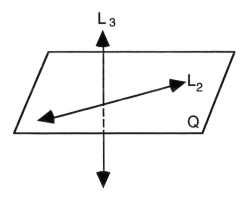

2. L_3 is not in plane Q. Not all the points in L_3 belong to the plane.

3. From the illustration, is P in the same plane as lines L_4 and L_5?

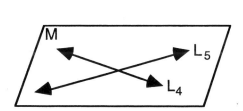

3. No, point P is not contained in plane M.

Planes, just as with lines, may intersect or may be parallel.

Definition 8.2 Two planes are parallel if they do not intersect.

Planes K and M are parallel to one another.

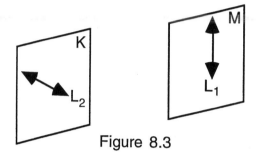

Figure 8.3

4. If two lines lie in parallel planes, are the lines necessarily themselves parallel?

4. No, the lines may be skew. See L_1 and L_2 in Figure 8.3.

Concept 8.1 If two planes intersect , the intersection will form a straight line.

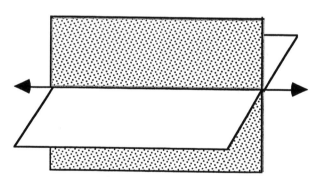

You can observe this in your environment by tracing the intersection of a wall of a room with the ceiling, by tracing the intersection of a side and top of a box, etc.

Concept 8.2 Two lines perpendicular to the same plane are parallel.

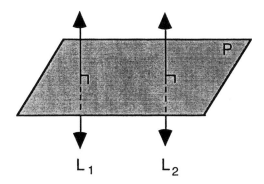

The vertical pieces of molding around a door are perpendicular to the floor. If the distance between these pieces of molding is measured, then the distance is always the same. (The strips of molding are parallel.)

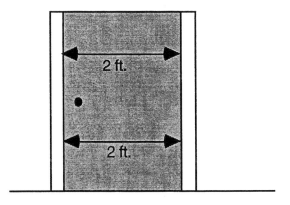

Concept 8.3	The intersection of a plane and a line not in that plane is a point.

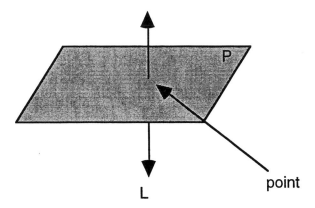

Take a sheet of paper (a plane) and a pencil (a line) and push the pencil through the paper. Pull the pencil out and observe the hole. The hole represents a "point".

Exercise 8.1

1. Indicate whether each statement is true or false.

   a. Two lines parallel to the same plane may be perpendicular to each other.

   b. Two intersecting planes form a straight line.

   c. If a line and a plane are parallel, then every line in the plane is parallel to the given line.

2. Complete the following sentences by filling in the blank with an appropriate work or phrase.

   a. A plane is determined by three _____ points.

   b. A plane is determined by a line and _____ .

3. Describe the intersection of each of the following:

   a. Two intersecting planes form _____ .

   b. A plane intersecting a line not in that plane forms a

      _____ .

8.2   Introduction to Volume and Surface Area

The geometric figures we have considered this far are two dimensional and fit in a plane. The geometric figures we will consider in this unit are three dimensional and occupy space.

Definition 8.3   A <u>solid</u> is a closed portion of space bounded by planes and/ or curved surfaces.

The following are examples of solids.

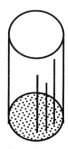
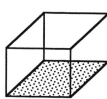
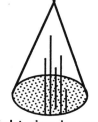

right circular cylinder rectangular solid right circular cone

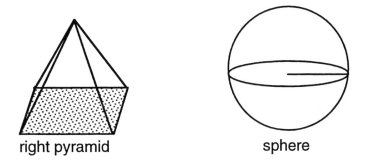

right pyramid   sphere

In solid geometry, we disregard the color, surface texture, and weight of the solid object. We are more concerned about the relationships of these solid objects to one another than their properties such as size and shape.

Definition 8.4   A prism is a solid bounded by planes on all sides.

The figure to the right is an example of a prism.

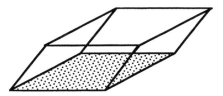

Definition 8.5   The volume of a solid is the measure of capacity and represents the space inside a solid. The volume equals the product of the area of the base and the altitude of the solid.

The volume of any spatial figure is the number of unit cubes that can fit into the solid figure.

8.3   Volume and Surface Area of a Rectangular Solid

Definition 8.6   A rectangular solid is a prism with each set of consecutive sides formed by perpendicular planes.

A set of rectangles can be bounded together to form a rectangular solid. See the figure below.

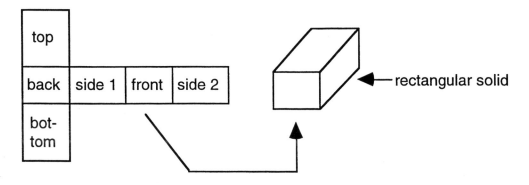

Definition 8.7	A <u>cube</u> is a rectangular solid where all of its sides are equal in measure.

The figure to
the right is
an example
of a cube.

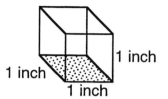

1 inch

1 inch

1 inch

Postulate 8.1	The volume, V, of a rectangular solid equals the product of the length, (L), width (W), and the height (H).

$$V = LWH$$

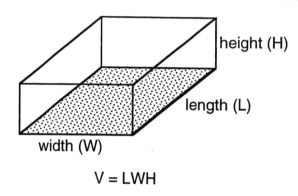

height (H)

length (L)

width (W)

$$V = LWH$$

Let's look at the volume of a rectangular solid 4 inches by 3 inches by 3 inches.

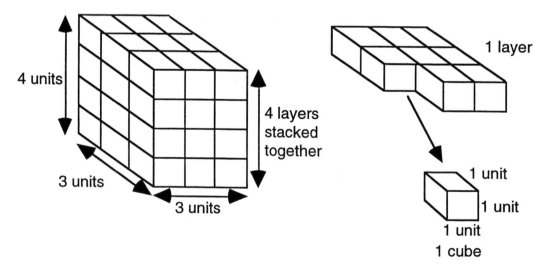

4 units

3 units

3 units

4 layers
stacked
together

1 layer

1 unit

1 unit

1 unit

1 cube

Notice there are 36 cubes in the solid. Therefore, the volume is 36 cubic units.

By the formula, $V = LWH$, the volume of this cube is $V = 4 \cdot 3 \cdot 3$ cubic units.

Example:

Find the volume of the following rectangular solid.

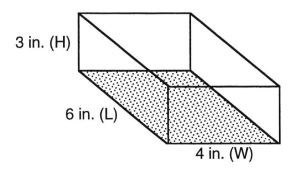

$V = LWH$

$V = (6 \text{ in.})(4 \text{ in.})(3 \text{ in.})$

$V = 72 \text{ cubic inches } = 72 \text{ cu. in. } = 72 \text{ in.}^3$

5. Find the volume of a rectangular solid with length = 3 cm., width equal 4 cm., and height = 2 cm.

5.
$V = (3 \text{ cm.})(4 \text{ cm.})(2 \text{ cm.})$
$V = 24 \text{ cu. cm. or}$
$V = 24 \text{ cm.}^3$

6. Find the volume of a rectangular solid with

$L = \dfrac{1}{2}$ ft., W = 5 ft., and H = 3 ft.

6.

$V = \left(\dfrac{1}{2} \text{ ft.}\right)(5 \text{ ft.})(3 \text{ ft.})$

$V = \dfrac{15}{2} \text{ ft.}^3$

$V = 7\dfrac{1}{2} \text{cu.ft. or } 7.5 \text{ cu.ft.}$

7. A rectangular glass fish tank, 4 ft. by 2 ft. by 3 ft., is filled with water. What is the volume of the tank?

7.
$V = (4 \text{ ft.})(2 \text{ ft.})(3 \text{ ft.})$
$V = 24 \text{ cu. ft. or } 24 \text{ ft.}^3$

Example:

If the volume of a rectangular solid is $8\dfrac{2}{3}$ cu. in., find the height given the

width is 13 in. and the length is $1\dfrac{1}{3}$ in.

$$V = LWH$$

$$8\frac{2}{3} = \left(1\frac{1}{3}\right)(13)H$$

$$\frac{26}{3} = \left(\frac{4}{3}\right)(13)H$$

$$\frac{26}{3} = \frac{52}{3}H$$

$$3\left(\frac{26}{3}\right) = 3\left(\frac{52}{3}\right)H$$

$$26 = 52H$$

$$\frac{26}{52} = H$$

$$\frac{1}{2}\ \text{in.} = H$$

$$0.5\ \text{in.} = H$$

Definition 8.8	The <u>surface area of a rectangular solid</u> is the sum of the areas of the six rectangles that are its sides.

Postulate 8.2	The surface area, A of a rectangular solid is given by the formula $A = 2LW + 2WH + 2LH$ where L is the length, W is the width, and H is the height.

Example:

Find the surface area of the rectangular solid in the figure below.

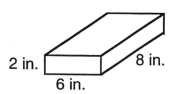

2 in.   6 in.   8 in.

$$A = 2LW + 2WH + 2LH$$
$$A = 2\cdot6\cdot8 + 2\cdot8\cdot2 + 2\cdot6\cdot2$$
$$A = 96 + 32 + 24$$
$$A = 152\ \text{sq. in. or } 152\ \text{in.}^2$$

8. Find the surface area of a rectangular solid with dimensions L = 6 ft., W = 5 ft., $H = 2\frac{1}{2}$ ft.

8.
$$A = 2\cdot6\cdot5 + 2\cdot5\cdot2\frac{1}{2} + 2\cdot6\cdot2\frac{1}{2}$$
$$A = 60 + 10\cdot\frac{5}{2} + 12\cdot\frac{5}{2}$$
$$A = 60 + 25 + 30$$
$$A = 115\ \text{sq. ft.}$$

Example:

Find the length of a rectangular solid with surface area of 90 sq. ft., width equal to 5 ft. and height equal to 2 ft.

$$90 = 2 \cdot L \cdot 5 + 2 \cdot 5 \cdot 2 + 2 \cdot L \cdot 2$$
$$90 = 10L + 20 + 4L$$
$$70 = 14L$$
$$5 \text{ ft.} = L$$

9. The surface area of a box is 128 sq. ft. The width is 6 ft. and the height is 4 ft. Find the length of the box.

9.
$$128 = 2 \cdot L \cdot 6 + 2 \cdot 6 \cdot 4 + 2 \cdot L \cdot 4$$
$$128 = 12L + 48 + 8L$$
$$128 = 20L + 48$$
$$80 = 20L$$
$$4 \text{ ft.} = L$$

Exercise 8.2

1. Name at least four examples of rectangular solids in your environment.

2. Find the volume and surface area of the following rectangular solids. Round the final answer to tenths.

   a. L = 5 ft., W = 4 ft., H = 7 ft.

   b. L = $2\sqrt{2}$ m., W = $5\sqrt{2}$ m., H = 3 m.

   c. L = $1\frac{1}{2}$ cm., W = 3 cm., H = $4\frac{1}{4}$ cm.

3. Find the length of a rectangular solid if the volume is 56 cu. dm., the width is 7 dm., and the height is 2 dm.

4. Find the width of a rectangular solid if the volume is $16\frac{2}{3}$ cu. ft., the length is $1\frac{2}{3}$ ft., and the height is 5 ft.

5. Find the length of a rectangular solid if the volume is $48\sqrt{6}$ cu. in., the width is $2\sqrt{2}$ in., and the height is $4\sqrt{3}$ in.

6.   The Jones family put a swimming pool in their backyard with length 25 ft., width 15 ft., and a uniform depth of 5 ft. Find the volume of the pool. (The pool is the shape of a rectangular solid.)

7.   Max wants to paint his wooden tool box black. If his tool box is 3 ft. long, 2 ft., wide and 2.5 ft. deep, find the surface area of the box. If he plans to use two coats of paint and a small can of paint covers 40 sq. ft., how many small cans of paint must he buy? (He can not buy a piece of a can.)

8.   If the surface area of a box is 280 sq. in., the width is 6 in., and the length is 10 in., find the height.

9.   Lucy's Publishing Company packs books in cubical shipping boxes 3 feet on each side. How many shipping boxes can be put in a moving van that has packing volume of 2025 cubic feet?

10. A freezer has inside dimensions of 6 feet, 4 feet and 2.5 feet. How many cubic feet of space are inside the freezer?

8.4 <u>Volume and Surface Area of a Right Pyramid</u>

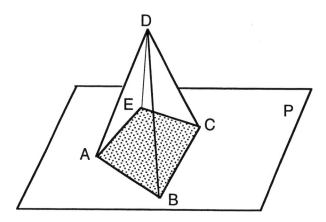

Given plane P with point D not in the plane and quadrilateral ABCE in P. The set of all line segments that join point D to a point of the quadrilateral ABCE form a pyramid. Quadrilateral ABCE is called the <u>base</u> of the pyramid. Note: The base of a pyramid may be any closed figure with line segments as sides. Therefore, a pyramid may have a base with three, four, or more sides.

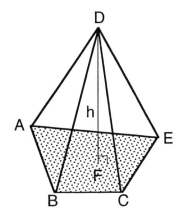

The <u>altitude</u> of the pyramid is the perpendicular line segment joining its vertex D to the base. $\overline{DF}$ (h) is the altitude.

We will confine our study to pyramids that have rectangular, square or triangular bases.

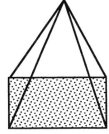

rectangular base

square base

triangular base

Postulate 8.3   The volume, V, of a pyramid is given by the formula
$$V = \frac{1}{3}Bh$$
where B is the area of its base and h is its height.

Example:

Find the volume of a pyramid with rectangular base of length 6 ft. and width 4 ft. The height of the pyramid is 5 ft.

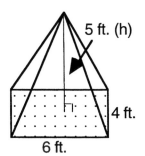

5 ft. (h)

4 ft.

6 ft.

B = Area of a rectangle

B = LW

B = 6·4

B = 24 sq. ft.

$V = \frac{1}{3}Bh$

$V = \frac{1}{3}·24·5$

V = 40 cu. ft.

Example:

Find the volume of a pyramid with a triangular base and height of 10 cm. The triangular base has height of 3 cm. and a base of 4 cm.

B = Area of a triangle

$B = \dfrac{1}{2} \cdot base \cdot height$

$B = \dfrac{1}{2} \cdot 4 \cdot 3$

$B = 6$ sq. cm.

$V = \dfrac{1}{3} Bh$

$V = \dfrac{1}{3} \cdot 6 \cdot 10$

$V = 20$ cu. ft.

Example:

The volume of a pyramid with a 6 in. by 6 in. square base is 72 cu. in. Find the height.

B = Area of a square

B = 6·6

B = 36 sq. in.

$V = \dfrac{1}{3} Bh$

$72 = \dfrac{1}{3} \cdot 36 \cdot h$

$72 = 12h$

6 in. = h

10. Find the volume of a right pyramid with a rectangular base having dimension, $L = 2\dfrac{5}{7}$ in.

and W = 12 in. The height of the pyramid is 10 in. Round your answer to tenths.

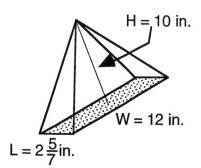

H = 10 in.

W = 12 in.

$L = 2\dfrac{5}{7}$ in.

10.

$B = 2\dfrac{5}{7} \cdot 12 = \dfrac{228}{7}$

$V = \dfrac{1}{3} Bh$

$V = \dfrac{1}{3}\left(\dfrac{228}{7} \text{ sq.in.}\right)(10 \text{ in.})$

$V = \dfrac{2280}{21}$

$V = 108\dfrac{12}{21}$ cu. in.

$V = 108\dfrac{4}{7}$ or 108.6 in.^{3}

11. Find the volume of a right pyramid if the rectangular base has L = 15 m. and W = 4 m. The height of the pyramid is 20 m.

11.

$$V = \frac{1}{3}Bh$$

$$B = 15 \cdot 4 = 60 \text{ sq.m.}$$

$$V = \frac{1}{3}(60 \text{ sq.m.})(20 \text{ m.})$$

$$V = 400 \text{ m.}^3$$

12. Find the height of a right pyramid if the volume is 24 cu. ft., and the rectangular base has L = 4 ft. and W = 6 ft.

12.

$$V = \frac{1}{3}Bh$$

$$B = 4 \cdot 6 = 24 \text{ sq.ft.}$$

$$24 \text{ft.}^3 = \frac{1}{3}(24 \text{ sq.ft.})h$$

$$24 \text{ft.}^3 = 8 \text{ ft.}^2 h$$

$$3 \text{ ft.} = h$$

13. Find the volume of a pyramid that has a square base with perimeter 16 cm. and its altitude is 7 cm. Round your answer to tenths.

13.

$$B = s^2 = 4^2 = 16 \text{ sq.cm.}$$

$$V = \frac{1}{3}(16 \text{ sq.cm.})(7 \text{ cm.})$$

$$V = \frac{1}{3}(112 \text{ cu.cm.})$$

$$V = 37\frac{1}{3} \text{ cu.cm.}$$

or 37.3 cm.^{3}

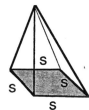

Perimeter = 4s

16 = 4s

4 cm. = s

14. The base of a pyramid is a triangle with area 16 sq. ft. If the height is 4 ft., find the volume to the nearest tenth.

14.

$$V = \frac{1}{3} \cdot 16 \cdot 4$$

$$V = \frac{64}{3}$$

$$V = 21\frac{1}{3} = 21.3 \text{ cu. ft.}$$

> **Postulate 8.4** The surface area of a right pyramid is the sum of the areas of its sides plus the base.

Example:

Find the surface area of a right pyramid with a square base. The square base has side of length 9 cm. The height of each triangular side of the pyramid is 12 cm.

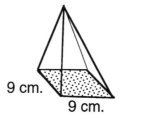

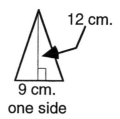

12 cm.

9 cm.
9 cm.

9 cm.
one side

$$\text{Area of base} = 9 \cdot 9 = 81 \text{ sq. cm.}$$

$$\text{Area of one side} = \frac{1}{2} \cdot 9 \cdot 12 = 54 \text{ sq. cm.}$$

There are four triangular sides.

$$\text{Total area} = \text{Area of four sides} + \text{Base}$$
$$= 4 \cdot 54 + 81$$
$$= 216 + 81$$
$$= 297 \text{ sq. cm. or } 297 \text{ cm.}^2$$

15. Find the surface area of a right pyramid with a square base. The square base has side of length 10 in. The height of each triangular side of the pyramid is 14 in.

15. Area of square the square base = (10)(10) = 100 sq.in.
Area of one triangular side =
$$\frac{1}{2} \cdot 10 \cdot 14 = 70 \text{ sq.in.}$$
There are four sides.
4(70) = 280 sq. in.
Surface area =
100 + 280 =
380 sq. in.

Exercise 8.3

1. Find the volume of the following pyramids with rectangular bases. Round off to tenths.

    a. L = $2\sqrt{3}$ in., W = $\sqrt{3}$ in., h = 4 in.

    b. L = $6\sqrt{7}$ m., W = $2\sqrt{7}$ m., h = $\sqrt{7}$ m.

2. In a pyramid with a rectangular base, if:

    a. V = $\dfrac{5}{6}$ cu.in., L = $\dfrac{1}{2}$ in., W = $\dfrac{3}{4}$ in., find h. Round off to tenths.

    b. V = $2\dfrac{5}{6}$ cu.cm., W = $1\dfrac{1}{8}$ cm., h = $2\dfrac{1}{3}$ cm., find L. Round off to tenths.

3. Find the height of a pyramid that has a rectangular base with L = 6 in. and W = 7 in. The volume of the pyramid is 180 cubic inches. Round off to tenths.

4. A pyramid has a triangular base. The triangular base has height of 7 in. and base of 6 in. If the height of the pyramid is 8 in., find the volume.

5. Give at least four examples of pyramids in your environment.

6. Find the surface area of the following pyramids with square bases.

    a. Side of square = 8 cm.; height of triangular side = 10 cm.

    b. Side of square = 4.5 in.; height of triangular side = 8.1 in. Round off to tenths.

8.5 Volume and Surface Area of a Right Circular Cylinder

A cylinder is a solid with a circle as top and bottom and a rectangle as its sides.

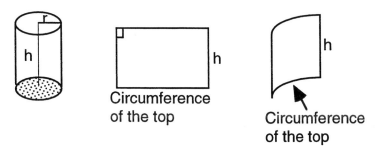

Circumference
of the top

Circumference
of the top

Postulate 8.5   The volume, V, of a right circular cylinder is given by the formula, $V = \pi r^2 h$, where r is the radius of the cylinder and h is the height.

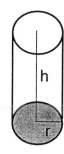

$$V = \pi r^2 h$$

Example:

Find the volume of the following right circular cylinder to the nearest hundredth. Use $\pi = 3.14$.

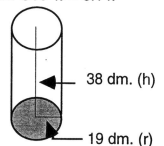

38 dm. (h)

19 dm. (r)

$V = \pi r^2 h$

$V = \pi (19\ dm.)^2 (38\ dm.)$

$V = \pi (361\ sq.dm.)(38\ dm.)$

$V = 13{,}718\pi$ cu. dm.

$V = 43{,}074.52$ cu. dm.

16. Find the volume of the given right circular cylinder to the nearest tenth. Use $\pi = 3.14$.

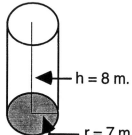

h = 8 m.

r = 7 m.

16.

$V = \pi r^2 h$

$V = \pi (7\ m.)^2 (8\ m.)$

$V = \pi (49\ sq.m.)(8\ m.)$

$V = 392\pi\ m.^3$

$V = 1{,}230.9\ m.^3$

17. Find the radius of a right circular cylinder if the volume is $6{,}480\ \pi$ cu. in. and h = 20 in.

17.

$6{,}480\pi\ in.^3 = \pi r^2 (20\ in.)$

$\dfrac{6480\pi\ in.^3}{20\pi\ in.} = \dfrac{\pi r^2 (20\ in.)}{20\pi\ in.}$

$324\ in.^2 = r^2$

$\sqrt{324\ in.^2} = r$

$18\ in. = r$

18. Two jars of the same brand of peanut butter stand on a shelf in a grocery store. The shorter jar has $\frac{1}{2}$ the height of the other jar but the diameter is twice the taller jar. Which jar has the greatest volume?

(Dimensions are given in the illustration. Round answers to the nearest tenth.)

18. $V_{s.j.} = \pi(2)^2\left(2\frac{1}{2}\right)$

$V_{s.j.} = 10\pi$

$V_{s.j.} = 31.4$ in.^{3}

$V_{l.j.} = \pi(1)^2(5)$

$V_{l.j.} = 5\pi$

$V_{l.j.} = 15.7$ in.^{3}

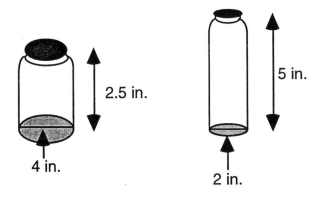

The shorter jar has the larger volume.

Postulate 8.6   The surface area, A, of a right circular cylinder is given by the formula, $A = 2\pi rh + 2\pi r^2$, where r is the radius of the cylinder and h is its height.

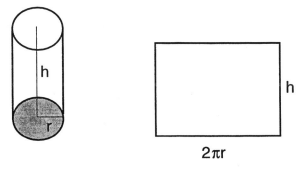

Area of the top of the cylinder $= \pi r^2$

Area of the bottom of the cylinder $= \pi r^2$

Area of the side of the cylinder $= 2\pi rh$

Therefore, the total surface area is $A = 2\pi rh + 2\pi r^2$

Example:

Find the surface area to the nearest tenth of a right circular cylinder with r = 6 cm. and h = 8 cm. Use π = 3.14 and round the answer to the nearest tenth.

$$A = 2\pi rh + 2\pi r^2$$
$$A = 2(3.14)(6)(8) + 2(3.14)(6^2)$$
$$A = 301.44 + 226.08$$
$$A = 527.5 \text{ sq. cm.}$$

19.

Find the surface area to the nearest tenth of a right circular cylinder with r = 5 in. and h = 7 in. Use π = 3.14 and round your answer to tenths.

19.
$$A = 2\pi rh + 2\pi r^2$$
$$A = 2(3.14)(5)(7) + 2(3.14)(5^2)$$
$$A = 219.8 + 157$$
$$A = 376.8 \text{ sq. in.}$$

Exercise 8.4

1. Find the volume and surface area of the following right circular cylinders. Use π = 3.14 and round the answer to the nearest tenth.

  a. r = 5 in., h = 12 in.

  b. r = 6 yd., h = 10 yd.

  c. diameter = 7 ft., h = 10 ft.

2. In a cylinder find r or h as indicated. Round answers to the nearest tenth.

  a. V = 1000 π cu. in., r = 10 in., find h.

  b. V = 448 π cu. cm., h = 7 cm., find r.

  c. V = 720 π cu. yd., r = 6 yd., find h.

  d. V = 96 π cu. ft., h = 6 ft., find r.

  e. V = $6\sqrt{2}$ π cu. m., h = $2\sqrt{2}$ m., find r.

3. Name at least four examples of right circular cylinders in your environment.

4. A cylindrical storage tank has a height of 25 ft. and a volume of 3600 π cu. ft. Find the radius of the base.

5.   One cylindrical oil tank has radius 5 ft. and height 6 ft. A second cylindrical tank has radius 4 ft. and height 8 ft. Which tank has the larger volume? How much larger? Which tank has the larger surface area? How much larger? Round answers to hundredths before comparing.

8.6 Volume and Surface Area of a Right Circular Cone

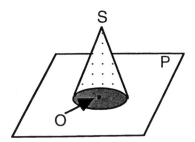

Given plane P with point S not in the plane and circle O in P. The set of all segments that join S to a point of the circle O form a cone. The circle O is called the base of the cone.

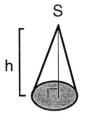

The altitude of the cone is the perpendicular line segment joining its vertex S to the plane of its base.

Postulate 8.7   The volume, V, of a right circular cone is given by the formula

$$V = \frac{1}{3}\pi r^2 h$$

where r is the radius of the base and h is the altitude of the cone.

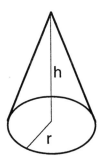

The altitude is h.

The radius is r.

Example:

Find the volume of the following right circular cone. Use $\pi = 3.14$ and round to the nearest tenth.

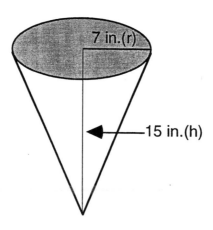

$$V = \frac{1}{3}\pi r^2 h$$

$$V = \frac{1}{3}\pi(7 \text{ in.})^2(15 \text{ in.})$$

$$V = \frac{1}{3}\pi(49 \text{ sq. in.})(15 \text{ in.})$$

$$V = 245\pi \text{ cu. in.}$$

$$V = 769.3 \text{ cu.in.}$$

20. Find the volume to the nearest tenth of a cone with diameter of 10 in. and height of 6 in. Use $\pi = 3.14$.

   a. Find the radius

   b. Find the volume.

20.

   a.
$$d = 2r$$
$$10 = 2r$$
$$5 = r$$

   b.
$$V = \frac{1}{3}\pi r^2 h$$

$$V = \frac{1}{3}\pi(5 \text{ in.})^2(6 \text{ in.})$$

$$V = \frac{1}{3}\pi(25 \text{ in.}^2)(6 \text{ in.})$$

$$V = 50\pi \text{ cu. in.}$$

$$V = 157.0 \text{ cu.in.}$$

21. A conical tank is $10\frac{1}{2}$ ft. deep and its circular top has a radius of 3 ft. How many cubic feet of water will it hold? Round the final answer to the nearest tenth.

21.

$$V = \frac{1}{3}\pi r^2 h$$

$$V = \frac{1}{3}\pi(3)^2\left(10\frac{1}{2}\right)$$

$$V = \underline{\hspace{2cm}}$$

$$V = 31\frac{1}{2}\pi \text{ cu. ft.}$$

$$V = 98.9 \text{ cu. ft.}$$

22. Find the height if the volume of a right circular cone is 500π cu. in. and r = 10 in.

22.

$$V = \frac{1}{3}\pi r^2 h$$

$$500\pi = \frac{1}{3}\pi(10)^2 h$$

$$500\pi = \frac{1}{3}\pi 100 h$$

$$3 \cdot 500\pi = 3 \cdot \frac{1}{3}\pi 100 h$$

$$1500\pi = 100\pi h$$

$$15 \text{ in.} = h$$

Postulate 8.8 The surface area, A, of a right circular cone is given by the formula

$$A = \pi rs + \pi r^2$$

where r is the radius of the base and s is its slant height.

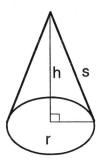

The height of the cone is h.
The radius of the base is r.
The slant height is s.
In a right circular cone
by the Pythagorean
Theorem $r^2 + h^2 = s^2$.

Example:

Find the surface area of a right circular cone with base of diameter 6 cm. and slant height of 8 cm. Use $\pi = 3.14$ and round the final answer to the nearest tenth.

$$d = 6 \text{ cm.}$$

$$r = 3 \text{ cm.}$$

$$A = \pi rs + \pi r^2$$
$$A = (3.14)(3)(8) + (3.14)(3)(3)$$
$$A = 75.36 + 28.26$$
$$A = 103.6 \text{ sq. cm.}$$

23. Find the surface area of a right circular cone with base of circumference 4π in. and slant height of 5 in. Use $\pi = 3.14$ and round to the nearest tenth.

23.

$$C = \pi d$$
$$4\pi = \pi d$$
$$4 = d$$
$$2 = r$$
$$A = \pi rs + \pi r^2$$
$$A = \pi(2)(5) + \pi(2)^2$$
$$A = 31.4 + 12.56$$
$$A = 44.0 \text{ sq. in.}$$

Exercise 8.5

1. Find the volume and surface area of the following right circular cones. Round the final answer to tenths.

    a. $r = 6$ m., $h = 8$ m., $s = 10$ m.

    b. $r = 2\sqrt{2}$ in., $h = 2\sqrt{2}$ in., $s = 4$ in.

    c. $d = 10$ cm., $h = 5$ cm., $s = 5\sqrt{2}$ cm.

    d. $C = 16\pi$ mm., $h = 6$ mm., $s = 10$ mm.

2. In a right circular cone if:

    a. $V = 75\pi$ cu. in., $h = 9$ in., find r.

    b. $V = 96\pi$ cu. ft., $h = 8$ ft., find r.

    c. $V = 196\pi$ cu. yd., $r = 7$ yd., find h.

    d. $V = \dfrac{200}{3}\pi$ cu. m., $h = 8$ m., find r.

e. $V = 15\sqrt{2}\pi$ cu. cm., $h = 5\sqrt{2}$ cm., find r.

f. $A = 21\pi$ sq. cm., $r = 3$ cm., find s.

3. A conical ant hill is 4 inches high with a base of 6π in. in circumference. Find the total volume of dirt (to the nearest tenth) that the hill contains.

4. Alice serves jello in a conical bowl that has a diameter of 4 in. If the bowl is 3 in. deep, how many cubic inches of jello are in the bowl? (Round to the nearest tenth.)

5. Name at least four examples of cones in your environment.

6. The circumference of the base of a cone is 6π cm. If the cone has slant height of 5 cm., find the surface area. (Round to the nearest tenth.)

8.7 Volume and Surface Area of a Sphere

In space, the set of all points at a given distance from a given point is called a
<u>sphere</u> having the given point as center.

Postulate 8.9   The volume, V, of a sphere is given by the formula
$$V = \frac{4}{3}\pi r^3$$
where r is the radius of the sphere.

Example:

Find the volume of a sphere with radius 4 ft. Round your answer to
tenths.

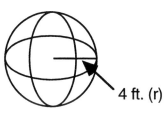

4 ft. (r)

$$V = \frac{4}{3}\pi r^3$$

$$V = \frac{4}{3}\pi(4 \text{ ft.})^3$$

$$V = \frac{4}{3}\pi\left(64 \text{ ft.}^3\right)$$

$$V = 85\frac{1}{3}\pi \text{ cu. ft. or ft.}^3$$

$$V = 267.9 \text{ ft.}^3$$

24. In a sphere if r = 5 m., find the volume to the nearest tenth.

24.

$$V = \frac{4}{3}\pi r^3$$

$$V = \frac{4}{3}\pi(5 \text{ m.})^3$$

$$V = \frac{4}{3}\pi\left(125 \text{ m.}^3\right)$$

$$V = 166\frac{2}{3}\pi \text{ m.}^3$$

$$V = 523.3 \text{ m.}^3$$

25. In a sphere if d = 3 cm., find the volume to the nearest tenth.

25.

$$2r = d$$

$$2r = 3$$

$$r = \frac{3}{2}$$

$$V = \frac{4}{3}\pi r^3$$

$$V = \frac{4}{3}\pi\left(\frac{3}{2}\right)^3$$

$$V = \frac{4}{3}\pi\left(\frac{27}{8}\right)$$

$$V = 4\frac{1}{2}\pi \text{ cm.}^3$$

$$V = 14.1 \text{ cm.}^3$$

26. In a sphere if V = $1333\frac{1}{3}\pi$ cu. ft., find the radius.

26. $V = \frac{4}{3}\pi r^3$

$$1333\frac{1}{3}\pi = \frac{4}{3}\pi r^3$$

$$\frac{4000}{3}\pi = \frac{4}{3}\pi r^3$$

$$3 \cdot \frac{4000}{3}\pi = 3 \cdot \frac{4}{3}\pi r^3$$

$$4000\pi = 4\pi r^3$$

$$\frac{4000\pi}{4\pi} = \frac{4\pi r^3}{4\pi}$$

$$1000 = r^3$$

$$10 \text{ ft.} = r$$

27. A spherical storage tank has radius 6 ft.

What is its volume in cubic feet? Round

your final answer to the nearest tenth.

27. $V = \frac{4}{3}\pi r^3$

$V = \frac{4}{3}\pi \cdot 216$

$V = 288\pi$ cu. ft.

$V = 904.3$ cu. ft.

Postulate 8.10   The surface area, A, of a sphere is given by the formula
$$A = 4\pi r^2$$
where r is the radius of the sphere.

Example:

Find the surface area of a sphere with diameter of 8 cm. Round your
answer to the nearest tenth.

$$d = 8$$
$$r = 4$$
$$A = 4\pi r^2$$
$$A = 4(3.14)(4)^2$$
$$= 201.0 \text{ sq. ft.}$$

28. Find the surface area of a sphere with $r = 3$ in.
Round the answer to tenths.

28.

$$A = 4\pi r^2$$

$$A = 4(3.14)(3)^2$$

$$A = 113.0 \text{ sq. in.}$$

29. How much material is needed to manufacture a balloon with radius of 5 ft.?

29.

$$A = 4\pi r^2$$
$$A = 4(3.14)(5)^2$$
$$A = 100\pi$$
$$A = 314 \text{ sq. ft.}$$

Exercise 8.6

1. Find the volume and surface area of the following spheres. Use $\pi = 3.14$ and round the final answer to the nearest tenth.

   a. $r = 3$ cm.

   b. $d = 12$ in.

   c. $r = 1.5$ ft.

   d. $r = 1\frac{3}{4}$ yd.

2. If the surface area, A, of a sphere is 4π sq. in., find r.

3. A jeweler wishes to make a hollow gold bead. The radius of the outside sphere is 3 mm. The radius for the inside sphere is 2 mm. What volume of gold is needed to make one bead? What volume of gold would be needed to make ten beads? Use $\pi = 3.14$ and round the final answer to the nearest tenth.

Section 8.8   Formulae Summary

In summary, the formulae you have studied in this unit are as follows:

Figure	Volume Formula
Rectangular Solid	$V = LWH$
Right Pyramid	$V = \frac{1}{3}Bh$
Right Circular Cylinder	$V = \pi r^2 h$
Right Circular Cone	$V = \frac{1}{3}\pi r^2 h$

Sphere	$V = \dfrac{4}{3}\pi r^3$

Figure	Surface Area Formula
Rectangular Solid	$A = 2LW + 2WH + 2LH$
Right Pyramid	Sum of the areas of its sides plus the area of the base.
Right Circular Cylinder	$A = 2\pi rh + 2\pi r^2$
Right Circular Cone	$A = \pi rs + \pi r^2$
Sphere	$A = 4\pi r^2$

Unit 8 Review

1. Find the volume and surface area of each of the following. Use $\pi = 3.14$ and round the final answer to the nearest tenth.

   a. right circular cylinder, d= 14 in., h = 5 in.

   b. right circular cone, r = 3 cm., h = 9 cm., s = $3\sqrt{10}$ cm.

   c. sphere, r = 9 dm.

2. Find the missing values.

   a. A right pyramid has volume 54 cu. yd. If its square base has a side measuring 4 yards, find h.

   b. A right circular cylinder has volume of $6\sqrt{2}\pi$ cu. m. If h = $3\sqrt{2}$ m., find r.

   c. A rectangular solid had volume of 728 cu. ft. If the length is 8 ft. and the width is $6\dfrac{1}{2}$ ft., find h.

3. Define the following terms:

   a. coplanar points

   b. volume

    c. parallel planes

    d. surface area

4.   Complete the following:

    a. The intersection of two planes forms a _____.

    b. The intersection of a plane and a sphere forms a _____.

    c. A plane intersecting a line not in that planes forms a _____.

5.   If a cylindrical pipe has the dimensions given in the diagram, find the radius and the volume of the material that is stored in the inner core. Use $\pi = 3.14$ and round the final answer to the nearest hundredth.

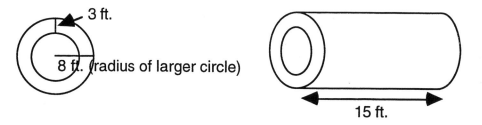

6.   An ice cream cone has inside dimensions 5 inches deep and 3 inches across the top. What volume of solid ice cream will the cone hold without overflowing? Use $\pi = 3.14$ and round the final answer to the nearest hundredth.

7.   Find the total volume of the solids shown below:

    a. The bottom of the figure is a rectangular solid. The top part is half of a cylinder. Use $\pi = 3.14$ and round the final answer to the nearest hundredth.

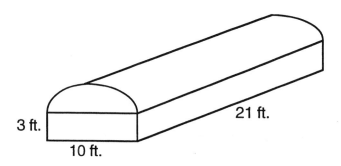

    b. The top and bottom of this figure are both right pyramids. The rectangular base (shaded portion) has length of 7 in. and width of 6 in. This base is common to both pyramids. The heights of each pyramid are shown in the drawing on the following page. Find the total volume of the figure.

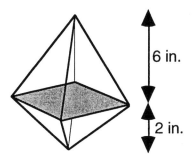

8. A metal ball has radius of 2 in. and a right cylindrical drinking glass is 6 in. tall with an inside radius of 2.5 in. Find the volume of each item. If the metal ball is dropped into the tall glass and the glass filled with water, determine what volume of water is needed. Round the final answer to tenths.

9. A homeowner wishes to pour enough concrete to form four steps leading to his front door. If the dimensions are given below, what volume of concrete would he need? (Each step has the same measure. Each step is a rectangular solid.)

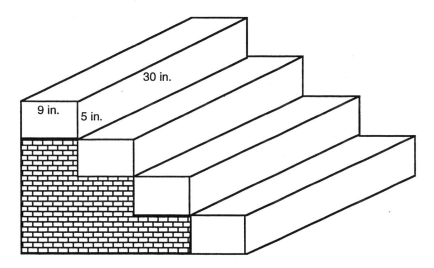

10. Ben has 10 party hats left over from a New Year's party. St. Patrick's Day is coming up and he plans to have another party but cannot afford new hats. He plans to buy green paint to paint the hats. Each hat is a cone with diameter 6 in. and slant height of 9 in. One coat of paint will be sufficient to do the job. If one jar of paint will paint 125 sq. in., how many jars will he need to buy?

Unit 9

Pythagorean Theorem With Applications

Learning Objectives:

The student will demonstrate his mastery of the following theorems and converse by writing them and by applying them to solutions of selected problems.

Theorem   In a right triangle with sides a, b, and c, the hypotenuse squared is equal to the sum of the squares of the sides. $\left(a^2 + b^2 = c^2\right)$

Converse   In a triangle with sides a, b, and c, if $a^2 + b^2 = c^2$, then the triangle is a right triangle.

Theorem   In a 30°-60° right triangle, the length of the side opposite the 30° angle is x. The length of the hypotenuse is twice x and the length of the side opposite the 60° angle is x multiplied by $\sqrt{3}$.

Theorem   In an isosceles right triangle, the hypotenuse is $\sqrt{2}$ times the length of one side.

Pythagorean Theorem With Applications

9.1   Introduction

One of the best known theorems in mathematics is probably this one, the Pythagorean Theorem. This theorem states that if unit squares are drawn on each of the three sides of a right triangle, the number of squares formed on the hypotenuse will equal in quantity to the sum of the square units formed on the other two sides.

The right triangle below has sides 3, 4, and 5 units. Squares A, B, and C are formed at each side. Notice that he sum of the squares A and B equal in number to the square C.

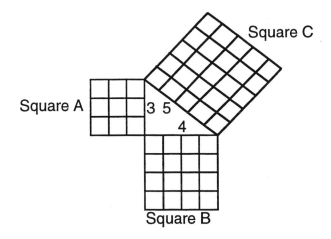

1.   a. Square A has _____ blocks.   1. a. 9
     b. Square B has _____ blocks.   b. 16
     c. Square C has _____ blocks.   c. 25

Note: The number of squares in A plus the number of squares in B equals the number of squares in C.

$$9 + 16 = 25$$
$$(3)^2 + (4)^2 = (5)^2$$

9.2 Pythagorean Theorem and Its Converse

Theorem 9.1   In a right triangle with sides a, b, and c, the hypotenuse squared is equal to the sum of the squares of the sides.

$$a^2 + b^2 = c^2$$

Example:

If the triangle below is a right triangle, find the hypotenuse to the nearest tenth.

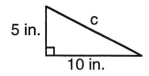

5 in.
c
10 in.

$$(5)^2 + (10)^2 = (c)^2$$
$$25 + 100 = c^2$$
$$125 = c^2$$
$$5\sqrt{5} = c$$
$$11.2 \text{ in. } = c$$

2. If the given triangle is a right triangle, find the length of the hypotenuse (c).

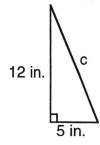

12 in.
c
5 in.

2.

$$5^2 + 12^2 = c^2$$
$$25 + 144 = c^2$$
$$169 = c^2$$
$$\sqrt{169} = c$$
$$13 \text{ in. } = c$$

Example:

A ladder that is 10 ft. long is placed against a building. The foot of the ladder is 5 feet from the base of the building. How far above the ground does the ladder touch the building? Round the final answer to tenths.

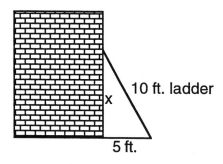

10 ft. ladder
x
5 ft.

We have to assume the building is perpendicular to the ground and the ground is a flat level surface. Therefore, the figure formed with the leaning ladder is a right triangle. The height, x, is found by solving:

$$x^2 + 5^2 = 10^2$$
$$x^2 + 25 = 100$$

$$x^2 = 75$$
$$x = \sqrt{75}$$
$$x = 5\sqrt{3} \text{ ft.}$$
$$x = 8.7 \text{ ft.}$$

The ladder will touch the building 8.7 ft. from the ground.

3.   A ladder that is 13 feet long is placed against a building. The foot of the ladder is 4 feet from the base of the building. How far above the ground does the ladder touch the building? Round answer to the nearest tenth.

3.

$$x^2 + 4^2 = 13^2$$
$$x^2 + 16 = 169$$
$$x^2 = 153$$
$$x = \sqrt{153}$$
$$x = 3\sqrt{17} \text{ ft.}$$
$$x = 12.4 \text{ ft.}$$

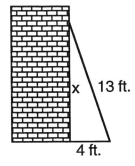

x   13 ft.

4 ft.

Example:

In a rectangle, the diagonal is 10 ft. and one side equals 5 ft. Find the other side and the area of the rectangle. Round answer to the nearest tenth.

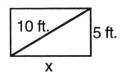

10 ft.   5 ft.

x

Recall a rectangle has all right angles. The diagonal divides the rectangle into two right triangles.

$$x^2 + 5^2 = 10^2$$
$$x^2 + 25 = 100$$
$$x^2 = 75$$
$$x = 5\sqrt{3} \text{ ft.}$$
$$x = 8.7 \text{ ft.}$$

Recall to find the area of a rectangle, the formula A = LW is needed.

$$A = 5(8.7) = 43.5 \text{ sq. ft.}$$

4. Each side of a square equals 7 cm. Find the length of the diagonal to the nearest tenth. Find the area of the square.

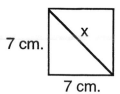

7 cm.

7 cm.

4.

$$7^2 + 7^2 = x^2$$
$$49 + 49 = x^2$$
$$98 = x^2$$
$$7\sqrt{2} = x$$
$$9.9 \text{ cm.} = x$$

$$A = s^2$$
$$A = 7^2$$
$$A = 49 \text{ cm.}^2$$

5. In a right triangle, one leg is two more than the second leg and the hypotenuse is 4 more than the second leg. Find all three sides of the triangle.

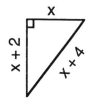

x

x + 2

x + 4

5.

$$(x+2)^2 + x^2 = (x+4)^2$$
$$(x^2 + 4x + 4) + x^2 = (x^2 + 8x + 16)$$
$$2x^2 + 4x + 4 = x^2 + 8x + 16$$
$$x^2 - 4x - 12 = 0$$
$$(x-6)(x+2) = 0$$

$$x - 6 = 0 \text{ or } x + 2 = 0$$
$$x = 6 \text{ or } x = -2$$
$$x = 6 \text{ side 1}$$
$$x + 2 = 8 \text{ side 2}$$
$$x + 4 = 10 \text{ hypotenuse}$$

Theorem 9.2   In a triangle with sides a, b, and c, if $a^2 + b^2 = c^2$, then the triangle is a right triangle. (This is the converse of Theorem 9.1.)

Example:

Show that 2, 1.5, 2.5 are sides of a right triangle.

The hypotenuse is the longest side. If these are sides of a right triangle, the hypotenuse would be 2.5.

Now, substitute the values into the formula, $a^2 + b^2 = c^2$.

$$a^2 + b^2 = c^2$$
$$2^2 + 1.5^2 = 2.5^2$$
$$4 + 2.25 = 6.25$$
$$6.25 = 6.25$$

The equation is a true statement; therefore, the figure is a right triangle.

6. Is a triangle with sides 6, 8, 10 a right triangle?

    First, choose c = 10 since the longest side is the hypotenuse.

    Now, does $6^2 + 8^2 = 10^2$?

6.

    Yes, 36+64=100

7. Is a triangle with sides 4, 4, and $4\sqrt{2}$ a right triangle?

    c = _____

    Does $4^2 + 4^2 = \left(4\sqrt{2}\right)^2$?

7.

    $c = 4\sqrt{2}$

    Yes, 16+16=32

8. Show that the triangle below is or is not a right triangle.

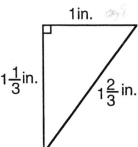

1in.

$1\frac{1}{3}$in.

$1\frac{2}{3}$ in.

8.   It is a right triangle.

$$1^2 + \left(1\frac{1}{3}\right)^2 = \left(1\frac{2}{3}\right)^2$$

$$1^2 + \left(\frac{4}{3}\right)^2 = \left(\frac{5}{3}\right)^2$$

$$1 + \frac{16}{9} = \frac{25}{9}$$

$$\frac{9}{9} + \frac{16}{9} = \frac{25}{9}$$

$$\frac{25}{9} = \frac{25}{9}$$

Exercise 9.1

1. Which of the following sets of numbers represent the lengths of the sides of a right triangle? Show why or why not?

    a. 3, 4, 5

    b. $1, 1\frac{1}{3}, 1\frac{2}{3}$

    c. $2\sqrt{2}, 3\sqrt{2}, 4\sqrt{2}$

    d. 8, 15, 17

2. In right triangle ABC, c is the length of the hypotenuse and a and b are the lengths of the legs. Round answers to tenths.

    a. If a = 2 cm. and b = 4 cm., find c.

    b. If a = 3 m. and c = 6 m., find b.

    c. If b = 9 in. and c = 10 in., find a.

3. An isosceles right triangle has hypotenuse 10 ft. Find the length of the sides and the area of the triangle.

4. An 11 ft. ladder is placed against a building. The foot of the ladder is 3 ft. from the base of the building. How far above the ground does the ladder touch the building? (Round answer to tenths)

5. A cable company technician needs to run a cable from a power pole to Mary's house. Use the drawing below and determine the length of the cable (to the nearest hundredth) the technician will need.

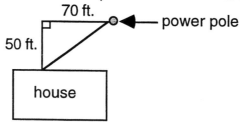

6. In a right triangle, one leg is one less than twice the second leg and the hypotenuse is seven less than three times the second leg. Find all three sides of the triangle.

7. Find the length of the diagonal of a rectangle whose length is 8 ft. and whose width is 12 ft. Round the final answer to hundredths.

8.   Find the area of a square whose diagonal is 8 cm. long.

9.3 Special Triangles-30°–60°Right Triangle

Theorem 9.3   In a 30°-60° right triangle, if the length of the side opposite the 30° angle is x, then the length of the hypotenuse is twice x and the length of the side opposite the 60° angle is x multiplied by the $\sqrt{3}$.

To begin looking at this theorem and it's development, begin with an equilateral triangle, $\triangle ABC$. By definition all three sides of an equilateral triangle are equal. Likewise, all three angles of the triangle can be shown to be equal by using Theorem 3.1. Since the sum of the interior angles of a triangle equal 180°, and all three angles are equal, they are each equal to 60°. Since all three sides are equal, label each as 2x.

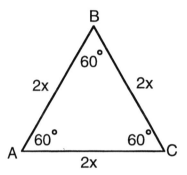

Now bisect $\angle B$ with line segment $\overline{BD}$. Since the sum of the interior angles of a triangle equal 180°, $\angle ADB$ and $\angle BDC$ are right angles. $\triangle ABD \cong \triangle CBD$ because of ASA = ASA. Therefore, $\overline{AD} = \overline{DC} = x$. Now, cutting the two triangles apart will give us two 30°-60° right triangles.

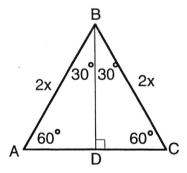

Looking only at one of them, let's develop a representation for $\overline{BD}$ in terms of x.

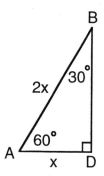

Using the Pythagorean Theorem, we can show that $\overline{BD} = x\sqrt{3}$.

$$a^2 + b^2 = c^2$$

$$x^2 + \left(\overline{BD}\right)^2 = (2x)^2$$

$$x^2 + \left(\overline{BD}\right)^2 = 4x^2$$

$$\left(\overline{BD}\right)^2 = 3x^2$$

$$\overline{BD} = x\sqrt{3}$$

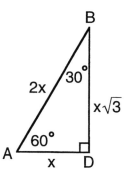

The sides x, 2x and $x\sqrt{3}$ are the sides of a 30°-60° right triangle.

Example:

Triangle ABC is a 30°-60° right triangle with hypotenuse 8 in. Find the other two legs.

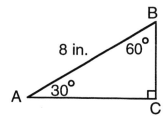

$\overline{AB}$ is the hypotenuse; therefore it is represented as 2x. $\overline{BC}$ is opposite the 30° angle; therefore, it is represented as x. $\overline{AC}$ is opposite the 60° angle; therefore, it is represented as $x\sqrt{3}$.

$$\overline{AB} = 2x$$
$$\overline{AB} = 8$$
$$\text{Therefore, } 2x = 8$$
$$x = 4$$
$$\overline{BC} = x = 4 \text{ in.}$$
$$\overline{AC} = x\sqrt{3} = 4\sqrt{3} \text{ in.}$$

9. Given the figure below, answer the following questions.

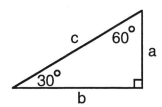

Which side is opposite the 30° angle in the above figure?

Which side is opposite the 60° angle in the above figure?

Which side is the hypotenuse?

10. According to Theorem 9.3, answer the following questions referring to the figure in item 9 above.

The length of side a is represented by _____ .

The length of side b is represented by _____ .

The length of the hypotenuse (side c) is represented by _____ .

9.

a

b

c

10.

x

$x\sqrt{3}$

2x

11. In $\triangle ABC$, $\overline{AB}$ = 10 ft. Find $\overline{AC}$ and $\overline{BC}$.

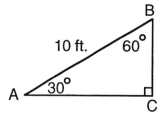

11.

$\overline{AB} = 2x$

$\overline{AB} = 10$, therefore

$2x = 10$

$x = 5$

$\overline{BC} = x = 5$ ft.

$\overline{AC} = x\sqrt{3} = 5\sqrt{3}$ ft.

12. In $\triangle ABC$, $\overline{BC}$ = 8 cm., find $\overline{AB}$ and $\overline{AC}$.

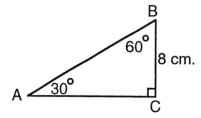

12.

$\overline{BC} = x$

$\overline{BC} = 8$ cm.; therefore

$x = 8$

$\overline{AB} = 2x = 16$ cm.

$\overline{AC} = x\sqrt{3} = 8\sqrt{3}$ cm.

13. In $\triangle ABC$, $\overline{AC}$ = 15 in., find $\overline{AB}$ and $\overline{BC}$.

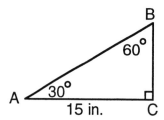

13.

$\overline{AC} = x\sqrt{3}$

$\overline{AC} = 15$ in.; therefore

$x\sqrt{3} = 15$

$\dfrac{x\sqrt{3}}{\sqrt{3}} = \dfrac{15}{\sqrt{3}}$

$x = \dfrac{15}{\sqrt{3}} \cdot \dfrac{\sqrt{3}}{\sqrt{3}}$

$x = \dfrac{15\sqrt{3}}{3}$

$x = 5\sqrt{3}$

$\overline{BC} = x = 5\sqrt{3}$ in.

$\overline{AB} = 2x = 10\sqrt{3}$ in.

Theorem 9.3 can be used in determining the altitude (height) of a parallelogram.

Example:

Find the area of parallelogram ABCD if $\overline{AD}$ = 15 cm., $\overline{CD}$ = 10 cm., and $\angle A = 30°$.

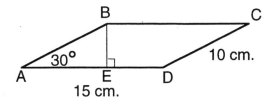

Since ABCD is a parallelogram $\overline{AB} = \overline{CD}$ because opposite sides of a parallelogram are equal. $\overline{AB}$ = 10 cm. $\triangle ABE$ is a 30°-60° right triangle. The hypotenuse is $\overline{AB}$ which is represented by 2x. The altitude is $\overline{BE}$ which is represented by x.

$$2x = 10$$
$$x = 5$$
$$\overline{BE} = 5$$

The area of a parallelogram is the base times the height. The base of parallelogram ABCD is $\overline{AD}$ = 15 cm.

$$A = bh$$
$$A = 15 \cdot 5$$
$$A = 75 \text{ sq.cm.}$$

14. Find the area of the following parallelogram according to the figure given.

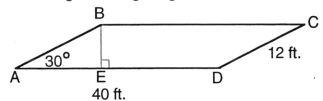

a. $\overline{AB}$ measures _____.

b. The height of parallelogram is _____ .

c. The area of parallelogram ABCD is _____ .

14.

a. 12 ft. since opposite sides of a parallelogram are equal.

b. $\overline{BE}$ = 6 ft. Theorem 9.3

c. $A = bh$
$A = (40)(6)$
$A = 240$ sq. ft.

15. Find the area of parallelogram MNOP

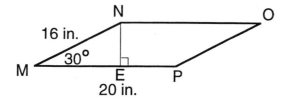

16 in.

30°

M   E   P
                    20 in.

a. $\overline{MN} =$ _____

b. $\overline{NE} =$ _____

c. Area = _____

15.

a. 16 in.

b. 8 in.

c. A = (20)(8)
    A = 160 sq. in.

16. ABCD is a parallelogram with $\overline{AD} = 60$ m.
     and $\overline{CD} = 24$ m. If $\angle BAD = x$ and $\angle ABC =$
     4x+30, find the value of x and the area of
     parallelogram ABCD.

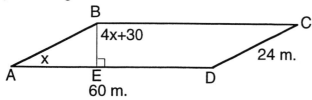

B

4x+30   C

x   24 m.

A   E   D
        60 m.

a. $(4x + 30) + (x) = 180°$ Why?

16.

a. Consecutive angles
    of a parallelogram
    are supplementary.
    $(4x + 30) + (x) = 180°$
              $5x + 30 = 180$
                   $5x = 150$
                    $x = 30$

b. Height = $\overline{BE} =$ _____

c. Area = _____

b. $\overline{BE} = 12$ m.

c. A = (60)(12)
    A = 720 sq. m.

Example:

     Find the altitude and area of an equilateral triangle whose side measures
     6 inches. Round the area to the nearest hundredth.

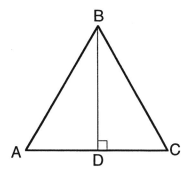

$\angle A = \angle ABC = \angle C = 60°$. The sum of the interior angles of a triangle equal 180°. Since all three angles of an equilateral triangle are equal, they are each equal to 60°. Since $\angle A = 60°$, then $\triangle ABD$ is a 30°-60° right triangle. $\overline{AB}$ is the hypotenuse of $\triangle ABD$ so is represented by 2x according to Theorem 9.3. Therefore,

$$2x = 6$$

$$x = 3$$

$\overline{BD}$ is the altitude and is opposite $\angle A = 60°$. By Theorem 9.3 $\overline{BD}$ is represented by $x\sqrt{3}$. Therefore,

$$\overline{BD} = x\sqrt{3}$$

$$\overline{BD} = 3\sqrt{3} \text{ in.}$$

The area of $\triangle ABC$ is

$$A = \frac{1}{2}bh$$

$$A = \frac{1}{2} \cdot 6 \cdot 3\sqrt{3}$$

$$A = 9\sqrt{3}$$

$$A = 15.59 \text{ sq. in.}$$

17. Find the altitude and area of equilateral $\triangle MNO$ if $\overline{NO}$ = 34 cm. Round the area to the nearest tenth.

17.

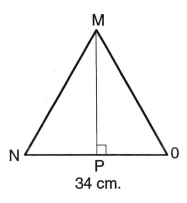

N   P   O

34 cm.

a. $\overline{MN}$ = _____

b. Altitude = $\overline{MP}$ = _____

a. 34 cm.

b.

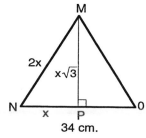

$2x = 34$

$x = 17$

$\overline{MP} = x\sqrt{3}$

$\overline{MP} = 17\sqrt{3}$ cm.

c. Area = _____

c.

$A = \dfrac{1}{2}bh$

$A = \dfrac{1}{2} \cdot 34 \cdot 17\sqrt{3}$

$A = 289\sqrt{3}$

$A = 500.6$ sq. cm.

Exercise 9.2

Solve.

1. The hypotenuse of a 30°-60° right triangle is 4 inches. Find the length of the legs.

2. The side opposite the 60° angle of a 30°-60° right triangle is 7 inches. What are the lengths of the other sides? Find the area to the nearest tenth of this triangle.

3. Find the altitude of an equilateral triangle if one side equals 10 feet.

4. One side of an equilateral triangle measures 3 m. Find the length of the altitude and the area of the triangle. Round the area to the nearest tenth.

5. The altitude of an equilateral triangle is 8 inches. Find the length of a side of the triangle. Leave answer in radical form.

6.   Find the value of x and the area of parallelogram RUTH.

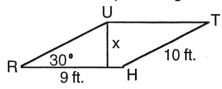

9.4 Special Triangles-Isosceles Right Triangles

> Theorem 9.4   In an isosceles right triangle, the hypotenuse is $\sqrt{2}$ times the length of one side.

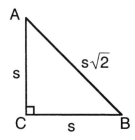

Given: $\triangle ABC$ is an isosceles right triangle

Prove: The hypotenuse is $\sqrt{2}$ times the length of one side.

Proof:

Statements	Reasons
1. $\triangle ABC$ is an isosceles right triangle	1. Given
2. $\overline{AC} = \overline{BC} = s$	2. Definition of isosceles triangle.
3. $s^2 + s^2 = \left(\overline{AB}\right)^2$	3. Pythagorean Theorem
4. $2s^2 = \left(\overline{AB}\right)^2$	4. Adding like terms
5. $s\sqrt{2} = \overline{AB}$	5. Taking the square root of both members of the equation.

Note:

If the triangle is isosceles, by definition two sides of the triangle are equal. By Theorem 3.1, if two sides of a triangle are equal, then the angles opposite those sides are equal.   By Theorem 4.9 the sum of the interior angles of a triangle equals 180°. If we let the two equal angles be x, then

$$x + x + 90° = 180°$$
$$2x + 90° = 180°$$
$$2x = 90°$$
$$x = 45°$$

This is why the Theorem 9.4 is sometimes called the 45°–45° right triangle theorem.

Example:

If one side of an isosceles right triangle equal 4 in., find the hypotenuse.

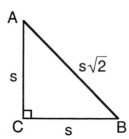

$s = 4$

The hypotenuse equals $s\sqrt{2}$.

Therefore, the hypotenuse equals $4\sqrt{2}$ in.

Example:

If the hypotenuse of an isosceles right triangle measures 25 inches, then find the measure of one of the equal sides. Round the answer to the nearest tenth.

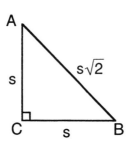

$$s\sqrt{2} = 25$$
$$s = \frac{25}{\sqrt{2}}$$
$$s = \frac{25}{\sqrt{2}} \cdot \frac{\sqrt{2}}{\sqrt{2}}$$
$$s = \frac{25\sqrt{2}}{2}$$
$$s = 12\frac{1}{2}\sqrt{2}$$
$$s = 17.7 \text{ in.}$$

18. In an isosceles right triangle if one of the equal sides has length 9 cm, find the length of the hypotenuse.

18.

$s = 9$

$s\sqrt{2} = 9\sqrt{2}$
The hypotenuse
has length $9\sqrt{2}$ cm.

19.   In an isosceles right triangle, if the hypotenuse is 8 cm, find the length of the other two sides.

A

8 cm.

C   B

19.

$$s\sqrt{2} = 8$$

$$s = \frac{8}{\sqrt{2}}$$

$$s = \frac{8}{\sqrt{2}} \cdot \frac{\sqrt{2}}{\sqrt{2}} = \frac{8\sqrt{2}}{2}$$

$$s = 4\sqrt{2} \text{ cm.}$$

Example:

If the side of a square is 10 dm., find the length of the diagonal.

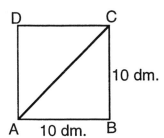

D   C

10 dm.

A   10 dm.   B

The diagonal of a square divides the square into two isosceles right triangles. The diagonal of the square is the hypotenuse of the isosceles right triangle. The length of the diagonal will be $s\sqrt{2} = 10\sqrt{2}$ dm.

Example:

Find the area of a square with diagonal 15 in.

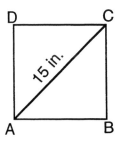

D   C

15 in.

A   B

Recall from the example above that the diagonal is the hypotenuse of an isosceles right triangle. Therefore,

$$s\sqrt{2} = 15$$

$$s = \frac{15}{\sqrt{2}} \cdot \frac{\sqrt{2}}{\sqrt{2}}$$

$$s = \frac{15\sqrt{2}}{2}$$

The area of a square is determined as follows:

$$A = s^2$$

$$A = \left(\frac{15\sqrt{2}}{2}\right)^2$$

$$A = \frac{225}{2}$$

$$A = 112.5 \text{ sq. in.}$$

20. If a square has a diagonal of length $5\sqrt{2}$ in., find the length of the sides of the square.

20.

$$s\sqrt{2} = 5\sqrt{2}$$

$$s = 5 \text{ in.}$$

21. If a square has a diagonal of length 11 ft., find to the nearest hundredth the length of the sides of the square.

21.

$$s\sqrt{2} = 11$$

$$s = \frac{11}{\sqrt{2}}$$

$$s = \frac{11\sqrt{2}}{2}$$

$$s = 5\frac{1}{2}\sqrt{2}$$

$$s = 7.78 \text{ ft.}$$

22. Find the area of an isosceles right triangle if the hypotenuse is 20 m.
   a.   Find the length of a side.

22.

$$s\sqrt{2} = 20$$

$$s = \frac{20}{\sqrt{2}}$$

$$s = \frac{20\sqrt{2}}{2}$$

$$s = 10\sqrt{2}$$

b.   Find the area.

$$A = \frac{1}{2}bh$$

$$A = \frac{1}{2}(10\sqrt{2})(10\sqrt{2})$$

$$A = 100 \text{ m.}^2$$

Exercise 9.3

1.   In an isosceles right triangle, if one leg is 13 cm., find the length of the hypotenuse.

2.   In an isosceles right triangle, if the hypotenuse is 16 ft., find the length of one of the legs of the triangle.

3.   Find the area of the an isosceles right triangle with hypotenuse of 6 m.

4.   In an isosceles right triangle, if the hypotenuse measures $41\sqrt{2}$ inches, then find the measure of one of the equal sides.

5.   If the area of an isosceles right triangle is $24\frac{1}{2}$ sq. ft., then find the measure of one of the equal sides.

6.   Find the area of an isosceles right triangle if one of the equal sides is 23 dm.

7.   Find the length of the diagonal of a square with side equal to 12 in.

8.   Find the area of a square with diagonal of 6 ft.

Unit 9 Review

I.   Which of the following sets of numbers can be lengths of the sides of a right triangle?

    1.   9, 23, 24   4. 6, 8, 10

    2. $\sqrt{2}, \sqrt{3}, \sqrt{5}$ 5. $1\frac{1}{5}, 1\frac{3}{5}, 2$

    3.   12, 35, 37   6. 120, 130, 50

II.   In each of the problems, find the length of the third side of the right triangle ABC. Round answers to the nearest tenth.

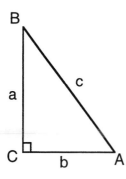

1. a = 5, b = 8, c = _____

2. c = $\sqrt{13}$, b = 3, a = _____

3. b = $\frac{2}{3}$, a = $\frac{1}{4}$, c = _____

4. a = $\sqrt{14}$, c = $\sqrt{26}$, b = _____

5. b = 0.3, a = 0.4, c = _____

6. c = 17, a = 15 , b = _____

III.   Solve the following:

1.   In an isosceles right triangle, find the lengths of the other sides if c = $5\sqrt{2}$ in.

2.   Find the altitude of an equilateral triangle with side of length 7 ft. Leave your answer in radical form.

3.   Find the length of the diagonal of a square with side 10 cm. Leave your answer in radical form.

4.   Find the length of a side of an equilateral triangle if the altitude is $8\sqrt{3}$ m.

5.   Find the length of a side of a square whose diagonal is of length 10 ft. Leave your answer in radical form.

6.   Find the area (to the nearest tenth) of an equilateral triangle with side equal to 26 in.

7.   Find the measure of the other sides if the hypotenuse of a 30°-60° right triangle measures $9\sqrt{2}$ cm. Leave your answer in radical form.

IV.   1.   In the parallelogram below, find the value of x, the height, and the area. ∠ABC = 5x.

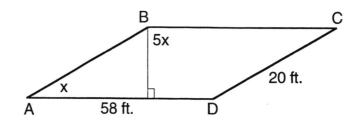

2. A ladder 25 ft. long is leaned against a building a distance of 6 ft. from the building. How far up the building does the ladder reach? Round the answer to hundredths.

3. In the parallelogram below, find the height and the area.

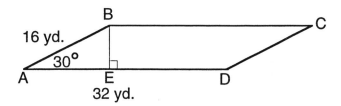

16 yd.

30°

B   C

A   E   D

32 yd.

4. A ramp is placed on top of a 5 ft stair case. The end of the ramp is 15 ft. from the base of the building. How long is the ramp? Round the answer to tenths.

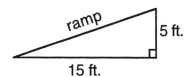

ramp   5 ft.

15 ft.

Unit 10

Ratio, Proportion, and Similarity

Learning objectives:

The student will demonstrate his mastery of the following definitions, property, and theorems by writing them and by applying them to solutions of selected problems:

Definitions: ratio, proportion, means, extremes, constant of proportionality, fourth proportional, mean proportional, similar triangles, and "~'.

Property: If $\dfrac{a}{b} = \dfrac{c}{d}$ and a, b, c, d $\neq$ 0, then ad = bc.
The product of the means equals the product of the extremes in a proportion.

Theorems:

1. Two triangles are similar if and only if two angles of one triangle are equal respectively to two angles of a second triangle.

2. If corresponding sides of two triangles are proportional, then the triangles are similar.

3. A line parallel to one side of a triangle divides the other two sides proportionately.

Ratio, Proportion, and Similarity

10.1 Basic Definitions

As part of our daily routine, frequently we make comparisons between any number of items. For example, we compare wins to losses in athletic events, weight gains vs. losses, the price per pound of meats, EPA ratings on automobiles in miles per gallon, the daily inflation index or even the P/E ratio of common stocks on the stock exchanges.

The comparisons of any two real numbers are termed ratios.

> Definition 10.1   A ratio is a comparison of two numbers, a and b indicated
>
> by their quotient, $\dfrac{a}{b}$, where b ≠ 0.

Quite simply, a ratio is a fraction.

Example:

There are 34 boys and 21 girls in a math class.

a.   Find the ratio of females to males.

To find the ratio of females to males, write a fraction with number of females as the numerator and the number of males as the denominator.
$$\frac{21\ \text{females}}{34\ \text{males}} = \frac{21}{34}$$

b.   Find the ratio of males to females.

To find the ratio of males to females, write a fraction with number of males as the numerator and the number of females as the denominator.
$$\frac{34}{21}$$

c.   Find the ratio of males to the whole class.

To find the ratio of males to the whole class, first determine the number of people in the class. 34 + 21 = 55 people in the class. Now, write the ratio requested.
$$\frac{34}{55}$$

d.   Find the ratio of females to the whole class.

To write the ratio of females to the whole class, write a fraction with the number of females as numerator and the number of people in the class as the denominator.

$$\frac{21}{55}$$

1. There are 15 females and 9 males in a biology class. | 1.

    a.   Find the ratio of females to males | a. $\dfrac{15}{9} = \dfrac{5}{3}$

    b.   Find the ratio of females to the entire class. | b. $\dfrac{15}{24} = \dfrac{5}{8}$

    c.   Find the ratio of males to females. | c. $\dfrac{9}{15} = \dfrac{3}{5}$

    d.   Is the ratio of males to females equivalent to the ratio of females to males? Show why or why not. | d. No $\dfrac{3}{5} \ne \dfrac{5}{3}$

Example:

Find the ratio of 3 days to one week.

In writing ratios all terms must have the same exact units of measure whenever a comparison is being made. Since one week is equal to seven days, the comparison will be made between 3 days and 7 days. Therefore, the ratio will be $\dfrac{3}{7}$.

2. Write the ratio of 4 ft. to 4 yds. | 2. Recall that 4 yds. is equivalent to 12 ft since there are 3 ft. per yd. Overall, 4 ft. to 4 yds is expressed as 4 ft. to 12 ft.

$\dfrac{4}{12} = \dfrac{1}{3}$

3. Find the ratio of 8 sec. to 1 hour. One hour is how many seconds? | 3.

3600 seconds

The ratio is _____.

$$\frac{8}{3600} = \frac{1}{450}$$

Example:

A recipe for pie crust uses 2 cups of flour and $\frac{2}{3}$ cup shortening. Find the ratio of flour to shortening.

The ratio of 2 cups flour to $\frac{2}{3}$ cup shortening is written as $\frac{(2)}{\left(\frac{2}{3}\right)}$.

It is worked as follows: $\frac{(2)}{\left(\frac{2}{3}\right)} = \left(\frac{2}{1} \div \frac{2}{3}\right) = \left(\frac{2}{1} \times \frac{3}{2}\right) = \frac{6}{2} = \frac{3}{1}.$

4. Find the ratio of 4 teaspoons of cinnamon to $2\frac{1}{3}$ teaspoons of sugar.

4.

$$\frac{4}{2\frac{1}{3}} = \frac{4}{1} \div 2\frac{1}{3}$$

$$= \frac{4}{1} \div \frac{7}{3}$$

$$= \frac{4}{1} \times \frac{3}{7}$$

$$= \frac{12}{7}$$

Definition 10.2   A <u>proportion</u> is a statement that two ratios are equal.

If $\frac{a}{b}$ and $\frac{c}{d}$ are two ratios, then $\frac{a}{b} = \frac{c}{d}$ is called a proportion where a, b, c, and d $\neq$ 0.

i.   b and c are called <u>means</u>.
ii. a and d are called <u>extremes</u>.

Example:

Is $\frac{2}{3} = \frac{14}{21}$ a true proportion?

Yes, it is a true proportion. $\dfrac{14}{21}$ reduces to $\dfrac{2}{3}$. Since $\dfrac{2}{3} = \dfrac{2}{3}$ is a true statement mathematically, the proportion is a true proportion.

5. Is $\dfrac{4}{20} = \dfrac{3}{15}$ a true proportion?

5. Yes, each fraction simplifies to $\dfrac{1}{5}$.

6. What two numbers are called the means in exercise 5 above?

6. 20 and 3

7. Is $\dfrac{2a}{6b} = \dfrac{12a}{16b}$ a true proportion?

7. False, $\dfrac{2a}{6b}$ and $\dfrac{12a}{16b}$ do not reduce to the same fraction.

8. What two numbers are called the extremes in exercise 7 above?

8. 2a and 16b

Definition 10.3   Two sequences of positive numbers a, b, c, . . . and p, q, r, . . . are <u>proportional</u> if and only if $\dfrac{a}{p} = \dfrac{b}{q} = \dfrac{c}{r} = \ldots = k$ (where k is the constant to which each ratio of the sequence is equal.) K is called the <u>constant of proportionality</u>.

Example:

Show that the following pair of sequences are proportional by finding the constant of proportionality.

$$4, 2, 3 \text{ and } 12, 6, 9$$

Examine the ratios $\dfrac{4}{12}, \dfrac{2}{6},$ and $\dfrac{3}{9}$. Since each simplifies to $\dfrac{1}{3}$ we may write

$\dfrac{4}{12} = \dfrac{2}{6} = \dfrac{3}{9} = \dfrac{1}{3} = k$. Therefore, the sequences are proportional with

constant of proportionality equal to $\dfrac{1}{3}$.

9. Show that the following pair of sequences are proportional.

$$2, 5, 15, 7 \text{ and } 8, 20, 60, 28$$

9.

a. Find the constant of proportionality.

a. $\dfrac{2}{8}=\dfrac{1}{4}, \dfrac{5}{20}=\dfrac{1}{4}$

$\dfrac{15}{60}=\dfrac{1}{4}, \dfrac{7}{28}=\dfrac{1}{4}$

$k=\dfrac{1}{4}$

b. Are the sequences proportional?

b. Yes

10. Determine whether of not the following pair of sequences are proportional.

10.

    10, 4, 6, 12, 14 and 5, 2, 4, 6, 8

a. Find the constant of proportionality.

a. $\dfrac{10}{5}=2, \dfrac{4}{2}=2$

$\dfrac{6}{4}=\dfrac{3}{2}, \dfrac{12}{6}=2$

$\dfrac{14}{8}=\dfrac{7}{4}$

Since $2 \neq \dfrac{3}{2} \neq \dfrac{7}{4}$, there is no constant of proportionality.

b. Are the sequences proportional?

b. No, because there is no constant of proportionality.

Exercise 10.1

1. Fill in the blank with the appropriate word or phrase.

    a. A _____ is the comparison of two numbers by their indicated quotient.

    b. A _____ is a statement that two ratios are equal.

    c. In comparing pairs of sequences, each ratio must be equal to the _____ before the pair of sequences are considered to be proportional.

2. Find the ratio of each of the following:

    a. In a basketball season, one team won 8 games and lost 6. Find the ratio of wins to losses.

    b. Find the ratio of losses to the total number of games played in part a.

    c. Find the ratio of 3 minutes to 4 hours.

    d. Find the ratio of $\dfrac{5}{4}$ cup of flour to $\dfrac{1}{8}$ cup of walnuts.

3. Determine if each of the following proportions is <u>true</u> or <u>false</u>.

    a. $\dfrac{3x}{6y} = \dfrac{3x}{9y}$

    c. $\dfrac{12y}{4x} = \dfrac{57y}{19x}$

    b. $\dfrac{10}{5} = \dfrac{\frac{1}{2}}{\frac{1}{4}}$

    d. $\dfrac{7}{8} = \dfrac{21}{25}$

4. Show that the following pairs of sequences are or are not proportional by finding the constant of proportionality.

    a. 1, 7, 11 and 3, 21, 33

    b. 18, 15, 39 and 8, 5, 13

    c. $\dfrac{1}{2}, \dfrac{1}{3}, \dfrac{1}{4}$ and $\dfrac{1}{3}, \dfrac{2}{9}, \dfrac{1}{6}$

10.2 Properties and Definitions Concerning Proportions

Algebraically, a proportion is an equation and the usual rules of algebra apply. The following property is very useful in working with proportions.

Property 10.1   If $\dfrac{a}{b} = \dfrac{c}{d}$ and a, b, c, and d ≠ 0, then ad = bc. The product of the means equals the product of the extremes in a proportion.

Example:

Determine if $\dfrac{2}{5} = \dfrac{4}{10}$ is a true proportion using Property 10.1.

Using Property 10.1,

$$\frac{2}{5} = \frac{4}{10}$$

$$(2)(10) = (5)(4)$$

$$20 = 20$$

we can see that $\frac{2}{5} = \frac{4}{10}$ is a true proportion.

11. Determine if $\frac{7}{4} = \frac{91}{52}$ is a true proportion
    using Property 10.1.

11.

$$\frac{7}{4} = \frac{91}{52}$$

$$(7)(52) = (91)(4)$$

$$364 = 364$$

Yes, $\frac{7}{4} = \frac{91}{52}$ is a
true proportion.

Definition 10.4   In a proportion $\frac{a}{b} = \frac{c}{d}$ and a, b, c, and d ≠ 0, d is known
as the <u>fourth proportional</u>.

Example:

In a proportion, find the fourth proportional to 2, 5, and 7.

Since the fourth proportional is d, the formula is

$$\frac{2}{5} = \frac{7}{d}$$

Use Property 10.1 to find the value of d.

$$\frac{2}{5} = \frac{7}{d}$$

$$(2)d = (5)(7)$$

$$2d = 35$$

$$d = \frac{35}{2}$$

12. In a proportion, find the fourth proportional
    to 3, 7, and 15 using Property 10.1.

    a. The proportion is _____.

12.

    a. $\frac{3}{7} = \frac{15}{d}$

b. The fourth proportional is _____.

b.
$$3d = 105$$
$$d = 35$$

13. In a proportion, find the fourth proportional to $\frac{1}{2}$, 3, and 4 using Property 10.1.

13.

a. The proportion is _____.

a. $\dfrac{\left(\frac{1}{2}\right)}{3} = \dfrac{4}{d}$

b. The fourth proportional is _____.

b.
$$\left(\frac{1}{2}\right)d = (4)(3)$$
$$\left(\frac{1}{2}\right)d = 12$$
$$2 \cdot \left(\frac{1}{2}\right)d = 2 \cdot 12$$
$$d = 24$$

Definition 10.5   In a proportion $\dfrac{a}{b} = \dfrac{c}{d}$ and a, b, c, and d ≠ 0, if b=c, then b and c are the <u>mean proportional</u> between a and d.

(For the remainder of this section, answers will be rounded to the nearest tenth.)

Example:

Find the mean proportional between 7 and 14. Round to the nearest tenth.

Let x be the mean proportional and use Property 10.1 to solve for x.

$$\frac{7}{x} = \frac{x}{14}$$
$$x^2 = 98$$
$$x = \pm\sqrt{98}$$
$$x = 7\sqrt{2}$$
$$x = 9.9$$

Note: The positive solution was used because the mean proportional is between 7 and 14, both positive numbers.

14. Find, to the nearest tenth, the mean proportional between 5 and 15

    a. The proportion is _____.

    b. The mean proportional is _____.

14.

    a. $\dfrac{5}{x} = \dfrac{x}{15}$

    b.
$$x^2 = (5)(15)$$
$$x^2 = 75$$
$$x = \pm\sqrt{75}$$
$$x = 5\sqrt{3}$$
$$x = 8.7$$

15. Find the mean proportional between 4 and 16.

    a. The proportion is _____.

    b. The mean proportional is _____.

15.

    a. $\dfrac{4}{x} = \dfrac{x}{16}$

    b.
$$x^2 = (4)(16)$$
$$x^2 = 64$$
$$x = \pm\sqrt{64}$$
$$x = 8$$

Given any three terms of a proportion, the values of the unknown term can be obtained by using Property 10.1.

Example:

Solve for x in the proportion $\dfrac{x}{\sqrt{7}} = \dfrac{6\sqrt{8}}{\sqrt{14}}$.

$$\frac{x}{\sqrt{7}} = \frac{6\sqrt{8}}{\sqrt{14}}$$
$$(\sqrt{14})x = (6\sqrt{8})(\sqrt{7})$$
$$\sqrt{14}x = 6\sqrt{56}$$
$$\frac{\sqrt{14}x}{\sqrt{14}} = \frac{6\sqrt{56}}{\sqrt{14}}$$

$$x = 6\sqrt{4}$$
$$x = 6 \cdot 2$$
$$x = 12$$

16. Solve for x. $\dfrac{x}{3} = \dfrac{4}{5}$

16.

$$5x = 3 \cdot 4$$
$$5x = \underline{\hspace{2cm}}$$
$$x = \underline{\hspace{2cm}}$$

$$5x = 12$$
$$x = \dfrac{12}{5}$$
$$x = 2.4$$

17. Solve for x. $\dfrac{x}{\sqrt{5}} = \dfrac{3\sqrt{2}}{\sqrt{10}}$

17.

$$\sqrt{10}x = \left(\sqrt{5}\right)\left(3\sqrt{2}\right)$$
$$\sqrt{10}x = \underline{\hspace{2cm}}$$
$$x = \underline{\hspace{2cm}}$$

$$\sqrt{10}x = 3\sqrt{10}$$
$$\dfrac{\sqrt{10}x}{\sqrt{10}} = \dfrac{3\sqrt{10}}{\sqrt{10}}$$
$$x = 3$$

18. Solve for x. $\dfrac{x}{x-3} = \dfrac{5}{3}$

18.

$$3x = 5(x-3)$$
$$3x = \underline{\hspace{2cm}}$$
$$x = \underline{\hspace{2cm}}$$

$$3x = 5x - 15$$
$$-2x = -15$$
$$x = \dfrac{15}{2}$$
$$x = 7.5$$

19. Solve for x. $\dfrac{x+3}{4} = \dfrac{x-3}{6}$

19.

$$6(x+3) = 4(x-3)$$
$$x = \underline{\hspace{2cm}}$$

$$6x + 18 = 4x - 12$$
$$2x = -30$$
$$x = -15$$

Example:

Solve for x. $\dfrac{4}{x-2} = \dfrac{x}{5}$

$$x(x-2) = 20$$
$$x^2 - 2x = 20$$

$$x^2 - 2x - 20 = 0$$

$$x = \frac{-(-2) \pm \sqrt{(-2)^2 - 4 \cdot 1 \cdot (-20)}}{2 \cdot 1}$$

$$x = \frac{2 \pm \sqrt{4 + 80}}{2}$$

$$x = \frac{2 \pm \sqrt{84}}{2}$$

$$x = \frac{2 \pm 2\sqrt{21}}{2}$$

$$x = \frac{2(1 \pm \sqrt{21})}{2}$$

$$x = 1 \pm \sqrt{21}$$

$$x = 5.6 \text{ or } x = -3.6$$

20. Solve for x. $\dfrac{3}{x-2} = \dfrac{x}{3}$

$$9 = x(x - 2)$$
$$\underline{} = x$$

20.

$$9 = x^2 - 2x$$
$$0 = x^2 - 2x - 9$$
$$x = \frac{2 \pm \sqrt{4 - 4 \cdot 1 \cdot (-9)}}{2 \cdot 1}$$
$$x = \frac{2 \pm \sqrt{4 + 36}}{2}$$
$$x = \frac{2 \pm \sqrt{40}}{2}$$
$$x = \frac{2 \pm 2\sqrt{10}}{2}$$
$$x = 1 \pm \sqrt{10}$$

$$x = 4.2 \text{ or } x = -2.2$$

21. Solve for x. $\dfrac{x+3}{4} = \dfrac{3}{x-4}$

$$x = \underline{}$$

21.

$$(x + 3)(x - 4) = (3)(4)$$
$$x^2 - x - 12 = 12$$
$$x^2 - x - 24 = 0$$

$$x = \frac{-(-1) \pm \sqrt{(-1)^2 - 4(1)(-24)}}{2 \cdot 1}$$

$$x = \frac{1 \pm \sqrt{1 + 96}}{2}$$

$$x = \frac{1 \pm \sqrt{97}}{2}$$

$$x = 5.4 \text{ or } x = -4.4$$

Exercise 10.2

In this exercise round all answers in 2 and 3 to the nearest tenth.

1. In a proportion, find the fourth proportional for each of the following:

    a. 3, 5, 12

    b. 8, 9, 4

    c. $\dfrac{2}{5}, \dfrac{3}{10}, \dfrac{1}{4}$

2. In a proportion, find the mean proportional between:

    a. 2 and 8

    b. 14 and 6

    c. 12 and 20

3. Solve for x.

    a. $\dfrac{11}{x} = \dfrac{5}{9}$

    d. $\dfrac{7}{x+1} = \dfrac{x}{6}$

    b. $\dfrac{x}{x-5} = \dfrac{4}{5}$

    e. $\dfrac{x+3}{5} = \dfrac{x+7}{x+10}$

    c. $\dfrac{x+5}{3} = \dfrac{x-13}{6}$

    f. $\dfrac{x+2}{x-5} = \dfrac{2x+1}{x-3}$

10.3 Similarity

Congruent figures may informally be described as "having the same size and shape". Similar figures may informally be described as "having the same shape, but not necessarily the same size" as illustrated in the figure below.

 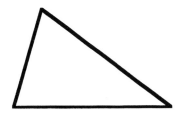

Similarity is a concept that photographers generally employ in the darkroom in printing pictures. By using a single negative under magnification, a photographer could enlarge or reduce the negative image as he desires. The overall shape of the image does not appear changed which suggests that although the line or curved segments may become enlarged, the measures of the corresponding angles or arcs remain constant.

Surveyors, housing contractors, and architects all deal with similarity in the use of designs, site plans, and blue prints.

In this unit, we will primarily be concerned with similarity involving triangles.

> Definition 10.6   Two triangles are <u>similar</u> if three angles of one triangle equal three angles of a second triangle and all corresponding sides are in proportion. The symbol used to denote similarity is "~".

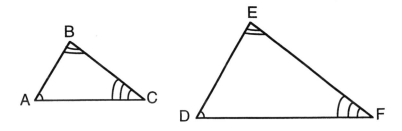

Given that $\triangle ABC \sim \triangle DEF$, then $\angle A = \angle D$, $\angle B = \angle E$, and $\angle C = \angle F$. The definition also states that corresponding sides are proportional. Use precautions in writing out the proportions. Be sure only corresponding sides are compared.

In the diagram above, $\overline{AB}$ corresponds to $\overline{DE}$, $\overline{BC}$ to $\overline{EF}$, and $\overline{AC}$ to $\overline{DF}$.

Hence, $\dfrac{\overline{AB}}{\overline{DE}} = \dfrac{\overline{BC}}{\overline{EF}} = \dfrac{\overline{AC}}{\overline{DF}}$.

> Theorem 10.1 Two triangles are similar if and only if two angles of one triangle are equal respectively to two angles of a second triangle.

This theorem is actually the statement and its converse combined.

Statement: If two triangles are similar, then two angles of one triangle
                    equal two angles of a second triangle.

Converse: If two angles of one triangle equal respectively to two
                    angles of a second triangle, then the triangles are similar.

Example:

    Given $\overline{SR} \parallel \overline{UV}$

    Prove: $\triangle SRT \sim \triangle VUT$

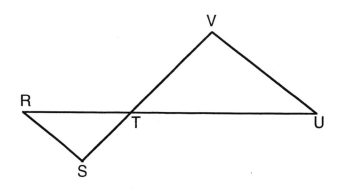

Statements	Reasons
1. $\overline{SR} \parallel \overline{UV}$	1. Given
2. $\angle R$ and $\angle U$ are alternate interior angles.	2. Definition of alternate interior angles.
3. $\angle R = \angle U$	3. If two lines are parallel, then pairs of alternate interior angles are equal.
4. $\angle RTS$ and $\angle VTU$ are vertical angles.	4. Definition of vertical angles.
5. $\angle RTS = \angle VTU$	5. Pairs of vertical angles are equal.
6. $\triangle SRT \sim \triangle VUT$	6. Theorem 10.1

22. Given: $\overline{MN} \perp \overline{PN}$ and $\overline{PQ} \perp \overline{PN}$ Prove: $\triangle MNO \sim \triangle QPO$ 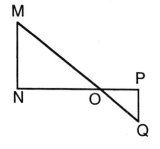	22.

Statements	Reasons
1. $\overline{MN} \perp \overline{PN}$ $\overline{PQ} \perp \overline{PN}$	1. Given
2. ∠N and ∠P are right angles.	2. Definition of perpendicular.
3. ∠N = ∠P	3. All right angles are equal.
4. ∠MON and ∠POQ are vertical angles.	4. Definition of vertical angles.
5. ∠MON = ∠POQ	5. Pairs of vertical ∠s are equal.
6. △MNO ~ △QPO	6. Thm. 10.1

23. Given: $\overline{ZY} \parallel \overline{WX}$
    Prove: △UZY ~ △UWX

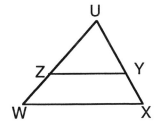

23.

Statements	Reasons
1. $\overline{ZY} \parallel \overline{WX}$	1. Given
2. ∠UZY and ∠W are corresponding angles. ∠UYZ and ∠X are corresponding angles.	2. Definition of corresponding angles.
3. ∠UZY = ∠W ∠UYZ = ∠X	3. If lines are parallel, then corresponding angles are equal.
4. △UZY ~ △UWX	4. Thm. 10.1

24. Given: $\overline{AB} \parallel \overline{DC}$ and $\overline{AD} \parallel \overline{BC}$
    Prove: $\triangle ADB \sim \triangle CBD$

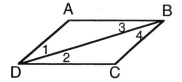

24.

Statements	Reasons
1. $\overline{AB} \parallel \overline{DC}$ $\overline{AD} \parallel \overline{BC}$	1. Given
2. $\angle 2$ and $\angle 3$ are alternate interior angles. $\angle 1$ and $\angle 4$ are alternate interior angles.	2. Definition of alternate interior angles.
3. $\angle 2 = \angle 3$ $\angle 1 = \angle 4$	3. If lines are parallel, then pairs of alternate interior $\angle$s are equal.
4. $\triangle ADB \sim \triangle CBD$	4. Thm. 10.1

Note: These triangles are also congruent by ASA = ASA with $\overline{BD}$ being the included side.

Example:

Given: $\overline{AB} \parallel \overline{DE}$, find $\overline{BC}$ and $\overline{DE}$.

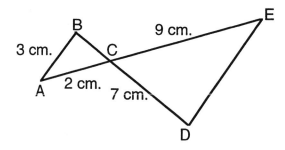

$\overline{AB} \parallel \overline{DE}$

$\angle B$ and $\angle D$ are alternate interior angles. $\angle A$ and $\angle E$ are alternate interior angles.

Given

Definition of alternate interior angles.

$\angle B = \angle D, \angle A = \angle E$ If lines are parallel, then pairs of alternate interior angles are equal.

$\triangle ABC \sim \triangle EDC$ Theorem 10.1

Since the triangles are similar, the sides are proportional by the definition of similarity. The proportions must be set up to compare corresponding sides.

$$\frac{\overline{AB}}{\overline{ED}} = \frac{\overline{AC}}{\overline{EC}} = \frac{\overline{BC}}{\overline{DC}}$$

Next substitute the values that were given into the proportion. $\overline{AB} = 3$ cm., $\overline{AC} = 2$ cm., $\overline{CE} = 9$ cm., and $\overline{CD} = 7$ cm. Therefore,

$$\frac{3}{\overline{ED}} = \frac{2}{9} = \frac{\overline{BC}}{7}$$

Not all of the values of the proportion were given; however, by using Property 10.1 (The product of the means equals the product of the extremes.) the unknowns can be found. Select a proportion that will give three known values such as

$$\left[\frac{3}{\overline{ED}} = \frac{2}{9}\right] \quad \text{and} \quad \left[\frac{2}{9} = \frac{\overline{BC}}{7}\right]$$

Now, solve each proportion for the unknown.

$$\frac{3}{\overline{ED}} = \frac{2}{9} \qquad\qquad \frac{2}{9} = \frac{\overline{BC}}{7}$$

$$(3)(9) = 2\overline{ED} \qquad\qquad (2)(7) = 9\overline{BC}$$

$$27 = 2\overline{ED} \quad \text{and} \quad 14 = 9\overline{BC}$$

$$\frac{27}{2} \text{ cm.} = \overline{ED} \qquad\qquad \frac{14}{9} \text{ cm.} = \overline{BC}$$

$$13.5 \text{ cm.} = \overline{ED} \qquad\qquad 1.\bar{5} \text{ cm.} = \overline{BC}$$

25. Given: $\overline{AB} \parallel \overline{DE}$ 25.
     Find $\overline{BC}$ and $\overline{ED}$.

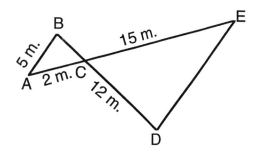

a. Why is $\triangle ABC \sim \triangle EDC$?

a. $\angle A = \angle E$ and $\angle B = \angle D$ because if lines are parallel, then pairs of alternate interior angles are equal. Therefore, by Thm. 10.1, the triangles are similar.

b. The sides are proportional in what way?

What values are substituted?

b. $\dfrac{\overline{AB}}{\overline{ED}} = \dfrac{\overline{AC}}{\overline{EC}} = \dfrac{\overline{BC}}{\overline{DC}}$

$\dfrac{5}{\overline{ED}} = \dfrac{2}{15} = \dfrac{\overline{BC}}{12}$

c. What two proportions should be selected

in order to solve for the unknown terms?

c. $\dfrac{5}{\overline{ED}} = \dfrac{2}{15}$

$\dfrac{2}{15} = \dfrac{\overline{BC}}{12}$

d. What is the value of $\overline{ED}$?

d.

$\dfrac{5}{\overline{ED}} = \dfrac{2}{15}$

$75 = 2\overline{ED}$

$\dfrac{75}{2} = \overline{ED}$

$37.5 \text{ m.} = \overline{ED}$

e. What is the value of $\overline{BC}$?

e.

$\dfrac{2}{15} = \dfrac{\overline{BC}}{12}$

$24 = 15\overline{BC}$

$\dfrac{24}{15} = \overline{BC}$

$1.6 \text{ m.} = \overline{BC}$

26. Jose' Oretgo estimated the distance (x) across the Ole' River by using the diagram below. Use his drawing to estimate the distance to the nearest tenth of a yard.

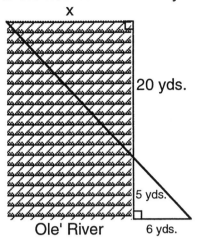

x

20 yds.

5 yds.

Ole' River   6 yds.

26.

$$\frac{6}{x} = \frac{5}{20}$$

$$5x = 120$$

$$x = 24 \text{ yds.}$$

27. Given: ΔDEF ~ ΔLMN
    Find $\overline{FE}$ and $\overline{DF}$.

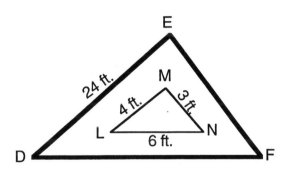

E

24 ft.   M
        4 ft.   3 ft.
    L   6 ft.   N

D   F

27.

$$\frac{\overline{LM}}{\overline{DE}} = \frac{\overline{MN}}{\overline{FE}} = \frac{\overline{NL}}{\overline{DF}}$$

$$\frac{4}{24} = \frac{3}{\overline{FE}} = \frac{6}{\overline{DF}}$$

$$\frac{4}{24} = \frac{3}{\overline{FE}}$$

$$72 = 4\overline{FE}$$

$$18 \text{ ft.} = \overline{FE}$$

$$\frac{4}{24} = \frac{6}{\overline{DF}}$$

$$144 = 4\overline{DF}$$

$$36 \text{ ft.} = \overline{DF}$$

28.

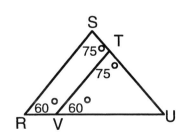

S
        T
75°
    75°
60°   60°
R   V   U

28.

a. Are △SUR and △TUV similar triangles?

a. Yes, by Thm. 10.1

b. If $\overline{SU}$ = 14 cm., $\overline{SR}$ = 8 cm., $\overline{UT}$ = 9.8 cm., find $\overline{TV}$.

b.

$$\frac{\overline{SU}}{\overline{UT}} = \frac{\overline{SR}}{\overline{TV}}$$

$$\frac{14}{9.8} = \frac{8}{\overline{TV}}$$

$$78.4 = 14\overline{TV}$$

$$5.6 \text{ cm.} = \overline{TV}$$

Example:

A man 6 feet tall casts a 10 foot shadow. In the same location and at the same time, a flagpole casts a 40 foot shadow. How high is the flagpole?

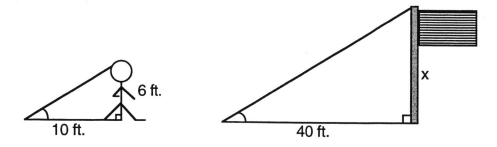

We must assume the man and the flagpole are perpendicular to the ground and the ground is a level surface. The sun's rays makes the same angle with the ground at the same time of day. Given the right angle where the boy meets the ground and where the flag pole meets the ground and given the angle of the sun is the same, by Theorem 10.1 the triangles are similar. Because the triangles are similar, the sides are proportional. The following is an example of one possible proportion that you could set up in order to solve for x:

$$\frac{6}{x} = \frac{10}{40}$$

$$10x = 240$$

$$x = 24 \text{ ft., height of the flagpole}$$

29. At 4 p.m. two trees side by side cast 10 ft. and 25 ft. shadows, respectively. If the first tree is 5 ft. tall, find the height of the second tree. (First, illustrate the exercise on a sheet of paper, then set up the proportion.)

29.

$$\frac{5}{x} = \frac{10}{25}$$

$$10x = 125$$
$$x = 12.5 \text{ ft.}$$

30. If a 6 foot man casts an 8 ft. shadow, at the same time and in the same location, how tall is a tree that casts a 20 ft. shadow ?

30.

$$\frac{6}{x} = \frac{8}{20}$$
$$120 = 8x$$
$$15 \text{ ft.} = x$$

31. A small tree, 3 feet tall, cast a shadow of 2 feet, and the large oak tree casts a shadow of 30 feet. Find the height of the large tree.

31.

$$\frac{3}{x} = \frac{2}{30}$$
$$90 = 2x$$
$$45 \text{ ft.} = x$$

Example:

In a scale drawing of two triangles, a smaller triangle has sides 4 ft., 5 ft. and 7 ft. The actual figure has one side 9 ft. long. (Recall in a scale drawing all of the angles in the smaller triangle are the same as those in the original triangle.) Round the final answer to tenths.

4 ft. △ 5 ft.   x △ y
    7 ft.   9 ft.

$$\frac{4}{x} = \frac{7}{9}$$
$$7x = 36$$
$$x = 5\frac{1}{7}$$
$$x = 5.1 \text{ ft.}$$

$$\frac{5}{y} = \frac{7}{9}$$
$$7y = 45$$
$$y = 6\frac{3}{7}$$
$$y = 6.4 \text{ ft.}$$

32. In a scale drawing of two triangles, a smaller triangle has sides 5 ft., 7, ft., and 9 ft. The actual figure has one side of 27 ft. Find the other sides.

32.

5 ft. △ 7 ft.   x △ y
    9 ft.   27 ft.

$$\frac{5}{x} = \frac{9}{27}$$
$$9x = 135$$
$$x = 15 \text{ ft.}$$

$$\frac{7}{y} = \frac{9}{27}$$
$$9y = 189$$
$$y = 21 \text{ ft.}$$

Theorem 10.2	If corresponding sides of two triangles are proportional, then the triangles are similar.

Example:

If the sides of two triangles were respectively 2, 3, 4 and 6, 9, 12, are the triangles similar?

First, find the ratios of the sides.

$$\frac{2}{6} = \frac{1}{3} \qquad \frac{3}{9} = \frac{1}{3} \qquad \frac{4}{12} = \frac{1}{3}$$

The sides of the two triangles are proportional with the constant of proportionality of $k = \frac{1}{3}$. Therefore, by Theorem 10.2, the triangles are similar.

33. If the sides of one triangle measure 10, 7, 5 and the sides of a second triangle measure 20, 14, and 10, are the triangles similar?

33.

Yes, their sides are proportional.
$$\frac{10}{20} = \frac{7}{14} = \frac{5}{10} = \frac{1}{2}$$
$$k = \frac{1}{2}$$

34. Are triangles with sides 2, 5, 6 and 3, $\frac{17}{2}$, 12 similar?

34.

No, their sides are not proportional.
$$\frac{2}{3} \neq \frac{5}{\left(\frac{17}{2}\right)} \neq \frac{6}{12}$$

35. Examine the following figures and decide whether or not these triangles are similar. State why.

35.

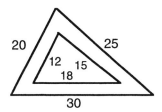

The sides are proportional and by theorem 10.2, the triangles are similar.

$$\frac{20}{12} = \frac{30}{18} = \frac{25}{15} = \frac{5}{3}$$

$$k = \frac{5}{3}$$

Exercise 10.3

1. Define similarity and give an example of this concept from your life experiences.

2. Given: $\overline{AB} \parallel \overline{DE}$, $\overline{AB}$ = 3 in., $\overline{BC}$ = 5 in., $\overline{CE} = 7\frac{1}{2}$ in., $\overline{AC}$ = 3 in.

    Find: $\overline{CD}$ and $\overline{DE}$

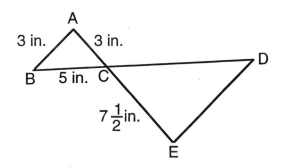

3. Are triangles with sides 3, 5, 7 and 12, 20, 28 similar?

4. A small pine tree, 8 feet tall, casts a shadow of 3 feet, and the large pine tree casts a shadow of 48 feet. Find the height of the larger tree.

5. A 5 foot woman casts a 6 foot shadow. In the same location and at the same time a flagpole casts a 30 foot shadow. How high is the flagpole?

6. ∆ABC ~ ∆DEF Find the other sides of the larger figure.

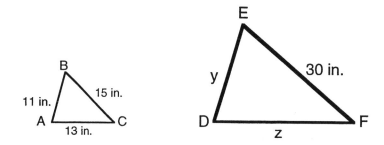

7.   Rays of light from the sun form shadows of upright objects on the ground. $\overline{PT}$ represents the height of a large monument; $\overline{TR}$ is a 126 ft shadow of the monument; $\overline{QS}$ represents a 10 ft. tree which casts an 18 ft. shadow, $\overline{SR}$. Find the height of the monument ($\overline{PT}$).

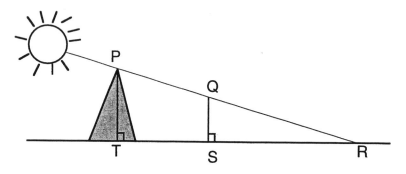

8.   Lin Le estimated the distance (x) across Lake Huyon by using the following diagram she drew. Find the distance across the lake.

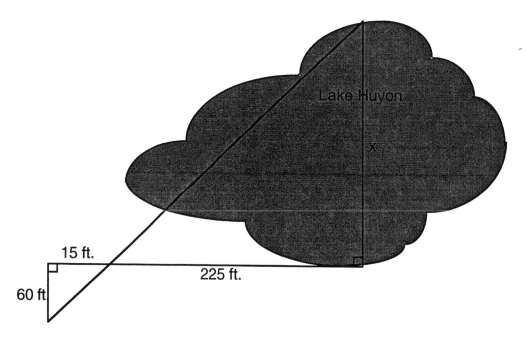

10.4 <u>Triangles and Proportions</u>

Theorem 10.3   A line intersecting two sides of a triangle and parallel to the third side divides the two intersected sides proportionately.

The proof of this theorem follows:

Given: △ABC with $\overline{DE} \parallel \overline{AC}$

Prove: $\dfrac{\overline{AD}}{\overline{BD}} = \dfrac{\overline{EC}}{\overline{BE}}$

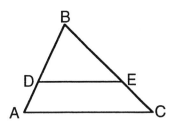

Statements	Reasons
1. $\overline{DE} \parallel \overline{AC}$	1. Given
2. ∠A and ∠BDE are corresponding angles. ∠C and ∠BED are corresponding angles.	2. Definition of corresponding angles.
3. ∠A = ∠BDE, ∠C = ∠BED	3. If two lines are parallel, then pairs of corresponding angles are equal.
4. △BAC ~ △BDE	4. Theorem 10.1
5. $\dfrac{\overline{AB}}{\overline{BD}} = \dfrac{\overline{BC}}{\overline{BE}}$	5. Definition of similarity
6. $\dfrac{\overline{AD}+\overline{BD}}{\overline{BD}} = \dfrac{\overline{BE}+\overline{EC}}{\overline{BE}}$	6. Substitution $\overline{AB} = \overline{AD}+\overline{BD};\ \overline{BC} = \overline{BE}+\overline{EC}$
7. $\dfrac{\overline{AD}}{\overline{BD}}+\dfrac{\overline{BD}}{\overline{BD}} = \dfrac{\overline{BE}}{\overline{BE}}+\dfrac{\overline{EC}}{\overline{BE}}$	7. Simplification
8. $\dfrac{\overline{AD}}{\overline{BD}}+1 = 1+\dfrac{\overline{EC}}{\overline{BE}}$	8. A quantity divided by itself equals one.
9. $\dfrac{\overline{AD}}{\overline{BD}} = \dfrac{\overline{EC}}{\overline{BE}}$	9. Equals subtracted from equals give equals.

Example:

Given: △ABC with $\overline{DE} \parallel \overline{AC}$, $\overline{BD}$ = 12 ft., $\overline{EC}$ = 3 ft., $\overline{BA}$ = 30 ft.

Find: $\overline{AD}$, $\overline{BE}$, and $\overline{BC}$

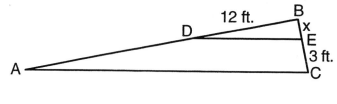

$$\overline{AD} = \overline{AB} - \overline{BD}$$

$$\overline{AD} = 30 - 12$$

$$\overline{AD} = 18 \text{ ft.}$$

To find $\overline{BE}$, use the proportion

$$\frac{\overline{BD}}{\overline{AD}} = \frac{\overline{BE}}{\overline{EC}}$$

$$\frac{12}{18} = \frac{x}{3}$$

$$18x = 36$$

$$x = 2$$

$$\overline{BC} = \overline{BE} + \overline{EC}$$

$$\overline{BC} = 2 + 3$$

$$\overline{BC} = 5 \text{ ft.}$$

36. Given: $\triangle ABC$ with $\overline{DE} \parallel \overline{AC}$, $\overline{BD} = 10$ ft.,
$\overline{EC} = 2$ ft., $\overline{BA} = 30$ ft.
    Find: $\overline{AD}$, $\overline{BE}$, and $\overline{BC}$

36.

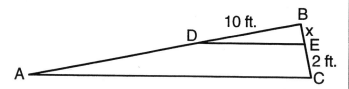

a. To find $\overline{BE}$, what proportion would you use?

$\overline{BE} =$ _____

a. Let $\overline{BE} = x$.

$$\frac{\overline{BD}}{\overline{AD}} = \frac{\overline{BE}}{\overline{EC}}$$

$$\frac{10}{20} = \frac{x}{2}$$

$$20x = 20$$

$$x = 1$$

$$\overline{BE} = 1 \text{ ft.}$$

b. To find $\overline{AD}$, what equation would you use?

$\overline{AD}$ = _____

b.

$\overline{AD} = \overline{AB} - \overline{BD}$

$\overline{AD} = 30 - 10$

$\overline{AD} = 20$ ft.

c. $\overline{BC}$ = _____

c.

$\overline{BC} = \overline{BE} + \overline{EC}$

$\overline{BC} = 1 + 2$

$\overline{BC} = 3$ ft.

37. Given: $\triangle RST$ with $\overline{UV} \parallel \overline{TS}$, $\overline{RV}$ = 9 cm.,
$\overline{VS}$ = 3 cm., and $\overline{RU}$ = 7 cm.

Find: $\overline{UT}$, $\overline{RS}$, and $\overline{RT}$

37.

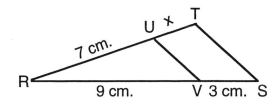

a. To find $\overline{UT}$, what proportion would you use?

$\overline{UT}$ = _____

a. Let $\overline{UT}$ = x.

$$\frac{\overline{RV}}{\overline{VS}} = \frac{\overline{RU}}{\overline{UT}}$$

$$\frac{9}{3} = \frac{7}{X}$$

$$9X = 21$$

$$X = \frac{21}{9}$$

$$X = 2\frac{1}{3} \text{ or } 2.\overline{3} \text{ cm.}$$

b. To find $\overline{RS}$, what equation would you use?

$\overline{RS}$ = _____

b.

$\overline{RS} = \overline{RV} + \overline{VS}$

$\overline{RS} = 9 + 3$

$\overline{RS} = 12$ cm.

c. Find $\overline{RT}$.

c. $\overline{RT} = \overline{RU} + \overline{UT}$

$$\overline{RT} = 7 + 2\frac{1}{3}$$

$$\overline{RT} = 9\frac{1}{3} \text{ or } 9.\overline{3} \text{ cm.}$$

38. Given: △WXY with $\overline{ZT} \parallel \overline{WX}$, $\overline{WY} = 12$ in., $\overline{XY} = 18$ in., and $\overline{WZ} = 5$ in.

Find: $\overline{YZ}$, $\overline{YT}$, and $\overline{XT}$

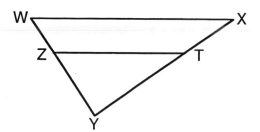

a. To find $\overline{YZ}$, what equation would you use?

$\overline{YZ} = $ _____

b. To find $\overline{YT}$, what proportion would you use?

$\overline{YT} = $ _____

c. Find $\overline{XT}$.

38.

a. $\overline{WY} = \overline{WZ} + \overline{ZY}$
   $12 = 5 + \overline{YZ}$
   $7 \text{ in.} = \overline{YZ}$

b.
$$\frac{\overline{WZ}}{\overline{ZY}} = \frac{\overline{XT}}{\overline{YT}}$$
$$\frac{5}{7} = \frac{18 - \overline{YT}}{\overline{YT}}$$
$$5\overline{YT} = 126 - 7\overline{YT}$$
$$12\overline{YT} = 126$$
$$\overline{YT} = 10.5 \text{ in.}$$

c. $\overline{YX} = \overline{YT} + \overline{XT}$
   $18 = 10.5 + \overline{XT}$
   $7.5 \text{ in.} = \overline{XT}$

Exercise 10.4

1. Given: $\overline{WV} \parallel \overline{TU}$ in △STU, $\overline{ST} = 8$, $\overline{SV} = 6$, and $\overline{VU} = 5$

Is $\dfrac{\overline{WT}}{8} = \dfrac{5}{6}$ a correct proportion?

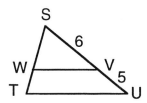

2. In △ABC, $\overline{DE}$ ‖ $\overline{AC}$, $\overline{AD}$ = 4 in., $\overline{BD}$ = 10 in., $\overline{BC}$ =15 in., and ∠BDE = 25°. Find $\overline{BE}$, $\overline{EC}$, and ∠A. Round answers to the nearest tenth.

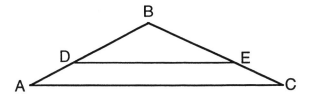

3. In △ABC, $\overline{AD}$ = 9 in., $\overline{BD}$ = 4 in., $\overline{EC}$ = 7 in., ∠A = 60°, ∠BDE = 60°, and ∠C = 80°. Find $\overline{BE}$, ∠BED, and ∠B. Round answers to the nearest tenth.

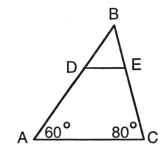

4. In △ABC, $\overline{DE}$ ‖ $\overline{BC}$. $\overline{AD}$ = a, $\overline{BD}$ = b, $\overline{AE}$ = c, and $\overline{EC}$ = d. Round answers to the nearest tenth.

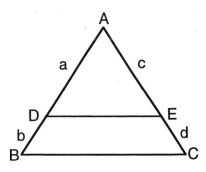

    a. a = 9 m., $\overline{AB}$ = 12 m., d = 7 m., find c.

    b. b = 4 m., a = 8 m., $\overline{AC}$ = 14 m., find d.

c. $\overline{AB} = 20$ m., $\overline{AC} = 26$ m., c $= 18$ m., find a.

Unit 10 Review

1. Fill in the blank with the appropriate word or phrase.

   a. A _____ is the comparison of two numbers by their indicated quotient.

   b. A _____ is a statement that two ratios are equal.

   c. In the proportion $\dfrac{a}{b} = \dfrac{c}{d}$ the numbers a and d are called the _____ of the proportion, and the numbers b and c are called the _____ of the proportion. The single term, d, is called the _____.

   d. Two triangles are called _____ if and only if three angles of one triangle are equal to three angles of the second triangle and all pairs of corresponding sides are in proportion. The symbol _____ is used to indicate such triangles.

   e. If the second and third terms of a proportion are equal, the second or third term is called the _____ between the first and fourth terms.

2. Are the triangles with sides 3, 5, 7 and 12, 20, 28 similar?

3. Given: $\overline{AB} \parallel \overline{DE}$, $\overline{AB} = 3$ cm., $\overline{BC} = 2$ cm., $\overline{CE} = 5$ cm., $\overline{CD} = 10$ cm.

   Find: $\overline{AC}$ and $\overline{DE}$

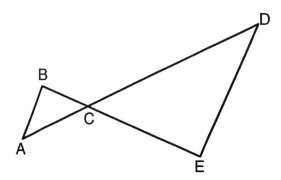

4. Find the fourth proportional to 3, 9, and 17.

5. Find the mean proportional between 11 and 21. Round to the nearest tenth.

6. Solve for x in each of the following. Round answers to the nearest tenth.

    a. $\dfrac{4}{3} = \dfrac{x+3}{5}$

    b. $\dfrac{2}{x+7} = \dfrac{x+5}{3}$

    c. $\dfrac{x}{\sqrt{5}} = \dfrac{6\sqrt{3}}{\sqrt{2}}$

    d. $\dfrac{x}{\sqrt{7}} = \dfrac{\sqrt{8}}{\sqrt{14}}$

    e. $\dfrac{x+6}{7} = \dfrac{-4}{x-5}$

    f. $\dfrac{x}{x-6} = \dfrac{5}{6}$

7. Which of the following proportions are true?

    a. $\dfrac{18}{9} = \dfrac{\left(\dfrac{1}{3}\right)}{\left(\dfrac{1}{2}\right)}$

    b. $\dfrac{7}{8} = \dfrac{21}{24}$

8. Find the ratio of 7 minutes to 2 hours.

9. A 7 foot upright pole near a vertical tree casts a 5 foot shadow. At the same time, find the height of the tree if its shadow is 35 feet.

10. Given: $\triangle ABC \sim \triangle DEF$

    Find x and y.

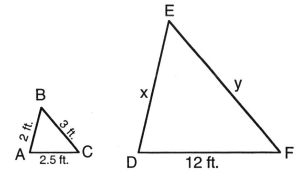

11. Given: $\overline{BD} \parallel \overline{AE}$, $\overline{AB} = 6$ ft., $\overline{BC} = 10$ ft., $\overline{DE} = 4$ ft., $\angle A = 40°$, $\angle CDB = 60°$
    Find: $\overline{DC}$, $\overline{AC}$, $\overline{CE}$, $\angle CBD$, $\angle E$, and $\angle C$
            Round answers to the nearest tenth.

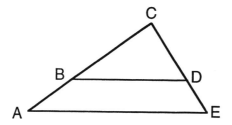

12. Given: $\overline{XY}$ ‖ $\overline{ON}$, $\overline{MO}$ = 21 in., $\overline{MX}$ = 16 in., $\overline{XN}$ = 8 in.

     Find: $\overline{MY}$, $\overline{YO}$, and $\overline{MN}$

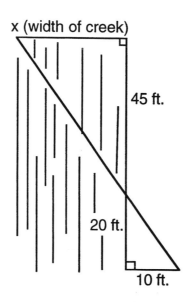

13. Sergo Popvo plans to build a bridge across a creek near his house. He
     steps off the distance and computes the width of the creek from the
     drawing below. Find the width of the creek to the nearest tenth.

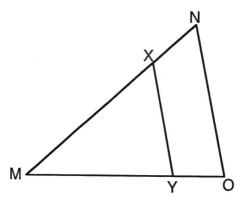

Unit 11

Basic Right Triangle Trigonometry

Learning objectives:

1. The student will demonstrate his mastery of the following definitions by writing them and by applying them to solutions of selected problems: tangent, sine, cosine.

2. The student will demonstrate his mastery of sine, cosine and tangent of 30°, 45°, and 60° by applying them correctly in problem solving.

3. The student will demonstrate his mastery of using the Square Root Table and Trigonometric Ratios Table by applying them correctly in problem solving.

Basic Right Triangle Trigonometry

11.1 Basic Definitions

The Greek word "trigonometry" means the measurement of triangles. In this unit, however, we will center our attention on the measurement of the acute angles of right triangles.

Study these two right triangles in Figure 11.1 and recall our discussion on similarity from Unit 10. If two angles of one triangle are equal to two corresponding angles of a second triangle, then the triangles are similar. $\Delta A_1B_1C_1 \sim \Delta A_2B_2C_2$ with $\angle B_1 = \angle B_2$ and $\angle C_1 = \angle C_2$.

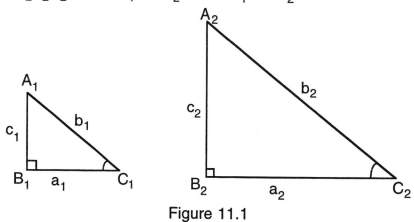

Figure 11.1

By the definition of similarity, the corresponding sides of the two triangles are proportional.

$$\frac{a_1}{a_2} = \frac{b_1}{b_2} = \frac{c_1}{c_2}$$

By interchanging the means in these equations, it is not difficult to obtain the following relationships. The corresponding ratios of the sides would equal:

$$\frac{a_1}{b_1} = \frac{a_2}{b_2} \text{ and } \frac{b_1}{c_1} = \frac{b_2}{c_2} \text{ and } \frac{a_1}{c_1} = \frac{a_2}{c_2}$$

As illustrated from the new sets of equations, we discovered that there are three basic ratios common to both triangles. The ratios are $\frac{a}{b}$, $\frac{b}{c}$, and $\frac{a}{c}$. These are called trigonometric ratios. The actual values for these three ratios do not depend on the size of the triangles but upon the measure of the acute angle involved. (Note: The measure of $\angle C$ in Figure 11.1 is the same in both triangles.)

Definition 11.1   The <u>tangent</u> (abbreviated as tan) of an acute angle of a right triangle is the ratio of the length of the opposite leg to the length of the adjacent leg.

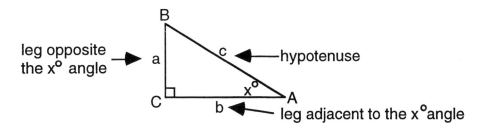

Figure 11.2

Study Figure 11.2. The legs are properly identified and labeled. Therefore, in reference to $\angle A$, <u>a</u> is the opposite leg and <u>b</u> is the adjacent leg.

$$\tan \angle A = \tan x° = \frac{\text{opposite leg}}{\text{adjacent leg}} = \frac{a}{b}$$

Example:

Find the tangent of $\angle Z$ in Figure 11.3.

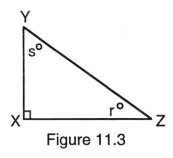

Figure 11.3

The hypotenuse is side $\overline{YZ}$.

In reference to $\angle Z$, the opposite leg is $\overline{XY}$.

In reference to $\angle Z$, the adjacent leg is $\overline{XZ}$.

$$\tan \angle Z = \tan r° = \frac{\text{opposite leg}}{\text{adjacent leg}} = \frac{\overline{XY}}{\overline{XZ}}$$

1.   Find the tangent of $\angle Y$ in Figure 11.3.

   The hypotenuse is side _____.

1.
$\overline{YZ}$

In reference to ∠Y, the opposite leg is

_____.

$\overline{XZ}$

In reference to ∠Y, the adjacent leg is

_____.

$\overline{YX}$

tan ∠Y = tan s° = _____

$\dfrac{\overline{XZ}}{\overline{YX}}$

Definition 11.2 The <u>sine</u> (abbreviated sin) of an acute angle of a right triangle is the ratio of the length of the opposite leg to the length of the hypotenuse.

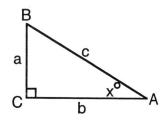

$$\sin \angle A = \sin x° = \frac{\text{opposite leg}}{\text{hypotenuse}} = \frac{a}{c}$$

Example:

In △XYZ find the tan r° and sin r°.

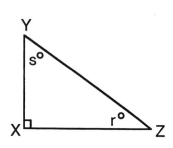

a. hypotenuse = $\overline{YZ}$

b. In reference to ∠Z, the opposite leg = $\overline{XY}$.

c. In reference to ∠Z, the adjacent leg = $\overline{XZ}$.

d. $\tan r° = \dfrac{\text{opposite leg}}{\text{adjacent leg}} = \dfrac{\overline{XY}}{\overline{XZ}}$

e. $\sin r° = \dfrac{\text{opposite leg}}{\text{hypotenuse}} = \dfrac{\overline{XY}}{\overline{YZ}}$

2.   Find sin ∠Y and tan ∠Y in △XYZ.   2.

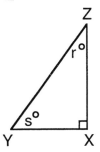

   a.   hypotenuse = _____   a. $\overline{YZ}$

   b.   In reference to ∠Y, the opposite leg is   b.
        _____. $\overline{XZ}$

   c.   sin ∠Y = sin s° = _____   c. $\dfrac{\overline{XZ}}{\overline{YZ}}$

   d.   In reference to ∠Y, the adjacent leg is   d.
        _____. $\overline{YX}$

   e.   tan ∠Y = tan s° = _____   e. $\dfrac{\overline{XZ}}{\overline{YX}}$

3.   Given △MNO, find the tangent and sine of   3.
      ∠M.

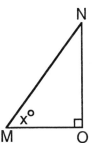

   a.   hypotenuse = _____   a. $\overline{MN}$

   b.   opposite leg = _____   b. $\overline{NO}$

   c.   adjacent leg = _____   c. $\overline{MO}$

   d.   tan x° = _____   d. $\dfrac{\overline{NO}}{\overline{MO}}$

e. sin x° = _____ | e. $\dfrac{\overline{NO}}{\overline{MN}}$

Definition 11.3 The <u>cosine</u> (abbreviated cos) of an acute angle of a right triangle is the ratio of the length of the adjacent leg to the length of the hypotenuse.

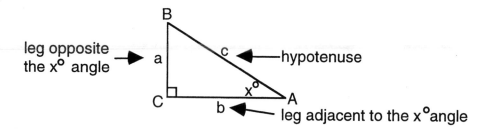

leg opposite the x° angle → a

c ← hypotenuse

C

b ← leg adjacent to the x°angle

x°

A

$$\cos \angle A = \cos x° = \dfrac{\text{adjacent leg}}{\text{hypotenuse}} = \dfrac{b}{c}$$

Example:

In △XYZ, find the cos ∠Z.

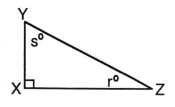

The hypotenuse is $\overline{YZ}$. In reference to ∠Z, the adjacent leg is $\overline{XZ}$.

$$\cos \angle Z = \cos r° = \dfrac{\text{adjacent leg}}{\text{hypotenuse}} = \dfrac{\overline{XZ}}{\overline{YZ}}$$

4.   Find the cos ∠Y for the ∠Y in the figure in the example above. | 4.

   a. The hypotenuse is _____. | a. $\overline{YZ}$

   b. In reference to ∠Y, the adjacent leg is _____. | b. $\overline{YX}$

   c. cos ∠Y = cos s° = _____ | c. $\dfrac{\overline{YX}}{\overline{YZ}}$

5.   Given △RUT, find the tangent, sine and cosine of ∠T. | 5.

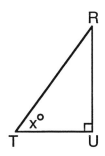

a. hypotenuse = _____

b. opposite leg = _____

c   adjacent leg = _____

d. tan x° = _____

e. sin x° = _____

f.   cos x° = _____

a. $\overline{RT}$

b. $\overline{RU}$

c. $\overline{UT}$

d. $\dfrac{\overline{RU}}{\overline{UT}}$

e. $\dfrac{\overline{RU}}{\overline{RT}}$

f. $\dfrac{\overline{UT}}{\overline{RT}}$

When the lengths of the legs and hypotenuse are known, these values may be substituted in the ratios and a numerical value found for the trigonometric ratios.

Example:

Find the tangent, sine, and cosine of ∠M.

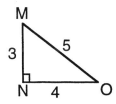

$$\tan \angle M = \frac{\text{opposite leg}}{\text{adjacent leg}} = \frac{4}{3}$$

$$\sin \angle M = \frac{\text{opposite leg}}{\text{hypotenuse}} = \frac{4}{5}$$

$$\cos \angle M = \frac{\text{adjacent leg}}{\text{hypotenuse}} = \frac{3}{5}$$

6. Using the drawing below, find the tangent, sine, and cosine of ∠A.

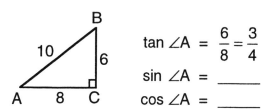

$\tan \angle A = \dfrac{6}{8} = \dfrac{3}{4}$

$\sin \angle A = $ _____

$\cos \angle A = $ _____

6.

$\sin \angle A = \dfrac{3}{5}$

$\cos \angle A = \dfrac{4}{5}$

7. Using the drawing below, find the tangent, sine, and cosine of ∠Y

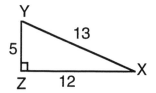

$\tan \angle Y = $ _____

$\sin \angle Y = $ _____

$\cos \angle Y = $ _____

7.

$\tan \angle Y = \dfrac{12}{5}$

$\sin \angle Y = \dfrac{12}{13}$

$\cos \angle Y = \dfrac{5}{13}$

8. Using △XYZ in item #7 above, find

$\tan \angle X = $ _____

$\sin \angle X = $ _____

$\cos \angle X = $ _____

8.

$\tan \angle X = \dfrac{5}{12}$

$\sin \angle X = \dfrac{5}{13}$

$\cos \angle X = \dfrac{12}{13}$

In summary, given right triangle, △XYZ below, the trigonometric ratios will be as listed below.

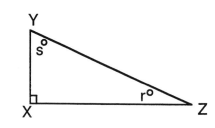

$$\sin \angle Z = \sin r° = \frac{\text{opposite leg}}{\text{hypotenuse}} = \frac{\overline{YX}}{\overline{YZ}}$$

$$\cos \angle Z = \cos r° = \frac{\text{adjacent leg}}{\text{hypotenuse}} = \frac{\overline{XZ}}{\overline{YZ}}$$

$$\tan \angle Z = \tan r° = \frac{\text{opposite leg}}{\text{adjacent leg}} = \frac{\overline{YX}}{\overline{XZ}}$$

$$\sin \angle Y = \sin s° = \frac{\text{opposite leg}}{\text{hypotenuse}} = \frac{\overline{XZ}}{\overline{YZ}}$$

$$\cos \angle Y = \cos s° = \frac{\text{adjacent leg}}{\text{hypotenuse}} = \frac{\overline{YX}}{\overline{YZ}}$$

$$\tan \angle Y = \tan s° = \frac{\text{opposite leg}}{\text{adjacent leg}} = \frac{\overline{XZ}}{\overline{YX}}$$

Exercise 11.1

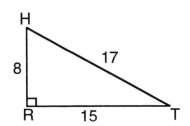

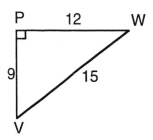

Determine the following trigonometric ratios:

1. cos ∠H   5. tan ∠O   9.   sin ∠V

2. sin ∠O   6. cos ∠W   10. cos ∠V

3. tan ∠H   7. tan ∠W   11. tan ∠T

4. sin ∠T   8. cos ∠M   12. sin ∠M

11.2   Trigonometric Ratios for Special Triangles

For some angles, the trigonometric ratios are not difficult to calculate. Specifically, let's examine the isosceles right triangle and the 30°–60° right triangle.

By Theorem 9.4, in an isosceles right triangle the hypotenuse is $\sqrt{2}$ times the length of one side. Recall the acute angles of an isosceles right triangle are both equal to 45°. In order to find the trigonometric ratios of a 45° angle, let's begin with an isosceles right triangle.

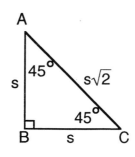

$$\sin \angle C = \sin 45° = \frac{s}{s\sqrt{2}} = \frac{1}{\sqrt{2}} = \frac{\sqrt{2}}{2}$$

$$\tan \angle C = \tan 45° = \frac{s}{s} = 1$$

$$\cos \angle C = \cos 45° = \frac{s}{s\sqrt{2}} = \frac{1}{\sqrt{2}} = \frac{\sqrt{2}}{2}$$

Example:

△ABC is an isosceles right triangle. Find sin ∠C, tan ∠C, and cos ∠C.

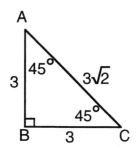

$$\sin \angle C = \sin 45° = \frac{3}{3\sqrt{2}} = \frac{1}{\sqrt{2}} = \frac{\sqrt{2}}{2}$$

$$\tan \angle C = \tan 45° = \frac{3}{3} = 1$$

$$\cos \angle C = \cos 45° = \frac{3}{3\sqrt{2}} = \frac{1}{\sqrt{2}} = \frac{\sqrt{2}}{2}$$

9.   Using △ABC in the example above, find tan ∠A, sin ∠A, and cos ∠A.

9.

$$\tan \angle A = \frac{3}{3} = 1$$

$$\sin \angle A = \frac{3}{3\sqrt{2}} = \frac{\sqrt{2}}{2}$$

$$\cos \angle A = \frac{3}{3\sqrt{2}} = \frac{\sqrt{2}}{2}$$

We can conclude that:

$$\begin{cases} \sin 45° = \dfrac{\sqrt{2}}{2} \\ \tan 45° = 1 \\ \cos 45° = \dfrac{\sqrt{2}}{2} \end{cases}$$

By Theorem 9.3, in a 30°–60° right triangle if the length of the side opposite the 30° angle is x, then the length of the hypotenuse is twice x and the length of the side opposite the 60° angle is x multiplied by the √3.

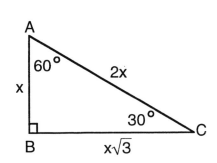

$$\sin \angle C = \sin 30° = \frac{x}{2x} = \frac{1}{2}$$

$$\tan \angle C = \tan 30° = \frac{x}{x\sqrt{3}} = \frac{\sqrt{3}}{3}$$

$$\cos \angle C = \cos 30° = \frac{x\sqrt{3}}{2x} = \frac{\sqrt{3}}{2}$$

$$\sin \angle A = \sin 60° = \frac{x\sqrt{3}}{2x} = \frac{\sqrt{3}}{2}$$

$$\tan \angle A = \tan 60° = \frac{x\sqrt{3}}{x} = \sqrt{3}$$

$$\cos \angle A = \cos 60° = \frac{x}{2x} = \frac{1}{2}$$

Example:

   $\triangle ABC$ is a 30°–60° right triangle. Find the sine, cosine and tangent of $\angle A$ and $\angle C$.

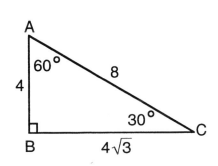

$$\sin \angle C = \sin 30° = \frac{4}{8} = \frac{1}{2}$$

$$\tan \angle C = \tan 30° = \frac{4}{4\sqrt{3}} = \frac{\sqrt{3}}{3}$$

$$\cos \angle C = \cos 30° = \frac{4\sqrt{3}}{8} = \frac{\sqrt{3}}{2}$$

$$\sin \angle A = \sin 60° = \frac{4\sqrt{3}}{8} = \frac{\sqrt{3}}{2}$$

$$\tan \angle A = \tan 60° = \frac{4\sqrt{3}}{4} = \sqrt{3}$$

$$\cos \angle A = \cos 60° = \frac{4}{8} = \frac{1}{2}$$

We can conclude that:

$$\begin{cases} \sin 30° = \dfrac{1}{2} \\[2mm] \tan 30° = \dfrac{\sqrt{3}}{3} \\[2mm] \cos 30° = \dfrac{\sqrt{3}}{2} \end{cases}$$

and that

$$\begin{cases} \sin 60° = \dfrac{\sqrt{3}}{2} \\[2mm] \tan 60° = \sqrt{3} \\[2mm] \cos 60° = \dfrac{1}{2} \end{cases}$$

Using the Square Root table in Appendix C, find the decimal approximations for $\sqrt{2}$ and $\sqrt{3}$. Now substitute these values into the trigonometric ratios listed.

Since $\sqrt{2} = 1.414$ and $\sqrt{3} = 1.732$ then:

$$\begin{cases} \sin 30° = \dfrac{1}{2} = 0.500 \\[2mm] \tan 30° = \dfrac{\sqrt{3}}{3} = \dfrac{1.732}{3} = 0.577 \\[2mm] \cos 30° = \dfrac{\sqrt{3}}{2} = \dfrac{1.732}{2} = 0.866 \end{cases}$$

$$\begin{cases} \sin 45° = \dfrac{\sqrt{2}}{2} = \dfrac{1.414}{2} = 0.707 \\[2mm] \tan 45° = 1 \\[2mm] \cos 45° = \dfrac{\sqrt{2}}{2} = \dfrac{1.414}{2} = 0.707 \end{cases}$$

$$\begin{cases} \sin 60° = \dfrac{\sqrt{3}}{2} = \dfrac{1.732}{2} = 0.866 \\[2mm] \tan 60° = \sqrt{3} = 1.732 \\[2mm] \cos 60° = \dfrac{1}{2} = 0.500 \end{cases}$$

These trigonometric values can be arranged in a table similar to the one shown below:

Degrees	sin x°	cos x°	tan x°
30°	0.500	0.866	0.577
45°	0.707	0.707	1.000
60°	0.866	0.500	1.732

Example:

Use the table to find the cosine of an angle that measures 30°.

First find the 30° angle under the column headed <u>degrees</u>. From this point move horizontally to the right and stop under the column for cosine. The value you find will be 0.866.

cos 30° = 0.866

10. Use the table to find the tangent of an angle   10.
     whose measure is 45°.   tan 45° = 1.000

Exercise 11.2

1. Without use of tables or a calculator, find the numerical value of the following. Leave your answer in simple radical form.

    a. sin 60°   d. sin 45°

    b. cos 45°   e. cos 30°

    c. tan 30°   f. tan 60°

2. Using the table developed in this section, find the numerical value of the following.

    a. cos 60°   d. tan 45°

    b. sin 30°   e. cos 45°

    c. sin 60°   f. tan 60°

11.3 <u>Reading the Trigonometric Table</u>

A complete table of trigonometric values can be found in Appendix D.

Example:

Using the Trigonometric Ratios Table in Appendix D, find the tangent, cosine, and sine of an 89° angle.

Locate the 89° measure in the fifth column under the <u>degree</u> heading.
From this point move horizontally to the right stopping at each new column.

The value you find for sine will be 1.000; .017 for cosine; 57.290 for tangent. Therefore,

$$\sin 89° = 1.000$$

$$\cos 89° = 0.017$$

$$\tan 89° = 57.290$$

11. Using the Trigonometric Ratios Table, find the value of each of the following:

    a. tan 37°

    b. sin 24°

    c. cos 63°

    d. tan 52°

    e. cos 20°

    f. sin 80°

11.

    a. 0.754

    b. 0.407

    c. 0.454

    d. 1.280

    e. 0.940

    f. 0.985

Example:

Using the Trigonometric Ratios table, find the measure of an angle, A, whose tangent equals 0.601.

First, locate the value 0.601 in the tangent column. Move horizontally to the left to the degree column. The measure you find will be 31°.

There, if tan $\angle A$ = 0.601, then $\angle A$ = 31°.

Example:

If tan $\angle A$ = 1.000, find $\angle A$ in the Trigonometric Ratios table.

tan $\angle A$ = 1.000

Therefore, $\angle A$ = 45°

12. Find the value of each angle.

    a. tan $\angle B$ = 1.732

    b. sin $\angle A$ = 0.707

    c. cos $\angle D$ = 0.866

12.

    a. $\angle B$ = 60°

    b. $\angle A$ = 45°

    c. $\angle D$ = 30°

d. sin ∠C = 0.391

e. cos ∠E = 0.259

d. ∠C = 23°

e. ∠E = 75°

Exercise 11.3

1.

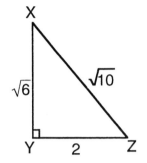

a. Find cos ∠Z.

b. Find tan ∠Z.

c. Find sin ∠Z.

2.   Using the Trigonometric Ratios table, find the numerical value of each.

a. tan 40°   b. sin 72°   c. cos 34°

3.   Using the Trigonometric Rations table, find the angle represented by each value.

a. tan ∠M = 0.384   b. sin ∠N = 0.999   c. cos ∠P = 1.000
     ∠M = _____   ∠N = _____   ∠P = _____

4.   Find the approximate measure of the angles of the triangle in exercise 1 above.

∠Z = _____

∠X = _____

11.4 Applications of Trigonometric Ratios

Example:

△ABC is an isosceles right triangle with one leg of length 7 in. Find the sine of ∠B.

$\overline{AC} = 7$ in.   Given

$\overline{CB} = 7$ in.   Definition of isosceles triangle

$\overline{AB} = 7\sqrt{2}$ in.   Theorem 9.4

$$\sin \angle B = \frac{\overline{AC}}{\overline{AB}} = \frac{7}{7\sqrt{2}} = \frac{\sqrt{2}}{2} = \frac{1.414}{2} = 0.707$$

Or, using the Trigonometric Ratios table, $\sin \angle B = \sin 45° = 0.707$.

Example:

Given trapezoid ABDC with $\angle A = 37°$, $\overline{AB} = 10$ in., $\overline{CD} = 8$ in., and $\overline{AC} = 5$ in., find the area of ABDC.

$$\sin 37° = 0.602$$

$$\sin 37° = \frac{h}{\overline{AC}}$$

$$(\sin 37°)(\overline{AC}) = h$$

$$(0.602)(5) = h$$

$$3.010 \text{ in.} = h$$

The area of trapezoid ABDC is calculated as follows:

$$A = \frac{1}{2}h(b_1 + b_2)$$

$$A = \frac{1}{2}(3.01)(8 + 10)$$

$$A = \frac{1}{2}(3.01)(18)$$

$$A = (3.01)(9)$$

$$A = 27.09 \text{ sq. in.}$$

13. In trapezoid ABCD, find the altitude and the area using the given measures. $\overline{AD}$ = 13 in., $\overline{BC}$ = 5 in., $\overline{AB}$ = 8 in. and $\angle A = 16°$.

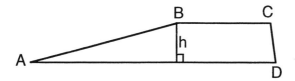

a. sin 16° = _____

b.

$$\sin 16° = \frac{h}{\overline{AB}}$$

$$(\sin 16°)(\overline{AB}) = h$$

$$\underline{\hspace{1cm}} = h$$

c. $A = \frac{1}{2}h(b_1 + b_2)$

14. In trapezoid ABCD, find the altitude and area using the measures that are given in the figure.

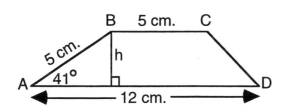

a. sin 41° = _____

b.

$$\sin 41° = \frac{h}{\overline{AB}}$$

$$(\sin 41°)(\overline{AB}) = h$$

$$\underline{\hspace{1cm}} = h$$

c. $A = \frac{1}{2}h(b_1 + b_2)$

13.

a. sin 16° = 0.276

b.

2.208 in. = h

c. A = 19.872 sq. in.

14.

a. sin 41° = 0.656

b.

h = 3.28 cm.

c. A = 27.88 sq. cm.

15. Find the altitude and the area of parallelogram RUTH using the measures given.

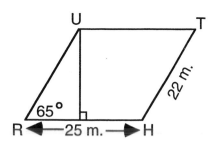

15.

a. sin 65° = _____

a. sin 65° = 0.906

b.

$$\sin 65° = \frac{h}{\overline{RU}}$$

$$(\sin 65°)(\overline{RU}) = h$$

$$\underline{\qquad} = h$$

b.

h = 19.932m.

c. A = bh

c. A = 498.3 sq. m.

16. In △ABC, ∠A = 50°, $\overline{AC}$ = 73 ft., and $\overline{AB}$ = 42 ft. Find the altitude and area of this triangle.

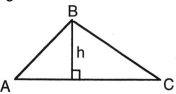

16.

a. sin 50° = _____

a. sin 50° = 0.766

b.

$$\sin 50° = \frac{h}{\overline{AB}}$$

$$(\sin 50°)(\overline{AB}) = h$$

$$\underline{\qquad} = h$$

b.

h = 32.172 ft.

c. $A = \frac{1}{2}bh$

c. A = 1174.278 ft.^{2}

17. In surveying for a new bridge, an engineer marked two points. One marking was placed on each side of the river. A third point, T, was

17.

marked such that $\overline{NT} \perp \overline{NO}$ and angle T
measures 44°. What is the distance across
the river from point N to O if $\overline{OT} = 80$ yd.?

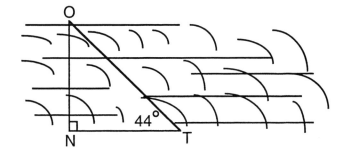

$$\sin 44° = \frac{\overline{ON}}{\overline{OT}}$$

$$\underline{\hspace{2cm}} = \overline{ON}$$

$$0.695 = \frac{\overline{ON}}{\overline{OT}}$$

$$(0.695)(80) = \overline{ON}$$

$$55.6 \text{ yd.} = \overline{ON}$$

In all of the previous examples sine of the angle was used. In the following
example cosine will be used. Tangent of the given angle may be used as well
as you will observe in item # 18 that follows later. Note: The trigonometric ratio
used depends on which sides of the right triangle are given.

Example:

A river is 20 yd. wide. A sail boat leaves shore at point B and its owner
wishes to tie up at point A. What is the distance from B to A. Round the
answer to the nearest hundredth.

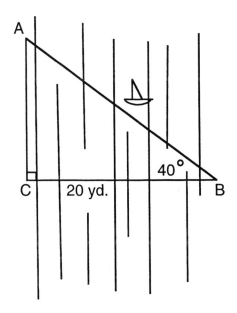

$$\cos 40° = \frac{20}{\overline{AB}}$$

$$0.766 = \frac{20}{\overline{AB}}$$

$$0.766\,\overline{AB} = 20$$

$$\overline{AB} = 26.11 \text{ yd.}$$

18. A six foot man observes the height of a tree 50 ft. away from him. If the man sights the top of the tree at an angle of 30° from the horizon, approximately (nearest hundredth) how tall is the tree?

18.

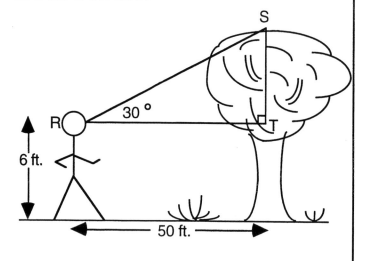

$$\tan 30° = \frac{\overline{ST}}{\overline{RT}}$$

$$0.577 = \frac{\overline{ST}}{50}$$

$$\underline{\qquad} = \overline{ST}$$

$\overline{ST}$ = 28.85 ft.

The height of the tree is approximately:

height of tree = $\overline{ST}$ + 6 ft. =

Height of tree = 34.85 ft.

Exercise 11.4

1. a. Given MNOP is a trapezoid with ∠M = 23°, $\overline{NO}$ = 12 in., $\overline{MP}$ = 27 in., and $\overline{MN}$ = 14 in. Find the area of trapezoid MNOP. Round the answer to the nearest thousandth.

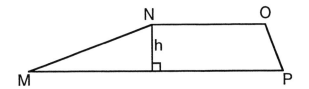

b. △ABC is an isosceles triangle with base $\overline{AC}$. If $\overline{AD}$ = 10 ft. and ∠A = 50°, find the area of △ABC to the nearest thousandth.

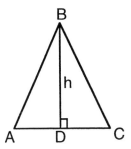

c. In parallelogram RSTU, ∠U = 17°, $\overline{ST}$ = 6 cm., and $\overline{RS}$ = 10 cm. Find the area of parallelogram RSTU to the nearest thousandth.

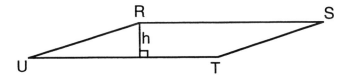

2. A tall radio tower is anchored by guy wires. One such wire, $\overline{XZ}$, was 175 ft. from the base of the tower. If ∠ZXY = 48°, find the length of $\overline{XZ}$. Round the final answer to hundredths.

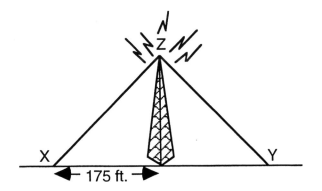

Unit 11 Review

1.

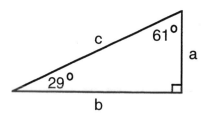

a. The leg opposite the 29° angle is _____ .

b. The leg adjacent to the 61° angle is _____ .

c. The hypotenuse is _____ .

d. The leg opposite the 61° angle is _____ .

e. The leg adjacent to the 29° angle is _____ .

2. Using the triangle in exercise 1 above, write the three trigonometric ratios for the 29° angle and the 61° angle in terms of a, b, and c.

    a. sin 29°   b. cos 29°   c. tan 29°

    d. sin 61°   e. cos 61°   f. tan 61°

3. Using the Trigonometric Ratios table, write the numeric values for the ratios found in exercise 2 above.

    a. sin 29°   b. cos 29°   c. tan 29°

    d. sin 61°   e. cos 61°   f. tan 61°

4.

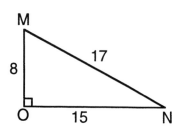

Fraction   Decimal

cos ∠M = _____   _____

tan ∠N = _____   _____

sin ∠N = _____   _____

Find the approximate measure of ∠N.

Find the approximate measure of ∠M.

5. Find the area of each of the following figures.

   a. STUW is a parallelogram with ∠S = 15°, $\overline{TU}$ = 18 ft., and $\overline{UW}$ = 10 ft. Find the area of parallelogram STUW.

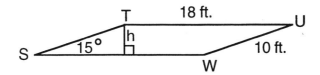

   b. Given △RQP with ∠R = 37°, $\overline{RP}$ = 5 cm., and $\overline{RQ}$ = 3 cm. Find the area of △RQP.

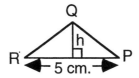

   c. Given trapezoid PMNO with ∠P = 43°, $\overline{MN}$ = 7 ft., $\overline{PO}$ = 15 ft., and $\overline{MP}$ = 6 ft. Find the area of trapezoid PMNO.

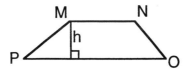

6. A surveyor wants to determine the distance between two points on opposite sides of a ditch. He measures $\overline{AB}$ and ∠B. If $\overline{AB}$ = 200 ft. and ∠B = 25°, then how far across does the ditch measure?

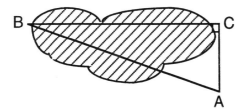

7. Without use of tables find the trigonometric ratio for the given special angle.

   a. sin 30°   b. cos 60°   c. tan 45°

   d. sin 60°   e. cos 30°   f. tan 60°

   g. sin 45°   h. cos 45°   i. tan 30°

8.   An angle of elevation is an angle formed by a horizontal line and a line of
     sight in the same plane. If the angle of elevation of the sun at a certain
     time measures 50°, find to the nearest foot the height of a building whose
     shadow is 20 feet long.

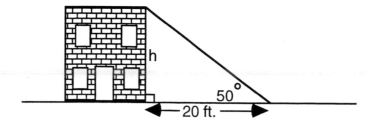

Unit 12

Circles and Sectors

Learning objectives:

1. The student will demonstrate his mastery of the following definitions and theorems by writing them and by applying them to solutions of selected problems:

    Definitions: circle, radius, center, chord, diameter, semicircle, tangent, point of tangency, secant, central angle, minor arc, major arc, inscribed angle, length of an arc, sector, circumcenter, and incenter.

    Theorems: 1. The measure of a central angle equals the measure of its intercepted arc.

    2. The measure of an inscribed angle is equal to one-half the measure of its intercepted arc.

    3. The ratio of the length of an arc of a circle to the circumference of the circle is the same as the ratio of the measure of the central angle of the arc to 360°.

    4. The ratio of the area of a sector of a circle to the area of the circle is the same as the ratio of the measure of the central angle of the arc to 360°.

    5. A line drawn from the center of a circle perpendicular to a chord bisects the chord and its intercepted arc.

    6. In the same circle, equal arcs have equal chords.

    7. In a circle, two chords are the same distance from the center of the circle if, and only if, they are equal.

    8. The perpendicular bisectors of the sides of a triangle meet at a point which is equidistant from the vertices of the triangle.

    9. The angle bisectors of a triangle meet in a point which is equidistant from the sides of the triangle.

2. The following constructions are required:

    a. To circumscribe a circle about a triangle.

b. To inscribe a circle within a triangle.

Circles and Sectors

12.1   Basic Definitions

Circles are in the environment everywhere: the top of the glass you had your juice from for breakfast; the top of your coffee cup; the plate you eat from; etc. The path a horse on a merry-go-round makes as the merry-go-round turns is a circle. The radius is the distance the horse is from the center of the merry-go-round and the center of the circle is the axle on which the merry-go-round turns.

To be more formal, recall the definition of a circle from Unit 7.

Definition 7.1	A <u>circle</u> is the set of all possible points a fixed distance from a given point. The fixed distance is called the <u>radius</u> of the circle and the given point is the <u>center</u>.

1.   a. In the diagram below, what is the radius?

     b. What is the center?

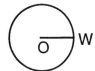

1. a. $\overline{OW}$

    b. O

Definition 12.1	A line segment is a <u>chord</u> if and only if its endpoints are points on the circle.

A specific type of chord that passes directly through the center of the circle is called a diameter. Because a diameter passes through the center of the circle, it can be defined in terms of the radius of a circle.

Definition 12.2	If two radii are joined to form a straight line segment, then this line segment is called a <u>diameter</u>.

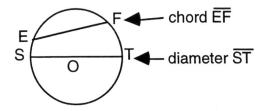

The measure of one diameter is equivalent to the length of two radii. ($d = 2r$, where d represents the diameter and r represents the radius.)

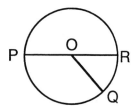

Radii $\overline{OP}$ and $\overline{OR}$ form diameter $\overline{PR}$.

$\overline{OR}$ and $\overline{OQ}$ do not form a diameter.

Definition 12.3   A diameter divides a complete circle into two equal parts. Each part is called a <u>semicircle</u>.

---

2.   Does a diameter always pass through the center of a circle?

| | 2. yes |

3.   Is a diameter a chord of a circle?

| | 3. yes |

4. $\overline{AB}$, $\overline{CD}$, and $\overline{EF}$ are all chords of the given circle. $\overline{CD}$ is a diameter. What two radii form $\overline{CD}$?

4.

$\overline{OD}$ and $\overline{OC}$

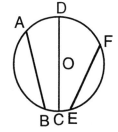

Definition 12.4   A line which intersects a circle at only one point is called a <u>tangent</u>. The point of intersection of the circle and tangent is called the <u>point of tangency</u>.

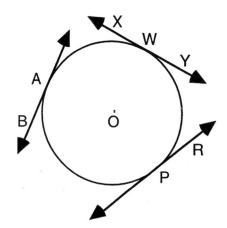

Figure 12.1

$\overleftrightarrow{AB}$ is a tangent with point of tangency, A. $\overrightarrow{XY}$ is a tangent with point of tangency, W.

5. Name another tangent and point of tangency in Figure 12.1.

    The tangent is _____ .

    The point of tangency is _____.

5.
$\overleftrightarrow{PR}$
P

Definition 12.5   A <u>secant</u> is a line which intersects a circle in two distinct points.

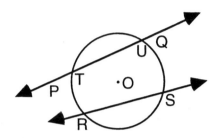

$\overrightarrow{PQ}$ and $\overleftarrow{RS}$ are secant lines. A line is a secant if and only if it contains a chord. In the figure above secant $\overrightarrow{PQ}$ contains chord $\overline{TU}$. Note: Secants and chords both intersect the circle in two distinct points. However, secants are lines and extend indefinitely beyond the circle. Chords are line segments and end on the circle.

6.

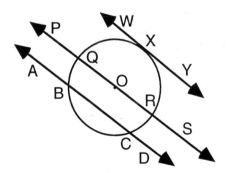

Given circle O:

a. Name the center.

b. Name two chords.

c. Name a diameter

6.

a. O

b. $\overline{BC}$, $\overline{QR}$

c. $\overline{QR}$

d. Name two secants.   d. $\overleftrightarrow{AD}$, $\overleftrightarrow{PS}$

e. Name two radii.   e. $\overline{OQ}$, $\overline{OR}$

f. Name a tangent.   f. $\overleftrightarrow{WY}$

g. Name the point of tangency.   g. X

Exercise 12.1

1. Explain why a diameter is a special type of chord.

2. Explain the relationship between the radius of a circle and the diameter of that same circle.

3. Explain the relationship between chord and secant.

4. Distinguish between secant and tangent.

5. In the circle to the right:

    a. Name the center.

    b. Name three radii.

    c. Name a diameter.

    d. Name three chords.

    e. Name a secant.

    f. Name a tangent.

    g. Name a point of tangency.

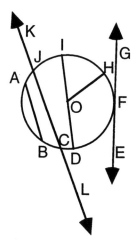

12.2   Angles in a Circle

> Definition 12.6   A central angle of a circle is an angle with vertex at the center of the circle and with sides as radii of the circle.

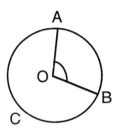

Figure 12.2

$\angle$AOB is a central angle in Figure 12.2.

The set of points between A and B divides the circle into two parts called arcs. Arcs are denoted by letters with the symbol ⌒.

> Definition 12.7   A minor arc is an arc that is less than half of a circle.

A minor arc is denoted by two letters with the arc symbol. $\overset{\frown}{AB}$ is a minor arc in Figure 12.2..

> Definition 12.8   A major arc is an arc that is more than half of a circle.

A major arc is denoted by three letters. It is larger than a semicircle. $\overset{\frown}{ACB}$ is a major arc. Since the entire circle measures 360°, a semicircle measures 180°, exactly half the measure of a circle.

> Theorem 12.1   The measure of a central angle equals the measure of the intercepted arc.

Example:

In the given diagram, if $\overset{\frown}{AB}$ = 89°, then find the central angle, $\angle$AOB.

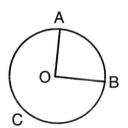

$\angle$AOB = 89° because $\overset{\frown}{AB}$ = 89°.

Example:

In the given diagram, if ∠AOB = 62°, find ⌢AB.

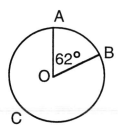

⌢AB = 62° because ∠AOB = 62°.

7. In the given diagram ∠AOB is a central angle.   7.
    Find ⌢AB. List the minor arc and the major arc.

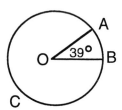

a. ⌢AB = _____   a. 39°

b. The minor arc is _____.   b. ⌢AB

c. The major arc is _____.   c. ⌢ACB

8. If ∠AOB is a central angle and ⌢AB = 70°,   8.
    then find ∠AOB and ⌢ACB.

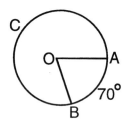

∠AOB = 70°

⌢AB + ⌢ACB = 360°
70° + ⌢ACB = 360°
⌢ACB = 290°

9.   If ∠AOB is a central angle, find $\overparen{AB}$, $\overparen{ACB}$,
      a major arc, and a minor arc.

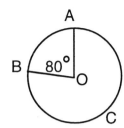

$\overparen{AB}$ = _____

$\overparen{ACB}$ = _____

Major arc = _____

Minor arc = _____

9.

80°

280°

$\overparen{ACB}$

$\overparen{AB}$

Definition 12.9   An <u>inscribed angle</u> is an angle whose vertex is on the
circle and whose sides are chords of the circle.

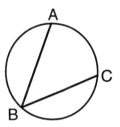

∠ABC is an inscribed angle.

Theorem 12.2   The measure of an inscribed angle is equal to one-half
the measure of its intercepted arc.

Example:

In the diagram below, if $\overparen{AC}$ = 112°, find ∠ABC.

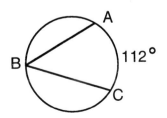

$$\angle ABC = \frac{1}{2}\overparen{AC} = \frac{1}{2}(112) = 56°$$

Example:

If ∠ABC = 39°, find $\overset{\frown}{AC}$.

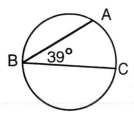

Solution: $\overset{\frown}{AC}$ = 2∠ABC = 2(39) = 78°

10. If $\overset{\frown}{AC}$ = 120°, find ∠ABC.

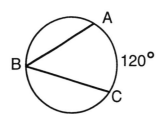

10. ∠ABC = 60°

11. If ∠ABC = 32°, find $\overset{\frown}{AC}$.

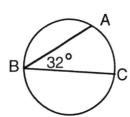

11. $\overset{\frown}{AC}$ = 64°

Exercise 12.2

1. Find the measures of central angle ∠AOB and of the inscribed angle
    ∠ACB. Identify the major arcs and the minor arcs.

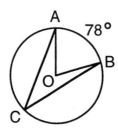

2. Point O is the center of the circle. If $\overline{DE}$ is the diameter, find ∠DOE, ∠COE, $\overarc{DC}$, and $\overarc{CE}$.

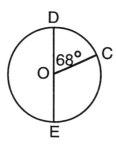

3. ∠ABC is an inscribed angle. If ∠ABC = 51°, find $\overarc{AC}$.

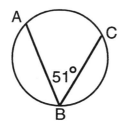

4. △ABC is an equilateral triangle. Find $\overarc{AC}$, $\overarc{AB}$, and $\overarc{BC}$.

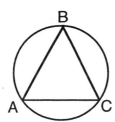

5. O is the center of the circle. ∠BAC = 30°, ∠COD = 30°, ∠1 = 105°
    Find ∠ABD, ∠BDO, $\overarc{BC}$, $\overarc{CD}$, $\overarc{AB}$, and $\overarc{AD}$.

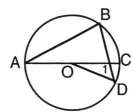

12.3   Arc Length and Area of a Sector

Recall the measure of an arc is the measure of its central angle.

> Definition 12.10   The length of an arc is the linear measure of the arc.

The length of an arc is how long the arc is should you cut it out, straighten it, and measure it with a ruler.

> Theorem 12.3   The ratio of the length of an arc of a circle to the circumference of the circle is the same as the ratio of the measure of the central angle of the arc to 360°. The length of an arc is expressed by the following equation:
>
> $$\frac{\text{Length of an arc (L)}}{\text{Circumference (C)}} = \frac{\text{Central Angle}}{360°}$$
>
> $$\frac{L}{C} = \frac{\text{Central Angle}}{360°}$$

Example:

Find the length of an arc whose central angle is 40° and whose circle has radius 6 in.

In finding the solution, find the circumference first. The formula for circumference is $C = 2\pi r$.

$$C = 2\pi r$$
$$C = 2\pi \cdot 6$$
$$C = 12\pi$$

Substituting C and the other values into the above formula to obtain:

$$\frac{L}{12\pi} = \frac{40°}{360°}$$
$$360L = 480\pi$$
$$L = \frac{480\pi}{360}$$
$$L = \frac{4}{3}\pi$$

Using $\pi = 3.14$ and approximating the answer to hundredths, L = 4.19 in.

12. Find the length of an arc whose central angle is 45° and whose circle has radius of 4 ft. Approximate the final answer to hundredths.

12.

Circumference = _____

$$C = 2\pi r$$
$$C = 2\pi \cdot 4$$
$$C = 8\pi$$
$$\frac{L}{8\pi} = \frac{45°}{360°}$$
$$360L = 360\pi$$
$$L = 1\pi$$
$$L = 3.14 \text{ ft.}$$

L = _____

13. Find the length of an arc whose central angle is 60° and whose circle has diameter 10 in. Approximate the final answer to hundredths.

13.

$$C = \pi d$$
$$C = 10\pi \text{ in.}$$
$$\frac{L}{10\pi} = \frac{60}{360}$$
$$L = \frac{5\pi}{3}$$
$$L = 5.23 \text{ in.}$$

Definition 12.11	A <u>sector</u> of a circle is the set of all possible points bounded by two radii and their intercepted arc.

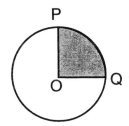

The shaded part represents a sector of a circle that can be described as a slice of pie.

Theorem 12.4	The ratio of the area of a sector of a circle to the area of the circle is the same as the ratio of the measure of the central angle of the arc to 360°. The area of a sector of a circle is expressed by this equation:

$$\frac{\text{Area of Sector}}{\text{Area of Circle}} = \frac{\text{Central Angle}}{360°}$$

Example:

Find the area of a sector with central angle 40° in a circle with radius 4 dm. Approximate the final answer to hundredths.

Area of Circle $= \pi r^2 = \pi \cdot 4^2 = 16\pi$ sq. dm.

$$\frac{\text{Area of Sector}}{\text{Area of Circle}} = \frac{\text{Central Angle}}{360°} \quad \underline{\text{or}} \quad \frac{A_{\text{sector}}}{A_{\text{circle}}} = \frac{\text{Central Angle}}{360°}$$

$$\frac{\text{Area of Sector}}{16\pi} = \frac{40°}{360°}$$

$$\frac{\text{Area of Sector}}{16\pi} = \frac{1}{9}$$

$$9(\text{Area of Sector}) = (1)(16\pi)$$

$$\text{Area of Sector} = \frac{16\pi}{9}$$

Area of Sector $= 5.58$ sq. dm.

14. Find the area of a sector with central angle 80° in a circle with radius 5 cm. Approximate the final answer to hundredths.

$A_{\text{circle}} = $ _____

$A_{\text{sector}} = $ _____

14.

$$A_{\text{circle}} = \pi r^2$$

$$A_{\text{circle}} = \pi 5^2$$

$$A_{\text{circle}} = 25\pi \text{ sq. cm.}$$

$$\frac{A_{\text{sector}}}{25\pi} = \frac{80}{360}$$

$$\frac{A_{\text{sector}}}{25\pi} = \frac{2}{9}$$

$$9(A_{\text{sector}}) = 50\pi$$

$$A_{\text{sector}} = \frac{50}{9}\pi$$

$$A_{\text{sector}} = 17.44 \text{ cm.}^2$$

Exercise 12.3

1. In each of the following find the length of the arc and the area of the sector. Approximate the final answer to hundredths. Use $\pi = 3.14$.

   a. central angle 90°, r = 10 ft.

   b. central angle 50°, r = $4\sqrt{2}$ cm.

   c. central angle 12°, d = 9 m.

2.   If the length of an arc is 20π m. and the circumference of the circle is 120π m., find the central angle.

3.   If the area of a sector is 3π sq. m. and the circle has radius 3 m., find the central angle.

4.   Find the area of the sector and length of the arc of the circle whose diameter is 4.5 in. and whose central angle is 50°. Round answer to hundredths.

5.   Mr. Jones planned to lay out his patio as illustrated below. One section (sector) of the patio would not be bricked in order to allow Mr. Jones space to plant his tree. Using the measurements in the illustration, find the area to the nearest hundredth of the patio that will be bricked.

2 ft.

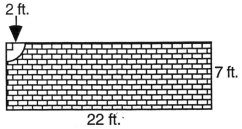

22 ft.

7 ft.

12.4   **Theorems Involving Circles**

Theorem 12.5	A line drawn from the center of a circle perpendicular to a chord bisects the chord and its intercepted arc.

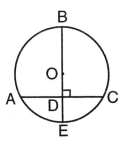

Given: O is the center of the circle with $\overline{OE} \perp \overline{AC}$

Prove (or conclusion): $\overline{OE}$ bisects $\overline{AC}$ which means $\overline{AD} = \overline{DC}$.
                       $\overline{OE}$ bisects $\overparen{AC}$ which means $\overparen{AE} = \overparen{EC}$.

Now, applying this theorem to the following example:

Example:

Given: $\overline{OE} \perp \overline{AC}$ and O is the center of the circle. $\angle EOC = 60°$, $\overline{DC} = 8$ in.

Find: $\overline{AC}$, $\overset{\frown}{EC}$, and $\overset{\frown}{AC}$

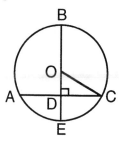

$\overline{OE}$ bisects $\overline{AC}$. Since $\overline{AD} = \overline{DC} = 8$ in, then $\overline{AC} = 16$ in.

$\angle EOC$ is a central angle. $\overset{\frown}{EC}$ has the same measure as its central angle. Therefore, $\overset{\frown}{EC} = 60°$. Since $\overline{OE}$ bisects $\overset{\frown}{AC}$, then $\overset{\frown}{AC} = 120°$.

15. Given: $\overline{OE} \perp \overline{AC}$ and O is the center of the circle. $\angle EOC = 71°$, $\overline{DC} = 7.5$ cm.

Find: $\overline{AC}$, $\overset{\frown}{EC}$, and $\overset{\frown}{AC}$

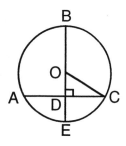

15. $\overline{AC} = 15$ cm.
        $\overset{\frown}{EC} = 71°$
        $\overset{\frown}{AC} = 142°$

16. Given: $\overline{OQ} \perp \overline{XY}$ and O is the center of the circle. $\angle XOQ = 85°$ and $\overline{XY} = 27$ in.

Find: $\overline{XP}$, $\overline{PY}$, $\angle QOY$, and $\overset{\frown}{QY}$

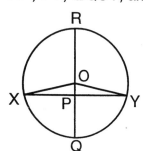

16.

$$\overline{XP} = \frac{1}{2}(27) = 13.5 \text{ in.}$$

$$\overline{PY} = \frac{1}{2}(27) = 13.5 \text{ in.}$$

$$\angle QOY = 85°$$

$$\overset{\frown}{QY} = 85°$$

Example:

If the radius of a circle is 8 inches and chord $\overline{AB}$ is 5 inches from the center of the circle, what is the measure of $\overline{AB}$?

Draw in radius $\overline{OB}$. $\triangle OEB$ is a right triangle. Use the Pythagorean Theorem to find $\overline{AB}$.

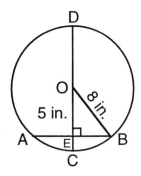

$$\overline{OE}^2 + \overline{BE}^2 = \overline{OB}^2$$
$$5^2 + \overline{BE}^2 = 8^2$$
$$25 + \overline{BE}^2 = 64$$
$$\overline{BE}^2 = 39$$
$$\overline{BE} = \sqrt{39}$$
$$\overline{AB} = 2\overline{BE} = 2\sqrt{39} \text{ in.}$$

or, to the nearest hundredth,

$$\overline{AB} = 12.49 \text{ in.}$$

17. Given: $\overline{OW} \perp \overline{MN}$ If the radius of a circle is ten inches and chord $\overline{MN}$ = 16 in., find $\overline{OA}$.

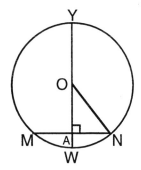

17.

If $\overline{MN}$ = 16 in.,

$$\overline{AN} = \frac{1}{2}(16) = 8 \text{ in.}$$

$\triangle OAN$ is a right triangle. Using the Pythagorean Theorem,

$$\overline{OA}^2 + \overline{AN}^2 = \overline{ON}^2$$
$$\overline{OA}^2 + 8^2 = 10^2$$
$$\overline{OA}^2 + 64 = 100$$
$$\overline{OA}^2 = 36$$
$$\overline{OA} = 6 \text{ in.}$$

Theorem 12.6   In the same circle, equal arcs have equal chords.

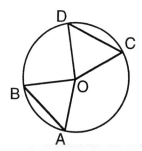

Given: $\overset{\frown}{AB} = \overset{\frown}{CD}$

Prove: $\overline{AB} = \overline{CD}$

Draw in radii $\overline{OB}$, $\overline{OA}$, $\overline{OD}$, and $\overline{OC}$.

Statements	Reasons
1. $\overset{\frown}{AB} = \overset{\frown}{CD}$	1. Given
2. $\angle BOA = \angle DOC$	2. The measure of a central angle equals the measure of its intercepted arc. Here the arcs are equal; hence, the angles are equal.
3. $\overline{OB} = \overline{OD}$, $\overline{OA} = \overline{OC}$	3. Radii of a circle are equal.
4. $\triangle BOA \cong \triangle DOC$	4. SAS = SAS
5. $\overline{AB} = \overline{CD}$	5. CPCTE

Theorem 12.7   In a circle, two chords are the same distance from the center of the circle if, and only if, they are equal.

This theorem is a theorem and its converse.

Statement 1:   If two chords are the same distance from the center of a circle, then these chords are equal.

Statement 2:
(the converse)   If two chords of a circle are equal, then they are the same distance from the center of the circle.

Example (using Statement 1):

In circle O, chords $\overline{AB}$ and $\overline{CD}$ are both 4 in. from the center of the circle. If $\overline{AB} = 6$ in., find the length of $\overline{CD}$.

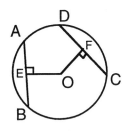

By Theorem 12.7, Statement 1, since $\overline{AB}$ and $\overline{CD}$ are both 4 in. from the center of the circle, then $\overline{AB} = \overline{CD} = 6$ in.

Example (using Statement 2):

In circle O, if $\overline{AB} = \overline{CD}$ and $\overline{OF} = 5$ ft., find $\overline{OE}$.

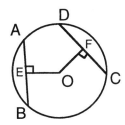

Since $\overline{AB} = \overline{CD}$, from Theorem 12.7, Statement 2, it can be concluded that $\overline{OE} = \overline{OF} = 5$ ft.

18. If $\overline{XW} = \overline{UV}$ and $\overline{OS} = 2$ in., find $\overline{OT}$. Tell why.

18.

$\overline{OT} = 2$ in. by Theorem 12.7, Statement 2.

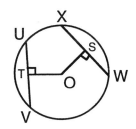

19. In the diagram in Exercise 18 above, $\overline{OT} = \overline{OS}$ and $\overline{UV} = 3.5$ cm., find $\overline{XW}$. Tell why.

19. $\overline{XW} = 3.5$ cm. by Theorem 12.7, Statement 1.

Exercise 12.4

1. Given: $\overline{BE}$ is a diameter. $\overline{BE} \perp \overline{AC}$, $\overline{DC} = 4$ m., $\overset{\frown}{AE} = 70°$

   Find: $\overline{AC}$, $\overset{\frown}{EC}$, and $\overset{\frown}{AC}$

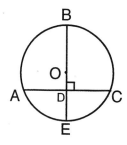

2.   Given: $\overline{OE} \perp \overline{AC}$, $\overline{AD}$= 2.3 ft., $\angle DOC = 42°$

     Find: $\overline{AC}$, $\overparen{EC}$, $\overparen{AE}$, $\overparen{AC}$, and $\angle OCD$

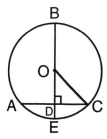

3.   If the radius of a circle is 10 in. and chord $\overline{AB}$ is 8 in. from the center of the circle, find the length of $\overline{AB}$ and $\overline{EC}$.

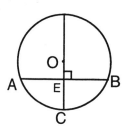

4.   If $\overline{AB} = \overline{DC}$ and $\overline{OX}$ = 4 ft., find the length of $\overline{OY}$.

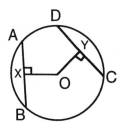

5.   If $\overline{OE} = \overline{OF}$ and $\overline{AB}$ = 2.5 mm., find $\overline{CD}$.

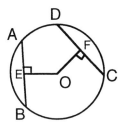

12.5   Inscribing and Circumscribing Circles

Theorem 12.8   The perpendicular bisectors of the sides of a triangle meet at a point which is equidistant from the vertices of a triangle.

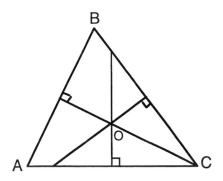

Figure 12.3

In △ABC, point O is the intersection of three perpendicular bisectors. This point is exactly the same distance from each vertex of the triangle.

Definition 12.12   The point of intersection of the perpendicular bisectors of the sides of a triangle is called the <u>circumcenter</u> of the triangle.

Point O in Figure 12.3 is called the circumcenter of the triangle.

Using Definition 12.12, it is possible to construct a point equidistant from the vertices and to circumscribe a circle about the triangle.

Construction 12.1   To Circumscribe a Circle About a Triangle

Step 1:   Draw a triangle ABC and label the vertices.

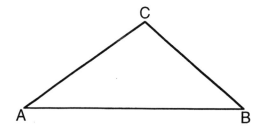

Step 2:   Now construct the perpendicular bisector of each side as
           demonstrated in Unit 1. Actually, it is sufficient to bisect only two
           sides of the triangle in locating the circumcenter. By constructing
           the third, a check on accuracy is obtained. If the third bisector
           intersects the first two in different points, it is advisable to start
           over.

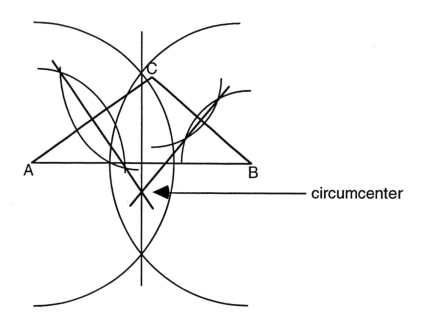

circumcenter

           In this example the circumcenter fell outside the triangle.
           However, this does not always occur. In obtuse triangles the
           circumcenter falls in the exterior of the triangle; in acute triangles
           it falls in the interior of the triangle; and, in right triangles, it lies
           on the hypotenuse.

Step 3:   Using the circumcenter as center of your compass and the
           distance from the circumcenter to either A, B, or C as the radius,
           draw a circle completely about the triangle.

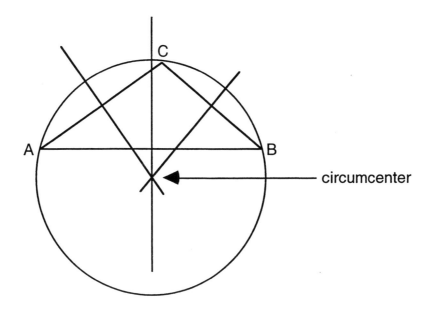

circumcenter

Theorem 12.9   The angle bisectors of a triangle meet in a point which is equidistant from the sides of the triangle.

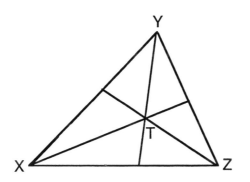

Figure 12.4

In △XYZ, point T is the intersection of the angle bisectors. This point is exactly the same distance from each of the sides of the triangle.

Definition 12.13   The point of intersection of the angle bisectors of a triangle is called an <u>incenter</u>.

Point T in Figure 12.4 is called the incenter of △XYZ. This definition is used to inscribe a circle within a triangle.

Construction 12.2   To inscribe a circle within a triangle

Step 1: Construct a triangle ABC and bisect each angle.

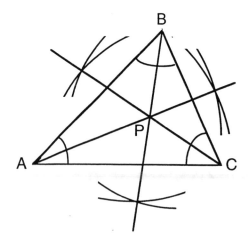

Again the incenter can be obtained by constructing only two angle bisectors. However, a third is an excellent check for accuracy. The incenter will always be inside the triangle.

Step 2: Construct a perpendicular from point P to any one of the sides.

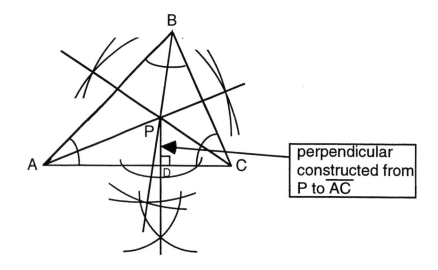

perpendicular constructed from P to $\overline{AC}$

Step 3: Using P as center and the length of $\overline{PD}$ as radius, construct a circle within triangle ABC.

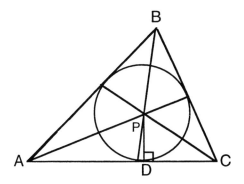

===============

Exercise 12.5

1. Follow the three steps in Construction 12.1 and locate the circumcenter of triangle ABC. Then, construct a circle about the figure such that the circle passes through A, B, and C.

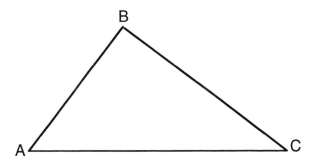

2. Using the steps in Construction 12.2, find the incenter of the given triangle and inscribe a circle within.

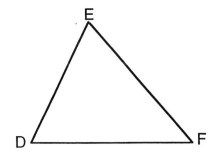

===============

Unit 12 Review

I.   Fill in the blanks with an appropriate word or phrase as discussed in this unit.

1. A _____ is the set of points a given distance from a fixed point. The given distance is a _____ of the circle and the fixed point is the _____.

2. If two radii are put together to form a straight line segment, this line segment is called a _____ of the circle.

3. A line segment whose endpoints are both on the circle is called a _____.

4. A line which intersects a circle in only one place is called a _____. The point where the line and circle intersect is called the _____.

5. A _____ is a line which intersects a circle in two distinct points.

6. A _____ of a circle is an angle with vertex at the center of the circle and with sides the radii of the circle.

7. An _____ is an angle whose vertex is on the circle and whose sides are chords of the circle.

8. A _____ of a circle is the set of all points bounded by two radii and their intercepted arc.

9. The point of intersection of the perpendicular bisectors of the sides of a triangle is called the _____.

10. The point of intersection of the angle bisectors of a triangle is called an _____.

II.   Find the solution for each of the following.

1.

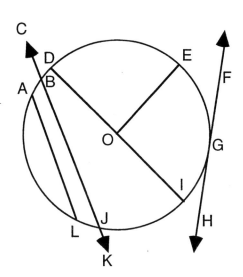

   a. Name the center.

   b. Name three radii.

   c. Name a diameter.

   d. Name three chords.

   e. Name a secant.

   f. Name a tangent.

   g. Name a point of tangency.

2. If ∠AOB is a central angle and $\overline{AC}$ is a diameter, find $\overset{\frown}{AB}$, $\overset{\frown}{BC}$ and $\overset{\frown}{AC}$. Name a major arc, a semicircle and a minor arc.

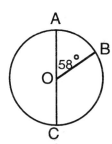

3. Given : ∠AEB = 55°, ∠D = 40°, and $\overset{\frown}{BD}$ = 90°

    Find: $\overset{\frown}{CD}$, $\overset{\frown}{AB}$, ∠BAD, ∠2, ∠CBD, $\overset{\frown}{AC}$, ∠ABD, and ∠ABC
               (Hint: Find the measures of ∠BAD, ∠ABC, ∠2, and ∠CBD
               first.)

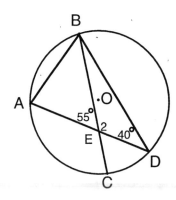

4. Find the length of the arc and the area of the sector in each of the following. Use π = 3.14 and round answers to hundredths.

   a. r = 6 ft., central angle = 45°

   b. d = 10√2 in., central angle = 80°

   c. r = 9 ft., central angle = $12\frac{1}{2}$°

5. Given: $\overline{AB} \perp \overline{CD}$ and O is the center of the circle. ∠EOD = 50°,
             $\overline{OE}$ = 3 in., $\overline{OD}$ = 5 in.

   Find: $\overline{DE}$, $\overline{CD}$, $\overset{\frown}{BD}$, $\overset{\frown}{CD}$, $\overset{\frown}{CF}$, $\overset{\frown}{AD}$, and $\overset{\frown}{AF}$.

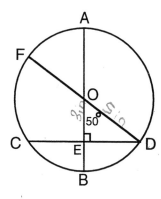

6. If $\overline{AB} = \overline{CD}$ and O is the center of the circle with $\overline{OS}$ = 9 yd., find the length of $\overline{OT}$.

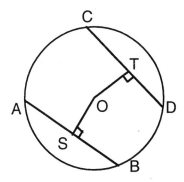

7. If $\overline{OE} = \overline{OF}$ and $\overline{AB} = 2\sqrt{3}$ mm., find $\overline{CD}$.

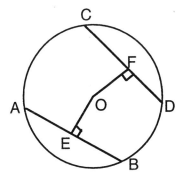

8. Given △ABC, circumscribe a circle about it.

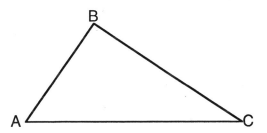

9. Given △DEF, inscribe a circle within it.

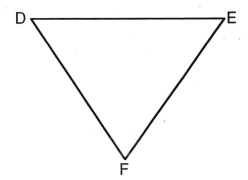

Unit 13

Coordinate Geometry

Learning Objectives:

1. The student will demonstrate his mastery of the following definitions, formulas, and implications by writing them and by applying them to solutions of selected problems.

Definitions: x-axis, y-axis, origin, quadrant, ordinate, abscissa, linear equation, slope, x-intercept, and y-intercept

Formulas: $\text{slope} = \dfrac{\text{rise}}{\text{run}}$

$\text{slope} = \dfrac{y_2 - y_1}{x_2 - x_1}$

$\text{midpoint} = \left(\dfrac{x_1 + x_2}{2}, \dfrac{y_1 + y_2}{2} \right)$

$y = mx + b$ (slope, y-intercept form of a straight line)

$y - y_1 = m(x - x_1)$ (point, slope form of a straight line)

$Ax + By = C$ (standard form of a straight line)

$\text{distance} = \sqrt{(x_2 - x_1)^2 + (y_2 - y_1)^2}$

Theorems:

1. Two lines are parallel if and only if they have the same slope.

2. Two lines are perpendicular if and only if their slopes are negative reciprocals of each other.

3. If (x_1, y_1) and (x_2, y_2) are the endpoints of a line segment, the midpoint of the line segment is determined by the formula:
    $\text{midpoint} = \left(\dfrac{x_1 + x_2}{2}, \dfrac{y_1 + y_2}{2} \right).$

4. If (x_1, y_1) and (x_2, y_2) are the endpoints of a line segment, the undirected distance from (x_1, y_1) to (x_2, y_2) is given by the formula:

$$\text{distance} = \sqrt{(x_2 - x_1)^2 + (y_2 - y_1)^2}.$$

2. The student will graph the equation of a straight line by three methods.

    a.   selection of points
    b.   slope, y-intercept
    c.   x-intercept, y-intercept

3. The student will write the equation of a straight line

    a.   given two points.
    b.   given a point and the slope.
    c.   given a point and a line to which it is parallel.
    d.   given a point and a line to which it is perpendicular.
    e.   given the x-intercept and y-intercept.
    f.   given the slope and y-intercept.
    g.   given the slope and x-intercept.

4. The student will plot points and describe their location in the Cartesian coordinate system.

5. The student will identify the slope of a line as positive, negative, zero, or no slope by inspecting the graph of the equation of the line.

Coordinate Geometry

13.1 Introduction

Coordinate geometry ties together some concepts from algebra and geometry. Rene' Descartes, a Frenchman, is credited with having developed a lot of the information in coordinate geometry.

In much the same way a road map helps a person along his journey, a Cartesian coordinate system helps to locate points in a plane.

Definition 13.1	In the Cartesian coordinate system the horizontal axis is called the x-axis.

Definition 13.2	In the Cartesian coordinate system the vertical axis is called the y-axis.

Definition 13.3	The x-axis and y-axis meet in a point called the origin.

Definition 13.4	The x-axis and y-axis divide the plane into four parts called quadrants.

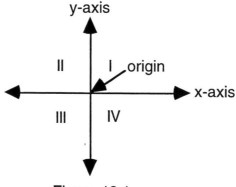

Figure 13.1

Quadrants are numbered counterclockwise. The positive side of the x-axis is to the right of the y-axis. The negative side of the x-axis is to the left of the y-axis. The positive side of the y-axis is above the x-axis and the negative side of the y-axis is below the x-axis. Points are plotted from ordered pairs. In an ordered pair, the x-coordinate comes first and the y-coordinate comes second. This is why it is called an ordered pair; the order in which the coordinates are placed must always be the same. Ordered pairs are written in the form (x,y).

Definition 13.5	In an ordered pair, (x,y), the x-coordinate is called the abscissa.

Definition 13.6   In an ordered pair, (x,y), the y-coordinate is called the ordinate.

In quadrant I both coordinates are positive. In quadrant II the abscissa is negative and the ordinate is positive. In quadrant III both coordinates are negative. In quadrant IV, the abscissa is positive and the ordinate is negative. Refer to Figure 13.2

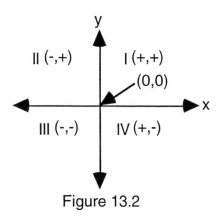

Figure 13.2

13.2   **Plotting Points**

Any point must fall in one of the four quadrants or on the axes. There are <u>eight</u> possibilities for locations of points: positive x-axis, first quadrant, positive y-axis, second quadrant, negative x-axis, third quadrant, negative y-axis, and fourth quadrant.

Taking an example of each case, let's begin with the positive x-axis. The point (4,0) falls on the <u>positive x-axis</u> a distance of four units to the right of the origin.

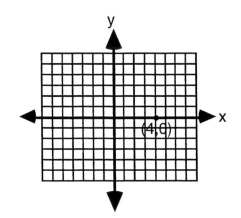

The point (3,2) falls in the
first quadrant a distance
of three units to the right
of the origin and two units
above the positive x-axis.

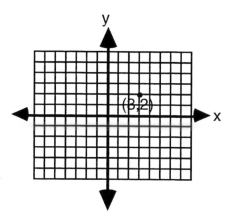

The point (0,3) falls on the
positive y-axis a distance
of three units above the
origin.

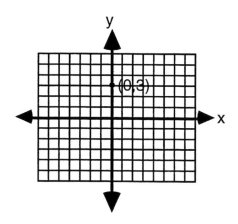

In the second quadrant the
abscissa is negative. Thus,
(-2,4) would be two units to
the left of the origin and
four units above the
negative x-axis.

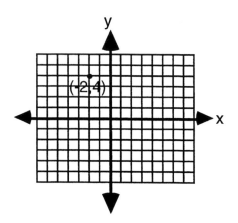

The point (-3,0) falls on the negative x-axis a distance of three units from the origin.

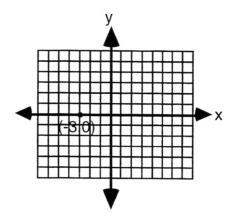

In the third quadrant both abscissa and ordinate are negative. To plot a point here move to the left of the origin and move below the negative x-axis. For example, (-2,-4) is two units to the left of the y-axis and four units below the negative x-axis.

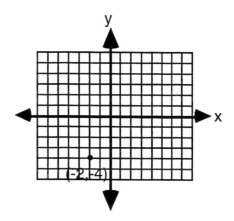

The point (0,-3) falls three units below the origin on the negative y-axis.

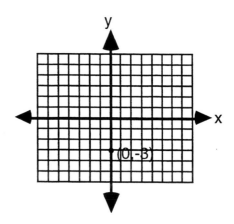

The point (4,-2) falls in the
<u>fourth</u> <u>quadrant</u> since the
abscissa is positive and
the ordinate is negative.
In plotting go to the right
of the origin four spaces
and go down two spaces
from here.

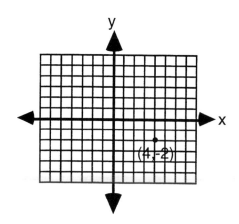

1. Plot the following points and
    describe the location of each
    point.

    a. (-6,0)
    b. (-2,-3)
    c. (5,1)
    d. (0,-2)
    e. (-3,4)
    f. (3,-5)
    g. (2,0)
    h. (0,6)
    i. (-1,4)
    j. (1,-4)

1.

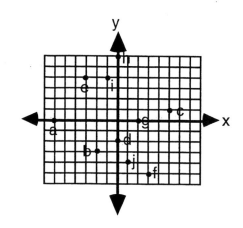

a. negative x-axis
b. quadrant III
c. quadrant I
d. negative y-axis
e. quadrant II
f. quadrant IV
g. positive x-axis
h. positive y-axis
i. quadrant II
j. quadrant IV

Exercise 13.1

1. Plot the following points and describe in words their location.

    a. (3,4)   b. (-2,-5)   c. (-3,0)

d. (0,-3)   e. (-2,4)   f. (2,-4)

g. (0,3)   h. (4,0)   i. (3,-1)

j. (6,3)   k. (1,-1)   l. (0,0)

13.3   Slope

Geometrically, any two points determine one and only one line in a plane. Hence, (3,1) and (5,3) determine a line as shown below.

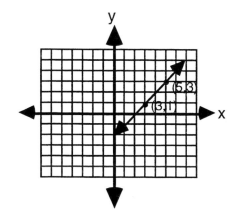

Sometimes we will need to discuss the steepness of a line or whether the line rises or falls. The term used to describe this concept is slope.

Definition 13.7   Slope is defined to be the rise (number of units one goes up or down) divided by the run (number of units one goes left to right or vice versa). $$slope = \frac{rise}{run}$$

Example:

Find the slope of the line through (3,1) and (5,3).

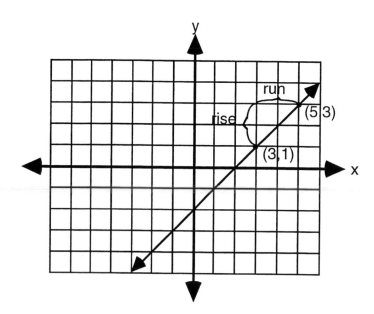

Solution: To go from the point (3,1) to (5,3) we go up two units and to the right two units. Up and to the right are both positive directions so

$$slope = m = \frac{rise}{run} = \frac{2}{2} = 1.$$

This means the slope is positive so the line rises as you view it from left to right.

2.   Find the slope of the line through (-2,3) and (1,5).

2.

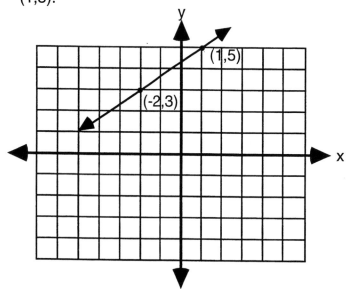

From(-2,3) to (1,5) go _____ (up or down) _____ units and go _____(left or right) _____ units.

up
2, right
3

Consequently, the slope $= m = \dfrac{\text{rise}}{\text{run}} = \underline{\quad}. \qquad \bigg| \qquad \dfrac{2}{3}$

This is one method for finding slope but depends heavily on being able to easily count units on a graph. Also, notice the slope formula, $m = \dfrac{\text{rise}}{\text{run}}$, can be obtained by systematically using another formula. The rise, the amount of up and down movement, is actually the difference in the y coordinates. The run, the amount of horizontal movement (left to right movement), is actually the difference in the x coordinates. Consequently,

$$\text{slope} = m = \frac{\text{difference in the y coordinates}}{\text{difference in the x coordinates}}$$

Note the differences must be taken in the same order. In formula notation, if (x_1, y_1) and (x_2, y_2) are any two points, then

$$\text{slope} = m = \frac{y_2 - y_1}{x_2 - x_1}$$

Example: Find the slope of the line through (-2,3) and (1,5).

Solution: Call the first point (x_1, y_1). That is, $(x_1, y_1) = (-2,3)$, so $x_1 = -2$ and $y_1 = 3$. Call the second point (x_2, y_2), so $x_2 = 1$ and $y_2 = 5$. Substituting into the formula gives:

$$m = \frac{y_2 - y_1}{x_2 - x_1} = \frac{5 - 3}{1 - (-2)} = \frac{2}{3}$$

Does it matter which point is (x_1, y_1) and which is (x_2, y_2)?

No, reversing the original roles, let $(x_2, y_2) = (-2,3)$ and $(x_1, y_1) = (1,5)$. Substituting into the formula,

$$m = \frac{y_2 - y_1}{x_2 - x_1} = \frac{3 - 5}{-2 - 1} = \frac{-2}{-3} = \frac{2}{3}.$$

Notice the same slope was obtained either way.

Example: Determine the slope of the line through (3,-4) and (-2,1) both

(a)   graphically, $\dfrac{\text{rise}}{\text{run}}$, and

(b)   algebraically, $m = \dfrac{y_2 - y_1}{x_2 - x_1}$.

Solution:

(a)

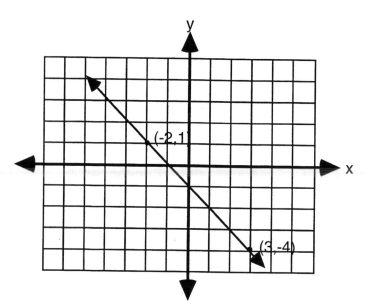

Graphically, beginning at (-2,1), the rise is down five units or negative five. Beginning with (-2,1), the run is over five or positive five. The slope is

$$m = \frac{rise}{run} = \frac{-5}{5} = -1.$$

(b) Algebraically, let $(x_1, y_1) = (3,-4)$ and $(x_2, y_2) = (-2,1)$. Substituting into the formula,

$$m = \frac{y_2 - y_1}{x_2 - x_1} = \frac{1-(-4)}{-2-3} = \frac{5}{-5} = -1.$$

3. Determine the slope of the line through (4,1) and (2,-3) both (a) graphically and (b) algebraically.

3.

(a)

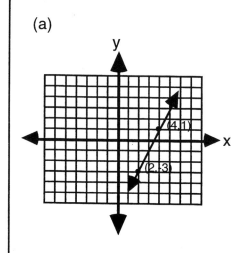

rise = 4 units
run = 2 units

$$m = \frac{rise}{run} = \frac{4}{2} = 2$$

(b)

$$m = \frac{-3-1}{2-4} = \frac{-4}{-2} = 2$$

The slope of a line must either be positive, negative, zero, or undefined, usually denoted as no slope.

If a line rises from left to right, then the slope is positive.

Example:

Two points on line L are (4,3) and (2,-1). Notice the line rises, viewing it from left to right. The slope,

$$m = \frac{3 - (-1)}{4 - 2} = \frac{4}{2} = 2$$

is positive.

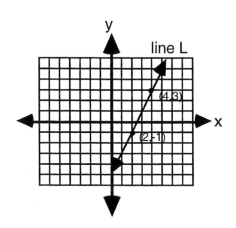

If a line falls from left to right, then the slope is negative.

Example:

Let (-3,3) and (3,-1) be two points on line W. Using the slope formula, the slope,

$$m = \frac{3 - (-1)}{-3 - 3} = \frac{4}{-6} = \frac{-2}{3}$$

Observe, the line falls from left to right and the slope is negative.

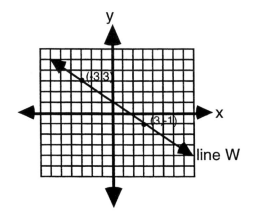

If a line is vertical, then it has no slope.

Example:

Let (5,3) and (5,-2) be two points on a vertical line, P. Substituting into the slope formla gives

$$m = \frac{3 - (-2)}{5 - 5} = \frac{5}{0}$$

which is undefined. This is called no slope. Notice that on this vertical line the x-coordinates are the same. This is true for all vertical lines. Because of this, the denominator of the slope formula becomes zero. Consequently, there is no slope.

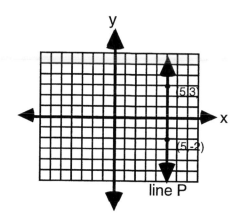

If a line is horizontal, then it has zero slope.

Example:

Let (1,3) and (4,3) be two points on line Q. The slope is

$$m = \frac{3 - 3}{1 - 4} = \frac{0}{-3} = 0$$

Observe here that the y-coordinates are the same which renders the numerator zero. This, in turn, makes the quotient zero.

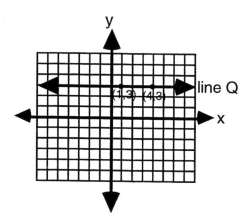

In summary, lines with positive slopes rise from left to right; lines with negative slopes fall from left to right; lines with no slope are vertical lines; and lines with zero slope are horizontal lines.

Example:

From the following diagrams, determine if the line has a positive slope, zero slope, negative slope, or no slope.

a.

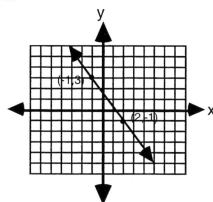

b.

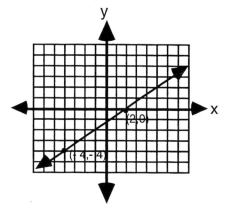

c.

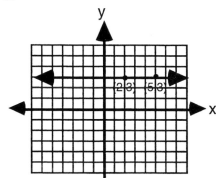

d.

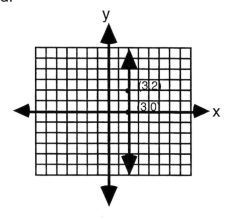

Solution:

a. The line falls from left to right so has negative slope.

b. The line rises from left to right so has positive slope.

c. The line is horizontal and has zero slope.

d. The line is vertical and has no slope.

4. From the diagrams below, determine if the lines have positive, negative, zero, or no slope.

4.

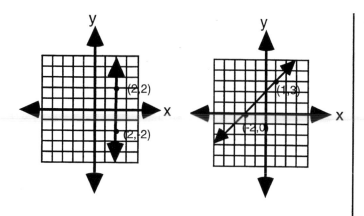

a.   no slope

b.   positive slope

c.   0 slope

d.   negative slope

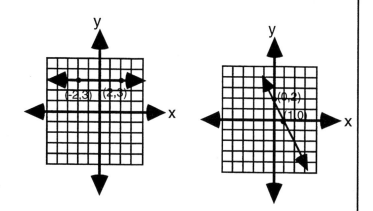

Exercise 13.2

1. Find the slope of the line determined by the given points.

   a. (0,4), (5,6)   b. (4,2), (7,-1)   c.   (-3,4), (3,-4)

   d. (4,7), (4,2)   e. (2,-3), (-3,-3)   f.   (1,2), (-3,-4)

2. Determine from the diagrams below if the lines have positive, negative, zero, or no slope.

a.

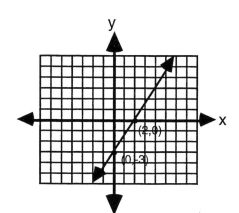

b.

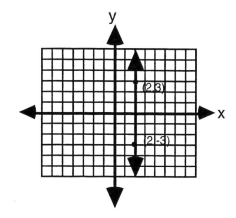

c.

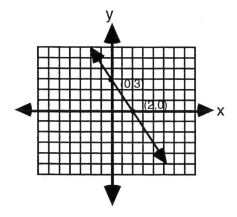

d.

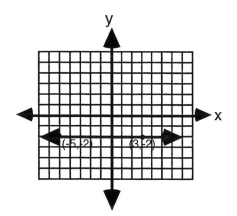

13.4 Graphing Lines

> Definition 13.8   A <u>linear equation</u> is an equation which can be written in the form $Ax + By = C$ where A and B are real numbers not both zero.

The graph of $Ax + By = C$ is a straight line. Graphs of straight lines are encountered in many fields of study: mathematics, statistics, engineering, business, accounting, biology, and others. This section will develop three methods for graphing lines:

1. selection of points

2. slope y-intercept

3. x-intercept, y-intercept

Method 1:   Selection of points

The steps in this method are as follows:

1. Solve the equation for y in terms of x.

2. Select three ordered pairs which satisfy the equation.

3. Plot the points and draw a line through them.

Example: Graph $3x + y = 4$

Step 1:   Solve the equation for y in terms of x.

$$3x + y = 4$$
$$(-3x) + 3x + y = (-3x) + 4$$
$$y = -3x + 4$$

Step 2: Select three ordered pairs which satisfy the equation.
Select three values for the x-coordinate and compute
corresponding values for the y-coordinate using the
equation in Step 1.

x	$y = -3x + 4$	y	ordered pair
0	$y = -3 \cdot 0 + 4$	4	(0,4)
1	$y = -3 \cdot 1 + 4$	1	(1,1)
2	$y = -3 \cdot 2 + 4$	-2	(2,-2)

Note: Care should be taken that the points are chosen
near the origin so the relative position of the line
to the origin can be seen.

Step 3: Plot the points.

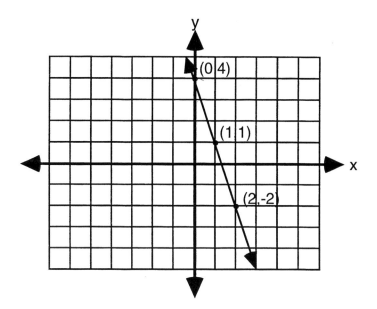

Example: Graph 3x + 2y = 6.

Step 1:

$$3x + 2y = 6$$
$$(-3x) + 3x + 2y = (-3x) + 6$$
$$2y = -3x + 6$$
$$\frac{1}{2}(2y) = \frac{1}{2}(-3x + 6)$$
$$y = \frac{-3}{2}x + 3$$

Step 2: Choose x values that are divisible by 2 so that the y
         values will be integers. This is not an essential
         requirement but does yield points which are easier to plot.

x	$y = \dfrac{-3}{2}x + 3$	y	(x,y)
0	$y = \dfrac{-3}{2} \cdot 0 + 3$	3	(0,3)
2	$y = \dfrac{-3}{2} \cdot 2 + 3$	0	(2,0)
-2	$y = \dfrac{-3}{2} \cdot -2 + 3$	6	(-2,6)

Step 3: Plot the points.

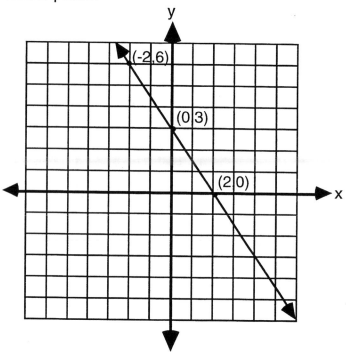

5. Graph $2x + 4y = 8$

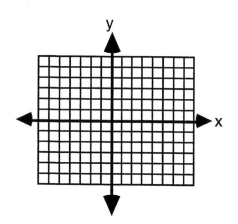

5. Step 1:

$$2x + 4y = 8$$
$$(-2x) + 2x + 4y = (-2x) + 8$$
$$4y = -2x + 8$$
$$\frac{1}{4}(4y) = \frac{1}{4}(-2x + 8)$$
$$y = \frac{-2x}{4} + \frac{8}{4}$$
$$y = \frac{-1}{2}x + 2$$

Step 2:

x	$y = \frac{-1}{2}x + 2$	y	(x,y)
0	$y = \frac{-1}{2} \cdot 0 + 2$	2	(0,2)
2	$y = \frac{-1}{2} \cdot 2 + 2$	1	(2,1)
-2	$y = \frac{-1}{2} \cdot -2 + 2$	3	(-2,3)

Step 3:

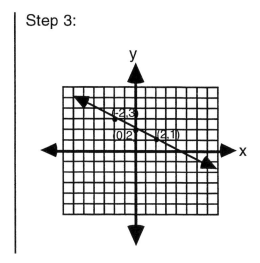

When A = 0, the general equation for a straight line, Ax + By = C, becomes By = C. The graphs of lines in this form are always horizontal.

Example: Graph 2y = 6

Step 1:   Solve for y.

$$2y = 6$$
$$\frac{1}{2} \cdot 2y = \frac{1}{2} \cdot 6$$
$$y = 3$$

Step 2:   Notice that no x term appears. A = 0. Hence, the equation is $y = 0 \cdot x + 3$. Any value can be chosen for x. Since 0 times any number is zero, y will always be 3.

x	$y = 0 \cdot x + 3$	y	(x,y)
0	$y = 0 \cdot 0 + 3$	3	(0,3)
2	$y = 0 \cdot 2 + 3$	3	(2,3)
-2	$y = 0 \cdot -2 + 3$	3	(−2,3)

Step 3:   Plot the points.

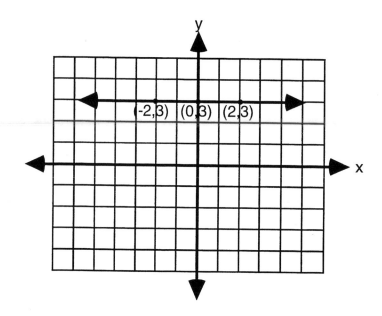

6. Graph 3y = -6

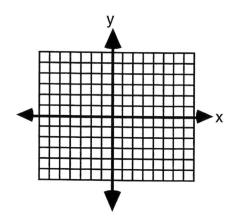

6. Step 1:

$$3y = -6$$

$$\frac{1}{3} \cdot 3y = \frac{1}{3} \cdot -6$$

$$y = -2$$

Step 2:

x	y = 0·x − 2	y	(x,y)
0	y = 0·0 − 2	-2	(0,-2)
1	y = 0·1 − 2	-2	(1,-2)
-1	y = 0·−1 − 2	-2	(-1,-2)

Step 3:

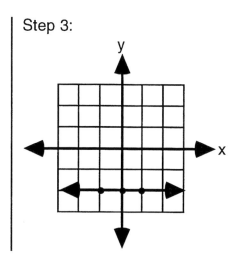

When B = 0, Ax + By = C becomes Ax = C. The graph of lines of this type is a vertical line. In this case y can be any number and x will always be the same. The selection of points method has to be adjusted to be used for this type of line. Observe the modifications in the next example.

Example: Graph 2x = 6

Step 1: The first problem with this equation and this method occurs here. We cannot solve for y. There is no y term. Hence, we will solve for x.

$$2x = 6$$
$$\frac{1}{2} \cdot 2x = \frac{1}{2} \cdot 6$$
$$x = 3$$

Step 2: In choosing values, notice that any value may be chosen for y. X is always the same. X's are not chosen and y's obtained, as in other examples, because the equation had to be solved for x instead of y. In this example y's are chosen and x's obtained.

y	$x + 0 \cdot y = 3$	x	(x,y)
0	$x + 0 \cdot 0 = 3$	3	(3,0)
2	$x + 0 \cdot 2 = 3$	3	(3,2)
-2	$x + 0 \cdot -2 = 3$	3	(3,-2)

Step 3:   Plot the points and draw the line.

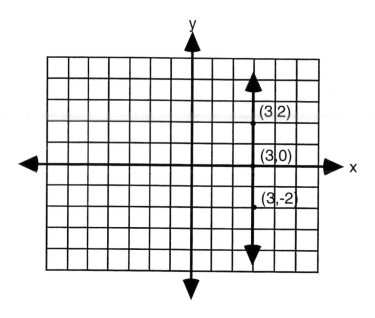

7. Graph $3x + 9 = 0$

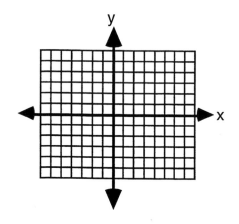

7. Step 1:

$$3x + 9 = 0$$
$$3x + 9 + (-9) = 0 + (-9)$$
$$3x = -9$$
$$\frac{1}{3} \cdot 3x = \frac{1}{3} \cdot -9$$
$$x = -3$$

Step 2:

y	$x + 0 \cdot y = -3$	x	(x,y)
0	$x + 0 \cdot 0 = -3$	-3	(-3,0)
2	$x + 0 \cdot 2 = -3$	-3	(-3,2)
-2	$x + 0 \cdot -2 = -3$	-3	(-3,-2)

Step 3:

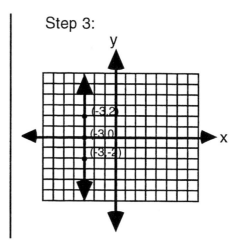

Definition 13.9   The point of intersection of the y-axis and a line is called the y-intercept. Its coordinates are (0,b).

Definition 13.10   The x-intercept is the point of intersection of the x axis and a line. Its coordinates are (a,0).

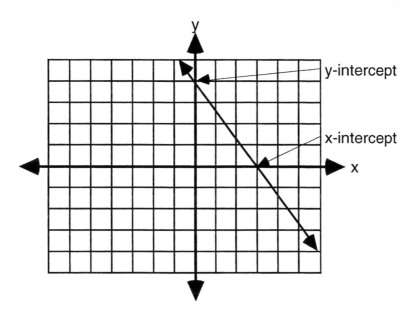

Definition 13.11   The slope y-intercept form of the straight line is $y = mx + b$, where m is the slope and b is the y-intercept.

The second method for graphing a straight line will use the slope y-intercept form of the straight line. The steps in this method are as follows:

1. Solve for y in terms of x. This transforms the equation into the $y = mx + b$ form where m is the slope and b is the y-intercept. The y-intercept is a point whose coordinates are (0,b).

2. Plot the y-intercept.

3. From the y-intercept, use the slope as rise over run to obtain other points. Connect the points with a straight line.

Example: Graph 3x + 2y = 8

Step 1:   Solve for y in terms of x.

$$3x + 2y = 8$$
$$(-3x) + 3x + 2y = (-3x) + 8$$
$$2y = -3x + 8$$
$$\frac{1}{2} \cdot 2y = \frac{1}{2} \cdot (-3x + 8)$$
$$y = \frac{-3}{2}x + 4$$

Compare $y = \dfrac{-3}{2}x + 4$ to

$$y = mx + b.$$

Observe the slope $m = \dfrac{-3}{2} = \dfrac{\text{rise}}{\text{run}}$; b, the y-intercept is 4.

Step 2:   Plot the y-intercept. The y-intercept is the point (0,4).

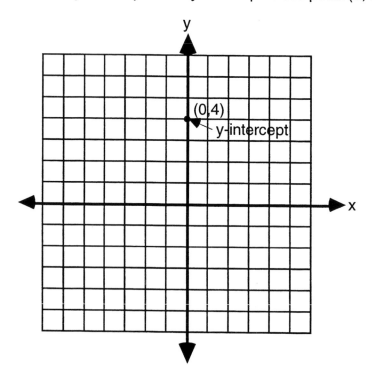

Step 3:   The slope is $\dfrac{-3}{2}$ which means from (0,4) come down three units

(-3) and go over two units (+2). Note that $\dfrac{-3}{2} = \dfrac{3}{-2}$; so, equivalently, one could go up three units (+3) and back two units (-2).

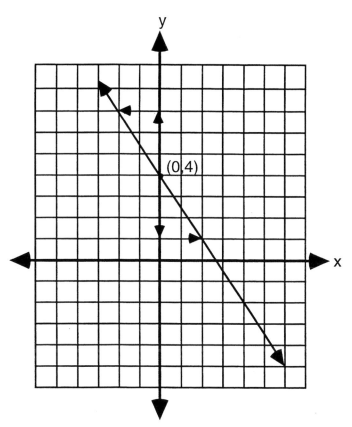

8. Using the second method, graph 2x + 3y = -3.

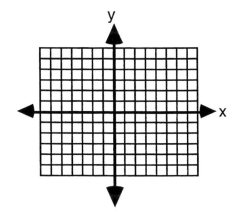

8. Step 1:

Solve the equation for y in terms of x.

$$2x + 3y = -3$$
$$(-2x) + 2x + 3y = (-2x) - 3$$
$$3y = -2x - 3$$
$$\frac{1}{3} \cdot 3y = \frac{1}{3} \cdot (-2x - 3)$$
$$y = \frac{-2}{3}x - 1$$

Step 2: Plot the y-intercept.

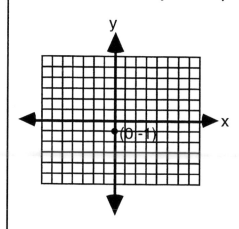

Step 3: The slope is $\dfrac{-2}{3}$ which means go down 2 and over three or up 2 and back 3.

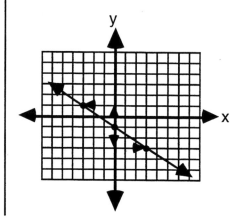

This method can likewise be applied to the case when A = 0 and, also, to the case when B = 0.

Example: Graph y = -2

In this equation A = 0. This equation can be written as $y = 0 \cdot x - 2$ where 0 is the slope and -2 is the y-intercept. A zero slope means there is zero rise but the run is not zero. Consequently, the graph is a horizontal line.

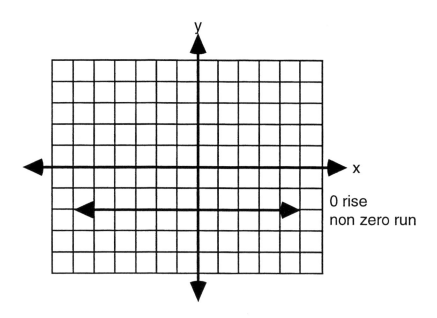

9. Graph y = 3

9. Writing y = 3 into y = mx + b form, $y = 0 \cdot x + 3$. The y-intercept is 3 and the slope is 0. This means that the rise is zero and the run is non zero.

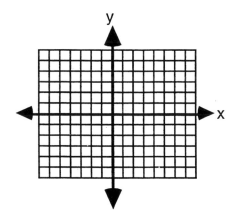

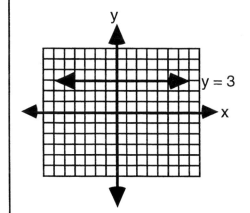

When B = 0, the equation cannot be written in the y = mx + b form. The equation is of the form Ax = C. This is a vertical line which has no slope (undefined slope). Recall the slope formula. To have no slope the denominator is zero which means the run is zero. The rise is non zero. There, likewise, is no y-intercept. These lines do not intersect the y-axis. In fact, they are parallel to it.

Example: Graph x = 4

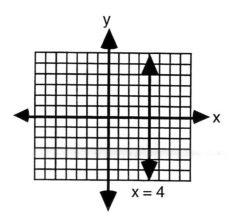

x = 4

10.   Graph x = -3

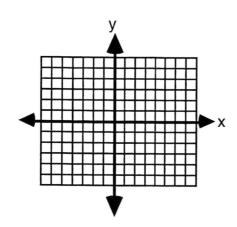

10.

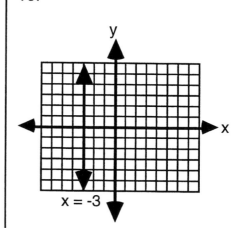

x = -3

The third and last method we will discuss to graph straight lines is the x-intercept, y-intercept method. The steps in this method are as follows:

    1. Find the y-intercept. Recall the y-intercept is a point (0,b).

    2. Find the x-intercept. Recall the x-intercept is a point (a,0).

    3. Plot the points and draw the line through the two points.

Example: Graph 2x + 3y = 6

    Step 1: Find the y-intercept. This point always has an x-coordinate of 0.
             Substituting x = 0 into the equation,

$$2x + 3y = 6$$
$$2 \cdot 0 + 3y = 6$$
$$3y = 6$$
$$\frac{1}{3} \cdot 3y = \frac{1}{3} \cdot 6$$
$$y = 2$$

So, the y-intercept is the point (0,2).

Step 2: Find the x-intercept. This point always has a y-coordinate of 0. Substituting y = 0 into the equation,

$$2x + 3y = 6$$
$$2x + 3 \cdot 0 = 6$$
$$2x = 6$$
$$\frac{1}{2} \cdot 2x = \frac{1}{2} \cdot 6$$
$$x = 3$$

So, the x-intercept is the point (3,0).

Step 3: Plot the points and draw the line.

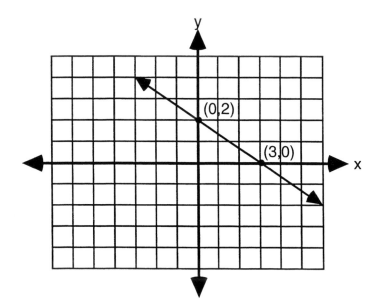

11. Using the third method, graph 4x - 2y = 8. | 11.

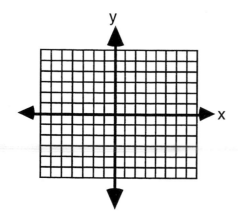

Let x = 0.

4x - 2y = 8

4·0 - 2y = 8

-2y = 8

$\frac{-1}{2}$·-2y = $\frac{-1}{2}$·8

y = -4

y - intercept = (0,-4)

Let y = 0.

4x - 2y = 8

4x - 2·0 = 8

4x = 8

$\frac{1}{4}$·4x = $\frac{1}{4}$·8

x = 2

x - intercept = (2,0)

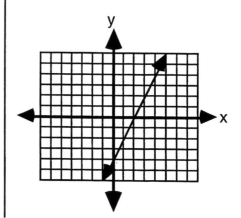

This method is particularly useful in that it precisely demonstrates where the line crosses both axes. Frequently, however, the x and y intercepts are fractions and plotting has to be approximate. This method is not especially useful for plotting lines which are parallel to the x-axis. Recall the lines are in the form By = C. These lines have a y-intercept but no x-intercept. Refer to the examples on pages 406 and 413. Likewise, this method is not useful for lines which are parallel to the y-axis. Recall these lines are of the form Ax = C. These lines have an x-intercept but no y-intercept. Refer to the examples on pages 408 and 414. Despite the non-usefulness of this method for equations of the types

By = C and Ax = C, it is very useful and very quick for graphing lines of the form Ax + By = C, where A, B, and C are not zero. Determining the x-intercept and y-intercept of a line are essential points in some studies of straight lines.

Exercise 13.3

1.   Graph using the selection of points method.

    a. $2x + 3y = 9$ d. $4x + 3y = 12$

    b. $5x - y = 2$ e. $3x - 9 = 0$

    c. $x - 2y = 6$ f. $2y + 6 = 0$

2.   Graph using the slope y-intercept method.

    a. $5x + 2y = 10$ d. $5y + 10 = 20$

    b. $2x - 3y = 9$ e. $3x - 5y = 20$

    c. $2x - 8y = 0$ f. $4x + 3y = 12$

3.   Graph using the x-intercept, y-intercept method.

    a. $2x - 7y = 14$ d. $2x + 3y = 24$

    b. $3x + 6y = 12$ e. $x - 2y = 4$

    c. $4x - 5y = 20$ f. $3x - 7y = -21$

13.5   Writing the Equation of a Straight Line

An essential topic in any study of straight lines is writing the equation of a line given various conditions. Writing the equation of a line is used in many subject areas: economics, business, statistics, accounting, engineering, physics, and mathematics to name a few.

Definition 13.12   The point slope form of a straight line is given by the equation $y - y_1 = m(x - x_1)$, where m is the slope and (x_1, y_1) is a known point on the line.

In writing the equation of a straight line there are two forms that are particularly useful: the point slope form defined above and the slope, y-intercept form, $y = mx + b$, where m is the slope and b is the y-intercept.

How do you decide which form to use? Frequently, it does not matter. In most cases, both forms can be easily used. No matter which form is used in determining the equation, the final answer should be left in standard form, $Ax + By = C$, where A, B, and C are integers and A is positive.

In the following examples, both methods are demonstrated. When you are working the problems, you need only select one method.

Example: Write the equation of the line in standard form which passes through the points (4,2) and (5,7).

Solution using the point slope form, $y - y_1 = m(x - x_1)$:

Determine the slope first. The slope, $m = \dfrac{y_2 - y_1}{x_2 - x_1} = \dfrac{7 - 2}{5 - 4} = \dfrac{5}{1} = 5.$

Either point can be used as (x_1, y_1) in the point slope form. Using $(x_1, y_1) = (4,2)$, substituting into the formula gives

$$y - y_1 = m(x - x_1)$$
$$y - 2 = 5(x - 4)$$
$$y - 2 = 5x - 20$$
$$y - 2 + 2 = 5x - 20 + 2$$
$$y = 5x - 18$$
$$-5x + y = -5x + 5x - 18$$
$$-5x + y = -18$$
$$-1(-5x + y) = -1(-18)$$
$$5x - y = 18 \text{ is the equation in standard form.}$$

Note: Suppose we had selected the point (5,7) instead of (4,2) to substitute. Would that have made any difference? No, for example:

$$y - y_1 = m(x - x_1)$$
$$y - 7 = 5(x - 5)$$
$$y - 7 = 5x - 25$$
$$y - 7 + 7 = 5x - 25 + 7$$
$$y = 5x - 18$$
$$-5x + y = -5x + 5x - 18$$
$$-5x + y = -18$$
$$-1(-5x + y) = -1(-18)$$
$$5x - y = 18 \text{ is the equation in standard form.}$$

Note that it is the same equation as was obtained above.

Solution using the slope y-intercept form:

Determine the slope first. The slope is $m = \dfrac{y_2 - y_1}{x_2 - x_1} = \dfrac{7-2}{5-4} = \dfrac{5}{1} = 5.$

Substitute this into the form $y = mx + b$ to obtain $y = 5x + b$. Use either point to obtain b. Using (4,2), that is $x = 4$ and $y = 2$, substitute these into the form to obtain b.

$$y = mx + b$$
$$y = 5x + b$$
$$2 = 5 \cdot 4 + b$$
$$2 = 20 + b$$
$$2 + (-20) = 20 + b + (-20)$$
$$-18 = b$$

Now, values for m and b have been obtained. Substitute them into the original form.

$$y = mx + b$$
$$y = 5x - 18$$
$$(-5x) + y = (-5x) + 5x - 18$$
$$-5x + y = -18$$
$$(-1)(-5x + y) = (-1)(-18)$$
$$5x - y = 18 \text{ is the equation in standard form.}$$

12. Write the equation for the line in standard form which passes through the points (3,-2) and (2,4).

Select either method you wish. You are encouraged to try both ways in order to decide which method is the easiest for you. Both methods are provided for your convenience.

12.

Solution using the point slope form:

$$m = \dfrac{4 - (-2)}{2 - 3} = \dfrac{6}{-1} = -6$$

Using (2,4) and the slope above,

$$y - y_1 = m(x - x_1)$$
$$y - 4 = -6(x - 2)$$

$$y - 4 = -6x + 12$$
$$6x + y - 4 = 6x - 6x + 12$$
$$6x + y - 4 = 12$$
$$6x + y - 4 + 4 = 12 + 4$$
$$6x + y = 16$$

Solution using the slope y-intercept form:

$$m = \frac{4 - (-2)}{2 - 3} = \frac{6}{-1} = -6$$

Using (2,4) substitute into
$$y = mx + b$$
$$4 = -6 \cdot 2 + b$$
$$4 = -12 + b$$
$$4 + 12 = -12 + b + 12$$
$$16 = b$$

Now, replace m and b with their values.
$$y = mx + b$$
$$y = -6x + 16$$
$$6x + y = 6x - 6x + 16$$
$$6x + y = 16$$

Example: Write the equation of the line in standard form which passes through (3,-2) and has slope $\frac{2}{5}$.

Solution using the point slope form:

Substitute directly into the formula
$$y - y_1 = m(x - x_1)$$
$$y - (-2) = \frac{2}{5}(x - 3)$$
$$y + 2 = \frac{2}{5}x - \frac{6}{5}$$

Multiplying both members by 5 to clear the equation of fractions, the equation becomes:

$$5(y + 2) = 5\left(\frac{2}{5}x - \frac{6}{5}\right)$$

$$5y + 10 = 2x - 6$$
$$-2x + 5y + 10 = -2x + 2x - 6$$
$$-2x + 5y + 10 = -6$$
$$-2x + 5y + 10 - 10 = -6 - 10$$
$$-2x + 5y = -16$$
$$-1(-2x + 5y) = (-1)(-16)$$

$2x - 5y = 16$ is the equation in standard form.

Solution using the slope y-intercept form $(y = mx + b)$:

Substitute the slope in first to obtain

$$y = \frac{2}{5}x + b$$

Now use the point (3,-2) to obtain b.

$$-2 = \frac{2}{5} \cdot 3 + b$$

$$-2 = \frac{6}{5} + b$$

$$5 \cdot -2 = 5\left(\frac{6}{5} + b\right)$$

$$-10 = 6 + 5b$$

$$-10 - 6 = 6 + 5b - 6$$

$$-16 = 5b$$

$$\frac{1}{5} \cdot -16 = \frac{1}{5} \cdot 5b$$

$$\frac{-16}{5} = b$$

Substitute m = $\frac{2}{5}$ and b = $\frac{-16}{5}$ into the following equation:

$$y = mx + b$$

$$y = \frac{2}{5}x - \frac{16}{5}$$

Simplifying:

$$5y = 5\left(\frac{2}{5}x - \frac{16}{5}\right)$$

$$5y = 2x - 16$$

$$-2x + 5y = -2x + 2x - 16$$

$$-2x + 5y = -16$$

$$-1(-2x+5y)=(-1)(-16)$$
$$2x-5y=16$$

13. Write the equation of the line in standard form which passes through $(-4,-2)$ and has slope $\dfrac{-3}{8}$.

Select either method you wish. Both solutions are provided for your convenience.

13.

Solution using the point slope form:

$$y-y_1=m(x-x_1)$$
$$y-(-2)=\frac{-3}{8}(x-(-4))$$
$$y+2=\frac{-3}{8}(x+4)$$
$$y+2=\frac{-3}{8}x-\frac{12}{8}$$
$$8(y+2)=8\left(\frac{-3}{8}x-\frac{12}{8}\right)$$
$$8y+16=-3x-12$$
$$3x+8y+16=3x-3x-12$$
$$3x+8y+16=-12$$
$$3x+8y+16-16=-12-16$$
$$3x+8y=-28$$

Solution using the slope y-intercept form:

$$y=mx+b$$
$$y=\frac{-3}{8}x+b$$
$$-2=\frac{-3}{8}\cdot-4+b$$
$$-2=\frac{3}{2}+b$$
$$2\cdot-2=2\left(\frac{3}{2}+b\right)$$
$$-4=3+2b$$
$$-4-3=3+2b-3$$

$$-7 = 2b$$

$$\frac{1}{2} \cdot -7 = \frac{1}{2} \cdot 2b$$

$$\frac{-7}{2} = b$$

$$y = \frac{-3}{8}x - \frac{7}{2}$$

$$8y = 8\left(\frac{-3}{8}x - \frac{7}{2}\right)$$

$$8y = -3x - 28$$

$$3x + 8y = 3x - 3x - 28$$

$$3x + 8y = -28$$

Example: Write the equation of the line in standard form with slope $\frac{-2}{3}$ and y-intercept 6.

Solution using the point slope form:

The y-intercept is where the line crosses the y-axis so its coordinates are (0,6). Using $m = \frac{-2}{3}$ and (0,6), substitute into the formula and simplify:

$$y - y_1 = m(x - x_1)$$

$$y - 6 = \frac{-2}{3}(x - 0)$$

$$y - 6 = \frac{-2}{3}x$$

$$3 \cdot y - 3 \cdot 6 = 3 \cdot \frac{-2}{3}x$$

$$3y - 18 = -2x$$

$$2x + 3y - 18 = 2x - 2x$$

$$2x + 3y - 18 = 0$$

$$2x + 3y - 18 + 18 = 0 + 18$$

$$2x + 3y = 18$$

Solution using the slope y-intercept form:

$$y = mx + b$$

$$y = \frac{-2}{3}x + 6$$

$$3 \cdot y = 3 \cdot \frac{-2}{3}x + 3 \cdot 6$$

$$3y = -2x + 18$$

$$2x + 3y = 2x - 2x + 18$$

$$2x + 3y = 18$$

14. Write the equation of the line in standard form with slope 3 and y-intercept 2.

Both types of solution are provided for your convenience.

14.
Solution using the point slope form:

The y-intercept is the point whose coordinates are (0,2).

$$y - y_1 = m(x - x_1)$$

$$y - 2 = 3(x - 0)$$

$$y - 2 = 3x$$

$$-3x + y - 2 = -3x + 3x$$

$$-3x + y - 2 = 0$$

$$-3x + y - 2 + 2 = 0 + 2$$

$$-3x + y = 2$$

$$-1(-3x + y) = -1 \cdot 2$$

$$3x - y = -2$$

Solution using the slope y-intercept form:

$$y = mx + b$$

$$y = 3x + 2$$

$$-3x + y = 2$$

$$-1(-3x + y) = -1 \cdot 2$$

$$3x - y = -2$$

Please note that for the rest of the examples and exercises in this section only one method of solution is provided. You may work any of the problems by either method.

Example: Write the equation of the line in standard form with x-intercept, 4 and y-intercept, -4.

Solution:

The x-intercept is the place where the line crosses the x-axis. The coordinates of this point are (4,0). The y-intercept's coordinates are (0,-4). The slope

$$m = \frac{-4-0}{0-4} = \frac{-4}{-4} = 1.$$

Using the slope y-intercept form and simplifying gives:

$$y = mx + b$$
$$y = x - 4$$
$$-x + y = -x + x - 4$$
$$-x + y = -4$$
$$-1(-x + y) = -1 \cdot -4$$
$$x - y = 4$$

15. Write the equation of the line in standard form which has x-intercept, 2, and y-intercept, 3.

15.

Solution:

x-intercept = (2,0)
y-intercept = (0,3)

$$m = \frac{3-0}{0-2} = \frac{3}{-2} = \frac{-3}{2}$$

$$y = mx + b$$

$$y = \frac{-3}{2}x + 3$$

$$2y = 2\left(\frac{-3}{2}x + 3\right)$$

$$2y = -3x + 6$$

$$3x + 2y = 3x - 3x + 6$$

$$3x + 2y = 6$$

Example: Write the equation of the line in standard form which passes through (4,3) and (4,-2).

Solution:

$$m = \frac{3-(-2)}{4-4} = \frac{5}{0} = \text{ no slope}$$

Since the slope is "no slope", neither formula can be used. Observe both x-coordinates are 4. Also, vertical lines are of the form, $Ax = C$ or $x = \frac{C}{A}$, where $\frac{C}{A}$ is the first coordinate of all points on the line. Therefore, the equation of the line is $x = 4$.

16. Write the equation of the line in standard form which passes through (2,2) and (2,-3).

16.

$$m = \frac{2-(-3)}{2-2} = \frac{5}{0} = \text{ no slope}$$

The equation of the line is $x = 2$.

Example: Write the equation of the line in standard form which passes through the points (0,4) and (5,4).

Solution:

$$m = \frac{4-4}{0-5} = \frac{0}{-5} = 0$$

Either form can be used for this problem. Using the point slope form:

$$y - y_1 = m(x - x_1)$$
$$y - 4 = 0(x - 0)$$
$$y - 4 = 0$$
$$y - 4 + 4 = 0 + 4$$
$$y = 4$$

Note: This is a horizontal line. The y coordinates are the same for both points. The equation is $y = 4$, 4 being the common y coordinate.

17. Write the equation in standard form of the line which passes through (2,2) and (-3,2).

17.

$$m = \frac{2-2}{2-(-3)} = \frac{0}{5} = 0$$

$$y - y_1 = m(x - x_1)$$
$$y - 2 = 0(x - 2)$$
$$y - 2 = 0$$
$$y - 2 + 2 = 0 + 2$$
$$y = 2$$

Theorem 13.1   Two lines are parallel if and only if they have the same slope.

Example: Determine if $2x + 3y = 7$ and $4x = -6y + 3$ are parallel.

Solution:

In order to determine if lines are parallel, their slopes need to be found and compared. One way to determine slope is to write the equation in the slope y-intercept form $y = mx + b$. Beginning with the first equation,

$$2x + 3y = 7$$
$$-2x + 2x + 3y = -2x + 7$$
$$3y = -2x + 7$$
$$\frac{1}{3} \cdot 3y = \frac{1}{3}(-2x + 7)$$
$$y = \frac{-2}{3}x + \frac{7}{3}$$

The slope is the coefficient of the x term. For this equation the slope is $\frac{-2}{3}$.

Using the same procedure for the second equation:

$$4x = -6y + 3$$
$$4x + 6y = -6y + 3 + 6y$$
$$4x + 6y = 3$$
$$-4x + 4x + 6y = -4x + 3$$
$$6y = -4x + 3$$
$$\frac{1}{6} \cdot 6y = \frac{1}{6}(-4x + 3)$$
$$y = \frac{-2}{3}x + \frac{1}{2}$$

For this equation the slope is $\dfrac{-2}{3}$. Both lines have the same slope. By Theorem 13.1, the lines are parallel.

18.   Determine if the lines $3x - 6y = 2$ and $2y = x + 3$ are parallel.

18.

Writing the equation in the $y = mx + b$ form:

$$3x - 6y = 2$$

$$-3x + 3x - 6y = -3x + 2$$

$$-6y = -3x + 2$$

$$\frac{-1}{6}(-6y) = \frac{-1}{6}(-3x + 2)$$

$$y = \frac{1}{2}x - \frac{1}{3}$$

The slope $m = \dfrac{1}{2}$.

For the second equation, writing it in the $y = mx + b$ form gives:

$$2y = x + 3$$

$$\frac{1}{2} \cdot 2y = \frac{1}{2}(x + 3)$$

$$y = \frac{1}{2}x + \frac{3}{2}$$

The slope $m = \dfrac{1}{2}$.

Since the slopes are the same, by Theorem 13.1 the lines are parallel.

Example: Find the equation of the line through (1,5) and parallel to the line $x + 6y = 2$.

Solution:

First, determine the slope of the given line by writing it in $y = mx + b$ form.

$$x + 6y = 2$$

$$-x + x + 6y = -x + 2$$

$$6y = -x + 2$$

$$\frac{1}{6} \cdot 6y = \frac{1}{6}(-x + 2)$$

$$y = \frac{-1}{6}x + \frac{1}{3}$$

The slope is $\frac{-1}{6}$.

Substitute the slope and coordinates of the point into the point slope form:

$$y - y_1 = m(x - x_1)$$

$$y - 5 = \frac{-1}{6}(x - 1)$$

$$y - 5 = \frac{-1}{6}x + \frac{1}{6}$$

$$6(y - 5) = 6\left(\frac{-1}{6}x + \frac{1}{6}\right)$$

$$6y - 30 = -x + 1$$

$$x + 6y - 30 = x - x + 1$$

$$x + 6y - 30 = 1$$

$$x + 6y - 30 + 30 = 1 + 30$$

$$x + 6y = 31$$

19. Determine the equation of the line in standard form that passes through (-1,-3) and is parallel to the line with equation $3x + 2y = 6$.

19.

Find the slope.

$$3x + 2y = 6$$

$$-3x + 3x + 2y = -3x + 6$$

$$2y = -3x + 6$$

$$\frac{1}{2} \cdot 2y = \frac{1}{2}(-3x + 6)$$

$$y = \frac{-3}{2}x + 3$$

$$m = \frac{-3}{2}$$

Write the equation:

$$y - y_1 = m(x - x_1)$$

$$y - (-3) = \frac{-3}{2}(x - (-1))$$

$$y + 3 = \frac{-3}{2}(x + 1)$$

$$y + 3 = \frac{-3}{2}x - \frac{3}{2}$$

$$2(y + 3) = 2\left(\frac{-3}{2}x - \frac{3}{2}\right)$$

$$2y + 6 = -3x - 3$$

$$2y + 6 - 6 = -3x - 3 - 6$$

$$2y = -3x - 9$$

$$3x + 2y = 3x + -3x - 9$$

$$3x + 2y = -9$$

Theorem 13.2   Two lines are perpendicular if and only if their slopes are negative reciprocals of each other.

That is, if the slope of one line is m, the slope of the line perpendicular to it is $\frac{-1}{m}$. Observe, $m \cdot \frac{-1}{m} = \frac{-m}{m} = \frac{-1}{1} = -1$. This gives a way to check if the slopes are negative reciprocals of each other. Find their product. If the product is -1, then the lines are perpendicular.

Example: Is the line x - 4y = 2 perpendicular to the line 4x + y = 3?

Solution:

Find the slope of the first equation.

$$x - 4y = 2$$

$$-x + x - 4y = -x + 2$$

$$-4y = -x + 2$$

$$\frac{-1}{4} \cdot -4y = \frac{-1}{4}(-x + 2)$$

$$y = \frac{1}{4}x - \frac{1}{2}$$

$$m = \frac{1}{4}$$

Determine the slope of the second line.

$$4x + y = 3$$
$$-4x + 4x + y = -4x + 3$$
$$y = -4x + 3$$

$$m = -4$$

Find the product of their slopes: $\dfrac{1}{4} \cdot (-4) = \dfrac{-4}{4} = -1$

Therefore, by Theorem 13.2, the lines are perpendicular.

20.   Is the line, 5x + 2y = 10, perpendicular to the line, 2x - 5y = 10?

20.

$$5x + 2y = 10$$
$$-5x + 5x + 2y = -5x + 10$$
$$2y = -5x + 10$$
$$\frac{1}{2} \cdot 2y = \frac{1}{2}(-5x + 10)$$
$$y = \frac{-5}{2}x + 5$$

$$m = \frac{-5}{2}$$

$$2x - 5y = 10$$
$$-2x + 2x - 5y = -2x + 10$$
$$-5y = -2x + 10$$
$$\frac{-1}{5} \cdot (-5y) = \frac{-1}{5}(-2x + 10)$$
$$y = \frac{2}{5}x - 2$$

$$m = \frac{2}{5}$$

Find the product of the slopes.
$$\frac{-5}{2} \cdot \frac{2}{5} = \frac{-10}{10} = -1$$

Example: Find the equation of a line in standard form that passes through (4,-2) and is perpendicular to x - 5y = 4.

Solution: First determine the slope of x - 5y = 4.

$$x - 5y = 4$$
$$-x + x - 5y = -x + 4$$
$$-5y = -x + 4$$
$$\frac{-1}{5} \cdot (-5y) = \frac{-1}{5}(-x + 4)$$
$$y = \frac{1}{5}x - \frac{4}{5}$$

The slope is $\frac{1}{5}$.

To determine the slope of the desired line, solve the following equation:

$$\frac{1}{5} \cdot m = -1$$

Note: The slope of the desired line is m. The slope of the given line is $\frac{1}{5}$. The product of any number and its reciprocal is -1. Since we are looking for the reciprocal, we will solve the equation.

$$\frac{1}{5} \cdot m = -1$$
$$5\left(\frac{1}{5} \cdot m\right) = 5(-1)$$
$$m = -5$$

Now, use the point slope form to obtain:

$$y - y_1 = m(x - x_1)$$
$$y - (-2) = -5(x - 4)$$
$$y + 2 = -5x + 20$$
$$5x + y + 2 = 5x - 5x + 20$$
$$5x + y + 2 = 20$$
$$5x + y + 2 - 2 = 20 - 2$$
$$5x + y = 18$$

21. Determine the equation in standard form of the line perpendicular to the line, 3x + y = 7 and passing through (-4,2).

21.

Find the slope:
$$3x + y = 7$$
$$-3x + 3x + y = -3x + 7$$
$$y = -3x + 7$$

m = -3

Find the slope of the line perpendicular to the given line:
$$-3 \cdot m = -1$$
$$\frac{-1}{3}(-3 \cdot m) = \frac{-1}{3}(-1)$$
$$m = \frac{1}{3}$$

Use the point slope form to find the equation of the line:
$$y - y_1 = m(x - x_1)$$
$$y - 2 = \frac{1}{3}(x - (-4))$$
$$y - 2 = \frac{1}{3}(x + 4)$$
$$y - 2 = \frac{1}{3}x + \frac{4}{3}$$
$$3(y - 2) = 3\left(\frac{1}{3}x + \frac{4}{3}\right)$$
$$3y - 6 = x + 4$$
$$-x + 3y - 6 = -x + x + 4$$
$$-x + 3y - 6 = 4$$
$$-x + 3y - 6 + 6 = 4 + 6$$
$$-x + 3y = 10$$
$$-1(-x + 3y) = -1(10)$$
$$x - 3y = -10$$

Exercise 13.4

1. Determine the equation of the following lines which meet the given conditions. Leave all answers in standard form.

   a. Passing through (3,4) and (-2,5).

   b. Passing through (4,5) and (4,-2).

   c. Passing through (3,3) and (-2,3).

   d. Passing through (4,2) and having slope 5.

   e. Passing through (-5,-4) and having slope $\dfrac{-2}{3}$.

   f. Passing through (4,5) and parallel to $2x - 7y = 6$.

   g. Passing through (-1,-4) and perpendicular to $x + 4y = 5$.

   h. Having x-intercept 3 and y-intercept -5.

   i. Having slope -3 and y-intercept -5.

   j. Having slope $\dfrac{-2}{3}$ and x-intercept -4.

13.6 Midpoint and Distance

Recall the definition of a midpoint. A midpoint is a point which divides a line segment into two equal parts.

> **Theorem 13.3:** If (x_1, y_1) and (x_2, y_2) are the endpoints of a line segment, then the midpoint of the line segment is determined by the formula:
>
> $$midpoint = \left(\frac{x_1 + x_2}{2}, \frac{y_1 + y_2}{2} \right)$$

Example: Find the midpoint of the line segment whose endpoints are (3,4) and (-5,3).

Solution:

Substitute the endpoints into the midpoint formula and simplify.

$$midpoint = \left(\frac{x_1+x_2}{2}, \frac{y_1+y_2}{2}\right)$$
$$= \left(\frac{3+(-5)}{2}, \frac{4+3}{2}\right)$$
$$= \left(\frac{-2}{2}, \frac{7}{2}\right)$$
$$= \left(-1, \frac{7}{2}\right)$$

22.　Find the midpoint of the line segment whose endpoints are (5,6) and (8,4).

22.

$$midpoint = \left(\frac{x_1+x_2}{2}, \frac{y_1+y_2}{2}\right)$$
$$= \left(\frac{5+8}{2}, \frac{6+4}{2}\right)$$
$$= \left(\frac{13}{2}, \frac{10}{2}\right)$$
$$= \left(\frac{13}{2}, 5\right)$$

Example:　Find the equation of the line with slope, $\frac{2}{3}$, which passes through the midpoint of (-3,4) and (7,-6).

Solution:　First determine the midpoint.

$$midpoint = \left(\frac{x_1+x_2}{2}, \frac{y_1+y_2}{2}\right)$$
$$= \left(\frac{-3+7}{2}, \frac{4+(-6)}{2}\right)$$
$$= \left(\frac{4}{2}, \frac{-2}{2}\right)$$
$$= (2,-1)$$

Using the point slope form, find the equation as follows:

$$y - y_1 = m(x - x_1)$$

$$y - (-1) = \frac{2}{3}(x - 2)$$

$$y + 1 = \frac{2}{3}x - \frac{4}{3}$$

$$3(y + 1) = 3\left(\frac{2}{3}x - \frac{4}{3}\right)$$

$$3y + 3 = 2x - 4$$

$$-2x + 3y + 3 = -2x + 2x - 4$$

$$-2x + 3y + 3 = -4$$

$$-2x + 3y + 3 - 3 = -4 - 3$$

$$-2x + 3y = -7$$

$$-1(-2x + 3y) = -1(-7)$$

$$2x - 3y = 7$$

Theorem 13.4	If (x_1, y_1) and (x_2, y_2) are the endpoints of a line segment, the undirected distance from (x_1, y_1) to (x_2, y_2) is given by the formula $$d = \sqrt{(x_2 - x_1)^2 + (y_2 - y_1)^2}$$

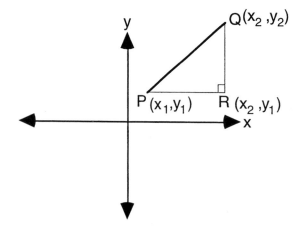

The formula can be derived as follows:

Let $P = (x_1, y_1)$ and $Q = (x_2, y_2)$. Draw $\overline{PR}$ parallel to the x-axis and $\overline{QR}$ parallel to the y-axis. $\overline{QR}$ is perpendicular to $\overline{PR}$ so $\triangle PQR$ is a right triangle. The coordinates of R are (x_2, y_1) since all points on a vertical line have the same x coordinates and all points on a horizontal line have the same y coordinates. The length of $\overline{PR}$ will be the difference in the x coordinates, $x_2 - x_1$. The length of $\overline{QR}$ will be the difference in the y coordinates, $y_2 - y_1$. Since $\triangle PQR$ is a right triangle, the Pythagorean Theorem applies. The notation $d(\overline{PQ})$ will be used to denote the distance from P to Q; $d(\overline{PR})$ will be used to denote the distance from P to R; and, $d(\overline{QR})$ will be used to denote the distance from Q to R.

$$d(\overline{PQ})^2 = d(\overline{PR})^2 + d(\overline{QR})^2$$
$$d(\overline{PQ})^2 = (x_2 - x_1)^2 + (y_2 - y_1)^2$$
$$d(\overline{PQ}) = \sqrt{(x_2 - x_1)^2 + (y_2 - y_1)^2}$$

Example: Find the undirected distance from (3,-2) to (-5,7). Round the answer to hundredths.

Solution: Let $(x_1, y_1) = (3,-2)$ and $(x_2, y_2) = (-5,7)$.

$$d = \sqrt{(-5-3)^2 + (7-(-2))^2}$$
$$d = \sqrt{(-8)^2 + 9^2}$$
$$d = \sqrt{64 + 81}$$
$$d = \sqrt{145}$$
$$d = 12.04$$

Note: The selection of (x_1, y_1) and (x_2, y_2) is arbitrary and may be reversed without changing the distance.

23. Find the length of the line segment connecting (-4,2) and (8,7).

23.

$$d = \sqrt{(8-(-4))^2 + (7-2)^2}$$
$$d = \sqrt{12^2 + 5^2}$$

$$d = \sqrt{144 + 25}$$
$$d = \sqrt{169}$$
$$d = 13$$

Example: Find the perimeter of the triangle whose vertices are (10,-1), (7,3), and (-3,2). Round the answer to the nearest hundredth.

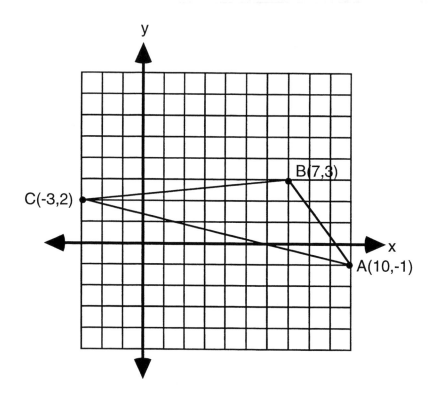

The perimeter is the sum of the length of the three sides.

$$d\left(\overline{BC}\right) = \sqrt{(7 - (-3))^2 + (3 - 2)^2}$$
$$d\left(\overline{BC}\right) = \sqrt{10^2 + 1^2}$$
$$d\left(\overline{BC}\right) = \sqrt{100 + 1}$$
$$d\left(\overline{BC}\right) = \sqrt{101}$$
$$d\left(\overline{BC}\right) = 10.05$$

$$\begin{cases} d(\overline{AB}) = \sqrt{(10-7)^2 + (-1-3)^2} \\ d(\overline{AB}) = \sqrt{3^2 + (-4)^2} \\ d(\overline{AB}) = \sqrt{9+16} \\ d(\overline{AB}) = \sqrt{25} \\ d(\overline{AB}) = 5 \end{cases}$$

$$\begin{cases} d(\overline{AC}) = \sqrt{(10-(-3))^2 + (-1-2)^2} \\ d(\overline{AC}) = \sqrt{13^2 + (-3)^2} \\ d(\overline{AC}) = \sqrt{169+9} \\ d(\overline{AC}) = \sqrt{178} \\ d(\overline{AC}) = 13.34 \end{cases}$$

The perimeter is 10.05 + 5 + 13.34 = 28.39 units.

24. Find the perimeter of the triangle with vertices A = (8,6), B = (-3,3), and C = (1,-1).

24.

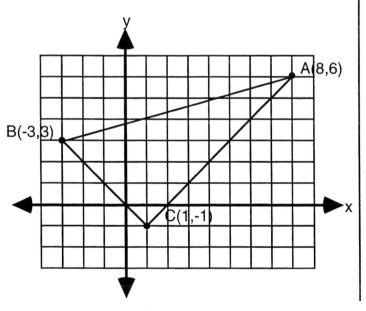

$$d\left(\overline{AB}\right) = \sqrt{(-3-8)^2 + (3-6)^2}$$

$$d\left(\overline{AB}\right) = \sqrt{(-11)^2 + (-3)^2}$$

$$d\left(\overline{AB}\right) = \sqrt{121+9}$$

$$d\left(\overline{AB}\right) = \sqrt{130}$$

$$d\left(\overline{AB}\right) = 11.40$$

$$d\left(\overline{BC}\right) = \sqrt{(-3-1)^2 + (3-(-1))^2}$$

$$d\left(\overline{BC}\right) = \sqrt{(-4)^2 + 4^2}$$

$$d\left(\overline{BC}\right) = \sqrt{16+16}$$

$$d\left(\overline{BC}\right) = \sqrt{32}$$

$$d\left(\overline{BC}\right) = \sqrt{16}\sqrt{2}$$

$$d\left(\overline{BC}\right) = 4\sqrt{2}$$

$$d\left(\overline{BC}\right) = 5.66$$

$$d\left(\overline{AC}\right) = \sqrt{(8-1)^2 + (6-(-1))^2}$$

$$d\left(\overline{AC}\right) = \sqrt{7^2 + 7^2}$$

$$d\left(\overline{AC}\right) = \sqrt{49+49}$$

$$d\left(\overline{AC}\right) = \sqrt{98}$$

$$d\left(\overline{AC}\right) = \sqrt{49}\sqrt{2}$$

$$d\left(\overline{AC}\right) = 7\sqrt{2}$$

$$d\left(\overline{AC}\right) = 9.90$$

The perimeter is
11.40 + 5.66 + 9.90 = 26.96
units.

Exercise 13.5

1. Find the midpoint of the following line segments.

   a. (4,2), (-7,6)

   c. $\left(\dfrac{1}{2},-3\right), \left(\dfrac{2}{3},5\right)$

   b. (5,-4), (-3,2)

   d. $\left(4\sqrt{2},3\sqrt{7}\right), \left(-2\sqrt{2},5\sqrt{7}\right)$

2. Find the length of the following line segments. Round answers to the nearest hundredth.

   a. (3,4), (5, -2)

   c. $\left(3\sqrt{2},4\right),\left(6\sqrt{2},-4\right)$

   b. (4,5), (-4,3)

   d. (4,-2), (6,-3)

3. Find the area and perimeter of the triangle whose vertices are (4,7), (4,10), and (6,7). Round the answers to the nearest hundredth.

Unit 13 Review

1. Describe each of the following terms:

   a. x-axis

   f. ordinate

   b. y-axis

   g. linear equation

   c. origin

   h. slope

   d. quadrant

   i. x-intercept

   e. abscissa

   j. y-intercept

2. Plot the following points and describe their location.

   a. (3,0)

   e. (-3,0)

   b. (4,6)

   f. (-2,-2)

   c. (0,-3)

   g. (0,4)

   d. (-3,2)

   h. (4,-2)

3.   Find the slope of the line through (4,6) and (-5,2).

4.   Determine if the slope of the following lines is positive, negative, zero, or no slope.

a.

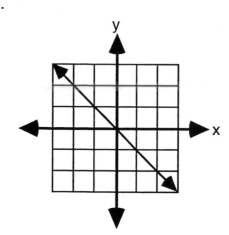

b.

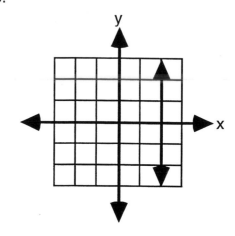

c.

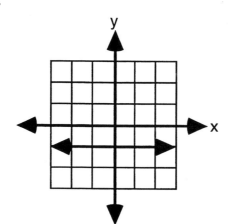

d.

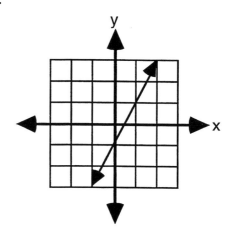

5.   Graph 3x - 2y = 12 using the selection of points method.

6.   Graph 4x - y = 8 using the slope y-intercept method.

7.   Graph 2x + 3y =12 using the x-intercept, y-intercept method.

8.   Determine the equation of the lines which meet the following conditions. Leave all answers in standard form.

a. Passes through (4,2) and (-4,3).

b. Passes through (5,-1) with slope 2.

c. Has slope $\frac{1}{2}$ and y-intercept 6.

    d. Has x-intercept 3 and y-intercept 6.

    e. Parallel to 2x - 4y = 2 and passes through (1,1).

    f. Perpendicular to 2x + 3y = 6 and passes through (-4,2).

    g. Passes through the midpoint of (-2,4) and (4,5) with slope 7.

9. Determine the length of the line segment joining (2,5) and (-4,-3).

10. Given the points A = (4,-3) and B = (-2,7), find

    a. the slope of $\overline{AB}$.

    b. the length of $\overline{AB}$. (Round answer to hundredths.)

    c. the midpoint of $\overline{AB}$.

    d. the slope of a line parallel to $\overline{AB}$.

    e. the slope of a line perpendicular to $\overline{AB}$.

    f. the equation in standard form of the line that passes through A and B.

11. Find the perimeter and area of a triangle whose vertices are (4,6), (4,-3) and (0,-3). Round answers to the nearest tenth.

Appendix A

Review of the Operations on Fractions

A.1 Addition and Subtraction

In adding or subtracting fractions, follow the following steps:

    a. Find the least common denominator (LCD).

    b. Change each fraction to an equivalent fraction having the LCD as the denominator.

    c. Add or subtract the numerators as indicated.

    d. Simplify the answer if necessary. Reduce your answer to lowest terms whenever possible.

Example: Subtract: $\dfrac{5}{6} - \dfrac{2}{9}$

    a. Find the LCD.

$$6 = 2 \cdot 3$$
$$9 = 3 \cdot 3$$

$$LCD = 2 \cdot 3 \cdot 3 = 18$$

    b. Change each fraction to an equivalent fraction.

$$\frac{5}{6} = \frac{}{18} \rightarrow \frac{5}{6} \times \frac{3}{3} = \frac{15}{18}$$

$$\frac{2}{9} = \frac{}{18} \rightarrow \frac{2}{9} \times \frac{2}{2} = \frac{4}{18}$$

    c. Subtract the numerators.

$$\frac{15}{18} - \frac{4}{18} = \frac{11}{18}$$

    d. Reduce the answer to lowest terms.

$$\frac{11}{18} \text{ is in lowest terms.}$$

Example: Add: $4\frac{2}{5}+2\frac{2}{3}+8 = 4\frac{2}{5}+2\frac{2}{3}+\frac{8}{1}$

a. Find the LCD.

$5 = 5 \cdot 1$

$3 = 3 \cdot 1$

$1 = 1 \cdot 1$

$LCD = 5 \cdot 3 \cdot 1 = 15$

b. Change the fraction portion of each mixed number to an equivalent fraction.

$$\frac{2}{5} = \frac{}{15} \rightarrow \frac{2}{5}\times\frac{3}{3} = \frac{6}{15}$$

$$\frac{2}{3} = \frac{}{15} \rightarrow \frac{2}{3}\times\frac{5}{5} = \frac{10}{15}$$

c. Add the numerators of the fractions. Add the whole numbers.

$$4\frac{6}{15}+2\frac{10}{15}+8 = 14\frac{16}{15}$$

d. Simplify the answer. Leave in lowest terms.

$$\frac{16}{15} = 1\frac{1}{15}$$

$$14\frac{16}{15} = 14+1\frac{1}{15} = 15\frac{1}{15}$$

Exercise A.1

Perform the indicated operations.

1. $\frac{3}{14}+\frac{5}{6}$

2. $3\frac{5}{8}+1\frac{11}{12}+\frac{5}{12}$

3. $3-\frac{5}{8}$

4. $6\frac{1}{3}-1\frac{2}{3}$

5. $15+2\frac{2}{5}$

6. $3\frac{4}{5}-2\frac{1}{2}$

7. $\dfrac{7}{8} - \dfrac{3}{4}$

8. $\dfrac{5}{8} - \dfrac{3}{8}$

9. $\dfrac{4}{12} + \dfrac{8}{15}$

10. $\dfrac{2}{9} + \dfrac{1}{9}$

The answers to this exercise can be found at the end of this appendix.

A.2 Multiplication of Fractions

One procedure for multiplying fractions involves the following steps:

  a. Change each whole number or mixed number to an improper fraction.

  b. Reduce when ever possible.

  c. Multiply numerators together and denominators together.

  d. If the answer is an improper fraction, then change it to a mixed number. Reduce to lowest terms.

Example: $1\dfrac{2}{3} \times 1\dfrac{4}{5} \times 2\dfrac{3}{4}$

  a. Change each mixed number to an improper fraction.

$$\dfrac{5}{3} \times \dfrac{9}{5} \times \dfrac{11}{4}$$

  b. Reduce when ever possible.

$$\dfrac{\overset{1}{\cancel{5}}}{\underset{1}{\cancel{3}}} \times \dfrac{\overset{3}{\cancel{9}}}{\underset{1}{\cancel{5}}} \times \dfrac{11}{4}$$

  c. Multiply numerators together and denominators together.

$$\dfrac{1 \times 3 \times 11}{1 \times 1 \times 4} = \dfrac{33}{4}$$

  d. If the answer is an improper fraction, then change it to a mixed number. Reduce to lowest terms.

$$\dfrac{33}{4} = 8\dfrac{1}{4}$$

Exercise A.2

1. $1\dfrac{1}{3}\times 2\dfrac{1}{8}$

2. $3\dfrac{1}{9}\times 9\times 1\dfrac{1}{8}$

3. $8\times\dfrac{1}{16}$

4. $1\dfrac{2}{3}\times 4\dfrac{1}{5}$

5. $\dfrac{3}{10}\times\dfrac{4}{9}\times\dfrac{12}{8}$

The answers to this exercise can be found at the end of this appendix.

A.3   Division of Fractions

One procedure for dividing fractions involves the following steps:

    a.   Change each whole number or mixed number to an improper fraction.

    b.   Invert the divisor.

    c.   Reduce when ever possible.

    d.   Multiply numerators together and denominators together.

    e.   If the answer is an improper fraction, then change it to a mixed number. Reduce to lowest terms.

Example: $10\dfrac{1}{2}\div 2\dfrac{1}{3}$

    a.   Change each mixed number to an improper fraction.

$$10\dfrac{1}{2}\div 2\dfrac{1}{3}$$

$$\dfrac{21}{2}\div\dfrac{7}{3}$$

    b.   Invert the divisor.

$$\dfrac{21}{2}\times\dfrac{3}{7}$$

c. Reduce when ever possible.

$$\frac{\overset{3}{\cancel{21}}}{2} \times \frac{3}{\underset{1}{\cancel{7}}}$$

d. Multiply numerators together and denominators together.

$$\frac{3 \times 3}{2 \times 1} = \frac{9}{2}$$

e. If the answer is an improper fraction, then change it to a mixed number.

$$\frac{9}{2} = 4\frac{1}{2}$$

Exercise A.3

1. $\dfrac{2}{3} \div \dfrac{7}{8}$ 2. $5\dfrac{2}{5} \div 6\dfrac{2}{5}$

3. $\dfrac{3\frac{1}{3}}{2\frac{1}{2}}$ 4. $4 \div \dfrac{1}{4}$

5. $2\dfrac{1}{2} \div \dfrac{5}{2}$

The answers to this exercise can be found at the end of this appendix.

Answers to Exercise A.1, A.2, and A.3

Answers A.1

1. $1\dfrac{1}{21}$ 3. $2\dfrac{3}{8}$ 5. $17\dfrac{2}{5}$ 7. $\dfrac{1}{8}$ 9. $\dfrac{13}{15}$

2. $5\dfrac{23}{24}$ 4. $4\dfrac{2}{3}$ 6. $1\dfrac{3}{10}$ 8. $\dfrac{1}{4}$ 10. $\dfrac{1}{3}$

Answers A.2

1. $2\frac{5}{6}$ 2. $31\frac{1}{2}$ 3. $\frac{1}{2}$ 4. 7   5. $\frac{1}{5}$

Answers A.3

1. $\frac{16}{21}$ 2. $\frac{27}{32}$ 3. $1\frac{1}{3}$ 4. 16   5. 1

Appendix B

Solving Linear Equations Using the Set of Rational Numbers

Recall the following properties from algebra that are useful for solving and simplifying equations:

a.   The Distributive Law:

   If a, b, and c are real numbers, then $a(b + c) = ab + ac$.

b.   The Addition Property of Equality:

   If $a = b$ and a, b, and c are real numbers, then $a + c = b + c$.

c.   The Multiplication Property of Equality:

   If $a = b$ and a, b, and c are real numbers, $c \neq 0$, then $ac = bc$.

d.   Substitution:

   If $a = b$, then b can be used for a in any expression.

Example 1: $-3x + 7 = 6x - 4$

Steps	Reasons
$-3x + 7 = 6x - 4$	
$-6x - 3x + 7 = -6x + 6x - 4$	Addition Property of Equality
$-9x + 7 = -4$	Substitution
$-9x + 7 - 7 = -4 - 7$	Addition Property of Equality
$-9x = -11$	Substitution
$\dfrac{-1}{9}(-9x) = \dfrac{-1}{9}(-11)$	Multiplication Property of Equality
$x = \dfrac{11}{9}$ or $1\dfrac{2}{9}$	Simplification

Example 2: $5(2x-3)-4 = 3x+9$

Steps	Reasons
$5(2x-3)-4 = 3x+9$	
$10x-15-4 = 3x+9$	Distributive Law
$10x-19 = 3x+9$	Substitution
$10x-19+19 = 3x+9+19$	Addition Property of Equality
$10x = 3x+28$	Substitution
$10x-3x = 3x+28-3x$	Addition Property of Equality
$7x = 28$	Simplification
$\dfrac{1}{7} \cdot 7x = \dfrac{1}{7} \cdot 28$	Multiplication Property of Equality
$x = 4$	Simplification

In the next two examples there are fractions. Fractions are usually cleared from the equation by using the Multiplication Property of Equality and multiplying by the least common denominator.

Example 3: $7x-\dfrac{5}{3} = 3$

Steps	Reasons
$7x-\dfrac{5}{3} = 3$	
$3\left(7x-\dfrac{5}{3}\right) = 3\cdot 3$	Multiplication Property of Equality
$21x-5 = 9$	Distributive Law

$$21x = 14$$ Substitution

$$\frac{1}{21} \cdot 21x = \frac{1}{21} \cdot 14$$ Multiplication Property of Equality

$$x = \frac{2}{3}$$ Simplification

Example 4: $\dfrac{7}{2}x + 5 = \dfrac{13}{3} - \dfrac{3}{4}x$

Steps   Reasons

$$\frac{7}{2}x + 5 = \frac{13}{3} - \frac{3}{4}x$$

$$12\left(\frac{7}{2}x + 5\right) = 12\left(\frac{13}{3} - \frac{3}{4}x\right)$$ Multiplication Property of Equality

$$42x + 60 = 52 - 9x$$ Distributive Law

$$42x + 60 - 60 = 52 - 9x - 60$$ Addition Property of Equality

$$42x = -9x - 8$$ Simplification

$$42x + 9x = -9x - 8 + 9x$$ Addition Property of Equality

$$51x = -8$$ Substitution

$$\frac{1}{51} \cdot 51x = \frac{1}{51} \cdot (-8)$$ Multiplication Property of Equality

$$x = \frac{-8}{51}$$ Simplification

Exercise B.1

1. $-3x - 5 = 2x + 6$

2. $2x - (x + 6) = 10$

3. $6 + 2x = 4(x - 2)$

4. $9 + 7x = 9x - 7$

5. $5x + \dfrac{1}{6} = 8$

6. $3x - \dfrac{1}{7} = 15$

7. $\dfrac{2}{9}y + 2 = \dfrac{y}{18} + 4$

8. $\dfrac{4}{3}x + 7 = \dfrac{5}{2}x - 1$

9. $\dfrac{1}{2}x - 10 = 12$

10. $\dfrac{9}{5}x + \dfrac{2}{3}x = \dfrac{2}{4}$

Answers to Exercise B.1

1. $-2\dfrac{1}{5}$ 2. 16 3. 7 4. 8 5. $1\dfrac{17}{30}$ 6. $5\dfrac{1}{21}$

7. 12 8. $6\dfrac{6}{7}$ 9. 44 10. $\dfrac{15}{74}$

APPENDIX C						
Table 1	SQUARE ROOTS (0 to 199)						
n	$\sqrt{n}$	n	$\sqrt{n}$	n	$\sqrt{n}$	n	$\sqrt{n}$
0	0.000	50	7.071	100	10.000	150	12.247
1	1.000	51	7.141	101	10.050	151	12.288
2	1.414	52	7.211	102	10.100	152	12.329
3	1.732	53	7.280	103	10.149	153	12.369
4	2.000	54	7.348	104	10.198	154	12.410
5	2.236	55	7.416	105	10.247	155	12.450
6	2.449	56	7.483	106	10.296	156	12.490
7	2.646	57	7.550	107	10.344	157	12.530
8	2.828	58	7.616	108	10.392	158	12.570
9	3.000	59	7.681	109	10.440	159	12.610
10	3.162	60	7.746	110	10.488	160	12.649
11	3.317	61	7.810	111	10.536	161	12.689
12	3.464	62	7.874	112	10.583	162	12.728
13	3.606	63	7.937	113	10.630	163	12.767
14	3.742	64	8.000	114	10.677	164	12.806
15	3.873	65	8.062	115	10.724	165	12.845
16	4.000	66	8.124	116	10.770	166	12.884
17	4.123	67	8.185	117	10.817	167	12.923
18	4.243	68	8.246	118	10.863	168	12.961
19	4.359	69	8.307	119	10.909	169	13.000
20	4.472	70	8.367	120	10.954	170	13.038
21	4.583	71	8.426	121	11.000	171	13.077
22	4.690	72	8.485	122	11.045	172	13.115
23	4.796	73	8.544	123	11.091	173	13.153
24	4.899	74	8.602	124	11.136	174	13.191
25	5.000	75	8.660	125	11.180	175	13.229
26	5.099	76	8.718	126	11.225	176	13.266
27	5.196	77	8.775	127	11.269	177	13.304
28	5.292	78	8.832	128	11.314	178	13.342
29	5.385	79	8.888	129	11.358	179	13.379
30	5.477	80	8.944	130	11.402	180	13.416
31	5.568	81	9.000	131	11.446	181	13.454
32	5.657	82	9.055	132	11.489	182	13.491
33	5.745	83	9.110	133	11.533	183	13.528
34	5.831	84	9.165	134	11.576	184	13.565
35	5.916	85	9.220	135	11.619	185	13.601
36	6.000	86	9.274	136	11.662	186	13.638
37	6.083	87	9.327	137	11.705	187	13.675
38	6.164	88	9.381	138	11.747	188	13.711
39	6.245	89	9.434	139	11.790	189	13.748
40	6.325	90	9.487	140	11.832	190	13.784
41	6.403	91	9.539	141	11.874	191	13.820
42	6.481	92	9.592	142	11.916	192	13.856
43	6.557	93	9.644	143	11.958	193	13.892
44	6.633	94	9.695	144	12.000	194	13.928
45	6.708	95	9.747	145	12.042	195	13.964
46	6.782	96	9.798	146	12.083	196	14.000
47	6.856	97	9.849	147	12.124	197	14.036
48	6.928	98	9.899	148	12.166	198	14.071
49	7.000	99	9.950	149	12.207	199	14.107

APPENDIX D							
Table 2			**TRIGONOMETRIC RATIOS**				
degrees	sin	cos	tan	degrees	sin	cos	tan
1	0.017	1.000	0.017	46	0.719	0.695	1.036
2	0.035	0.999	0.035	47	0.731	0.682	1.072
3	0.052	0.999	0.052	48	0.743	0.669	1.111
4	0.070	0.998	0.070	49	0.755	0.656	1.150
5	0.087	0.996	0.087	50	0.766	0.643	1.192
6	0.105	0.995	0.105	51	0.777	0.629	1.235
7	0.122	0.993	0.123	52	0.788	0.616	1.280
8	0.139	0.990	0.141	53	0.799	0.602	1.327
9	0.156	0.988	0.158	54	0.809	0.588	1.376
10	0.174	0.985	0.176	55	0.819	0.574	1.428
11	0.191	0.982	0.194	56	0.829	0.559	1.483
12	0.208	0.978	0.213	57	0.839	0.545	1.540
13	0.225	0.974	0.231	58	0.848	0.530	1.600
14	0.242	0.970	0.249	59	0.857	0.515	1.664
15	0.259	0.966	0.268	60	0.866	0.500	1.732
16	0.276	0.961	0.287	61	0.875	0.485	1.804
17	0.292	0.956	0.306	62	0.883	0.469	1.881
18	0.309	0.951	0.325	63	0.891	0.454	1.963
19	0.326	0.946	0.344	64	0.899	0.438	2.050
20	0.342	0.940	0.364	65	0.906	0.423	2.145
21	0.358	0.934	0.384	66	0.914	0.407	2.246
22	0.375	0.927	0.404	67	0.921	0.391	2.356
23	0.391	0.921	0.424	68	0.927	0.375	2.475
24	0.407	0.914	0.445	69	0.934	0.358	2.605
25	0.423	0.906	0.466	70	0.940	0.342	2.747
26	0.438	0.899	0.488	71	0.946	0.326	2.904
27	0.454	0.891	0.510	72	0.951	0.309	3.078
28	0.469	0.883	0.532	73	0.956	0.292	3.271
29	0.485	0.875	0.554	74	0.961	0.276	3.487
30	0.500	0.866	0.577	75	0.966	0.259	3.732
31	0.515	0.857	0.601	76	0.970	0.242	4.011
32	0.530	0.848	0.625	77	0.974	0.225	4.331
33	0.545	0.839	0.649	78	0.978	0.208	4.705
34	0.559	0.829	0.675	79	0.982	0.191	5.145
35	0.574	0.819	0.700	80	0.985	0.174	5.671
36	0.588	0.809	0.727	81	0.988	0.156	6.314
37	0.602	0.799	0.754	82	0.990	0.139	7.115
38	0.616	0.788	0.781	83	0.993	0.122	8.144
39	0.629	0.777	0.810	84	0.995	0.105	9.514
40	0.643	0.766	0.839	85	0.996	0.087	11.430
41	0.656	0.755	0.869	86	0.998	0.070	14.301
42	0.669	0.743	0.900	87	0.999	0.052	19.081
43	0.682	0.731	0.933	88	0.999	0.035	28.636
44	0.695	0.719	0.966	89	1.000	0.017	57.290
45	0.707	0.707	1.000				

Appendix E

Using a Protractor To Measure an Angle

Step 1:

To measure an angle, place the cross mark of the protractor on the vertex of the angle and the straightedge of the protractor on one side of the angle.

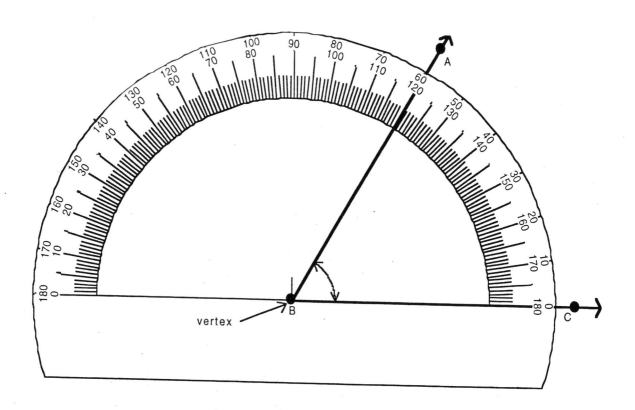

Figure E.1

Step 2:

As in Figure E.1, the side of the angle along the straightedge of the protractor is to the right of the cross mark and the upper scale on the protractor is used to measure the angle. ∠ABC measures 60°.

Note: In the case that your protractor's scales are reversed, then reverse the instructions and use the lower scale on your protractor. ∠ABC still will measure 60°.

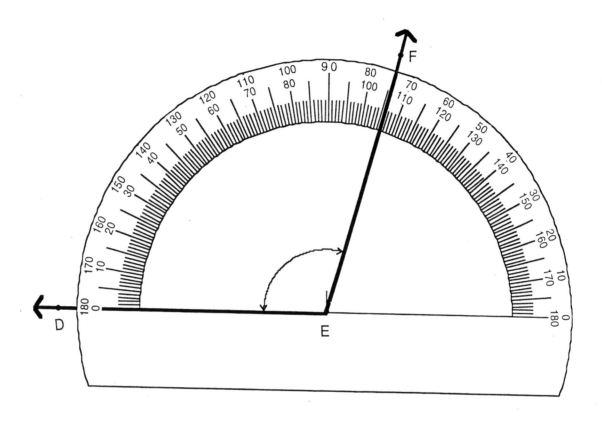

Figure E.2

Step 3:

As in Figure E.2, the side of the angle along the straightedge of the protractor is to the left of the cross mark. Use the lower scale on the protractor to measure the angle. ∠DEF = 106°.

Remember: In the case that your protractor's scales are reversed, then use your upper scale. ∠DEF will still be 106°.

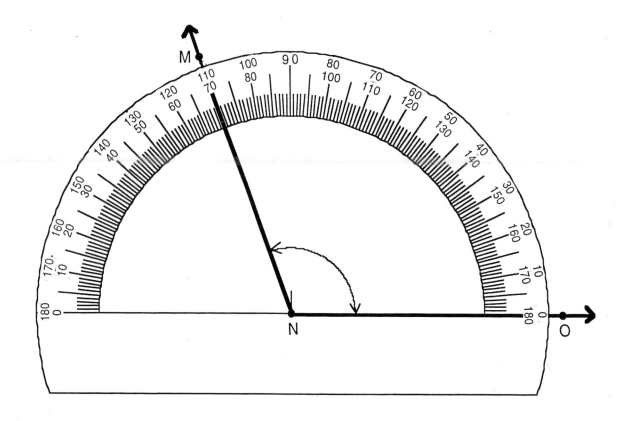

Figure E.3

In Figure E.3, as in Figure E.1, the side of the angle along the straightedge of the protractor is to the right of the cross mark. Using the upper scale, ∠MNO measures 110°.

Exercise E.1

1.   Use a protractor to measure each of the following angles.

    a.   b.

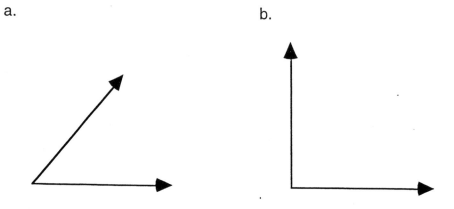

c.

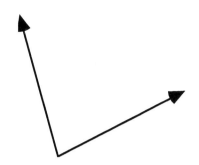

d.

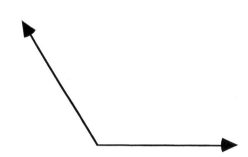

2.   Use a protractor to draw each angle as described below:

   a. ∠RML = 35°   b. ∠MNQ = 135°

   c. ∠C = 172°   d. ∠1 = 78°

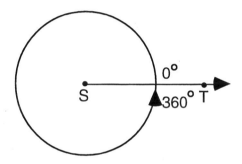

A ray that is rotated about its endpoint on a flat surface will eventually get back to its starting point. The measure of the ray's starting position is 0°. The measure of one complete rotation is 360°. The measure of $\frac{1}{2}$ rotation is exactly $\frac{1}{2}$ of 360°, or 180°.

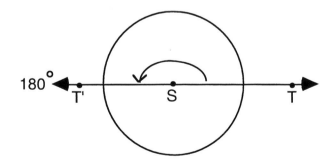

Therefore, $\overrightarrow{ST}$ rotated to $\overrightarrow{ST'}$ measures 180°.

Using a protractor, ∠T'ST would still measure 180°.

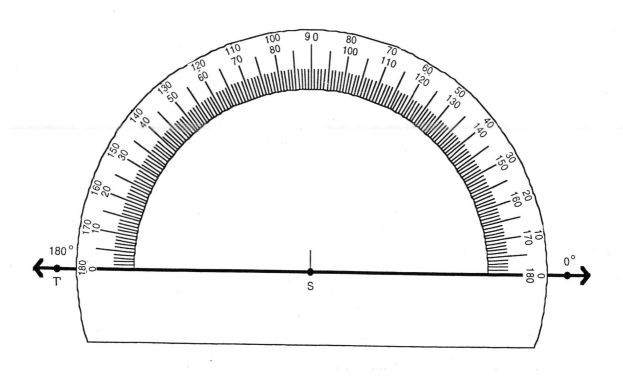

Figure E.4

Answers to Exercise E.1

1.   a. 53°   b. 90°   c. 80°   d.   122°

2.   a.   b.

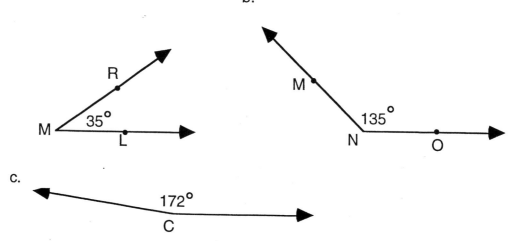

d.

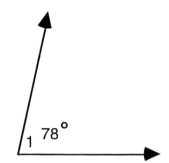

Appendix F

Answers to Exercises

Unit 1 Answers

Exercise 1.1, page 11

1. a. A and B   b. yes   c. 4 cm.; yes

2. $2c + (c+3) + (3c-3) = 12$

$$6c = 12$$
$$c = 2$$

$\overline{XY} = 4$ cm.
$\overline{YZ} = 5$ cm.
$\overline{ZW} = 3$ cm.

Exercise 1.2, pages 24-26

1. $\angle 1, \angle ABC, \angle CBA, \angle B$

2.

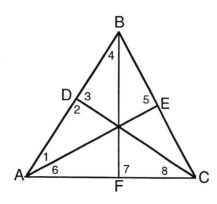

3.

   a. 68°, acute

   b. 180°, straight

   c. 59°, acute

   d. 120°, obtuse

4.

	Supplement	Complement
a.	150°	60°
b.	60°	none
c.	$(180-x)°$	$(90-x)°$
d.	135°	45°

5.

$(5N+7) + 2N + (N+29) = 180$

$$8N + 36 = 180$$
$$8N = 144$$
$$N = 18°$$

$\angle XYT = 36°$, acute
$\angle TYS = 97°$, obtuse
$\angle SYZ = 47°$, acute

6.
$$x + (x - 30) = 90$$
$$x = 60°$$
$$x - 30 = 30°$$

7.
$$x + (5x + 12) = 90$$
$$x = 13°$$
$$5x + 12 = 77°$$

8.
$$x + x = 180 \quad \text{(Both}$$
$$2x = 180 \quad \text{angles}$$
$$x = 90° \quad \text{are } 90°.)$$

9.
$$\left(\frac{2}{3}x + 10\right) + x = 180$$
$$x = 102°$$
$$\frac{2}{3}x + 10 = 78°$$

10.
$$(3x - 20) + x = 90$$
$$x = 27\frac{1}{2} = 27.5$$
$$3x - 20 = 62\frac{1}{2} = 62.5$$

Exercise 1.3, page 41

1. Refer to Construction 1.3.

2. Refer to Construction 1.1.

3. Refer to Construction 1.2.

Unit 1 Review, pages 41-45

1. See definitions in unit.

2. a. angle, vertex, $\angle$ b. complementary   c. supplementary

3. defined terms, undefined terms, theorems, and postulates

4. a.
$$x + \frac{2}{3}x = 90$$
$$x = 54°$$
$$\frac{2}{3}x = 36°$$

   b.
$$x + 5x = 180$$
$$x = 30°$$
$$5x = 150°$$

   c.
$$(4x + 20) + x = 90$$
$$x = 14°$$
$$4x + 20 = 76°$$

   d.
$$x + 2x = 180$$
$$x = 60°$$
$$2x = 120$$

5. a. Follow the steps in Construction 1.1.
   b. Follow the steps in Construction 1.2.
   c. Follow the steps in Construction 1.3.

6. i.   90°, right   ii.   51°, acute   iii.   112°, obtuse   iv.   180°, straight

7. i.   points D and X   ii.   yes   iii.   midpoint

8. Endpoint; no, the rays not only have a different direction but also have different endpoints.

9.   a.

$$(30x - 60) + (2x + 20) + x = 180$$

$$x = 6\frac{2}{3} = 6.\overline{6}$$

$$\angle DBE = 6\frac{2}{3}° = 6.\overline{6}°$$

$$\angle CBE = 33\frac{1}{3}° = 33.\overline{3}°$$

$$\angle ABC = 140°$$

b.

$$(2x - 9) + (x + 3) = 90$$

$$x = 32°$$

$$\angle ABD = 55°$$

$$\angle DBC = 35°$$

$$\angle ABC = 90°$$

10.   a.
$\angle 2 = \angle 3$ because supplements of equal angles are equal.

$\angle 1 = 110°$

$\angle 2 = 70°$

$\angle 3 = 70°$

b.
$\angle 4 = 95°$, supplementary to $\angle 5$

$\angle 6 = 95°$, vertical to $\angle 4$

$\angle 7 = 85°$, vertical to $\angle 5$

Unit 2 Answers

Exercise 2.1, page 50

1. a. X, Z, N
   b. △XZN, △YZM, △YMO, △MNO, △NOX, △YOX, △XYM, △YMN, △YXN, △MXN, △ZMX, △ZYN

2. 18 m.

3. No; this figure is not a closed three sided figure.

Exercise 2.2, page 56

1. a. isosceles triangle, right triangle
   b. obtuse triangle, scalene triangle
   c. acute triangle, scalene triangle
   d. equilateral triangle, equiangular triangle

Exercise 2.3, page 63

1. See Construction 2.2.

2. See Construction 2.1.

3. 45 inches

4. $2x + 8 = 32$
   $x = 12$ inches

5. $\frac{1}{2}x + 2x = 41\frac{1}{2}$

   $x = 16\frac{3}{5} = 16.6$ inches

   $Base = 8\frac{3}{10} = 8.3$ inches

6. $3x = 69$
   $x = 23$ inches

7. a. No, it wouldn't be a closed figure.
   b. No, this figure is not closed.
   c. Yes, an acute triangle has three acute angles.

Exercise 2.4, pages 71-72

1. $\angle M = \angle P$, $\angle MNO = \angle PNO$, $\angle PON = \angle MON$, $\overline{OP} = \overline{OM}$, $\overline{MN} = \overline{PN}$, $\overline{ON} = \overline{ON}$

2. a. $\overline{PR} = \overline{AB}$, $\overline{RQ} = \overline{BC}$, $\overline{PQ} = \overline{AC}$, $\angle P = \angle A$, $\angle R = \angle B$, $\angle Q = \angle C$
   b. $\overline{LM} = \overline{CU}$, $\overline{MN} = \overline{UT}$, $\overline{LN} = \overline{CT}$, $\angle L = \angle C$, $\angle M = \angle U$, $\angle N = \angle T$

3. $\triangle DCF \cong \triangle ABE$

Exercise 2.5, pages 75-78

1.

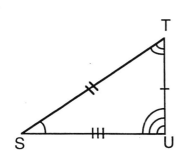 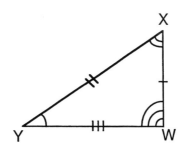

2. $\triangle DEF \cong \triangle HIG$

3. a. yes   b. no   c. no   d. yes

4. a. yes   b. no   c. yes   d. yes

5. a. ∠R and ∠U   b. $\overline{RU}$ and $\overline{RT}$ c. $\overline{RT}$ d. ∠T

Exercise 2.6, pages 83-84

1. yes; SSS = SSS   2. yes; SSS = SSS   3. yes; SAS = SAS

4. yes: ASA = ASA   5. no   6. no

Unit 2 Review, pages 84-87

1. The definitions may be found throughout the unit.

2. a. no   b. no   c. yes; SAS = SAS
   d. yes; SSS = SSS   e. yes; ASA = ASA   f. yes; SAS = SAS

3. a. equilateral triangle   b. isosceles triangle   c. equiangular triangle
   d. right triangle   e. obtuse triangle   f. acute triangle or
                                                            equiangular triangle

4. a. equal sides   equal angles   b equal sides   equal angles
   $\overline{DC} = \overline{DC}$ ∠A = ∠B $\overline{PT} = \overline{RS}$ ∠P = ∠R
   $\overline{BD} = \overline{AC}$ ∠ADC = ∠BCD $\overline{TQ} = \overline{SQ}$ ∠PQT = ∠RQS
   $\overline{DA} = \overline{CB}$ ∠ACD = ∠BDC $\overline{PQ} = \overline{RQ}$ ∠QTP = ∠QSR

   c. equal sides   equal angles
   $\overline{PS} = \overline{RT}$ ∠P = ∠R
   $\overline{SQ} = \overline{TQ}$ ∠PQS = ∠RQT
   $\overline{PQ} = \overline{RQ}$ ∠PSQ = ∠RTQ

5. △AFC ≅ △DEB which is the same as △FCA ≅ △EBD which is the same as △CAF ≅ △BDE

6. 2x + 5 = 23   7. (x+5) + (x+7)+(x+2) = 59   x + 5 = 20 ft.
      x = 9 inches   x = 15   x + 7 = 22 ft.
                                                             x + 2 = 17 ft.

8. See Construction 2.1 and Construction 2.2

9. a. △ABC overlaps △DCB   b. △AEC overlaps △DEB

Unit 3 Answers

Exercise 3.1, page 92

1. Converse: If you live in the United States, then you line in Virginia.

Contrapositive: If you don't live in the United States, then you don't live in Virginia.

Inverse: If you don't live in Virginia, then you don't live in the United States.

2. Converse: If you can fly a plane, then you can operate a car.
   Contrapositive: If you can't fly a plane, then you can not operate a car.
   Inverse: If you can't operate a car, then you can not fly a plane.

3. Converse: If the triangle is equilateral, then it is not scalene.
   Contrapositive: If the triangle isn't equilateral, then it is scalene.
   Inverse: If the triangle is scalene, then it isn't equilateral.

4. Converse: If a triangle is not a right triangle, then it is an acute triangle.
   Contrapositive: If the triangle is a right triangle, then it is not an acute triangle.
   Inverse: If a triangle is not an acute triangle, then it is a right triangle.

5. Converse: If it is cloudy, then it is raining.
   Contrapositive: If it is not cloudy, then it is not raining.
   Inverse: If it is not raining, then it is not cloudy.

Exercise 3.2, pages 96-97

1. $\angle 1$ and $\angle 3$ are equal because they are complements of the same angle ($\angle 2$).

2. Reflexive Law: Any quantity is equal to itself.

3. $\angle 1$ and $\angle 2$ are vertical angles. Pairs of vertical angles are equal.

4. $\angle 1$ and $\angle 2$ and $\angle 3$ and $\angle 4$ are pairs of supplementary angles. If $\angle 2 = \angle 3$, then $\angle 1 = \angle 4$ since supplements of equal angles are themselves equal.

5. a. They are equal sides of an isosceles triangle.
   b. Halves of equal line segments are equal.

Exercise 3.3, pages 101-103

1.

Statements	Reasons
1. $\angle S = \angle T$, $\overline{SR} = \overline{TU}$, $\overline{SR} \perp \overline{RU}$ and $\overline{TU} \perp \overline{RU}$	1. Given
2. $\angle R$ and $\angle U$ are right angles.	2. Definition of perpendicular lines.
3. $\angle R = \angle U$	3. All right angles are equal.
4. $\triangle SRP \cong \triangle TUP$	4. ASA = ASA

2.

Statements	Reasons
1. $\overline{MO}$ and $\overline{NP}$ bisect each other.	1. Given
2. $\overline{NQ} = \overline{QP}$ and $\overline{MQ} = \overline{QO}$	2. Definition of bisector.
3. $\angle NQM$ and $\angle OQP$ are vertical angles.	3. Definition of vertical angles.
4. $\angle NQM = \angle OQP$	4. Pairs of vertical angles are equal.
5. $\triangle NQM \cong \triangle OQP$	5. SAS = SAS

3. In this problem, the triangles may be easier to see if they are pulled apart first.

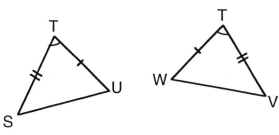

Statements	Reasons
1. $\overline{WT} = \overline{UT}$, $\overline{ST} = \overline{TV}$	1. Given
2. $\angle T = \angle T$	2. Reflexive
3. $\triangle WTV \cong \triangle UTS$	3. SAS = SAS

4.

Statements	Reasons
1. $\angle 2 = \angle 3$, $\overline{AB} = \overline{CD}$, $\angle A = \angle D$	1. Given
2. $\angle 1$ and $\angle 2$ are supplementary. $\angle 3$ and $\angle 4$ are supplementary.	2. Definition of supplementary.
3. $\angle 1 = \angle 4$	3. Supplements of equal angles are themselves equal.
4. $\triangle ABE \cong \triangle DCE$	4. ASA = ASA

5.

Statements	Reasons
1. $\triangle XYZ$ is isosceles. $\overline{XO} = \overline{OZ}$	1. Given
2. $\overline{XY} = \overline{ZY}$	2. Definition of isosceles triangle.
3. $\overline{YO} = \overline{YO}$	3. Reflexive Law
4. $\triangle XOY \cong \triangle ZOY$	4. SSS = SSS

Exercise 3.4, pages 105-109

1. 1. Given
   2. Definition of vertical angles.

3. Pairs of vertical angles are equal.
4. ASA = ASA
5. CPCTE

2. 1. Given
   2. If two angles of a triangle are equal, then the sides opposite these angles are equal.
   3. ASA = ASA
   4. CPCTE

3. 1. Given
   2. Reflexive Law
   3. SSS = SSS
   4. CPCTE

4. 1. Given
   2. If two angles of a triangle are equal, then the sides opposite those angles are equal.
   3. Reflexive Law
   4. Equal quantities subtracted from equal quantities are equal.
   5. Definition of supplementary angles.
   6. Supplements of equal angles are equal.
   7. SAS = SAS
   8. CPCTE

5. 1. Given
   2. Definition of midpoint.
   3. Definition of midpoint.
   4. Definition of vertical angles.
   5. Pairs of vertical angles are equal.
   6. SAS = SAS
   7. CPCTE

6. 1. Given
   2. Definition of bisector.
   3. Reflexive law
   4. ASA = ASA
   5. CPCTE

7. 1. Given
   2. Definition of perpendicular lines.
   3. All right angles are equal.
   4. Definition of perpendicular bisector.
   5. Reflexive Law
   6. SAS = SAS
   7. CPCTE

Unit 3 Review, pages 109-111

1. hypothesis; conclusion

2. Converse: If I pass geometry, then I studied hard.
   Inverse: If I don't study hard, then I won't pass geometry.
   Contrapositive: If I don't pass geometry, then I didn't study hard.

3. Yes
   If a theorem is proven valid, its converse is not necessarily true. Its converse is not a logical equivalent of the theorem; and, therefore, must be proven itself valid.

4. SSS = SSS, SAS = SAS, ASA = ASA

5.

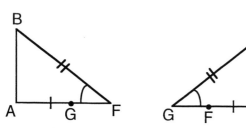

   1. Given
   2. Reflexive Law
   3. Equals added to equals are equal. $\left(\overline{AG}+\overline{GF}=\overline{GF}+\overline{FE}\right)$
   4. SAS = SAS

6. 1. Given
   2. Reflexive Law
   3. ASA = ASA

7. 1. Given
   2. Definition of midpoint.
   3. SAS = SAS
   4. CPCTE
   5. If two sides of a triangle are equal, then the angles opposite those sides are equal.

8. 1. Reflexive Law
   2. Given
   3. Definition of bisector.
   4. Given
   5. Definition of perpendicular lines.
   6. All right angles are equal.
   7. SAS = SAS
   8. CPCTE
   9. Definition of isosceles triangle.

9. 1. Given
   2. Definition of bisector.
   3. Definition of supplementary angles.
   4. Supplements of equal angles are equal.
   5. Reflexive Law
   6. ASA = ASA
   7. CPCTE

Unit 4 Answers

Exercise 4.1, pages 125-127

1. $\angle 1 = 123°$ Supplementary to $\angle 2$ $\angle 6 = 57°$ Corresponding to $\angle 2$
   $\angle 3 = 57°$ Vertical to $\angle 2$ $\angle 7 = 57°$ Vertical to $\angle 6$
   $\angle 4 = 123°$ Vertical to $\angle 1$ $\angle 8 = 123°$ Vertical to $\angle 5$
   $\angle 5 = 123°$ Alternate interior to $\angle 4$

   (Note: Other reasons may be acceptable.)

2. $\angle 4$ and $\angle 7$ are
   supplementary angles.

   $2x + (x + 4) = 180°$

   $$x = 58\frac{2}{3}° = 58.\overline{6}°$$

   $$2x = 117\frac{1}{3}° = 117.\overline{3}°$$

   $$x + 4 = 62\frac{2}{3}° = 62.\overline{6}°$$

3. $\angle 2$ and $\angle 7$ are alternate interior
   angles.

   $3x - 2 = x + 4$

   $x = 3$

   $3x - 2 = 7°$

   $x + 4 = 7°$

4. $\angle 3$ and $\angle 7$ are
   corresponding angles.

   $2x - 10 = x + 4$

   $x = 14$

   $x + 4 = 18°$

   $2x - 10 = 18°$

5. skew lines

6. alternate interior angles
   alternate exterior angles
   corresponding angles

7. l ∥ m where $\angle 1$ and $\angle 2$ are supplementary angles. $\angle 3$ and $\angle 4$ are
   supplementary angles.

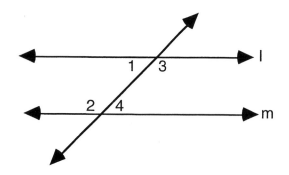

8. 1. Given
   2. Definition of alternate interior angles.
   3. If lines are parallel, then pairs of alternate interior angles are equal.
   4. Reflexive
   5. SAS = SAS

9. 1. Given
   2. Definition of alternate interior angles.
   3. If lines are parallel, then pairs of alternate interior angles are equal.
   4. Definition of vertical angles.
   5. Pairs of vertical angles are equal.
   6. ASA = ASA
   7. CPCTE

Exercise 4.2, pages 139-142

1. $\angle BCA = 50°$; $\angle BCD = 130°$ 2. 27°, 35°, 118° since x = 37

3. $21\frac{1}{9}° = 21.\bar{1}°, 42\frac{2}{9}° = 42.\bar{2}°, 116\frac{2}{3}° = 116.\bar{6}°$ 4. 58°, 32° since x = 19

5. $\angle DAC = 45°$ $\angle DAC$ and $\angle ACB$ are alternate interior angles.
   $\angle CAB = 30°$ $\angle CAB$ and $\angle ACD$ are alternate interior angles.
   $\angle D = 105°$ Theorem 4.9
   $\angle B = 105°$ Theorem 4.9

6. $\angle C = 43°$; $\angle B = 94°$ Triangle ABC is isosceles.

7. $\angle 1 = 60°$, $\angle 2 = 120°$, $\angle 3 = 71°$, $\angle 4 = 109°$, $\angle 5 = 49°$, $\angle 6 = 131°$
   The exterior angles of $\triangle CGE$ are $\angle 4$, $\angle DEC$, $\angle 2$, $\angle ACG$, $\angle 6$, and $\angle EGH$.

8. See Construction 4.1.

9. a. Given
   b. The sum of the interior angles of a triangle equals 180°.
   c. Substitution
   d. Equals subtracted from equals give equals.
   e. ASA = ASA   *See explanation on page 142.

Exercise 4.3, page 146

1. $\overline{AC} = 5.4$ cm.; $\overline{BC} = 6$ cm.   2. 40 cm.

3. $\angle T = 47°$, $\overline{LH} = 6\dfrac{1}{2} = 6.5$ ft., $\angle ULH = 58°$, $\angle U = 75°$

Exercise 4.4, page 148

1. They are perpendicular to the same line.

2. See the steps in Construction 4.2.

Unit 4 Review, pages 149-152

1. 1. Equal alternate interior angles
    2. Equal alternate exterior angles
    3. Equal corresponding angles
    4. Interior angles on the same side of the transversal interior to the two lines are supplementary.

2. $\angle 2 = 30°$, $\angle 4 = 60°$, $\angle 5 = 90°$, $\angle 6 = 90°$

3. $\angle 1 = 60°$, $\angle 2 = 30°$, $\angle 3 = 60°$, $\angle 4 = 30°$

4. Refer to the unit for the definitions.

5. Refer to Construction 4.2.

6.

$\angle 1 = 155°$	$\angle 8 = 136°$	$\angle 15 = 25°$
$\angle 2 = 25°$	$\angle 9 = 136°$	$\angle 16 = 155°$
$\angle 3 = 25°$	$\angle 10 = 44°$	$\angle 17 = 111°$
$\angle 4 = 155°$	$\angle 11 = 136°$	$\angle 18 = 111°$
$\angle 5 = 136°$	$\angle 12 = 44°$	$\angle 19 = 69°$
$\angle 7 = 44°$	$\angle 13 = 155°$	

7. 2. Definition of perpendicular.
    3. All right angles are equal.
    4. Lines perpendicular to the same line are parallel.
    5. Definition of a transversal.
    6. Definition of alternate interior angles.
    7. If two lines are parallel, then pairs of alternate interior angles are equal.
    8. ASA = ASA

8. $2x + 6 = 4x$
$$x = 3$$
The angle measures are both $12°$.

9. The perimeter of $\triangle STU = 15$ in.

10. Refer to Construction 4.1.

11. $28\frac{1}{3} = 28.\overline{3}°$, $96°$, $55\frac{2}{3} = 55.\overline{6}°$

12. $(2x - 7) + (3x + 2) = 90$
$$x = 19$$
$$\angle B = 31°; \ \angle C = 59°$$

13. $\angle 1 = 50°$, $\angle 2 = 90°$, $\angle 3 = 130°$, $\angle 4 = 40°$, $\angle 5 = 50°$, $\angle 6 = 40°$,
$\angle 7 = 50°$, $\angle 8 = 50°$, $\angle 9 = 130°$

Unit 5 Answers

Exercise 5.1, pages 171-173

1. $\angle A = 94°$, $\angle B = 86°$, $\angle C = 94°$ 2. 15 in.   3. $43°$

4. side $= 18\frac{3}{4}$ m. or 18.75 m.; angle $= 16°$

5. $\angle A = 1°$, $\angle C = 1°$, $\angle D = 179°$, $\angle B = 179°$

6. 1. Given
   2. Definition of transversal.
   3. If two angles on the same side of the transversal interior to the two lines are supplementary, then the lines are parallel.
   4. Definition of parallelogram.

7. By the definition of parallelogram,
$$\overline{AB} = \overline{DC} \qquad \overline{AB} = x - 1 = 8 - 1 = 7$$
$$(x - 1) = (2x - 9) \qquad \overline{DC} = 2x - 9 = 16 - 9 = 7$$
$$x = 8 \qquad \overline{BC} = 3x - 17 = 24 - 17 = 7$$
By the definition of parallelogram , $\overline{BC} = \overline{AD} = 7$. From above, since $\overline{AB} = \overline{DC} = \overline{BC} = \overline{AD} = 7$, the figure is a rhombus.

8. $\overline{QS} = 6$ in.   By Theorem 5.5 the diagonals of a rectangle are equal.
$\overline{QT} = 3$ in., $\overline{PT} = 3$ in. A rectangle is a parallelogram. By Theorem 5.6, the diagonals of a parallelogram bisect each other.

9. $\angle 1 = 60°$, $\angle 2 = 60°$, $\angle 3 = 30°$, $\angle 4 = 30°$, $\angle 5 = 90°$, $\angle 6 = 90°$, $\angle A = 60°$,
$\angle D = 120°$

Exercise 5.2, pages 175-177

1. a. $\overline{EF} = 14$ cm.   b. $\overline{BC} = 18$ ft.   c. $\overline{WX} = 17$ dm.

2. a. 11   b. 2   c. 25

3. legs = 25 in., $\overline{EF}$ = 25 in., $\angle 1 = 35°$, $\angle B = 145°$

Unit 5 Review, pages 177-180

I. 1. quadrilateral   2. A, B, C, and D; $\overline{DC}$, $\overline{CB}$, $\overline{AB}$, and $\overline{AD}$; opposite; consecutive

   3. parallelogram   4. rectangle   5. square   6. rhombus

   7. trapezoid; bases   8. isosceles trapezoid   9. median

II. 1. 37   2. x = 4, $\angle B = 105°$, $\angle A = \angle DAC + \angle CAB = 75°$

   3. $\overline{AB} = \overline{DC} = 22$ dm., $\overline{CB} = \overline{AD} = 8$ dm.

   4. $x = 61\frac{1}{3} = 61.\overline{3}°$, $(x+3) = 64\frac{1}{3} = 64.\overline{3}°$, $(2x-7) = 115\frac{2}{3} = 115.\overline{6}°$

   5. $x = 47°$ 6. $\overline{QS} = 8$ in.

   7. $\overline{BE} = 5$ in., $\overline{CE} = 8$ in. By Theorem 5.6, the diagonals of a parallelogram bisect each other.

   8. $\overline{BE} = 6$ in., $\overline{CE} = 8$ in., $\angle B = 120°$, $\angle 1 = 60°$. $\angle 2 = 60°$, $\angle 3 = 30°$, $\angle 4 = 30°$, $\angle 5 = 90°$

   9. $\overline{AB} = 13$ cm., $\angle 2 = 60°$ Since $\overline{AB} \parallel \overline{PQ}$, $\angle 1 = \angle 2$ because they are corresponding angles.

   10. $\overline{AB} = 30$ ft., $\overline{AE} = \overline{BD} = 30$ ft.   11.   x = 2, $\overline{WR} = 21$, $\overline{YZ} = 7$

Unit 6 Answers

Exercise 6.1, pages 187-188

1. a. Order Property II   b. Order Property III   c. Order Property IV

   d. Order Property V, Part 1   e. Order Property V, Part 2

   f. Order Property V, Part 2   g. Order Property I

   h. Order Property III   i. Order Property II

   j. Order Property V, Part 2   k. Order Property I

l.   Order Property IV   m. Order Property II

n. Order Property V, Part 1

2. a. -6 < 5   b. x < y or x = y or x > y   c. -12 > -16

d. (3x + 1) - 1 > 0 - 1 or 3x > -1

3. a. 2x + 2 > 0   b. y ≥ 0   c. w ≤ 0   d. 0 < z ≤ 78

e. 2 < x < 10   f. $x^2 > 4$ g. -3 < x ≤ 7

Exercise 6.2, page 191

1. a. x > -2   b. x > -6   c. -2 ≥ x or x ≤ -2

d. x ≥ -4   e. $x \geq \dfrac{7}{12}$ or x ≥ .58$\bar{3}$ f. $x < \dfrac{-3}{8}$ or x < -.375

g. $x \leq -8\dfrac{2}{5}$ or x ≤ -8.4   h. $\dfrac{7}{12} \geq y$ or y ≤ .58$\bar{3}$

i. $x \geq 1\dfrac{1}{5}$ or x ≥ 1.2   j. x > 0   k. x > 0

l. $x \leq \dfrac{-7}{2}$ or x ≤ -3.5

Exercise 6.3, pages 196-197

1. $\overline{DC}$ is the longest; $\overline{BC}$ is the shortest by Theorem 6.3.

2. $\overline{AB}$ is the longest; $\overline{BC}$ is the shortest.

3. $\overline{PQ}$

4. ∠ZNY is the largest; ∠Y is the smallest by Theorem 6.2

5. Yes, by Theorem 6.1 and Corollary 4.2, page 138.

Unit 6 Review, pages 197-199

1. a. Order Property II   b. Order Property III

c. Order Property IV   d. Order Property V, Part 1

e. Order Property V, Part 2

2. a. -4 < 8   b. c < d or c = d or c > d   c. 12 < 32

3. a. 3x - 5 > 0   b. y ≤ 0   c. −21 ≤ z < 0   d. 3 < y < 11

4. a. $x > \dfrac{2}{5}$ or x > 0.4   b. $y \le 15\dfrac{1}{3}$ or $y \le 15.\overline{3}$ c. x > −7

   d. y ≤ −6   e. $\dfrac{-1}{2} < x$ or x > −0.5   f. x > 1

   g. $x \le 3\dfrac{1}{2}$ or x ≤ 3.5   h. 3 ≤ c or c ≥ 3   i. $-6\dfrac{2}{3} > x$ or $x < -6.\overline{6}$

5. a. $\overline{DC}$ is the shortest side which is opposite the smallest angle.
      $\overline{AC}$ is the longest side which is opposite the largest angle.
      Theorem 6.3

   b. $\overline{AB}$

   c. The largest angle is ∠F which is opposite the longest side. The smallest
      angle is ∠E which is opposite the shortest side (Theorem 6.2).

   d. By the definition of exterior angle, ∠9 = ∠5 + ∠XYZ thus ∠XYZ = 54°.
      The sum of the interior angles of a triangle equal 180° so ∠YXZ = 72°.
      By Theorem 6.3 $\overline{YZ}$ must be longer than $\overline{XZ}$ and $\overline{XY}$.

Unit 7 Answers

Exercise 7.1, page 209

I. 1. $4\sqrt{2}$ 2. $6\sqrt{2}$ 3. $\dfrac{\sqrt{3}}{4}$ 4. $8\sqrt{2}$ 5. $\dfrac{\sqrt{3}}{3}$ 6. $\sqrt{7}$

   7. $20\sqrt{6}$ 8. 18   9. $3\sqrt{5}$ 10. $\sqrt{3}$ 11. $15\sqrt{3}$ 12. $40\sqrt{6}$

   13. $\sqrt{5}$ 14. $9\sqrt{3}$ 15. 360   16. $30\sqrt{6}+48$ 17. $\dfrac{11}{4}\sqrt{3}+3$

   18. $140\sqrt{3}$ 19. $256\sqrt{3}$ 20. $8\sqrt{7}$

Exercise 7.2, pages 214-215

I. 1. $\{-2,2\}$

2. $\left\{-\dfrac{3}{2},\dfrac{3}{2}\right\}$ or $\{-1.5,1.5\}$

3. $\left\{-\dfrac{1}{5},\dfrac{1}{5}\right\}$ or $\{-0.2,0.2\}$

4. $\left\{-\dfrac{\sqrt{5}}{6},\dfrac{\sqrt{5}}{6}\right\}$ or $\{-0.37,0.37\}$

5. $\left\{-\dfrac{2\sqrt{3}}{3},\dfrac{2\sqrt{3}}{3}\right\}$ or $\{-1.15,1.15\}$

6. $\left\{-\dfrac{3\sqrt{3}}{4},\dfrac{3\sqrt{3}}{4}\right\}$ or $\{-1.30,1.30\}$

7. $\left\{-\dfrac{\sqrt{15}}{6},\dfrac{\sqrt{15}}{6}\right\}$ or $\{-0.65,0.65\}$

8. $\left\{-\dfrac{3\sqrt{10}}{8},\dfrac{3\sqrt{10}}{8}\right\}$ or $\{-1.19,1.19\}$

II. 1. $\{3,5\}$

2. $\left\{\dfrac{1}{3},\dfrac{5}{4}\right\}$ or $\{.33,1.25\}$

3. $\left\{\dfrac{-2}{5},0\right\}$ or $\{-0.4,0\}$

4. $\left\{\dfrac{-10}{3},\dfrac{3}{2}\right\}$ or $\{-3.33,1.5\}$

5. $\left\{\dfrac{-3}{2},\dfrac{3}{2}\right\}$ or $\{-1.5,1.5\}$

6. $\left\{\dfrac{-3}{2},2\right\}$ or $\{-1.5,2\}$

7. $\left\{\dfrac{3}{2},\dfrac{3}{2}\right\}$ or $\{1.5,1.5\}$

8. $\left\{\dfrac{-5}{2},\dfrac{2}{5}\right\}$ or $\{-2.5,0.4\}$

III. 1. $\{-1,-5\}$

2. $\left\{\dfrac{-\sqrt{14}}{2},\dfrac{\sqrt{14}}{2}\right\}$ or $\{-1.87,1.87\}$

3. $\left\{1,\dfrac{3}{2}\right\}$ or $\{1,1.5\}$

4. $\{-1-2\sqrt{3},-1+2\sqrt{3}\}$ or $\{-4.46,2.46\}$

5. $\left\{\dfrac{-\sqrt{21}}{3},\dfrac{\sqrt{21}}{3}\right\}$ or $\{-1.53,1.53\}$

6. $\left\{\dfrac{1-\sqrt{19}}{3},\dfrac{1+\sqrt{19}}{3}\right\}$ or $\{-1.12,1.79\}$

7. $\left\{\dfrac{-2-\sqrt{2}}{2},\dfrac{-2+\sqrt{2}}{2}\right\}$ or $\{-1.71,-0.29\}$

8. $\left\{\dfrac{1}{2},\dfrac{1}{2}\right\}$ or $\{0.5,0.5\}$

Exercise 7.3, pages 223-225

1. a. 120 sq. in.   b. 120 sq. ft.   c. 7 sq. yd.   d. 53.9 sq. m.

2. a. 2 in.
b. $\dfrac{\sqrt{14}}{5}$ or .75 cm.
c. $1\dfrac{1}{3}$ or 1.33 mm.

3. a. 12 sq. in.
b. 13 sq. in.
c. $9\dfrac{3}{8}$ or 9.38 sq. in.

4. 12 ft., 15 ft.
5. 288 ft.
6. $900

7. 25 sq. ft.
8. $2\dfrac{1}{4} = 2.25$ sq. in.

Exercise 7.4, pages 227-228

1. a. 24 sq. in.
b. $22\dfrac{2}{3}$ or 22.67 sq. ft.
c. $126\sqrt{10}$ or 398.45 sq. yd.

d. $25\dfrac{2}{3}$ or 25.67 sq. cm.
e. 205 sq. dm.

2. a. 8 m.
b. 17 cm.
c. $3\dfrac{1}{3}$ or 3.33 mi.
d. 570 m.

3. 9 ft., 12 ft.
4. 3 yd., 7 yd.

Exercise 7.5, pages 231-232

1. a. 30 sq. in.
b. $7\dfrac{1}{2} = 7.5$ sq. ft.
c. $\dfrac{\sqrt{35}}{2}$ or 2.96 sq. cm.

d. 2 sq. m.
e. $\dfrac{1}{6}$ or 0.17 sq. mi.

2. a. 8 ft.
b. $\dfrac{28\sqrt{3}}{3}$ or 16.17 in.
c. 9 yd.

3. 18.92 sq. m.
4. $90 = \dfrac{1}{2}x(x+3)$; base = 15 in.
5. 16 cm.
6. 24 tiles

Exercise 7.6, pages 235-236

1. a. 91 sq. m.
b. 350 sq. cm.
c. 120 sq. mm.
d. $2\dfrac{17}{24}$ or 2.71 sq. in.

2. a. 5 mi.
b. 16 m.

3. 6 ft., 4 ft.
4. 42 ft.

5. $40 = \frac{1}{2}x[(2x-1)+x]$; altitude $= 5\frac{1}{3}$ cm. or 5.33 cm.

6. 5 cm., 15 cm.   7. 1440

Exercise 7.7, page 242

1.   <u>Area</u>   <u>Circumference</u>

    a. 225π m.^{2} or 706.5 m.^{2} 30π m. or 94.2 m.

    b. 12π cm.^{2} or 36.78 cm.^{2} $4\sqrt{3}\pi$ cm. or 21.75 cm.

    c. $\frac{9}{4}\pi$ ft.^{2} or 7.07 ft.^{2} 3π ft. or 9.42 ft.

2. a. 12 m.   b. 22.5 cm.   c. 5 m.   d. $4\sqrt{3}$ in. or 6.93 in.

3. $A_{track} = 16\pi$ sq. ft.$+160$ sq. ft. or 210.24 sq. ft.

Unit 7 Review, pages 243-246

1. a. 9 sq. in.   b. 16 sq. yd.   c. 38 sq. m.   d. 96 sq. m.   e. 16 sq. m.

2. $2\sqrt{3}$ in. or 3.46 in.; $8\sqrt{3}$ in. or 13.86 in.

3. 21 m.   4. 6 cm.   5. 5 ft.   6. 40.5 sq. in.

7. $7+\sqrt{69}$ or 15.31 cm.   8. 42 sq. ft.   9. base $= 13$; altitude $= 11$

10. 140 sq. in.   11. 2 in., 4 in.   12. $1\frac{2}{9}$ ft. or 1.22 ft.

13. 4 gal., $60   14. 2

15.   <u>Circumference</u>   <u>Area</u>

    a. $4\frac{2}{3}\pi$ cm. or 14.65 cm. $\frac{49}{9}\pi$ sq. cm. or 17.10 sq. ft.

    b. $10\sqrt{2}\pi$ ft. or 44.41 ft. 50π ft.^{2} or 157.00 ft.^{2}

    c. 1.6π dm. or 5.02 dm. 0.64π dm.^{2} or 2.01 dm.^{2}

    d. 12π in. or 37.68 in. 36π in.^{2} or 113.04 in.^{2}

16. a. 3 m.   b. 5 ft.   c. 4.7 cm.   d. $8\sqrt{2}$ in. or 11.31 in.

17. $\text{Area}_{\text{field}} = 77 \text{ ft.}^2 + \dfrac{49}{8}\pi \text{ ft.}^2$ or $77 + 19.23 = 96.23 \text{ ft.}^2$

18. a. circle, radius, center   b. diameter   c.   circumference

Unit 8 Answers

Exercise 8.1, page 252

1.   a. True   b. True   c. False

2.   a. noncollinear   b. point not on that line

3.   a. straight line   b. point

Exercise 8.2, pages 257-258

1.   Answers may vary.

2.   Volume   Surface Area

     a. 140 cu. ft.   166 sq. ft.

     b. 60 cu. m.   99.4 sq. m.

     c. $19\dfrac{1}{8}$ or 19.1 cu. cm.   47.3 sq. cm.

3.   4 dm.   4. 2 ft.   5. 6 in.   6. 1,875 cu. ft.

7.   2 cans   8. 5 in.   9. 75 boxes   10. 60 cu. ft.

Exercise 8.3, page 263

1.   a. 8 cu. in.   b. $28\sqrt{7}$ or 74.1 cu. m.

2.   a. $6\dfrac{2}{3}$ or 6.7 in.   b. $3\dfrac{5}{21}$ or 3.2 cm.

3. $12\dfrac{6}{7}$ or 12.9 in.   4. 56 cu. in.   5. Answers may vary.

6.   a. 224 sq. cm.   b. 93.15 or 93.2 sq. in.

Exercise 8.4, pages 266-267

1.   Volume   Surface Area

   a. 300π or 942.0 cu. in.   533.8 sq. in.

   b. 360π or 1130.4 cu. yd.   602.9 sq. yd.

   c. 122.5π or 384.7 cu. ft.   296.7 sq. ft.

2.   a. 10 in.   b. 8 cm.   c. 20 yd.   d. 4 ft.   e. $\sqrt{3}$ or 1.7 m.

3.   Answers may vary   4. 12 ft.

5.   Volume of first tank   471 cu. ft.
     Volume of second tank   401.92 cu. ft.
     Difference = 69.08 cu. ft. The first tank has the larger volume.
     Surface area of first tank   345.4 sq. ft.
     Surface area of second tank   301.44 sq. ft.
     Difference = 43.96 sq. ft. The first tank has the larger surface area.

Exercise 8.5, pages 270-271

1.   Volume   Surface Area

   a. 301.4 cu. m.   301.4 sq. m.

   b. 23.7 cu. in.   60.6 sq. in.

   c. 130.8 cu. cm.   189.5 sq. cm.

   d. 401.9 cu. mm.   452.2 sq. mm.

2.   a. 5 in.   b. 6 ft.   c. 12 yd.   d. 5 m.   e. 3 cm.   f. 4 cm.

3. 12π or 37.7 in.^{3} 4. 4π cu. in. or 12.6 in.^{3}

5.   Answers may vary   6. 75.4 sq. cm.

Exercise 8.6, page 274

1.   Volume   Surface Area

   a. 36π or 113.0 cm.^{3} 36π or 113.0 cm.^{2}

   b. 288π or 904.3 in.^{3} 144π or 452.2 sq. in.

   c. 4.5π or 14.1 ft.^{3} 9π or 28.3 sq. ft.

d. $\dfrac{343}{48}\pi$ or 22.4 yd.^{3} $\dfrac{49}{4}\pi$ or 38.5 yd.^{2}

2.   1 in.   3. One bead 79.6 cu. mm.; 10 beads 796 cu. mm.

Unit 8 Review, pages 275-277

1.   Volume   Surface Area

a. 245π or 769.3 in.^{3} 168π or 527.5 in.^{2}

b. 27π or 84.8 cm.^{3} 117.6 cm.^{2}

c. 972π or 3052.1 cu. dm. 324π or 1017,4 sq. dm.

2.   a. $10\dfrac{1}{8} = 10.125$ yd.   b. $\sqrt{2}$ m.   c. 14 ft.

4.   a. straight line   b. circle   c. a point

5. $r = 5$ ft., $V = 375\pi$ or 1177.5 ft.^{3} 6. $V = 3.75\pi$ or 11.8 cu. in.

7.   a. $V = 262.5\pi + 630$ or 1454.3 ft.^{3} b. 112 cu. in.

8. $V_{sphere} = 10\dfrac{2}{3}\pi$ in.^{3}; $V_{glass} = 37\dfrac{1}{2}\pi$ in.^{3}

Volume of water needed = $37\dfrac{1}{2}\pi - 10\dfrac{2}{3}\pi = 26\dfrac{5}{6}\pi$ or 84.3 in.^{3}

9.   5400 cu. in.   10.   10 jars

Unit 9 Answers

Exercise 9.1, pages 284-285

1.   a. Right triangle   b. Right triangle

$3^2 + 4^2 = 5^2$ $(1)^2 + \left(\dfrac{4}{3}\right)^2 = \left(\dfrac{5}{3}\right)^2$

$9 + 16 = 25$ $1 + \dfrac{16}{9} = \dfrac{25}{9}$

c. Not a right triangle   d. Right triangle

$\left(2\sqrt{2}\right)^2 + \left(3\sqrt{2}\right)^2 = \left(4\sqrt{2}\right)^2$ $8^2 + 15^2 = 17^2$

$8 + 18 \neq 32$ $64 + 225 = 289$

2. a.   c = 4.5 cm.   b. b = 5.2 m.   c. a = 4.4 in.

3. side = $5\sqrt{2}$ ft.; area = 25 sq. ft.   4. 10.6 ft.

5. 86.02 ft.   6. 8, 15, 17   7. 14.42 ft.   8. 32 sq. cm.

Exercise 9.2, pages 292-293

1. 2 in., $2\sqrt{3}$ in.   2. $\dfrac{7\sqrt{3}}{3}$ in., $\dfrac{14\sqrt{3}}{3}$ in., A = 14.1 in.^{2}

3. $5\sqrt{3}$ ft.   4. altitude = $\dfrac{3\sqrt{3}}{2}$ m.; area = 3.9 sq. m.

5. $\dfrac{16\sqrt{3}}{3}$ in.   6. x = 5 ft.; area = 45 sq. ft.

Exercise 9.3, page 297

1. $13\sqrt{2}$ cm.   2. $8\sqrt{2}$ ft.   3. 9 sq. m.   4. x = 41 in.

5. x = 7 ft.   6. Area = 264.5 sq. dm.   7. $12\sqrt{2}$ in.   8. 18 ft.^{2}

Unit 9 Review, pages 297-299

I. 1. no   2. yes   3. yes   4. yes   5. yes   6. yes

II. 1. 9.4   2. 2   3. 0.7   4. 3.5   5. 0.5   6. 8

III. 1. 5 in.   2. $\dfrac{7}{2}\sqrt{3}$ ft.   3. $10\sqrt{2}$ cm.   4. 16 m.   5. $5\sqrt{2}$ ft.

6. 292.7 sq. in.   7. $\dfrac{9}{2}\sqrt{2}$ cm., $\dfrac{9}{2}\sqrt{6}$ cm.

IV.   1. x = 30; height = 10 ft; area = 580 ft.^{2} 2. 24.27 ft.

3. height = 8 yd.; area = 256 sq. yd.   4. 15.8 ft.

Unit 10 Answers

Exercise 10.1, pages 305-306

1.   a. ratio   b. proportion   c. constant of proportionality

2. a. $\dfrac{4}{3}$ b. $\dfrac{3}{7}$ c. $\dfrac{1}{80}$ d. $\dfrac{10}{1}$

3. a. no   b. yes, both ratios reduce to 2

    c. yes, both ratios reduce to $\dfrac{3y}{x}$ d. no

4. a. $\dfrac{1}{3}$ b. none   c. $\dfrac{3}{2}$

Exercise 10.2, page 312

1. a. 20   b. $4\dfrac{1}{2}$ c. $\dfrac{3}{16}$

2. a. 4   b. 9.2   c. 15.5

3. a. 19.8   b. -20   c. -23   d. -7, 6
    e. -8.6, 0.6   f. 0.1, 7.9

Exercise 10.3, pages 323-324

1. Refer to definition in the unit. Examples may vary.

2. $\overline{CD}$ = 12.5 in., $\overline{ED}$ = 7.5 in.

3. $\dfrac{3}{12} = \dfrac{5}{20} = \dfrac{7}{28} = k$; yes, $k = \dfrac{1}{4}$.   4. 128 ft.

5. 25 ft.   6. y = 22 in. and z = 26 in.   7. 70 ft.   8. 900 ft.

Exercise 10.4, pages 328-330

1. No, the proportion should be $\dfrac{\overline{WT}}{8} = \dfrac{5}{11}$.

2. $\overline{BE}$ = 10.7 in., $\overline{EC}$ = 4.3 in., $\angle A = 25°$

3. $\overline{BE}$ = 3.1 in., $\angle BED = 80°$, $\angle B = 40°$

4. a. c = 21 m.   b. 4.7 m.   c. 13.8 m.

Unit 10 Review, pages 330-332

1. a. ratio   b. proportion   c. extremes, means, fourth proportional
    d. similar, ~   e. mean proportional

2.   Yes, the sides are proportional. $k = \dfrac{1}{4}$

3. $\overline{AC} = 4$ cm., $\overline{DE} = 7.5$ cm.   4. d = 51   5. 15.2

6.   a. 3.7   b. -8.6, -3.4   c. 16.4   d. 2   e. -2, 1   f. -30

7.   a. no   b. yes   8. $\dfrac{7}{120}$ 9. 49 ft.   10. x = 9.6 ft., y = 14.4 ft.

11. $\overline{DC} = 6.7$ ft., $\overline{AC} = 16$ ft., $\overline{CE} = 10.7$ ft., $\angle CBD = 40°$, $\angle E = 60°$, $\angle C = 80°$

12. $\overline{MY} = 14$ in., $\overline{YO} = 7$ in., $\overline{MN} = 24$ in.   13. 22.5 ft.

Unit 11 Answers

Exercise 11.1, page 341

1. $\cos \angle H = \dfrac{8}{17}$ 2. $\sin \angle O = \dfrac{3}{5}$ 3. $\tan \angle H = \dfrac{15}{8}$ 4. $\sin \angle T = \dfrac{8}{17}$

5. $\tan \angle O = \dfrac{3}{4}$ 6. $\cos \angle W = \dfrac{12}{15} = \dfrac{4}{5}$ 7. $\tan \angle W = \dfrac{9}{12} = \dfrac{3}{4}$

8. $\cos \angle M = \dfrac{3}{5}$ 9. $\sin \angle V = \dfrac{12}{15} = \dfrac{4}{5}$ 10. $\cos \angle V = \dfrac{9}{15} = \dfrac{3}{5}$

11. $\tan \angle T = \dfrac{8}{15}$ 12. $\sin \angle M = \dfrac{4}{5}$

Exercise 11.2, page 345

1. a. $\dfrac{\sqrt{3}}{2}$ b. $\dfrac{\sqrt{2}}{2}$ c. $\dfrac{\sqrt{3}}{3}$ d. $\dfrac{\sqrt{2}}{2}$ e. $\dfrac{\sqrt{3}}{2}$ f. $\sqrt{3}$

2. a. 0.500   b. 0.500   c. 0.866   d. 1.000   e. 0.707   f. 1.732

Exercise 11.3, page 347

1. a. $\cos \angle Z = \dfrac{\sqrt{10}}{5}$ b. $\tan \angle Z = \dfrac{\sqrt{6}}{2}$ c. $\sin \angle Z = \dfrac{\sqrt{15}}{5}$

2. tan 40° = 0.839; sin 72° = 0.951; cos 34° = 0.829

3. $\angle M = 21°$; $\angle N = 87°$ or 88°; $\angle P = 1°$

4.

$$\cos \angle Z = \frac{\sqrt{10}}{5} = .632 \qquad \tan \angle X = \frac{\sqrt{6}}{3} = .8162$$
$$\angle Z = 51° \qquad\qquad\qquad \angle X = 39°$$

Exercise 11.4, pages 352-353

1. a. 106.743 sq. in.   b. 596 sq. ft.   c. 17.54 sq. cm.

2. 261.58 ft.

Unit 11 Review, pages 354-356

1. a. a   b. a   c. c   d. b   e. b

2. $\sin 29° = \dfrac{a}{c}$ $\cos 29° = \dfrac{b}{c}$ $\tan 29° = \dfrac{a}{b}$

   $\sin 61° = \dfrac{b}{c}$ $\cos 61° = \dfrac{a}{c}$ $\tan 61° = \dfrac{b}{a}$

3. $\sin 29° = 0.485$ $\cos 29° = 0.875$ $\tan 29° = 0.554$
    $\sin 61° = 0.875$ $\cos 61° = 0.485$ $\tan 61° = 1.804$

4. $\cos \angle M = \dfrac{8}{17} = 0.471$; $\tan \angle N = \dfrac{8}{15} = 0.533$; $\sin \angle N = \dfrac{8}{17} = 0.471$
    $\angle N = 28°$; $\angle M = 62°$

5. a. 46.62 sq. ft.   b. 4.515 sq. cm.   c. 45.012 sq. ft.

6. $\overline{BC} = 181.2$ ft.

7. a. 0.500   b. 0.500   c. 1.000   d. 0.866   e. 0.866   f. 1.732
   g. 0.707   h. 0.577

8. 24 ft.

Unit 12 Answers

Exercise 12.1, page 362

1. A diameter has endpoints on the circle but its segment also passes through the center of the circle whereas other chords do not pass through the center.

2. A diameter is formed by two radii placed end to end. The measure of a diameter therefore equals the measure of two radii.

3. A chord is contained within a secant line. A secant is a line that passes through a circle intersecting it in two points. However, a chord is a line segment that has its endpoints at the intersection of the secant and the circle.

4. A secant line intersects a circle in two points and a tangent line has only one point of intersection.

5. a. center-point O   b. radii- $\overline{OH}$, $\overline{OI}$, $\overline{OD}$ c. diameter- $\overline{ID}$

   d. chords- $\overline{AB}$, $\overline{JC}$, $\overline{ID}$ e. secant- $\overleftrightarrow{KL}$ f. tangent- $\overleftrightarrow{GE}$
   g. point of tangency-point F

Exercise 12.2, pages 366-367

1. $\angle AOB = 78°$; $\angle ACB = 39°$; minor arcs: $\overparen{AB}$, $\overparen{BC}$, $\overparen{AC}$; major arcs: $\overparen{ABC}$, $\overparen{ACB}$, $\overparen{CAB}$

2. $\overparen{DC} = 68°$; $\angle DOE = 180°$; $\overparen{CE} = 112°$; $\angle COE = 112°$

3. $\overparen{AC} = 102°$ 4. $\overparen{AB} = \overparen{BC} = \overparen{AC} = 120°$

5. $\angle ABD = 75°$; $\angle BDO = 45°$; $\overparen{BC} = 60°$; $\overparen{DC} = 30°$; $\overparen{AD} = 150°$; $\overparen{AB} = 120°$

Exercise 12.3, pages 370-371

1.   Arc Length   Area of the Sector

   a. 5π ft. or 15.7 ft. 25π sq. ft. or 78.5 sq. ft.

   b. $\dfrac{10\sqrt{2}}{9}\pi$ cm. or 4.93 cm. $\dfrac{40}{9}\pi$ cm.^{2} or 13.96 cm.^{2}

   c. 0.3π m. or 0.94 m. $\dfrac{27}{40}\pi$ m.^{2} or 2.12 m.^{2}

2. central angle = $60°$ 3. central angle = $120°$

4. length of arc = $\dfrac{5}{8}\pi$ in. or 1.96 in.; area of sector = $\dfrac{45}{64}\pi$ sq. in. or 2.21 sq. in.

5. $A_{patio} = 150.86$ ft.^{2}

Exercise 12.4, pages 375-377

1. $\overline{AC}$ = 8 m.; $\overparen{EC}$ = 70°; $\overparen{AC}$ = 140°

2. $\overline{AC}$ = 4.6 ft.; $\overparen{EC}$ = 42°; $\overparen{AE}$ = 42°; $\overparen{AC}$ = 84°; $\angle OCD$ = 48°

3. $\overline{AB}$ = 12 in.; $\overline{EC}$ = 2 in.   4. $\overline{OY}$ = 4 ft.   5. $\overline{CD}$ = 2.5 mm.

Exercise 12.5, page 381

1. See steps in Construction 12.1.

2. See steps in Construction 12.2.

Unit 12 Review, pages 382-385

I. 1. circle, radius, center   2. diameter   3. chord
   4. tangent, point of tangency   5. secant   6. central angle
   7. inscribed angle   8. sector   9. circumcenter   10. incenter

II. 1. a. point O   b. $\overline{OD}, \overline{OE}, \overline{OI}$ c. $\overline{DI}$ d. $\overline{AL}, \overline{DI}, \overline{JB}$ e. $\overline{KC}$
    f. $\overline{FH}$ g. point G

2. $\overparen{AB}$ = 58°; $\overparen{AC}$ = 180°; $\overparen{BC}$ = 122°; major arc = $\overparen{ACB}$;
   minor arc = $\overparen{AB}$ or $\overparen{BC}$; semicircle = $\overparen{ABC}$ or $\overparen{AC}$

3. $\overparen{CD}$ = 30°; $\overparen{AB}$ = 80°; $\angle BAD$ = 45°; $\angle 2$ = 125°; $\angle CBD$ = 15°;
   $\overparen{AC}$ = 160°; $\angle ABD$ = 95°; $\angle ABC$ = 80°

4. a. $\frac{3}{2}\pi$ ft. or 4.71 ft; $\frac{9}{2}\pi$ sq. ft. or 14.13 sq. ft.

   b. $\frac{20\sqrt{2}}{9}\pi$ in. or 9.87 in.; $\frac{100}{9}\pi$ sq. in. or 34.89 sq. in.

   c. $\frac{5}{8}\pi$ ft. or 1.96 ft.; $\frac{45}{16}\pi$ sq. ft. or 8.83 sq. ft.

5. $\overline{DE}$ = 4 in.; $\overline{CD}$ = 8 in.; $\overparen{BD}$ = 50°; $\overparen{CD}$ = 100°; $\overparen{CF}$ = 80°;
   $\overparen{AD}$ = 130°; $\overparen{AF}$ = 50°

6. $\overline{OT}$ = 9 yd.   7. $\overline{CD}$ = $2\sqrt{3}$ mm.   8. See Construction 12.1

9. See Construction 12.2

Unit 13 Answers

Exercise 13.1, pages 392-393

1. a. Quadrant I
    b. Quadrant III
    c. Negative x - axis
    d. Negative y - axis
    e. Quadrant II
    f. Quadrant IV
    g. Positive y - axis
    h. Positive x - axis
    i. Quadrant IV
    j. Quadrant I
    k. Quadrant IV
    l. Origin

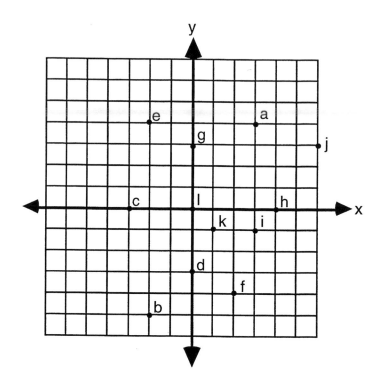

Exercise 13.2, pages 400-401

1. a. $\dfrac{2}{5}$ b. -1 c. $\dfrac{-4}{3}$ d. no slope   e. 0   f. $\dfrac{3}{2}$

2. a. positive   b. no slope   c. negative   d. zero

Exercise 13.3, page 417

1. a.

x	y
0	3
3	1
-3	5

b.

x	y
0	-2
1	3
-1	-7

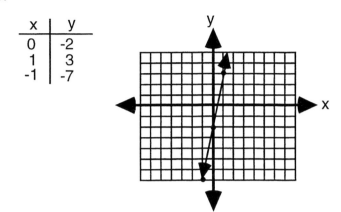

c.

x	y
0	-3
2	-2
-2	-4

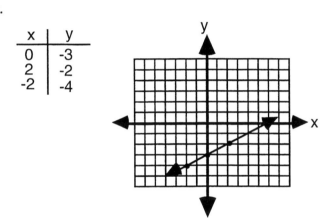

d.

x	y
0	4
3	0
6	-4

e.

x	y
3	1
3	0
3	-1

f.

x	y
1	-3
0	-3
-1	-3

2. a. slope = $\dfrac{-5}{2}$, y-intercept = 5   b. slope = $\dfrac{2}{3}$, y-intercept = -3

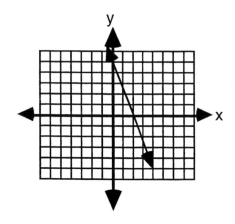
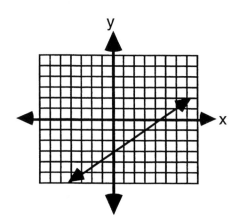

c. slope = $\dfrac{1}{4}$, y-intercept = 0

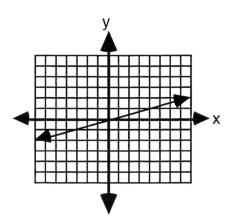

d. zero slope, y-intercept 2

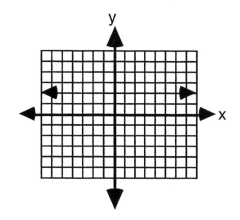

e. slope = $\dfrac{3}{5}$, y-intercept = -4

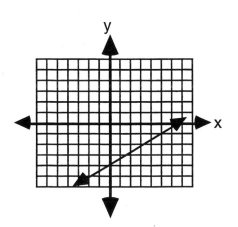

f. slope = $\dfrac{-4}{3}$, y-intercept = 4

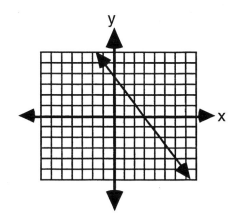

3. a. x-intercept = 7, y-intercept = -2

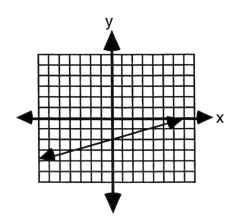

b. x-intercept = 4, y-intercept = 2

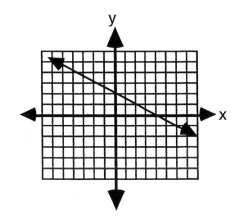

c. x-intercept = 5, y-intercept = -4   d. x-intercept = 12, y-intercept = 8

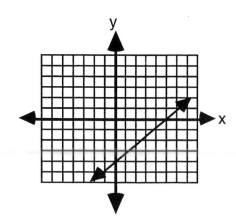

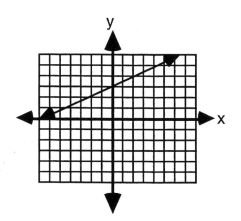

Note: Each block represents 2.

e. x-intercept = 4, y-intercept = -2   f. x-intercept = -7, y-intercept = 3

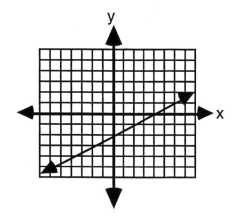

Exercise 13.4, page 434

1. a. x + 5y = 23   b. x = 4   c. y = 3   d. 5x - y = 18
    e. 2x + 3y = -22   f. 2x -7y = -27   g. 4x - y = 0   h. 5x - 3y = 15
    i. 3x + y = -5   j. 2x + 3y = -8

Exercise 13.5, page 441

1. a. $\left(\dfrac{-3}{2},4\right)$ b. (1,−1)   c. $\left(\dfrac{7}{12},1\right)$ d. $\left(\sqrt{2},4\sqrt{7}\right)$

2. a. 6.32   b. 8.25   c. 9.06   d. 2.24

3. Perimeter = 8.61 units; area = 3 square units

Unit 13 Review, pages 441-443

1. Refer to body of the unit for the definitions.

2. a. Positive x - axis
    b. Quadrant I
    c. Negative y - axis
    d. Quadrant II
    e. Negative x - axis
    f. Quadrant III
    g. Positive y - axis
    h. Quadrant IV

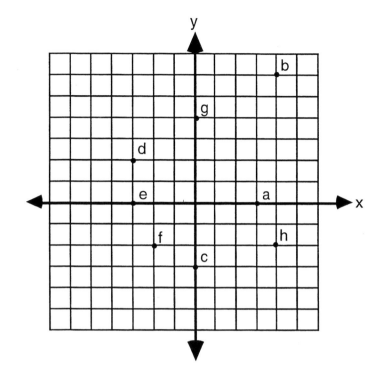

3. $\dfrac{4}{9}$ 4. a. negative   b. no slope   c. 0 slope   d. positive

5.

x	y
0	-6
2	-3
4	0

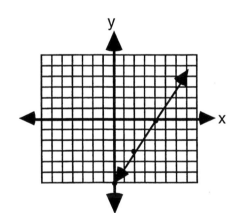

6. slope = 4, y-intercept = -8

7. x-intercept = 6, y-intercept = 4

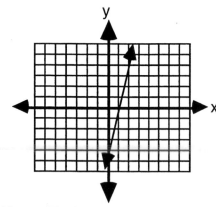

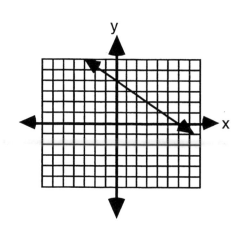

Note: Each square represents two.

8. a. x + 8y = 20   b. 2x - y = 11   c. x - 2y = -12   d. 2x + y = 6

    e. x - 2y = -1   f. 3x - 2y = -16   g. 14x - 2y = 5

9. 10

10. a. $\dfrac{-5}{3}$ b. 11.66   c. (1,2)   d. $\dfrac{-5}{3}$ e. $\dfrac{3}{5}$

    f. 5x + 3y = 11

11. Perimeter = 22.8 units; area = 18 square units

Index

AAS = AAS, 142
Abscissa, 388
Acute angle, 1, 17
Acute triangle, 46, 54
Addition property
    of equal line segments, 93
    of order, 181
Adjacent angles, 1, 18
Alternate exterior angles, 112
    definition of, 117
    equal, 119
Alternate interior angles, 112
    definition of, 117
    equal, 119
Altitude, 46
    construction of the
        altitude of a triangle, 58
    of a cone, 267
    of a cylinder, 264
    of a parallelogram, 225
    of a pyramid, 259
    of a rectangular solid, 254
    of a trapezoid, 232
    of a triangle, 57, 228
Angle(s), 1
    acute, 17
    adjacent, 18
    alternate exterior, 117
    alternate interior, 117
    bisector of, 38
    central, 363
    complementary, 21
    construction of bisector, 1, 38
    copying an, 39
    corresponding, 117
    cosine of, 333
    definition, 13
    degree measure of, 15-17
    exterior, 132
    included, 73
    inscribed in an arc, 365
    naming an, 14
    obtuse, 17
    of parallelogram, 162
    right, 17
    sine of, 333

    straight, 18
    supplementary, 22
    symbol for, 13
    tangent of, 333
    of triangle, 47
    vertex of, 13
    vertical, 32
Angle bisector, 1
    construction of, 38
    definition of, 38
Arcs
    length of, 368
    major, 363
    minor, 363
Area, 200
    formulas, 243
    of a circle, 240-242
    of a parallelogram, 225-228
    of a rectangle, 216-225
    of a sector, 369
    of a square, 221
    of a trapezoid, 232-236
    of a triangle, 228-232
ASA Postulate, 46, 80, 97
Axes, 388
Axiom, 1
Base(s)
    of a cone, 267
    of an isosceles triangle, 52
    of a pyramid, 258
    of a trapezoid, 233
Bisector
    construction of angle bisector, 38
    construction of perpendicular
        bisector of a line segment, 35
    of an angle, 38
    of a line segment, 1, 34
    perpendicular, 1
Center of a circle, 236, 359
Central angle
    definition, 363
    measure of, 363
Chord(s)
    definition, 359
    equal, 374
    theorems dealing with, 371